P9-DOG-201

FREE AND FAITHFUL IN CHRIST

For freedom Christ has set us free (Gal 5:1)

BERNARD HÄRING

Free and Faithful in Christ

Moral Theology for Clergy and Laity

VOLUME 1
General Moral Theology

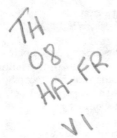

CROSSROAD · NEW YORK

1982
The Crossroad Publishing Company
575 Lexington Avenue, New York, NY 10022

Copyright © Bernard Häring 1978. all rights reserved. No part of this
book may be reproduced, stored in a retrieval system, or transmitted, in
any form or by any means, electronic, mechanical, photocopying, re-
cording, or otherwise, without the written permission of
The Crossroad Publishing Company.

Printed in the United States of America

LIBRARY OF CONGRESS CATALOGING IN PUBLICATION DATA

Häring, Bernhard, 1912–
Free and faithful in Christ.

Includes indexes.
Contents: v. 1. General moral theology—v. 2. The
truth will set you free.
1. Christian ethics—Catholic authors. I. Title.
BJ1249.H36   1982   241'.042   81-22155
ISBN 0-8245-0308-2 (v.1)   AACR2

CONTENTS

Chapter Three
CREATIVE LIBERTY AND FIDELITY IN RESPONSIBILITY

Chapter Six
CONSCIENCE: THE SANCTUARY
OF CREATIVE FIDELITY AND LIBERTY

Chapter Seven
TRADITIONS, LAWS, NORMS AND CONTEXT

xi

Chapter Eight
SIN AND CONVERSION

Synthesis
FREEDOM, FIDELITY AND ADORATION

ACKNOWLEDGEMENTS

My gratitude to God, who gave me the freedom and strength to begin and to finish this volume, flows over into thankfulness to those who helped and encouraged me in the work.

In first place, my heartfelt thanks to Mrs. Josephine Ryan who took the responsibility for correct English and who, through her constructive criticism, challenged my imagination and led to greater accuracy of thought and expression. Without being sure of her always generous and competent assistance, I probably would not have decided to do the original writing in English, since it is not my mother tongue.

I also thank Fr. Charles E. Curran who read the manuscript carefully before it went to the publisher, and made some very good suggestions.

I received most generous help in transcription of the thirty tapes and the retyping of many pages from Sr. Joyce Gadoua S.C.J., from Mrs. Alice Parody, Mrs. Jody Schaden, Mrs. Virginia Malachowsky and Ms. Phyllis LaVoie.

A word of appreciation goes also to Sr Mary Gallagher for her patient work on the index.

B.H.

Introduction

Twenty-five years after completing my three-volume work, *The Law of Christ*, I attempt anew to offer a comprehensive presentation of Catholic Moral Theology.[1] It is not because I want to disown my earlier effort but in this quarter of a century as much has happened as in a given century of the past, and perhaps even more.

In these years I not only had the opportunity to see a worldwide response to *The Law of Christ* but was also engaged in a unique learning process through the Second Vatican Council and through my various activities that always meant both listening and an effort to respond. The Ecumenical Council sensitized my already great interest in ecumenism and equally deepened my passionate interest in the Third World. Since the Council, I have spent a considerable portion of my yearly academic vacation working in Africa, Asia and Latin America, and U.S.A., and in doing so I became more and more aware that my writings were still too European. Now again I write, of course, as a man of European background and North American experience, but I do so in a warm and enduring friendship with the people of the Third World.

I hope that this new comprehensive moral theology will express with equal clarity and urgency the Christocentric approach of *The Law of Christ*. It is always Christ who was, who comes and will come to manifest the Father to us and to draw us together in his liberating love. I also feel a strong sense of continuity in my effort to present responsibility and co-responsibility as key concepts in a Christian ethics for people of today. I want, however, to verify and deepen the vision of responsibility in Jesus Christ by giving greater attention to its expression in creative liberty and creative fidelity.

1

Liberty, liberation and fidelity are at the very heart of the "signs of the times". We try to decipher these signs in community, listening to one another, sharing our experiences and reflections, and being fully committed to each other in Jesus Christ. Each of us has a specific background that gives us our particular place at the window in the common tower from which we watch the events.

Born in a rather medieval little town in southwestern Germany before World War I, my childhood was marked by a loving family but also by the heartbreaking experiences of anguish and loss caused by the war. As a student I came into contact with the work of such groundbreaking thinkers as Max Weber and Max Scheler, and with such great representatives of personalism as Martin Buber and Ferdinand Ebner. I was an enthusiastic follower of the liturgical renewal. But what most influenced my thinking about moral theology was the mindless and criminal obedience of Christians to Hitler, a madman and tyrant. This led me to the conviction that the character of a Christian must not be formed one-sidedly by a leitmotif of obedience but rather by a discerning responsibility, a capacity to respond courageously to new value insights and new needs, and a readiness to take the risk.[2]

Years of contact with the Russian and Polish populations during the war, my activity as a teacher of graduate students of all nationalities, colours, cultures and classes, the Ecumenical Council, and my apostolate in the various continents were all testing the son of a farmer in his sense of continuity of life. Altogether, it was an experience of liberation from tribal thoughts and visions, an experience of openness to others, of "being with" others and serving them. And it was an experience within the Church to which I am firmly dedicated, as one who believes in her mission to be and to become even more a visible and effective sign of God's liberating love. There our Lord calls us to be faithful to him, the Lord of history, and to the best of all traditions. But I suffer with the Church when I see parts of her enslaved by dead traditions in contradiction with our faith in a living God who works with his people at all times.

New knowledge and experiences of freedom and liberation at a time of profound and rapid change, new challenges to broaden the horizons of freedom and to incarnate it in man's total environment and life, but also new threats to its very existence and to its right understanding, make liberty a main concern for a responsible Christian ethicist. We have to ask ourselves how, as people of this time and age, we can come to a better understanding of "the perfect law of liberty" (Jas 1:25).

Whenever I think or speak about liberty, there rings in my heart the word, "fidelity to Christ", the Faithful One, who is Liberty incarnate and our Liberator. All too frequently today we find approaches to both liberty and fidelity that make them seem to be adversaries. But it is my firm conviction that true freedom and commitment to the liberation of all people at all levels can and must join hands with fidelity. This becomes evident when we look at these two qualities in the light of Jesus Christ and understand them as creative. The liberty for which Christ has freed us cannot reveal its responsive and creative dynamics without an equally creative fidelity to the Lord of history. This includes fidelity to the best of tradition and, above all, fidelity to our fellowmen, in gratitude to those who have gone before us and in responsibility to those who will come after us.

We are living at a time of fundamental decisions for or against liberty and fidelity, and each person and community should realize that we are all involved. We cannot choose one or the other; we can only have both together in their creativeness. Either we make a conscientious and solidary option for creative liberty and fidelity or we lose sight of continuity of life and thus become vulnerable to all kinds of manipulation.

My perception of the social dimension of the individual person has been sharpened and made more concrete by the experience of the last twenty-five years; but the personalism which I have untiringly proposed has nothing to do with individualistic narrowness. It is a personalism that confronts each of us with God, with our fellowmen and with all of creation.

The new experience and ongoing reflection about liberty, liberation and fidelity require also a new strategy of liberation. Our response to the Lord of history and to the most urgent needs of humankind calls for creating healthy public opinions, sensitizing the consciences of each and all, and building communities whose economic, cultural, social and political structures will incarnate the values of liberty and fidelity in the whole life of our times. Thus we invite a creative understanding of commitment to liberty and fidelity.

Despite a certain trend towards conservatism in parts of the Church and society, I am convinced that we have moved into a new era that will be determined by people who live by their own conscience and are particularly qualified to act as discerning members of community and society. Of course there still exists, and probably always will exist, a number of people who understand fidelity as staying where they were born and where they were located by conditionings and by the will of others; but the era in which almost everyone was content to be born and to live as a member of a certain church or "organized religion" is over. The people who will shape the future of believers of all religions are those who have the courage to make their own choice, whatever pain may be involved, and to do so with personal responsibility. We want to help form a generation whose members will live their own lives as discerning people and with the creativity and fidelity that characterizes those who believe in the living God.

For these and many other reasons, I believe that a distinctively Christian moral theology for this new era has to be a theology of responsibility essentially marked by liberty, fidelity and creativity. This new vision lends courage and guidance to the rethinking of a number of doctrines, traditions, teachings and practices, and to distinguishing the deposit of faith from ideologies, taboos and other obscuring factors. This must be done, however, with utmost concern for fidelity to the Lord and his people in the covenant, and for freedom as a sign of our faith in redemption.

In all of this, creative liberty and fidelity should be not only key concepts in the efforts of analysis and new synthesis but also the pattern and character of all those who engage in the work. Again and again we must ask the question: How free are we in our thinking and in our sharing of experience and reflections? Do we consciously live in the presence of the Lord of history? How well do we use and broaden the freedom which today's

Church and society give us to think and speak honestly as free persons?

We have also to discern past efforts of moral theologians and ethicists in view of previous situations that have frequently and substantially limited not only their freedom to share with others but also their very freedom to search with absolute honesty and courage. We shall, therefore, turn our attention to the great prophetic figures throughout history who have had the charisms of creativity and fidelity, and who, even in the midst of conflict, were as faithful as they were bold in bringing their contributions into the common heritage.

TITLE OF THE BOOK

Like the name of a person, the title of a book should indicate a programme. It should be chosen not just to attract attention but to reveal the book's main purpose and character.

The name of my first comprehensive moral theology, *The Law of Christ*, evidently referred to Galatians 6:2, with its emphasis on Christ who, in his own person, is our Law, our Way, our Life. The immediate context, "Bear the burden of each other and thus fulfil the law of Christ", inferred a saving solidarity as the heart of the law of Christ as he reveals it in his own person, in his life and in his death. It is a law of love and of unity in love; and in its light we see the total message of the epistle to the Galatians, the message of freedom in Jesus Christ.

The title of this book, *Free and Faithful in Christ*, reveals its identity and main programme. It is not an abridged or revised edition of *The Law of Christ*, but I hope the reader will find in it a continuity of the thought and message of the earlier book, centering on the love of Jesus Christ. With the Apostle of the Gentiles, I see in Christ's love the greatest manifestation of God's creative love and liberty. His saving justice reveals God's creative fidelity to his own name as Father. Christ, who comes from the Father and leads us to the Father, remains always the focal point of our reflection.

A Christocentric moral theology tries to synthesize theocentrism and Christian anthropocentrism. The very origin, countenance and goal of freedom is love; and we cannot understand the fullness of love revealed in Jesus Christ unless we see it as given in total freedom, total fidelity, and with its specific quality of creativity.

In making creative freedom and fidelity in Christ the main theme of this moral theology, we cannot forget the other key concept — solidarity. Our call to share in the free, faithful and creative love of Jesus Christ brings forth and fosters the bonds of a saving solidarity among the children of God, setting us free from the solidarity and bondage of sin.

FOUNDATIONS

Moral theology, as I understand it, is not concerned first with decision-making or with discrete acts. Its basic task and purpose is to gain the right vision, to assess the main perspectives, and to present those truths and values which should bear upon decisions to be made before God.

Since we are dealing with Christian ethics, we have to avoid with utmost care the fabrication of our own perspectives and preferences. We can gain the necessary vision of wholeness only by listening to the word of God and, in the light of his word, searching the signs of the times. Hence, I present first the main perspectives of the Old and New Testaments as biblical theology and a biblically oriented moral theology have worked them out. Only then do I try to discern the main patterns that respond faithfully to the biblical perspectives and, at the same time, creatively meet the signs of the times.

In order to understand the purpose and relevance of these perspectives the reader has to be aware that the author does not follow the trend of those who confine moral theology practically to "normative ethics": his first intention is to form a Christian mind set and that profound vision which is essential for Christian maturity.

---

[1] Cf. my book *Das Gesetz Christi. Moraltheologie für Priester und Laien,* first published in German, Erich Wewel Verlag, Freiburg, 1954; English tr. by Edwin Kaiser, *The Law of Christ,* The Newman Press, Westminster/Md. 1961, 1963, 1966 (3 volumes). The work is translated into fourteen languages.

[2] About the impact of the war experience on my thinking see my book *Embattled Witness,* Seabury Press, New York, 1976, esp. pp. 67-72.

Chapter One

Biblical perspectives: vision of wholeness

It would be an exercise in futility and alienation to begin with a catalogue of norms taught by the Old and New Testaments, without first presenting a vision of wholeness with the main patterns and the historical context. Our first task, therefore, is to "grasp the pre-eminent themes of divine revelation", insofar as they "nourish our own spiritual lives".[1]

Vatican II gave a clear-cut programme for our present efforts in moral theology when it said, "Theological disciplines should be renewed by livelier contact with the mystery of Christ and the history of salvation. Special attention needs to be given to the renewal of moral theology. Its scientific exposition should be more thoroughly nourished by scriptural teaching. It should show the loftiness of the calling of the faithful in Christ, and their mission to bring forth fruit in love for the life of the world".[2]

In earlier years it was an unfortunate custom to refer to Scripture only after having presented one's own system, and to do so particularly in order to present proof-texts for the norms already established once and forever. Our quite different approach is to look first and mainly to the biblical perspective to find, in a vision of wholeness, the value and meaning of Christian life. Then, at the proper time, we shall look to the guidelines and norms presented in the Bible, always aware of a certain historical context, and in view of fidelity and creativity throughout history.

I. BIBLICAL PERPECTIVES: OLD TESTAMENT

Moral theology has much to learn from the great and all-pervading perspectives of the Old Testament. There, the great themes that are particularly fruitful for ethics overlap and integrate each other.[3] Frequently they are the key to a better understanding of the New Testament and the history of the Church.

1. God's word and calling

Unlike the philosophy of Aristotle and others, the Bible does not present God in a perspective of causality as, for instance, the prime mover of men. Mainly, it presents God in a perspective of his creative word and call to fellowship. "God spoke and it was". This is the great vision of the book of Genesis and, indeed, of the entire Old and New Testaments.

The theme of God's creative word becomes solemn when it is a matter of people made in his image and likeness. "Then God said, 'Let us make man in our own image after our likeness; and let them have dominion over the fish of the sea, and over the birds of the air, and over the cattle, and over all the earth', so God created man in his own image, in the image of God he created him; male and female he created them, and God blessed them" (Gen 1:26-27).

God's creative word is a calling, for we are to be not only images of our Creator by freedom in shaping the earth, but also and above all, to be with him in freedom. God calls us to himself and thus offers us repose and peace. The great theme of the Sabbath introduces, again and again, the vision of adoration and liberty. Man can be free only as an adorer, finding his peace and abode with God. In contrast to the pagan religions, the creation history is a liberating word. The believer in Yahweh knows no taboos; he can make free disposition of all things. However, there is an absolute limit: the dignity, before God, of each and every person.

2. God's call to repentance and salvation

Out of a sinful world, God calls Noah to fidelity and trust in him. Indeed, God calls all people to repentance and thus to salvation. The story of Noah symbolizes God's abiding concern for the salvation of humankind: salvation through an exodus of repentance and trust. God's call and the gift of his covenant [4] are infinitely merciful, but those who refuse to respond with faith and repentance are mercilessly warring against themselves, condemning themselves to perdition (cf. Ex 6:10).

3. God's call: election and promise

God calls Abraham to another exodus: "Go from your country and your kindred and your father's house to the land that I will show you" (Gen 12:1). His call for an exodus is election and promise. It is blessing for Abraham and for all his descendants insofar as they put their faith in him as pilgrims before the face of God, responding trustfully and faithfully to his calling.

The great theme becomes more perceptible here. History is understood as the history of God with his people. God calls them to shape their history by courageous faith, by fidelity to God's calling, which is always election and promise for those who walk with him. He is presented as the God of our forefathers, God of the past, present and future history.[5] As he has protected the patriarchs who trusted in him, so will he be with all men who have faith in him and respond to his calling, even a calling to the exodus, with all its frustration and suffering.

4. God's calling: liberation and covenant

God calls Moses and manifests his saving fidelity. He calls Moses into the desert to live the exodus personally, and there to experience God's powerful presence, to know him, the Holy One, the Liberator. The story of Moses embodies the prophets' and the people's trustful response to God. It also manifests, however, the history of distrust and its terrifying consequences.

God's saving and liberating action becomes the main motif for life. He makes a new covenant with Moses and the people, and all of Israel's morality is covenant morality,[6] a shared response in gratitude and fidelity. Israel's liberty will always depend upon her gratitude for God's liberating action and on his fidelity to the covenant. Again, God manifests himself as the

Lord of history. History's events depend, however, also upon his people's response.

5. The people's repentance and God's calling of charismatic leaders

Whenever people forget God and become unfaithful to the covenant, they are in distress and hopelessly embattled with their enemies. But when they repent and call upon him, responding to his promise of mercy, God intervenes by calling and sending charismatic leaders.[7]

This is one of the great themes of the Old Testament, especially of the book of Judges and the two books of Samuel. God has called humankind by his word. He graciously listens to his people when they sincerely turn to him and call upon his mighty help. The charismatic leader, who puts all his trust in the Lord and responds creatively to God's calling, configures the history of Israel. Liberation happens only in the realm of conversion and of God's undeserved mercy.

6. God elects and rejects kings

A perspective that is all-pervasive in the Old Testament is the value and the ambiguity of authority. Already in Genesis 3:16, the abuse of power — male domineering over female — becomes the chief symbol and reality of the fall away from God. Where people do not adore God, they will yield to the lust for power which is, again and again, the cause of destructiveness and disunity. The charismatic leaders directly sent by God, like Moses, Gideon and Samuel, serve the good of the people without looking for power and dynasties. They are real symbols of God's gracious reign. A healthy charismatic authority is a great blessing, coming from God.

The Old Testament presents then the whole history of kings as a striking symbol of the ambiguity of earthly kingdom and power. Involved is not just the sin of the kings themselves but also the sin of the people who want a king to serve as symbol and cause for their own power among nations. This makes the institution of monarchy a constant source of curse (cf. 1 Sam 8).

Even so, God's intentions are for peace and salvation. He gives to Saul, David, and to many other kings, a chance to be a sign of his gracious election, to be anointed by his Spirit if they abide in the covenant and call their people to covenant fidelity. But again and again Israel's kings and their priests acted just like the kings of sinful nations who did not know God.

God is with the kings when they listen to the prophets and are zealous in preserving faith in the one true God. He blesses kings if they trust in him and manifest concern for justice, unity and peace. Disunity, and hence decay, is presented mainly as a result of the misuse of authority. This is one of the outstanding themes of the books of Samuel, the books of the Kings and of Chronicles. It is also a particular message of the prophets.

7. *God calls prophets and they respond*

We accept the Old Testament in all its parts; however, we look on it as a whole. It gives us startling insights into the ups and downs of the chosen people. There are stories and other texts within the books of the Old Testament that manifest on the one hand, God's revelation, but on the other hand, Israel's very imperfect grasp of it because of imperfect readiness to respond wholeheartedly and trustfully.

The summit of the Old Testament is the history of the prophets. They are characterized as men of vision, seized by God, who calls them and sends them. They are given a profound experience of God, which, however, is never severed from history, from the joys and sorrows, the needs, hopes and anguishes of the people of their times.

The history of ethical prophetism gives a unique vision of the ever-present perspectives, "the sacred and the good".[8] The prophets experience at the same time God's holiness and his mercy. By their discernment and boldness, they restore the synthesis between the vertical and the horizontal, between the experience of God's holiness and people's commitment to justice, mercy and peace. They unmask the atheism of ritualism and of all forms of religion that do not bear fruit in love, justice, mercy.[9]

Mary synthesizes the history of ethical religious prophetism when her life-song spells out, "Holy is his name; his mercy sure from generation to generation towards those who fear him" (Lk 1:50). Those who do not show mercy towards the widow, the orphan, the immigrant worker, the disadvantaged and persecuted, manifest their hidden atheism. They do not know the holy God.

The prophets are not authorities for the sake of their own prestige; they are called and sent by God. Their whole life says, "Lord, here I am, call me; Lord, here I am, send me". For his mission, the prophet receives neither salary nor honours. He is totally at the service of God and his fellowmen; and for this he has frequently to suffer and even to die.

For the most part, the prophets are men and women who do not belong to the priestly family of Aaron or to the tribe of Levi. Prophetism cannot be institutionalized, as is proved by the false prophets who wanted to please the kings and the mighty, and who tried to institutionalize their profitable position. Yet some of the prophets are also priests, and thus symbolize the true mission of the priest as God has willed it.

The history of the priests in Israel is a great tragedy. Aaron, whom God himself has chosen to assist the charismatic leader, Moses, and to teach Israel how to adore God, misleads and seduces Israel to make religion a symbol of its own power. This will always happen where the priestly class seeks status, symbols and power (cf. Ex 32:1-30).

God wills priests to preserve fidelity in Israel. The priest is meant to teach the people how to adore God with their whole life. He should cultivate a grateful memory of God's saving deeds and thus call the people to fidelity in the covenant.

Where priests think and act as members of a privileged caste, they are alienated; they have no God-experience, no wisdom and no discernment. Through their ritualism and legalism they become a source of alienation to the entire people. Their lack of fidelity and of creative liberty is unmasked by the prophets and by their own unwillingness to listen to the prophets. But in spite of all this, God sends prophets again and again as a sign of his fidelity that renews and saves his people.

While the decay of the priestly class leads Israel to such narrowness and self-centredness that they join in the power struggle of nations, the prophets call Israel to be a sign before all nations. They shake the false self-consciousness of Israel who, looking only to herself and her achievements, had come to think she was by herself a superior or chosen nation among other nations.

8. *The Servant of Yahweh*

To my mind, the summit of the Old Testament, and especially of the history of the ethical and religious prophetism, is Second Isaiah, who presents the "Servant of Yahweh" (Is 40ff). Israel is clearly called to be a servant among the nations. Only thus will Israel herself be saved, and all nations will be blessed in the name of the God of Israel. When she puts her faith and trust in the Lord and accepts the role of humble servant, as witness among the nations, Israel is a sign of God's blessing and gracious presence.

This is the heart of the prophetic message: that God will finally call and send One who is fully,faithfully and creatively the Servant of God and men. This is the messianic hope. It is hope for peace, justice and unity among all nations, wrought by the Servant of God. And the role of Israel will depend on how she responds to this calling to be, herself, a servant among the nations.

9. *The covenant and the law*

God's call to Noah, to Abraham, to Jacob, Moses and all of Israel issues in a covenant. God commits himselfs to his saving covenant. By the very gift of the covenant and the saving action that brings it forth, God grants Israel the gift of the Law. But the Law is not something externally added to the covenant; it flows from it. If Israel gratefully and humbly accepts and celebrates the covenant, she will respond in fidelity, observing the statutes by which God wants to protect her on the road of her history.

The holy people of Israel — prophets, priests and others — understand that the way the holy God acts with Israel is a call to holiness (cf. Lev 19: "the code of holiness"). The law is not an imposition or a burden to make life hard for Israel. As much as the covenant, and with the covenant and through it, the law is a gracious gift of God. Therefore the true Israelite rejoices in observing the law of the covenant.

In the best of Israel's priestly and prophetic tradition, there is not a boring repetition of law. Again and again, according to historical circumstances, it is, rather, an explanation of the benefit and deep meaning of the covenant. The work of the prophets is, above all, to help people to interiorize the law and to receive it as a gift, a guide and a light that makes Israel truly free, responsive and creative.

The prophets proclaim and foster the hope that God will fulfil his covenant and his law, and will find a people responsive and faithful in the covenant. This becomes the heart of the messianic hope as it reaches its summit in the songs of the Servant of Yahweh. It becomes the unifying theme of the great prophets. "Behold the days are coming, says the Lord, when I will make a new covenant with the house of Israel and the house of Judah, not like the covenant which I made with their fathers when I took them by the hand to bring them out of the land of Egypt, my covenant which they broke, though I was their husband, says the Lord. But this is the covenant which I will make with the house of Israel after those days, says the Lord: I will put my law within them, and I will write it upon their hearts; and I will be their God and they shall be my people. And no longer shall each man teach his neighbour and teach his brother, saying, 'Know the Lord', for they shall all know me, from the least of them to the greatest, says the Lord; for I will forgive their iniquity and I will remember their sin no more" (Jer 31:31-34).

God promises to repeat the miracles he did when he rescued Israel from Egypt and when he gathered the dispersed Israelites from exile. He will bring them all home to his own heart, will gather them and unite them in his fatherly justice. He will give them a new heart and a new spirit. "For I will take you from the nations, and gather you from all the nations, and bring you into your own land. I will sprinkle clean water upon you, and you shall be clean from all your uncleannesses, and from all your idols I will cleanse you. A new heart I will give you, and a new spirit I will put within you. Indeed, I will put my own spirit within you" (Ez 36:24-26).

Thus the main perspectives of the Old Testament merge into the one "Good News" of conversion as God's gracious word and work and the people's grateful acceptance and response. It is a message and call for each of them and all of them.

The faithfulness of the response is the work of the Spirit. Here, one other great perspective, present throughout the Old Testament, comes to its summit; the Spirit who gives life and brings forth the harvest of creativity and fidelity.

II. BIBLICAL PERSPECTIVES: NEW TESTAMENT

Throughout the Old Testament, it becomes ever more clear that religion is not a philosophy about ideas but a history of the living God with his people, and that everything depends upon how the people listen to God, receive his message and his messengers, and respond to him. The New Testament proves even more the impossibility of reducing faith and morality to a system of laws or a philosophy of ideas.

At the very heart of the New Testament is Christ, the Son of David, the Son of Man, the Son of the living God.[10] This is the newness of Christian ethics: that the Father has given us everything and, indeed, has given us himself by sending us his beloved Son, his Word incarnate. "Out of his full store we have all received grace upon grace; for while the law was given through Moses, grace and truth came through Jesus Christ. No one has ever seen God; but God's only Son, he who is nearest to the Father's heart, has made him known" (Jn 1:16-18).

1. *Christ is the New Covenant*

Covenant (*berith*) is the key concept and leitmotif of the Old Testament. The people of Israel are called in the covenant, and they respond to the calling through covenant morality: through lives freely lived in faithfulness to the covenant. It would be strange to think that this main perspective of the Old Testament would be lacking in the New Testament. Rather, it is still, and even more, the heart of the matter. Christ was foretold as "the covenant of the people". "I am the Lord. I have called you in righteousness, I have taken you by the hand and kept you; I have given you as the covenant to the people, the light of the nations" (Is 42:6).

When Christ chose to be baptized with others in a general baptism in the Jordan, he revealed his will to bear the sin-burden of all in saving solidarity. Then the Spirit came visibly upon him and the voice was heard saying, "This is my Son, my beloved, on whom my favour rests" (Mt 3:17). This solemn word of the theophany evidently refers to the first song of the Servant of Yahweh, in which the Messiah is foretold as the covenant of the people. The song begins with the word, "Behold my servant, my chosen, on whom my favour rests" (Is 42:1). The Father thus manifests him as the Messiah, the Christ, the Anointed. "I have put my Spirit upon him" (Is 42:1).

That Christ is the fulfilment of the covenant and is, himself, the new covenant, is expressed in many forms. He it is who takes upon himself the sin-burden of all mankind. He is the brother who gives all humanity the unique freedom to call his Father their Father. That he is one with the Father and one with us is the central truth of his farewell discourses and his high-priestly prayer: He is in us, and we have life with the Father only in him and by his Spirit. "We here declare to you the eternal life which dwelt with the Father and was made visible to us. What we have seen and heard, we declare to you so that you and we together may share in a common life, that life which we share with the Father and his Son, Jesus Christ, and we write this in order that the joy of us all may be complete" (1 Jn 1:3-4).

Having revealed clearly his oneness with the Father and his solidarity with us, Jesus declares the covenant-law to "love one another as I have loved you" (Jn 15:12). But already he has taught his disciples that the love he speaks of is not just a sentimental feeling but a serving love. "Do you understand what I just did for you? You address me as 'Teacher' and 'Lord' and fittingly enough, for that is what I am. But if I washed your feet — I who am Teacher and Lord — then you must wash each other's feet. What I just did was to give you

an example: as I have done, so must you do . . . Once you
know these things, blest will you be if you put them into practice" (Jn 13:12-17).

It is in view of this covenant morality that Paul speaks
of the "law of Christ". "Bear the burden of each other, and
in this way you will fulfil the law of Christ" (Gal 6:2). In and
with Christ, in a solidarity of liberating love, we fulfil his law.

The love which we receive and can share in Jesus Christ
is that Thou-I-We relationship which exists between the Father
and the Son in the Holy Spirit. It is that common life which
Russian theology calls *Sobornost*, a communion which is the
source of all true liberation. In that infinite freedom in which
the Father shares his life with the Son, through the Spirit, he
also decides to share his life, his Son and his Spirit with us.
In that love, we are all made one in Christ.

The Pauline gospel of "life in Christ Jesus" is not only a
mystical ethics of Thou and I; it is equally the covenant
morality of the new fellowship, the new solidarity, of those
who are in Christ Jesus. Justin has explained well these dimensions of the New Testament in his *Dialogue with Tryphon*.[11]
Repeatedly he calls Christ "the Law and the Covenant". By
Jesus' saving solidarity with us in his life, death and resurrection, and by sending us his Spirit, he gives us a share in his
fellowship and covenant. We are thus freed from solidarity in
sin and the fear of death.

2. *Christ is the Prophet*

Christ is not "one of the prophets" but *The* Prophet. Filled
with the Spirit, driven by the Spirit and anointed by the Spirit,
he makes visible by his life and death the synthesis of love
of God and love of neighbour. On the cross he entrusts himself
to the Father and, at the same time, gives himself to his
brothers and sisters, so that they, too, may have life in the
Spirit.

He alone knows the Father and can make him known to
those whom he baptizes by the Holy Spirit. By all that he
says and does, and especially by the Paschal Mystery, he makes
the Father visible as holiness and mercy. It is he who brings

the history of the prophets to its summit as the "saving conflict", the final liberator from empty ritualism and deadly
legalism. He teaches us to adore the Father "in spirit and
truth". "God is Spirit, and those who worship him must
worship him in spirit and truth" (Jn 4:24). Thus he sets us
free from alienation and estrangement.

He who is *The* Prophet does not institutionalize a school of
prophets who would automatically possess the Spirit; but those
who truly believe in him, trust in him, and adore the Father
with him, will have a share in his prophetic role. They will not
endlessly repeat Christ's words to long-dead generations but
will proclaim his word, his total message, in creative faithfulness to the living God in their own times.

3. *Christ is the One who baptizes his disciples by fire and
the Spirit*

Christ is driven by the Spirit to give himself totally for
his brothers and sisters, to be the living Gospel for the poor,
and the liberator of the oppressed. By baptism in the Holy
Spirit his call to discipleship becomes truth in liberation. Those
who are in Jesus Christ, believe in him, and are baptized
by the Spirit, are known by their harvest of the Spirit: "love,
joy, peace, patience, kindness, goodness, fidelity, gentleness and
self-control" (Gal 5:22). Those who are baptized by the Spirit
and "belong to Christ Jesus have crucified their selfishness
with its passions and desires. If the Spirit is the source of our
life, let the Spirit also direct our course" (Gal 5:22-25).

Whoever lives in faith, gratitude, creativity and fidelity on
the level of the Spirit is no longer under the fear of the law.
Through radical adoration and thanksgiving, those who follow
Christ see their very gifts received from God as their "law"
to meet the needs of their fellowmen. Thus Christians can
experience that they are "no longer under law but under
grace" (Rom 6:14). In a new spirit of freedom they can cry,
"Abba, Father", and know that the Father of our Lord Jesus
Christ is also their Father. "The Spirit you have received is not
a spirit of slavery leading you back into a life of fear, but a
Spirit that makes you children, enabling you to cry, 'Abba,

Father'. In that cry, the Spirit of God joins with our spirit in testifying that we are God's children; and if children, then heirs" (Rom 8:14-16).

James speaks of "the perfect law, the law that makes us free" (Jas 1:25). We can understand what he means through Paul's message of the law of the Spirit, and through John the Baptist's promise, ratified by Christ in the Pentecost, that Christ will baptize us in the Holy Spirit. Those who live on the level of the Eucharist, the covenant in the blood of Jesus, praising God with a grateful memory, are no longer like slaves under law. They bring the harvest of justice and peace.

4. Christ is the One who was, who comes, and will come

The great theme of God's history with humankind comes to its completion in Christ. He is the Emmanuel, God-with-us. He who was from the beginning is with us as our life, our truth, our way. He who is the fulfilment of all of God's promises is the Faithful One, and the Spirit he sends us will carry through his promises creatively until the final coming of Christ.

The basic virtues or character of the disciples of Christ cannot easily be expressed by the four cardinal virtues of Hellenistic philosophy. It is, rather, the eschatological virtues that characterize the patterns of his disciples. It is ongoing thanksgiving for what the Lord has done, and joyful anticipation of the final fulfilment, in vigilance and readiness for the present opportunities. All of Christian life is a sharing in the history of redemption and liberation. In this perspective, the sacramental life of the Church is a fruitful source of creative liberty and fidelity.

This fundamental theme of history and of the eschatological virtues has to be seen always in the light of Christ, the Covenant, the Faithful One. It is not a good sign if Christians are scrupulous about the very words of many laws, yet fail to show fidelity to the great law of compassion and mercy proclaimed by Jesus Christ in life and death. "Be compassionate as your Father is compassionate" (Lk 6:36).

The history which we share in Jesus Christ is the history of both fidelity and mercy in holiness.

5. *Christ is the eternal Word of the Father, incarnate in our history*

He is the Word in whom all things are made, and the Word who took upon himself our flesh, our humble human existence. He is the final Word of the Father to us, in whom the Father gives himself; the Word who breathes the Spirit.

Christ lives in and by the Word that comes from the Father. He is the Covenant for all of humankind by living the unique covenant, the hypostatic union of the eternal Word of the Father and the human nature of Jesus of Nazareth.

Jesus is not only the Word of the Father to us; he is also the perfect response. Thus he is the rallying call, inviting and enabling us, by his Spirit, to listen to him and to join him in his adoring, trusting and loving response to the Father. His call to discipleship is, therefore, a call to creative responsibility in freedom and fidelity.

Christ is the life-giving Word. He brings us to the fullness of life and makes each of us truly an image and likeness of the Father, in him, with him and through him, by his life-giving Spirit.

It is in this perspective that we should see the sacraments entrusted to the Church by Jesus Christ. His decisive word about the Eucharist, in which we celebrate the new and everlasting covenant, is that "the Spirit alone gives life; the flesh is of no avail; the words which I have spoken to you are both spirit and life" (Jn 6:62-63). In the Eucharist, Christ shares with us his body and his blood, and he reminds us that by the power of the Holy Spirit he has given himself up for us. By the same Spirit, he enables us freely to give ourselves as total gift to him, in trust and readiness to fulfil our mission, which is to share in his mission.

6. *Jesus is the Truth*

He speaks the truth and acts out the liberating truth which is manifestation of the absolute freedom in which God shares with us his life, his truth, his love.

Jesus is the living Gospel. From the Father he sends us "the Spirit of truth". "When he comes, who is the Spirit of truth, he will guide you into all the truth; for he will not speak on his own authority but will tell only what he hears; and he will make known to you the things that are coming" (Jn 16:13).

The truth which Jesus Christ made evident, even to the point of giving his life for us, is that God is absolute freedom in self-giving love, and that we, too, discover our true selves when we put to death our selfishness and give ourselves trustfully to Christ and his Gospel, in the service of our brethren. Through the gift of the Holy Spirit, we can realize that faithful, generous and creative love is liberty and commitment to the liberation of all. Through the gift of the Spirit of truth, the disciples of Christ learn to discern true love from its counterfeits.

7. *Jesus is Lord*

The Son of the living God made himself the servant of all. He was infinitely rich but chose to enrich us all in his poverty. He whom the Father manifests as the Lord gave himself up on the cross as the ultimate sign of his saving solidarity with us.

The Lordship of Jesus Christ is an important theme and perspective in a distinctively Christian ethics. It exposes all the enslaving cosmic powers, "the authorities and potentates of this dark world" (Eph 6:12). Jesus, the Lord who becomes Servant, teaches us the right use of authority and points the way to healthy authority structures in the Church and in the world. Whoever believes in him and confesses him as Lord will never domineer, and will be free from prejudice against any race, class, colour or sex, and from all other vices that disown the one Father of all and the one Lord, Jesus Christ.

The Spirit by whom Jesus Christ is risen from the dead teaches us genuine responsibility, solidarity, humble and creative exercise of authority in creative obedience to the Lord. Jesus Christ, our Lord, lived obedience even unto death. It was not obedience to an external law but to his mission to make manifest the liberating power of love for the Father and trust in him (cf. Phil 2:5-11). For Christian morality this means, "Let your bearing towards one another arise out of your life in Christ Jesus" (Phil 2:5). In this way we confess that "Jesus Christ is Lord, to the glory of God the Father" (Phil 2:11).

8. *Jesus Christ is our Justice and our Peace*

By his whole life, and especially his death and resurrection, and the mission of the Holy Spirit, Jesus Christ reveals to us the saving justice of the Father, who even takes care of his alienated and rebellious children. Like Jesus himself, his saving justice and messianic peace are undeserved gifts of the Father. We have no title to receive these gifts. It is only the inner and absolute freedom of God's love that sends us Jesus, our Peace and our Justice.

Justification by grace and faith, and peace as the gift of the risen Lord, set us free to live according to the Eucharist. In a liberated spirit of praise and thanksgiving for the peace and justice embodied and brought by Christ and wrought in us by the Holy Spirit we can realize our mission to be committed, in fidelity, to justice and peace for all people and on all levels. The law of faith that entrusts us to Jesus, our Peace and saving Justice, does not allow for any particularism. It is commitment to unity in diversity, and requests diversity as a sign of that unity which marks Christ's peace and justice.

9. *The call to discipleship*

Christ, who is the Word incarnate and the total life-response for all humanity, calls us to be his disciples. He calls each by name and bestows special charisms on each; but his call is a rallying call. The Synoptics describe it as a gracious invitation to follow Christ and to share his companionship, and thus to be friends with one another. By Paul and John, it is presented in more sacramental symbolism as a "life in Christ Jesus" that determines all our relationships.

We look also to the concrete examples of Jesus Christ and his disciples. But we are never stereotypes, nor are the events of our lives carbon copies of earlier times. Only for those who live with Christ and in and for Christ, and are guided by his Spirit, does imitation make sense and reveal its creative qualities.

III. THE BIBLE AND NORMATIVE ETHICS

Those who understand moral theology merely as "normative ethics", in the limited sense of prohibitive norms, will scarcely appreciate the importance of these biblical dimensions and perspectives. In the last ten years there have been continuing discussions on two themes which sometimes did not seem to be related to each other: first, on the use of the Bible in normative ethics; second, on the specifically Christian character of moral theology.[12] An attentive analysis of these writings shows the following trend. Those authors who minimize or exclude a specifically Christian content of normative moral theology come from that tradition of manuals which presented a rather static code morality or an ethics of principles and norms which could be well controlled. Although reacting against the controller, they continue to look just for norms regarding the common element in decisions. This is very evident in one of the latest publications, Franz Boeckle's *Fundamentalmoral*.[13] He is treating the biblical basis of moral theology almost exclusively in the chapter on "How to argue about norms". He wants a creative moral theology and is opposed to the old legalism. But he does not give enough attention to the prophetic tradition in the Bible, he does not treat the theme of "on-going conversion", he thoroughly misunderstand what the best theologians meant with *Zielgebot* (goal commandments), interpreting it as utopia or "mere ideal". He insists on the importance of the biblical message of the "kingdom of God" and the radical "yes" to it but he has practically no bridge between this faithful "yes" and the static norms. And, of course, these norms do not yield very much in favour of a distinctively Christian ethics.

A moral theology of creative liberty and fidelity finds its distinctively Christian quality in the light of the dynamic dimensions and perspectives which we find in the Bible. Their normative value is quite different from any kind of norms fitting external controls. They are, however, binding — and at the same time liberating — guidelines, norms in a very broad but real sense. They depend thoroughly on faith and thus are distinctively Christian. This does not exclude that generous people not professing Christian faith might, in one way or the other, be guided by the same dynamics.

For all those who truly know and love Jesus Christ, and thus can share his love to the Father and join God in his love to all people, the faithful adherence to these perspectives and guidelines leads to an ever increasing knowledge of the Way, the Truth and the Life they are to follow. "This is the eternal life, to know you who alone are truly God, and whom you have sent, Jesus Christ" (Jn 17:3).

In all these perspectives of the Old and especially of the New Testament, there is no place for a mere code morality or an allowance to confine oneself to static norms. It is always the dynamics of salvation truth, of fidelity to the "Good News" that bears in itself joy and peace, and manifests the gifts of God and thus directs our life. Doubtless there are norms in the sense of guidelines or "goal commandments" and norms which indicate what opposes the kingdom of justice, peace and love, and therefore contradicts the new life in Christ; but the efficacy and clarity of these norms are in the salvation truth that makes us know God and know man in his dignity and his total vocation.

At this point, the reader may ask, "What, then, might be the impact of the present discussion on the historical Jesus and, in addition, the impact of a more critical reading of the New Testament?" My response is that it cannot diminish but rather should strengthen the Christocentric vision.

An eminent historian, Eric Osborn, says that in the patristic period, discipleship retains and even intensifies its focus on the person of Jesus Christ.[14] While I would not go all the way with Ernst Käsemann in his historical criticism of biblical texts, I would agree with him when he says, "The discussions on the historical Jesus have made positive contributions to the understanding of Christian discipleship. It has underlined the particularity of Jesus, his sovereignty over his followers, his immediacy and clarity, and the identity of the crucified and risen Lord. In one word, the study of the historical Jesus confronts us with his Lordship".[15]

The less we get lost in discussions about individual sayings and norms, the more we turn our attention, in faith, to Jesus. He is not only the presupposition but the centre of the New Testament. Thus the real history of Jesus is "always happening afresh; it is now the history of the exalted Lord, but it does not cease to be the earthly history it once was, in which the call and claim of the Gospel are encountered".[16]

A wise use of the discussion on the historical Jesus seems to lead to a greater sense of immediacy, to "a shift from narrative to invitation to share trust".[17] This, however, must never be understood in the sense of heresy: that is, of picking out what we like. On the contrary, "No aspect of Jesus saves us but the whole life touches our life as a whole".[18]

I agree with Eric Osborn that, "The disciple is a follower rather than an imitator, but the one thing that he must know is the cross. He follows Jesus by taking up his cross. What lives on in the community of faith should be the love which came in the crucified Lord".[19]

This does not mean, however, that we are confined to only a general perspective. If, in the community of believers, we know all about Jesus that we can know, then our vision and our love will not only increase our creative freedom but will also evidence creative fidelity in the whole content of our lives.

Throughout the whole treatise we shall have opportunity to return to the problem of hermeneutics and the proper use of scripture in Christian ethics.[20] We shall address ourselves to this difficult question especially in Chapter Seven, regarding whether and how abiding moral norms can be found in the Bible.

NOTES

1 *Optatam totius* (Decree on Priestly Formation), 16.
2 l.c.
3 This section is greatly indebted to W Eichrodt, *Theology of the Old Testament*, 2 vols, London, 1961-1967; J. Hempel, *Das Ethos des Alten Testaments*, Berlin, 3rd ed. 1964; G. von Rad, *Old Testament Theology*, 2 vols, New York, 1962-1965; P. van Imschoot, *Theology of the Old Testament*, Tournai-New York, 1975; R.B. Laurin, *Contemporary Old Testament*

Theologians, Valley Forge, 1970; P. van Imschoot, "L'ésprit de Jahvè, principe de vie morale dans l'Ancien Testament", *Ephem. Th. Lovan.* 16 (1939), 457-467; J.L. McKenzie, *A Theology of the Old Testament,* Garden City/N.J., 1974.

4 J. Hempel, l.c., 202, gives a great relevance to the story of the covenant with Noah.

5 Cf. A. Gelin, *Key Concepts of the Old Testament,* New York, 1955, IX: "The Old Testament is the history of the people that lived the great realities — election, promise, covenant, kingdom, exile, community"; see also E. Jacob, *Theology of the Old Testament,* New York, 1958, 183-232: "God, the Lord of History". History gives the faith reality, while faith makes history understandable. God acts in history and gives his word of interpretation to prophets.

6 I follow here W. Eichrodt who has convincingly shown how fruitful it is to study the whole Old Testament in the perspective of the Covenant. Those who criticized him have not yet succeeded to propose an equally central key concept.

7 On "charismatic leaders" see W. Eichrodt, l.c., I, 289-392, compared with I, 293-456: the official leaders, namely the priests and the kings. It can scarcely be overlooked that the priests became frequently "the king's priests".

8 Cf. B. Häring, *Das Heilige und das Gute,* Krailling vor München, 1950; R. Otto, *The Idea of the Holy. An Inquiry into the non-rational factor in the idea of the divine and its relation to the rational.* London-Oxford-New York, 1976

9 W. Eichrodt, l.c.. I, 356; cf. M. Buber, *Der Glaube der Propheten,* München, 1950; G. von Rad, *Die Botschaft der Propheten,* München, 2 ed., 1970.

10 Among the many studies on the moral message of the New Testament, see: O. Preisker, *Das Ethos des Urchristentums,* Gutersloh, 1949; T.W. Manson, *Ethics and the Gospel,* London, 1960; A. Schulz, *Nachfolge und Nachahmung,* München, 1962; A. Humbert, "L'observance des commandements dans les écrits Johanniques", *Studia Moralia* (Rome) I (1963), 187-219; R. Schnackenburg, *Moral Teaching of the New Testament,* London, 1954; Id., *Christliche Existenz nach dem Neuen Testament,* München, 1967; C. Spicq, *Théologie morale du nouveau Testament,* 2 vols, Paris, 1965; N. Lazure, *Les valeurs morales de la théologie Johannique,* Paris, 1965; J. Jeremias, *The Central message of the New Testament,* London, 1965; P. Stuhlmacher, *Gerechtigkeit Gottes bei Paulus,* 2nd ed., Göttingen, 1966; H.D. Betz, *Nachfolge und Nachahmung Jesus Christi im Neuen Testament,* Tübingen, 1967; M. Hengel, *Nachfolge und Charisma,* Berlin, 1968; H.D. Wendland, *Ethik des Neuen Testaments,* Eine Einführung, Göttingen, 1970; J. Ziesler, *Righteousness in Paul,* Cambridge. 1972; R. Schwager, *Jesus-Nachfolge,* Freiburg, 1973; J.L. Holden, *Ethics of the New Testament,* New York, 1973; J.T. Sanders, *Ethics in the New Testament,* Philadelphia, 1975; P. Hoffmann and V. Eid, *Jesus von Nazareth und eine christliche Ethik. Sittliche Perspektiven der Verkündigug Jesu,* Freiburg-Basel-Wien, 1975; Chr. Dietzfelbinger, *Die Antithesen der Bergpredigt,* München, 1975; B. Birch & L.L. Rasmussen, *Bible and Ethics in Christian Life,* Minneapolis, 1976; C.T. Montague, S.M., *The Holy Spirit: Growth of a Biblical Tradition,* New York, 1976.

11 Cf. Justin, *Dialogue with the Jew Tryphon,* chs. 11-24, PG 497, 528.

12 This is not the moment to offer a full treatment of this burning question on the identity of Christian ethics, since this would practically mean to anticipate a great part of the whole book. I hope that the reader will have a clear idea on this point at the end. But the few things said in the text indicate the main thrust. It is, for the author, a fundamental matter to be kept in mind in each chapter. The basis is an anthropology in the light of Christ, the priority of faith over and above works, the fecundity of faith "bearing fruit in love and justice"; the emphasis on the eschatological

virtues and correspondingly on the *kairòs*, the history of salvation giving meaning to all of history, a specifically Christian understanding of creative liberty and fidelity (see esp. chapters III and IV); the vision of the fundamental option in the light of the primacy of faith and grace (ch. V); that reciprocity of consciences that is possible by a "life in Christ" (ch. VI); the understanding of "natural law", human experience and co-reflection within the law of Christ, without renouncing a rational argumentation on matters of strictly normative ethics in dialogue with all men (ch. VII); emphasis on Christian community for the formation of a Christian way of life and thought-pattern, on solidarity of salvation as against solidarity of perdition seen in the call to a fundamental and on-going decision (ch. VIII). For those who have followed or are studying this problem I want to indicate that my position comes very close to James M. Gustafson as expressed in his books: *Christ and the Moral Life*, New York, 1968; *Christian Ethics and the Community*, Philadelphia, 1971; and esp.: *Can Ethics be Christian?*, Chicago and London, 1975. See also: E. LeRoy Long, *A Survey of Christian Ethics*, New York, 1967; R. Remond (ed.), *Morale humaine, morale chrétienne*, Bruxelles, 1967; J.B. Nelson, *Moral Nexus: Ethics of Christian Identity and Community*, Philadelphia, 1971; A. Auer, *Autonome Moral und christlicher Glaube*, Dusseldorf, 1971; F. Compagnone, *La specificità della morale cristiana*, Bologna, 1972; R. McCormick, "Notes on Moral Theology", in *Theological Studies*, 38 (1977), 65ff (survey and evaluation of some articles on this subject); H. Rotter, *Christliches Handeln. Seine Begründung und Eigenart*, Graz-Köln, 1977; H. Halter, *Paulinische Kriterien für das Proprium Christlicher Moral*, Freiburg, 1977; J. Ratzinger, *Einführung in das Christentum*, 12 ed., 1977, esp. 197-221.

13 F. Böckle, *Fundamentalmoral*, München, 1977.

14 E. Osborn, *Ethical Patterns in Early Christian Thought*, Cambridge, 1976.

15 E. Käsemann, "The Problem of the Historical Jesus", in *Essays on the New Testament Themes*, London, 1964, 64.

16 l.c., 47.

17 L.E. Keck, *A Future Historical Jesus*, London, 1972, 134.

18 l.c., 192

19 E. Osborn, l.c., 197.

20 J. Etienne, "Théologie morale et renouveau biblique", in *Eph. Theol. Lovan.*, 4o (1964), 232-241; W. Crotty, "Biblical Perspectives in Moral Theology", in *Theological Studies*, 26 (1965), 574-596; E. Hamel, "L'usage de l'Ecriture en théologie morale", in *Gregorianum*, 46 (1966), 77-84; J.M. Gustafson, "The Place of Scripture in Christian Ethics: A Methodological Study", in *Interpretation*, 24 (197o), 439-455; H.J. Baden, "Ethischer Pluralismus im Neuen Testament", in *Theologie der Gegenwart*, 19 (1976), 13-17; E. Hamel, "La théologie more entre l'Ecriture et la raison", in *Gregorianum* 56 (1976), 275-319.

Chapter Two

How free and creative was and is moral theology?

I. THE LIMITED SCOPE OF THIS ENDEAVOUR

The task of moral theology is not only to reflect on the vocation of the faithful as they understand it. The moral theologian surely must listen to and learn from the faithful, but he has also a ministry to help believers to understand all of Christian life as specifically marked by creative freedom and fidelity and by genuine responsibility. Therefore, first of all, he has to ask himself whether he, too, lives his calling: whether he is on the right wavelength and can share the experience of these qualities with his fellow Christians. It is not only a question of how he lives his calling but also how free he actually is to communicate an understanding of Christian morality that truly expresses creative liberty and fidelity in loving response to the Lord's own love.

Moral theology is creative in the service of God only when it is faithful to the word of God and to the best of tradition. It can equally be said that it is faithful only when it recognizes the creative presence of God and his calling us to share creatively in the shaping of human history. Hence, in examining past history in order to learn faithfully and creatively, our question is: how faithful was past theology and is present theology to the prophetic history, to the bible, and to those men and women who particularly embodied the patterns of Christ the prophet?

Because of the pervading interdependence between the self-understanding and structures of the Church and the quality of freedom, fidelity and creativity embodied in the cultural environment of an era, we also have to examine these inter actions. However, we do not favour determinism. We cannot simply make excuses because of an unfavourable environment, for we believe that, again and again, the Holy Spirit calls prophets to shape the world around them.

We look also at all of past history and present endeavours in the basic perspectives and patterns of creative freedom and fidelity. How well explained and understood is the essential connection between adoration of God "in spirit and truth" and genuine fidelity and responsibility? Is the interdependence of culture and religious expression an ever-present perspective and structural element in theology? In various periods and schools, how central was the understanding of creative love in the light of God's freedom to give himself to us and to call humanity to share freely and creatively in his history with his people?

In a study about the presence or partial absence of creative fidelity and freedom in theology and religious teaching, the categories of a sociology of knowledge, as proposed by Max Scheler, can be particularly helpful.[1] He distinguishes three quite different types of approach to the search for truth: (1) *Heilswissen*, the knowledge of salvation; (2) *Seinswissen*, the knowledge of being; (3) *Harrschaftswissen*, the knowledge of dominion or control.

Heilswissen is searching for truth and witnessing to truth that is concerned mainly with salvation as coming from God: this, in personal wholeness, integrity and integration, with healthy relationships in the sight of God and with a longing for greater wholeness and salvation. It implies trust in God which leads to good relationships and thus helps to discover one's own and the other's inner resources. It is characterized by joyous, grateful faith as response to God's revealing himself as salvation.

Seinswissen refers to the "knowledge of truths in themselves", to all philosophical speculation primarily concerned with the metaphysical categories of being and beings. It is concerned with truths but with no specific focus on salvation, personal wholeness or healthy human relations.

There is, however, throughout the ages, an existential philosophy that gives main attention to the ultimate meaning of human life, the dignity and freedom of the human person, the purpose of community and society, in view of human relationships. This kind of philosophy belongs to *Heilswissen* in a broader sense. We shall ask, therefore, what kind of philosophy is congenial to salvation truth.

Herrschaftwissen is concerned with the structure of society, especially the meaning and purpose of authority and authority structure in interaction with the whole frame of the economic, cultural and political processes, relations and structures. It gives particular attention to the questions of social and international justice and peace.

Focusing on healthy exercise of authority and the historically best constitution of society, this knowledge of dominion touches fundamental problems related to wholeness and health of society and, at least indirectly, to the wholeness and health of the individual person. Unfortunately, however, it frequently forgets the supreme dignity of the person. If it is authentic knowledge about the meaning and purpose of societal structures and authority and the best possible process of decision-making, it is not at all opposed to salvation knowledge. But the sociology of knowledge finds many instances of "knowledge of dominion" that ignores the fundamental issue of creative liberty.

Such a vision and practice of dominion is surely not challenged by a *Seinswissen* for which the person is not much more than a subsumption (a case) of the abstract category of being. If the two degenerate forms of knowledge of being and dominion are wedded, the person is treated almost as a cog in the wheel. It is the kind of knowledge useful for the manipulator who not only tries to get hold of things but also of people.

I repeat that knowledge of dominion is not, of itself, evil. On the contrary, it is beneficial when it truly aims at promoting the common good through sound organization and administration, thus creating space for creative liberty and fidelity.

But whenever, in practice, it takes first place over and above salvation knowledge, it becomes a dangerous threat to human wholenesss, integrity and freedom. This is especially true when it happens in the realm of religion.

Both Max Scheler and Max Weber hold that organized religion, especially if it develops a whole system of promotion, honours and privileges, tends to give prime importance to "spiritual" power (dominion) and organization. It becomes bureaucratic, and presents an institutional temptation by empowering sinful men to domineer over others. Against this kind of religion Karl Barth and, with a different emphasis and perspective, Bonhoeffer were putting their hope in a "religion-less Christianity". Practically, this meant the priority of faith and salvation knowledge, and assigning organization and hierarchical structures wholly to the service of integration of faith and life.

The sociology of knowledge outlined here helps us as a paradigm to understand the past and present history of moral theology. Expressed in more biblical terms, we give special attention to one of the pressing themes of the Old and New Testament: the conflict between the prophets and the priestly class (not to be confused with genuine priests).

Whenever priests understood and organized themselves as a privileged class, strongly linked with the prevailing political power in mutual support of their respective positions of power, the priests' religious "knowledge" became routine, formalism. They lost the sense of wholeness and the spirit of true adoration. Religious training then led to the knowledge of many laws but without any integration in the one great law of God's love, mercy and saving justice. Lack of fidelity to God's compassionate love was over-compensated by thousands of rules that served neither the witness of faith nor growth in holiness.

It is my conviction that we cannot properly evaluate the past history of moral theology without giving specific attention also to how the authority structures and the understanding of authority itself in Church and society, along with the patterns of political and economic authority and the very structure of family, have influenced the patterns of life in the Church, including the ministry of theology.

II. CREATIVE FIDELITY IN THE APOSTOLIC CHURCH

One of the earliest examples of creative liberty and fidelity in the apostolic Church is seen in the conflict that arose because of the cultural diversities of the believers. The first clash between the Jews born and raised in Judea and those coming from the Diaspora called for a creative solution by giving a greater share in decision-making to representatives of the Hellenistic Jews. The solution, a new ministry of deacon, enriched the early Church through evangelization beyond Judea and Galilee by a pioneering group (cf. Acts 6:1-8). In this paradigm we see a proper, courageous and creative use of authority in resolving the conflict; and it seems not too bold to say that the seven deacons turned out to be the more prophetic group in comparison with the rather static established Church in Jerusalem.

A second important event in apostolic times shows the leader of the apostles, Simon Peter, in a most creative charismatic role. There is spontaneity in his temperament, but it is clear that this is a divine charism that somehow had to be forced upon Peter through a profound God-experience. When, after a vision, Peter was invited to preach the gospel in the house of a gentile Roman officer, Cornelius, he still did not know what the outcome would be. He needed a special intervention of God who bestowed the gifts of the Spirit on the new believers before they were baptized. Under divine inspiration, this motivated Peter not to impose on them the circumcision and all the other Jewish customs that would have ensued. It was not easy for Peter to win the agreement of the Church in Jerusalem. But here, creative freedom goes hand in hand with the patience and gentleness shown by the charismatic leader. This (Acts 10:11-18) is a classical case of genuine salvation knowledge.

The third creative breakthrough shows not Peter but Paul, the prophet among the apostles, challenging the established Church when Peter had yielded to the pressure of a conservative Jewish group. Thus arose the famous Antioch conflict where Paul publicly withstood Peter (Gal 2:9-21). He did not at all deny the supreme authority of Peter, but he publicly blamed his inconsistency. Peter accepted the challenge humbly, but the conflict continued and nearly fractured the young Church. For Paul, it was a matter of giving the first place to Christ who is our life, our truth and our law. Consciously or unconsciously, others were still giving first place to law in its written form and traditional make up, while Christ was looked upon more as the law enforcer. Yet the creative liberty of Paul had its bearing on the Church's mission through a common solution reached in the Council of Jerusalem (Acts 15:1-35).

Because of the prophetic word of Paul, the prophetical initiative of Stephen, Philip and the other deacons, and the charismatic leadership in the apostolic Church, Christianity could spread all over the known world of that time. The gospel was not impeded by a canon law like the one which hindered the Church's mission work from the sixteenth to the twentieth century in Asia and Africa.

Whenever theology remains faithful to the biblical approach, there will be no separation between dogma and morality, and no theology severed from evangelization and pastoral ministry. Rather, all theology will affirm and serve the primacy of salvation truth.

III. THE CHURCH FATHERS

1. *The early Church Fathers*

The first who tried a synthesis, a constructive encounter with the prevailing philosophy of Platonism, was Justin (martyred ca. 161). Being in dialogue with both pagan philosophy and Jewish culture, he presents Christ to Jews and Gentiles as *Logos kay Nomos* (the Word and the Law). The seed of the Word is present in all of creation and in people's hearts. Everywhere there are "the seeds of the Logos". All people have some knowledge of God's love and law. Justin's approach suffered, however, by a certain onesidedness because he ascribes too great a role to Moses whom he considered as the first writer and as influencing all the pagan writers. In his famous *Dialogue with the Jew, Tryphon*, he presents Christ as the *Nómos*, "the

Law and the Covenant", in perfect continuity with the central role of the covenant pattern in Old Testament law.[2]

2. Clement of Alexandria

Clement of Alexandria (died ca. 214) is, no doubt, one of the most courageous theologians in creative dialogue with the prevailing thought patterns of his culture. "No one denies his importance for the history of Christian morals".[3] Faithful to the Bible, he develops the main patterns such as discipleship, righteousness, the all-embracing reality of love as gift, goal and commandment, and the relationship between faith and freedom. His chief writings are *Protrepticus* (Exhortation), *Paedagogos* (Instructor) and *Stromateis* (Miscellanies).

The centre and sum of Clement's teaching is the true knowledge of Jesus Christ. Being deeply involved in the fight against Gnosticism, he is creative and constructive in presenting the Christian as the one who lives the true form of Gnosis.[4] He presents a good deal of philosophical speculation (*Seinswissen*) but always integrates it with a salvation perspective and intention. While using Platonic philosophy, he carefully avoids certain pitfalls. He rejects, for instance, the stoic antagonism of body and soul and strongly emphasizes the goodness of the body. However, it is not surprising that he, too, occasionally uses expressions that are characteristic of the patterns of thought in his culture: "The body is only a husk which is wrapped around us for our earthly journey, so that we may be able to enter this common place of correction".[5]

Clement also uses the prevailing ethical idea of the Stoics, *apatheia*; but he gives it a quite new direction. It is no longer the stoic self-sufficiency but the inner freedom and peace that allow creative discipleship. His theology gives place to the primacy of love. "The act of loving the Father with all our strength and power makes us free from decay. For the more a person loves God, the more closely he enters into God".[6]

A main pattern and theme for Clement is that the human person is created in the image and likeness of God. The moral life is seen as responding to this vocation. To him, the perfect "Gnostic" is Jesus Christ, and those who come to know Christ and, through him, the Father, are true "Gnostics". Thus he brings to the foreground the all-embracing goal-commandment, "Let your goodness have no limits, just as the goodness of the heavenly Father knows no bounds" (Mt 5:48).

Clement does not allow Christians to avoid their responsibility to the earthly city: they should, rather, know their vocation to be "salt for the earth". Disciples of Christ can live a truly Christian life in a big city like Alexandria. They are not compelled to renounce wealth, but they will make generous use of it if they really understand the discipleship of Christ. For this purpose Clement wrote his book, *Quis Dives Salvetur?* ("What Rich Man Can Be Saved?"). Faithful to the mystery of the incarnation and redemption, he consistently teaches the mission of Christ's disciples to be light in the world and for the world.[7]

Against Manicheism, Clement purposefully defends the goodness of marriage as well as the vocation of celibacy for the kingdom of God. At times, however, he seems reluctant simply to acknowledge the moral goodness of conjugal intercourse. Some of his restrictions and negative expressions seem to have had more influence on the later tradition than his generally balanced vision. We do not do justice to Clement by quoting only accidental lapses into expressions similar to the Stoics', as, for instance, his description of conjugal intercouse as a "kind of minor epilepsy, an incurable disease. Note the harm it does: the whole person is lost in the unconsciousness of the intercourse".[8] Such expressions as this only prove that even thinkers as creative as Clement do not completely escape the influence of the spirit of their era.

3. Origen

The most creative theologian of the early Greek Church, and surely one of the most influential pioneers in theological synthesis and inquiry, is Origen (born 184 or 185; died ca. 254).[9] He had probably been a student under Clement of Alexandria, and was distinguished by the breadth of his knowledge in profane and sacred literature. True to the rule of faith as it was kept in his time, he looked for a deeper understanding of fundamental questions that still concern us today.

For Origen, Christ is the centre of history. The virtues

are mediated by Christ. Against the Valentinians, Origen strongly defends freedom of the will. He teaches the vocation of all Christians to holiness, and can be considered the creator of spiritual theology. All of his theology has a pastoral and spiritual note. He not only taught and preached the gospel of Jesus Christ but also witnessed to Christ under terrible and prolonged tortures. In the search for deeper understanding of faith in the formation of a Christian élite and in the dialogue with unbelievers, Origen proved, again and again, his fidelity and courage. He truly knew what discipleship meant.

The influence of Origen on the early Church was great. During his lifetime he not only suffered from the enemies of the Church but sometimes also from Church authorities. Because in his youth he had castrated himself in a wrong understanding of Matthew's gospel (Mt 19:12), Bishop Demetrius not only refused him ordination to the priesthood but also banned him from Alexandria when a Palestinian bishop had ordained him. However, during most of his life he found a Church and environment favourable to his charism as a zealous and creative explorer of revealed truth.

After Origen's death, and especially after the end of the fourth century, his influence was not always what it might have been. His enemies distorted many of his words, taking them out of context, and his admirers sometimes did no better. By that time, Origenism was feeling the attack of people who had only "knowledge of dominion". The emperor Justinian forced an ecumenical council (ca. 550) to put Origen's name on the list of heretics in Canon 11. That, however, was not approved by Pope Vigilius. The three following councils nevertheless repeated condemnations, always under the influence of knowledge of control and dominion, and not so much on behalf of salvation knowledge.

4. St Basil

St Basil the Great (330-379) was surely one of the most influential Fathers of the Greek Church. He is an eminent example of creative fidelity, concerned about faith and its moral implications. For him, a true believer is seized by an intense desire to follow Christ. At a time when the official Church, and especially the bishops, became too tied up with imperial power — a Church in the service of the emperor — Basil was one of the great leaders of monachism. He is the father of almost all the oriental monasteries throughout the ages.

At its beginning, the monachist movement was a non-violent protest against the worldliness of a Church in service to the empire. St Basil represents the charismatic, the enthusiastic Church. He gives special emphasis to the Holy Spirit and the charisms of the Spirit. He sees clearly that all the charisms, and particularly those of the monks, are for the common good. Since his time, schools, hospitals and other social works have been a part of the religious community.

Basil did not want to set up a sect like that of Qumran, severed from the Church. On the contrary, he wanted the monachism of the religious to become the inspiration of all Christians. He left no doubt that the vocation to holiness is for all; but in view of the concrete situation of his time, marked by a "Church of the empire" and bishops as a superior social class, he insisted that a life in holiness outside the model community was very difficult.

The heart of Basil's spirituality and morality is love in the discipleship under the guidance of the Holy Spirit. His writings are thoroughly nourished by Holy Scripture, and the same is particularly true of his monastic rule. However, where he touches on matters of righteousness, he strongly stresses obedience, although everyone is directed to be obedient to the grace of the Holy Spirit. He greatly influenced the future by his stress on self-denial and a more platonic attitude towards the body as a prison of the soul. His rigorism, however, is tempered by a childlike simplicity and by a healing approach to those who are transgressors of the law. "Basil's faith is more static than Clement's".[10] This applies also to the way he uses moral imperatives of the gospel, although never severed from the gifts of the Holy Spirit.

St Basil was a great admirer of God's creation, even though he does not really include the human body in this admiration. He believed, however, in an inborn law present to all, so he too has influenced positively the tradition of natural law theories.

5. St John Chrysostom

In his courage, his vision, his enthusiasm and sanity, and in his charism, John Chrysostom (died 407) embodies the prophetic tradition probably more than most of the great theologians. He truly honours Christ the Prophet. His hero is Paul, the apostle to the Gentiles, and he is Paul's most fervent and faithful interpreter in his emphasis on faith and love in the discipleship of Jesus Christ. Like the prophets, he is clearly on the side of the poor, the oppressed and underprivileged; and, like the prophets of old, he paid in his own body for being a prophet. He was exiled and treated badly. He died when he was led to an even more miserable place of exile on the Black Sea. His guards had been instructed to treat him as harshly as possible and not to let him recover. His last word were "Glory to God for all things".

"As a moralist, he is at the same time creative and profound".[11] All his life and writings manifest the absolute priority of knowledge of salvation. As patriarch of Constantinople he gave striking example of a truly Christian and prophetic exercise of authority, although it cost him enormous suffering and persecution. At the same time, he followed Christ the Prophet, showing great love even to those who persecuted him. He was a prophet also in the way he tried to convert priests who wanted to belong to a superior social class. He praised martyrdom for faith, but gave equal praise to those who offer their lives for any other of God's commandments, especially if commitment to justice and to the rights of the poor and oppressed are involved.[12] It is no wonder that, in the matter of slavery, he was much more clear-sighted than most of his contemporaries. He did not see how slavery could ever be in accordance with God's providence for all humanity or with the dignity of persons created in the image of God. He strongly urged believers either to free the slaves or to treat them as brothers with kindness and reverence.

Chrysostom is also very positive about the importance of work for the Christian's personal development and for service to the brethren. He does not tolerate any gap between faith and daily life. Because of his own prophetic gift and his great veneration for St Paul, he has no tendency towards legalism.

He praises virginity but not in opposition to marriage. "It is wrong to denigrate marriage in order to praise virginity".[13] As a pastor, he greatly values family life: "Make your home a church".[14] He is not anti-feminist. Perhaps only Gregory of Nazianzus among the Church Fathers has a more courageous and positive outlook on marriage. Neither Gregory nor Chrysostom minimize the importance of the body, although they, too, promoted radical self-denial in the discipleship of the Crucified.

Against those who think that monasteries have no meaning, John Chrysostom defends monks. However, he urges monks to be ready for service to others, and especially ready for mission work. "How much better were it for you to become less zealous and to profit others than, remaining on the heights, to look down upon your dying brothers. For how shall we overcome our enemies if one part of us pays no heed to virtue, and those who pay heed to it will stay far from the line of battle?" [15]

Chrysostom's Christian doctrine of natural law is fully developed and in no way severed from the Lordship of Jesus Christ. He insists that all people are endowed with moral knowledge. "When God created man at the beginning he gave to him a natural law. What is natural law? It shapes and corrects the conscience within us when it provides knowledge which is capable, of itself, of distinguishing what is good from what is not good".[16]

External circumstances did not favour Chrysostom's prophetic courage and creativity. He is a sign that God can send prophets under the most unfavourable conditions if those called are truly responsive to the call.

6. St Ambrose

St Ambrose (339-397) is one of the great churchmen who combines, in an outstanding way, salvation truth with authentic knowledge of authority. He was so loved as governor of the province Aemilia-Liguria (seated in Milan) that after the death of the Arian bishop the people spontaneously called for him as bishop. He was able to unite the people again in the Catholic faith.

Like Chrysostom, Ambrose was never the "king's priest".

His prophetic courage brought him sharp opposition from Empress Justina. He called the mighty ones to penance, to justice and clemency. He was a great teacher of faith. Although not a speculative theologian, he brought the thought of Origen and Basil the Great home to the Latin Church. As a pastor, he addressed many moral problems in a very practical way. He wrote for his priests the book *De Officiis* (on the duties of a good pastor and of all believers), borrowing particularly from Cicero's book of the same title. He was, however, critical, discerning regarding the use of pagan philosophy. Like others, he adopted the system of the four cardinal virtues from Stoic ethics trying to give them an authentically Christian content. He influenced the Latin Church above all through his disciple, St Augustine, whom he had received into the Catholic Church.

7. St Augustine

Augustine of Hippo (354-430) is perhaps the most creative, the most imaginative thinker of Christian antiquity and like Chrysostom is marked by a dedication to Christ and his Church. Augustine, however, had greater influence in the western Church, since he wrote in Latin. Throughout the centuries he has been a fascinating figure, due to his warm humanity, his sincerity, his confidence in God and his capacity to present an attractive synthesis of Christian doctrine and ethics. "He is the crowning end of Christian antiquity, its last and greatest thinker".[17]

St Augustine has treated almost all of the major perspectives of Christian morality, and has done so in great depth and with an unmatched knowledge of the human heart. He has anticipated much of the knowledge uncovered by modern depth psychology. "The genius of Augustine is unique in its versatile mastery of all the literary genres in his ethical writings: vivid description, profound handling of principles, captivating manifestation of emotions, practical moral exhortation, epistolatory admonition, spiritual guidance. Even the diverse methods found within Catholic moral theology, the scholastic and mystic, æsthetic and casuistic, find their models in his work".[18]

Like his personality, Augustine's theology reveals a great complexity. He went a long way from Manicheism to Platonism and finally to Christ; and only gradually did he free himself from some manichean trends. He always remained a Platonist and so influenced all of western theology until Thomas Aquinas, and even beyond that time.

Always and everywhere, Augustine extols the bounty of God's grace, and faith as an undeserved gift. On the other hand, he has not denied free will, although he realizes that the mystery of predestination on one hand and free will on the other cannot be explained by a human being. Against the Manicheans and Pelagians, Augustine strongly asserts the reality of sin. He calls the Church herself "a mixed body". Sin is a terrifying reality but man cannot excuse himself. God offers his grace to all, and those who pray and put their trust in God will receive freedom in Christ.

Like the Church Fathers of the East of whom we have already written, Augustine teaches a natural law by which God guides the conscience of all people. God never has abandoned humankind. Like Cicero, Augustine defines virtue as "a natural disposition consistent with nature and reason".[19] However, he does not think highly of the virtues of the heathen but thinks that they are, rather, more like splendid vices.

More than many earlier theologians, Augustine succeeds in integrating the four cardinal virtues into the one great vision of redeemed, Christlike love. He sees the divine gift of love, responded to by man, as at the heart of all virtues: "So that temperance is love, keeping the self entire and uncorrupt for the beloved. Courage is love, bearing everything gladly for the sake of the beloved. Righteousness is love, serving the beloved only, and therefore ruling well. And prudence is love, wisely discerning what helps it and what hinders it".[20] Without love, no virtue really counts. Love unites us with God and with fellowman. It makes us truly the Church, and makes the Church "the one Christ loving himself".[21]

The love of God, always united with the love of neighbour, is for Augustine everywhere visible as the centre of morality. "Virtue is simply nothing but the highest love of God".[22] Probably the most quoted word of St Augustine is "Love and do what you will".[23] However, it must be read in the context and in its original meaning. He does not say *"ama"* but "*dilige*", which means "have a pure and right love". St Augustine's vision of love is not at all that unstructured or agnostic love which Joseph Fletcher and other extreme situation ethicists have in mind. He tells us to be careful about whom we love and how we love, and that we can learn love from Jesus Christ under the guidance of the Holy Spirit.

One of St Augustine's weakest points is his outlook on sexuality and marriage; but there, too, he makes many sensible observations although, especially in his early writings, there is still much of his manichean background. But because he is nevertheless such a creative and faithful theologian, it is not surprising that the Augustinian vision of marriage had a great and often unfortunate impact on the Church in succeeding centuries. In the encyclical *Casti Connubii*, for instance, St Augustine is quoted thirteen times; and it is not uninteresting to read the context of all the quotes made in that encyclical.[24]

IV. A TIME OF REPETITION

For theology in general and moral theology in particular, the period from the end of the sixth to the end of the twelfth century was barren. There was little activity beyond the compiling of summaries. Fidelity was not creative; rather, it was frequently misunderstood as never-changing repetition.

To some extent the Iro-Scottish Church was creative in the matter of the sacrament of penance, mitigating and adjusting the rather rigid discipline of the Roman Church. The Irish and Scottish monks did this not without some relation to the oriental monks. However, the penitential books that influenced the whole western Church for almost twelve hundred years were creative in the wrong sense: they added more and more kinds of penance for the various sins. The *Penitential* of Burchard is a pertinent example. It lists not less than twenty varieties of homicide, each with its own appropriate penance determined according to the social rank of the person who was killed! [25] In all of this, there was too much knowledge of dominion, of the controller, so that the wisdom of the "knowledge of salvation" was somehow blocked.

V. A CENTURY OF CREATIVE THEOLOGY AND RENEWAL

1. *The blessing of St Francis and St Dominic*

The great religious movements at last brought a new creativity into the theology of morals. Mystical theology was enriched by St Bernard of Clairvaux, Eckart, Tauler, Henry Suso and many others. The greatest contributions were made by members of the two mendicant orders, the Franciscans and Dominicans. Here again, serious learning met with enthusiasm of faith. Alexander Hales (died 1245) and St Bonaventure (1221-1274) and later Duns Scotus (died 1308) enriched the Church by "teaching of wisdom". There was no such thing as a separate moral theology. They studied all of theology as a message of salvation. Union with Christ, the gifts of faith and grace, the sacramental reality: all this was presented in its own richness as bringing fruit in love and justice for the life of the world.

The Dominicans gave to the Church such splendid teachers as Albert the Great (1193-1280) who, in the breadth of his knowledge, is comparable to Clement and Origen, and his disciple, St Thomas Aquinas (died 1274).

2. *A saint innovator*

In the recent past centuries, Thomas Aquinas has been presented consistently as the glory and bulwark of the Catholic faith. However, we should remind ourselves of what it meant in those times to be such a creative theologian. Avery Dulles tells of this. To his contemporaries, Thomas Aquinas "was not the 'common doctor' but a controversial innovator, not a canonized saint but the purveyor of a dangerous new brand of secular philosophy, not a strong bulwark but a teacher widely suspected of heresy . . . At Paris, where he did his later studies, the Dominicans were regarded as a strange, unwholesome breed, neither monks nor seculars, defiant of all the traditional categories. Not surprisingly, the Dominican house of studies became a sign of contradiction. The life style of St Thomas and his Dominican brothers might not have excited disapprobation had it not been combined with a second revolutionary stance: the acceptance of Aristotle as the master of theological and scientific method. Thomas had to begin his teaching career in the midst of violent controversy. On many occasions the university students were forbidden to attend his classes. After he died, the bishop of Paris and the archbishop of Canterbury condemned numerous theses which St Thomas had defended".[27]

Thomas Aquinas was truly creative in a pastoral sense. It was not arbitrariness when he tried to meet Aristotle's thought which was already widespread in Europe and was, for many, a temptation to abandon faith. Instead of presenting sterile apologetics, Thomas entered into a most fruitful dialogue, working out a new synthesis without abandoning what was good in the Augustinian tradition. Aquinas was very well versed in the Bible, and his moral teaching, thoroughly integrated into the whole vision of faith, has at its very heart "the law of the Spirit which gives us life in Christ Jesus".

In a certain sense, Thomas Aquinas was the innovator of a systematic moral theology. However, it is erroneous to present separately the second part of the theological *Summa*, which treats mainly of ethical questions, as a system cut off from the first and third parts. Not only does he treat important moral questions in the third part of the *Summa* — such as "moral life in accordance with the sacraments of faith" — but, above all, the second part was never thought of as an independent moral theology. For St Thomas as for St Bonaventure, there is only one theology and that is the doctrine of salvation that teaches us to know God and to know man, to love God and serve man.

While Thomas Aquinas offers a considerable body of philosophical speculation (what Max Scheler would call *Seinswissen*) it is all subordinated to the knowledge of salvation. It is presented with a pastoral mind.

Not unlike Chrysostom, Thomas Aquinas is a model of the creative and faithful theologian in circumstances that did not always favour these qualities. He had much less to suffer than Chrysostom, but it cannot be deplored enough that his beneficial influence was greatly stifled by office holders in the Church at a time when it was most needed. Later, Thomism did not serve its main purpose because it became too repetitious. The formulations of Aquinas were simply repeated unimaginatively, without his courageous encounter with the spirit of the era and without his sound vision of the signs of the times.

3. *The impact of Nominalism*

The Nominalism that prevailed after the thirteenth century, largely through the great influence of William of Ockham (1349), can be called creative; yet in many aspects it does not deserve the praise of "faithful in Christ". It emphasized, and sometimes overemphasized, individual freedom and the unique value of the singular and the individual, but it lost sight of the solidarity of salvation.

4. *Thomas Aquinas vindicated*

In the sixteenth century, the work of Thomas Aquinas was finally no longer suspect and found its great commentators. Some of them, like Thomas De Vio, Cardinal Cajetan (died 1534), and the Dominican Francis of Vitoria (died 1536), are imposing figures of the Thomistic renaissance. Especially Francis Vitoria was most sensitive to the new problems arising in a new era.

VI. ORIGIN OF THE ROMAN CATHOLIC MORAL THEOLOGY

1. *A new purpose and new environment of moral theology*

It is important to remind ourselves that the moral theology that most of us were taught in our seminaries twenty or thirty years ago is a rather recent product. Through fifteen centuries the Catholic Church had nothing like that. It is not "the" tradition but is one late tradition; and as we shall see, it was never unchallenged within the Roman Catholic Church. That there is nothing similar in the Orthodox or Protestant Churches is no wonder, since this type of moral theology came into being only after the great separation.

Although the Thomistic revival of Christian moral theology was concerned with human rights and with international justice — the relations between and among nations — a rather striking privatizing tendency also soon became apparent. And this goes hand in hand with the new purpose of moral teaching: the "administration of the sacrament of penance".

On the one hand, a truly Catholic reform, whose most noble representatives were, among others, St Teresa of Avila and St John of the Cross, was giving the Church profound works on a spirituality that, at least partially, continued the tradition of the great Church Fathers of whom we have spoken. On the other hand there was developing a moral theology just for the solution of cases in the confessional. In this theology, the confessor's role was understood chiefly as a judge. Not only had he to know whether the penitent had sinned but also whether he had committed a grave sin (frequently equated with mortal sin) and to determine accurately the number and species of all these mortal sins. Such a moral theology no longer promotes the patterns of discipleship, of that righteousness that comes from God's justifying action and in loving response to his call to become ever more the image and likeness of his own mercy. All this was left out or at least left to dogmatic or spiritual theology.

The goal of systematic moral theology was now to determine the doctrinal principles underlying the correct solution of cases for the confessional. The result was a gradual development of an independent and self-sufficient moral discipline, although it considered itself self-sufficient only by incorporating all determinations of canon laws and frequently those of civil laws. It became one-sidedly an ethics of obedience while it was also an ethics of control through the confessor.

The new perspective and purpose led to a rapid development of the problematic of "theological opinion" — opinion that could safely be followed by the confessor or/and by the penitent. The source of moral knowledge was no longer Holy Scripture but chiefly law and the declarations of the magisterium which were also conceived in the perspective of abiding laws. The exercise of the magisterium was too much linked with the earthly power of the bishops, especially of the popes.

When the patristic and medieval tradition on natural law was presented in this new framework, it became deeply affected by a legalistic tendency. The emphasis was no longer on the law inborn in man and discovered by conscience in the reciprocity of consciences, but rather on the authoritative decision of what natural law prescribes for all people of all times. There was little consciousness of the interdependence of moral knowledge with the total cultural, social, political structures and environment.

It would be unfair to say that all this endeavour was sterile There were, throughout all this time, many moralists who tried to integrate the new knowledge of their times about man. But in view of the whole historical context — including the heavy hand of the universal Roman Inquisition and other inquisitions and censorships — a prophetic spirit could not flourish. This moral theology, for instance, presented reasons for the existence of slavery instead of being a prophetic voice for the radical abolishment of such an abominable institution. Most of the manuals showed little interest in matters of social and international justice, for this was not considered a matter for the ordinary penitent. They surely did not foster a consciousness of everyone's responsibility in the cultural, social and political spheres.

The work of theologians has to be seen always within the frame of society and Church and their respective self-understanding. The prevailing concern of one part of this new Roman Catholic moral theology was to enforce the laws of Church and state. The emphasis was on man-made laws. Church law was also understood as being enforced by the political community while, at the same time, the Church enforced the law and order of the political community. And since the self-understanding of the Church was static, as was also the understanding of human nature and natural law, a desire for change was considered one of the greatest sins.

This attitude produced the system of "tutiorism", whereby the literal application of the law was to prevail in all matters of doubt. Close to the same rigid approach came "probabiliorism", which taught that the presumption always favours the literal application of the law unless much stronger reasons can be presented for freedom to seek the good in a different way. Natural law principles were proposed as if they were part of a codified law. Scripture, too, was understood as a static system of laws; hence, any quote from the Bible could enforce a law in a literal, fundamentalist understanding.

On the other side were numerous pastors and theologians — mostly Probabilists — who were much more aware of the dynamic character of history, of human nature and of natural law, and were mainly concerned with respect for the consciences of sincere people. By no means did they deny the validity of law and order. Under the given circumstances they did not dare to challenge the authoritarian regimes and the staggering number of laws and penal sanctions. Within the given system, however, they gave priority to people's conscience as long as it was sincere. Therefore they taught that in cases where the validity, justice or correct application of a law might be in doubt, creative liberty should prevail.

Frequently these moralists were profoundly compassionate pastors, and their concern in proposing the system of probabilism was to follow the main pattern of the Bible, "Be compassionate as your heavenly Father is compassionate" (Lk 6:36). It cannot be denied that some people would take advantage of their arguments and opinions in order to find the easy way out, but this does not at all diminish the merits of those numerous moralists — especially in the Society of Jesus — who were keenly aware that all too many laws and sanctions stifle the freedom and creativity of the faithful.

They were also concerned not to make it impossible for dedicated Christians to be present in economic and cultural spheres. There was, for instance, the very sharp and clearly defined position of the official Church, prohibiting the taking of any form of interest for loans. In order to avoid guilt complexes or rebellion against the official Church, or withdrawal from the world, many moralists found arguments and reasons for allowing a moderate rate of interest. While their way of arguing, in view of the clearcut teaching of the official Church, was sometimes artificial, their motives, intentions and intrinsic reasons were valid.

Since the rigorists and tutiorists could see no moral value except in the observance of law, they easily labelled these Probabilists as "laxists", or men aiming to undermine morality. To oppose any part of the codes of law was, for them, to undermine morality. Even Blaise Pascal seems to have been not quite free from this misunderstanding when he undertook his fight against the moral teaching of the Jesuits.[28]

The Jansenists, who bitterly fought against the Probabilists, were perhaps even more entangled in legalistic thinking than those whom they were blaming. It is true that Probabilists, even when their concern was clearly for a better understanding of fidelity and in favour of liberty, did sometimes use arguments that, on legal grounds, were distorted.

Meanwhile, the Carmelites of Salamanca, keeping themselves out of the heat of the vigorous theological quarrels, patiently composed their *Cursus Theologiæ Moralis* (1665-1724). This is, without doubt, the most comprehensive and significant work in moral theology of that time. However it, too, is affected by the whole situation of a Church in self-defence, a Church too much linked with a totalitarian type of political system.

2. *St Alphonsus Liguori*

St Alphonsus Liguori (1696-1787) is honoured by the Church as patron of moral theologians and confessors.[29] His work and his contribution to the history of moral theology can be evaluated only in view of the situation of Church and society in which he made his efforts to bring balance into moral theology and to fight against Jansenism. Alphonsus, founder of the Redemptorists, was, above all, a pastor dedicated to the marginal people, the poor and the oppressed. He and his confreres bound themselves by an explicit vow to give preference to these marginal people.

Against Jansenistic pessimism, St Alphonsus' essential message is, "Plentiful is redemption with the Lord". When he began to write, he was not at all intending to propose a systematic moral theology for all times. On the contrary, he was simply moved by pastoral zeal. At that time, the Society of Jesus was already strongly embattled and the Probabilists were suspect. He himself had been taught by a Dominican who followed a rather rigid probabiliorism, but as soon as Alphonsus dedicated himself to the poor and the marginal people, he saw that this system was not suited to his purpose.

He did embrace probabilism, but in view of the situation in the Church he carefully called it "aequiprobabilism", which means that when an upright conscience has equally or almost equally good reasons for creative use of freedom in view of present needs, it is not bound by law which is, in itself or in its concrete application, doubtful. Law should have no right to stifle creative freedom unless it has clearly stronger reasons for doing so.

In spite of warnings on all sides, Alphonsus also consistently taught that confessors should not unsettle the good conscience of penitents by referring to law, whether natural law or merely Church or state law, when he can foresee that the penitent cannot truly interiorize this law or precept.

The whole theological effort of St Alphonsus against Jansenism is a theology of divine mercy. He therefore strongly opposes the Thomistic system's teaching about predestination and the distinction between "efficacious" and merely "sufficient" graces. In that system it seemed that God would exclude great numbers of people from salvation by his own decrees. While the elect would receive graces "efficacious" to merit salvation, others would be given graces called "sufficient", which would be sufficient for accountability but unproductive of the good works for which they are given, and therefore would metaphysically determine unavoidable failure and consequent condemnation. No wonder that the opponents of this theory responded by the prayer, *A gratia sufficienti libera nos Domine*: "From 'sufficient' grace, deliver us, O Lord!"

St Alphonsus's theology, like the whole Catholic moral theology of the past centuries, was chiefly concerned with helping confessors to form mature and peaceful consciences. He had given much time to helping scrupulous persons, and therefore instructed confessors not to lead people into unnecessary anxiety. He wrote a number of books specifically destined for confessors, one of which was the *Homo Apostolicus*, "The Apostolic Man". This is probably the most mature of the saint's work in the field of penitential moral theology. It went through one hundred and eighteen editions. Not less helpful is his *Confessor of Country People*. Against the prevailing theological theory that saw the confessor's role above all as a judge, St Alphonsus, in full awareness of the situation, assigned first role to making visible the compassionate love of the heavenly Father, as Christ did.

One can fully appreciate the charism of creative liberty and fidelity in Alphonsus only by giving attention to his more numerous and widespread writings on a truly Christian life. In almost all his books, he repeatedly refers to St Augustine's word, "Have true love and do what love wills". The most beautiful of his works is *The Art of Loving Jesus Christ*. This is a kind of moral theology for lay people as well as for priests. It presents the true countenance of love and applications of love, in the form of a commentary on the thirteenth chapter of the first letter of St Paul to the Corinthians.

This is what St Alphonsus understood as the ideal moral theology. His constant theme is on the vocation of all Christians to holiness; but he was thoroughly against Jansenism which would allow place in the Church only to perfected people. His vision was one of ongoing conversion, and he saw the priest as a patient guide who encourages people to take one step after another.

VII. RENEWAL OF MORAL THEOLOGY IN THE NINETEENTH CENTURY

1. *Reliving the broader tradition*

As we have shown, the individualistic moral theology was never unchallenged. For instance, Cardinal Berulle, founder of the French school of spirituality which gave the Church great saints, always presented a spirituality and morality based on the sacramental experience of life in Christ, who is the supreme sacrament. Where members of his school preached the gospel, they preserved whole areas from Jansenism and dechristianization.

A scientific and systematic effort to renew moral theology took place in the faculties of German state universities. These efforts were possible because the theological faculties at state universities enjoyed greater academic freedom than teachers in the seminaries. The best known moralists who presented a totally different type of manual from those of the legalistic

and casuistic schools are John Michael Sailer (1751-1832).
John Baptist Hirscher (1788-1865), and Francis Xavier
Linsenmann (1835-1898).

2. *John Michael Sailer*

Sailer [30] gave to his comprehensive text on moral theology
the characteristic subtitle, "Not only for Future Catholic Pastors
but also for Every Educated Christian". Like Rosmini in Italy,
he was shocked by the gap between the clergy and educated
lay people. As the great Church fathers of East and West have
done, so Sailer entered into active dialogue with the thought
patterns of his times. He follows the emphasis on creative
fidelity, righteousness in response to God's own saving justice,
and discipleship and love as the all-embracing response to God.

Both in the goal he sets for himself and in the spiritual
fervour of his language, he resembles St Francis de Sales whom
he greatly admired. But he does not content himself with
imparting practical advice for spiritual progress as did Francis
in his masterly treatises. Sailer's purpose and plan includes
the entire edifice of teaching Christian life, a systematic presentation of the perfect goal of that life. But far from Jansenistic
harshness, he allows patient, ongoing progress towards the
ideal. At the heart of his moral theology is the theme of ongoing
conversion.

Sailer must be appreciated in the light of his times. He
belongs to the Romantic period, and his ideal of personality
is influenced by it. Therefore he insists on the use and development of all of God's individual gifts in all their diversity, but
also in the spirit of solidarity, since everything is given in view
of the upbuilding of the mystical body of Christ.

In view of Sailer's creativity as a theologian and his distinctively Christian fidelity to the Church, it is almost
unbelievable how much he had to suffer from Church and state
establishments. Even saints were denouncing him as a controversial and suspect theologian. However, he finally received
appreciation from the official Church and was nominated bishop
of Regensburg.

3. John Baptist Hirscher

Not less creative was John Baptist Hirscher.[31] He presents the whole Christian moral teaching in the pattern of the Synoptics: that is, the realization of the kingdom of God on earth. In theological depth he yields to Sailer, whom he greatly admired, but he exceeds him in greater psychological insights. More realistic and equally aware of the age in which he lived, he gave a more dynamic and rigorous presentation of thought, though he occasionally fell short of Sailer's mystic loftiness.

Sublime in conception and happy in execution, Hirscher's moral theology nevertheless suffered from the defects which are inevitable in the enterprise of pioneers. He gratefully accepted critique and improved each of his later editions. His work found ready acceptance among Catholics and Protestants; but when one of his books, in which he blamed the methods of the Neo-scholastics, was put on the Index of forbidden books, he was not only discredited in the eyes of many Catholics but also suffered a loss of self-confidence. And this was so because he was not only loyal but also devout in his fidelity to the official Church.

4. Francis Xavier Linsenmann

A number of other outstanding and creative theologians worked in the same direction as Sailer and Hirscher, and would deserve to be mentioned. The most important continuer of this renewal was Francis Xavier Linsenmann (1855-1898) of the Tübingen school. He dedicated a long series of studies to the fundamental problems of law and liberty.[32] He was convinced that moral theology should follow the spirit of St Paul and give primary attention to the freedom of the sons and daughters of God. He considered as sterile and futile a moral theology concerned only with what is proscribed by law. "Only a tiny portion of the good expected from us is circumscribed by law. An immense area of free moral activity lies open before us".[33] Therefore Linsenmann considered it one of the major tasks of moral theology to uncover the deeper meaning of freedom as following of Christ under the grace of the Holy Spirit.

His manual of moral theology (1878) is a happy synthesis

of speculative and practical method, with openness to the Spirit and to the opportunities of his age. Always he emphasizes the normative value of growth and ongoing conversion. That his work did not meet with the recognition and success it deserved is most unfortunate. It did not correspond with the static self-understanding of the Church that had prevailed after Vatican I and was, indeed, a strong force since the Congress of Vienna in 1816, and even more since 1848, when many Christians and office holders in the Church decided to withstand all change as if it were sin and danger.

One of the strengths of the German effort to renew Catholic moral theology was its contact with the prevailing spirit of the age, a constructive dialogue with the most influential philosophies, and the fact that the manuals were written in the German language. But in the long run this became also a handicap, since none of the manuals were ever translated into other languages and, therefore, beyond the German-speaking countries, had no major impact on the whole of moral theology in the Catholic Church.

VIII. TWO GREAT CONVERTS TO THE CATHOLIC CHURCH: ECUMENICAL DIMENSION

In a perspective of creative fidelity and depth of inner freedom, John Henry Cardinal Newman and Vladimir Sergeevich Solovyev cannot be highly enough esteemed. They are two giants in ecumenical and spiritual theology.

1. John Henry Newman

John Henry Newman (1801-1890) is an example of prophetic priesthood. Circumstances, at least as far as the institutional Church was concerned, did not make his prophetic role easier than the priestly and kingly powers in old Israel did for the prophets of old. But his genius was supported by warm friendships and, above all, by the inner strength of his spirituality.

As an Anglican priest he was censored by the University of Oxford and by twenty-four Anglican bishops, mainly because of his dynamic understanding of doctrine. Fully aware that much in the Catholic Church of his time did not reflect the vision he expressed in his famous *Essay on the Development of Christian Doctrine* (1845), he became a fervent member of the Roman Catholic Church. His article *On Consulting the Faithful in Matters of Doctrine*, published in *The Rambler*, occasioned accusations in Rome and his removal as editor of *The Rambler*. The clouds of suspicion hung over him most of his priestly life, yet his autobiography, *Apologia pro Vita Sua*, witnesses to his serenity and inner peace.

Despite all the accusations that were sent to Rome and had found strong echoes in the Roman Curia, Pius IX personally invited Newman to assist in the sessions of the First Vatican Council. Newman, however, excused himself. Although he believed in infallibility as it was finally defined in Vatican I, he considered its solemn declaration not opportune, and did not want to enter the arena of disputes in Rome. He preferred the solitude of his Oratory in Birmingham. His book, *Letter to the Duke of Norfolk*, is probably the most constructive presentation of the doctrine of infallibility in relation to conscience. It reconciled many Catholics and Anglicans with Newman. No moral theologian can ignore the great vision of Newman on conscience and on genuine religious authority.

Newman's theology and life was thoroughly nourished by Holy Scripture and by study of the Church Fathers. He insisted on the continuity of the Old and New Testaments through the prophetic tradition. He also was convinced that God had given a prophetic spirit to people outside Israel, and he envisioned everything in view of Christ the Prophet.

Although the institution and a great part of the history of the cardinalate does not belong to the prophetic aspect of the Church, it was a consoling gesture when Leo XIII named as cardinal this man who had suffered so much from traditionalists in the Church, and from parts of the institutional Church. That honour changed nothing in the simplicity of his life.

In the Second Vatican Council, the theology and spirit of Cardinal Newman, and of Rosmini whom he highly venerated, were effectively present. Both were most loyal sons of a Church that made them suffer so much.

2. *Vladimir Sergeevich Solovyev*

Vladimir Sergeevich Solovyev (1853-1900),[34] although coming from a different tradition, resembles Newman in the breadth of his knowledge and vision and in the depth of his spirituality. No more than Newman can Solovyev be labelled a "moralist"; indeed, he was sometimes not very kind in his expressions about western moralism severed from Wisdom.

A renewal of moral theology in the perspective of the gospel and of the prophets should give special attention to Solovyev's writings. The official Russian Church did not treat him favourably. The Holy Synod of 1889 forbade him to write further on religious matters. His conversion to the Roman Catholic Church was, in his eyes, by no means a separation from the Orthodox Church. He lived in loving and faithful relationships with these two parts of a separated Christianity in the hope of unity. His writings are of great service to ecumenism, which will be fostered by a theology that overcomes the division between spirituality and moral theology.

IX. CONCLUSION:
A NEW KAIROS FOR CREATIVE THEOLOGY

The renewal of moral theology is not a matter just for moral theologians. Dogmatic theologians like John Adam Möhler, Rosmini, Newman, Solovyev and, in our time, men like Henri de Lubac, Yves Congar, Karl Rahner, and notable theologians of other churches, have explored the salvation dimension and the prophetic strength of the deposit of faith.

Biblical renewal brings moral and dogmatic theology together again. A great turning point for the whole of Catholic theology came through the encyclical *Divino afflante Spiritu* of Pius XII in 1943. It opened for biblical scholars and all theologians an era of liberty and thus of greater fidelity to the Gospel.

The Second Vatican Council has given great impetus to the renewal of Catholic moral theology. The deepened self-understanding of the Church set forth in the *Pastoral Constitution on the Church in the Modern World*, which should be read in the perspective of the prophetic tradition of Israel and the

Church, the *Decree on Ecumenism*, surely one of the most prophetic documents of Church history, the *Declaration on Religious Liberty*, which can mean liberation from a prepotent "knowledge of dominion", and, finally, the short but forceful appeal for a profound renewal of moral theology in view of the lofty vocation of the believers in Christ (*Priestly Formation*, 16): all these present a great challenge for moral theology today to enter into a new phase of creativity in freedom and fidelity. These two aspects cannot be severed from each other.[35]

NOTES

1 Cf. M. Scheler, *Die Wissensformen und die Gesellschaft*, Leipzig, 1926, reprint Basel-München, 1960.
2 *Dialogus cum Tryphone judaeo*, c. 11, n. 2 PG 6, 497; c. 24, n. 1 PG 6, 528; cf. E.F. Osborn, *Justin Martyr*, Tübingen, 1973.
3 E.F. Osborn, *Ethical Patterns in Early Christian Thought*, Cambridge, New York/Melbourne, 1976, 51.
4 Cf. H. Chadwick, *Early Christian Thought and Classical Tradition. Studies in Justin, Clement and Origen*, New York, 1966; O. Prunet, *La morale de Clement d'Alexandria*, Paris, 1966.
5 Cf. E.F. Osborn, *The Philosophy of Clement of Alexandria*, Cambridge, 1967.
6 *Protrepticus*, 11, 117.
7 E.F. Osborn, *Ethical Patterns of Early Christian Thought*, 52.
8 Clement, *Paidagogos*, II PG 8, 511 A.
9 Cf. H.T. Kerr, *The First Systematic Theologian: Origen of Alexandria*, Princeton, 1958; G. Teichtweier, *Die Sündenlehre des Origines*, Regensburg, 1958; G. Gruber, *Zoë, Wesen, Stufen und Mitteilung des wahren Lebens bei Origines*, München, 1962.
10 E.F. Osborn, l.c., 101.
11 A. Puech, *St-Jean Chrysostome et les moeurs de son temps*, Paris, 1891, 325.
12 Chrysostom, *Against the Jews*. 6, 7, PG48, 916.
13 *On virginity*, 9, PG 48, 539-540.
14 In Ps. XLI, 2, PG 55, 158.
15 *Homily on 1 Cor.* 6, PG 61, 53-54.
16 *On Statues*, 12, 3, PG 49, 131.
17 E. Troeltsch, *Augustin, die Christliche Antike und das Mittelalter*, München und Berlin, 1915, 6f; cf. M.T. Clark, *Augustine, Philosopher of Freedom*, New York, 1958.
18 J. Mausbach. *Die Ethik des hl. Augustinus*, Freiburg, 1929, I, 47.
19 *On 63 Diverse Questions*, 31, 1, PL 40, 20.
20 *On the Morals of the Catholic Church*, I, 15, 25, PL 32, 1322.
21 *On the Epistle of John*, 10, 3, PL 35, 2056.
22 *On the Morals of the Catholic Church*, 15, 25, PL 32, 1322.
23 *On the Epistle of John*, 7, 8, PL 35, 2033.
24 See my book *Love is the Answer*, Denville, 1970.
25 Migne, PL 140, 853 DC.

[26] E. Gilson, *Saint Thomas d'Aquin*, Paris, 1925; A. Dempf, *Die Ethik des Mittelalters*, München-Berlin, 1927; O. Lottin, *Psychologie et morale aux XIIe et XIIIe siecles*, Louvain, 1942/54.

[27] A. Dulles, S.J., "The Revolutionary Spirit of Thomas Aquinas", in *Origins*, Feb. 1975, 543f.

[28] Blaise Pascal, *Lettres Provinciales* (1656).

[29] Cf. K. Keusch, *Die Aszetik des hl. Alfons Maria von Liguori*, Paderborn, 1926.

[30] G. Fischer, *Johann Michael Sailer und Immanuel Kant*, Freiburg, 1953.

[31] J. Scharl, *Gesetz und Freiheit. Die theologische Begründung der christlichen Ethik bei J.B. Hirscher*, München, 1941.

[32] *Tübinger Theol. Quartalschrift* 53 (1871), 64-114; 221-277; 54 (1972), 3-49; 193-254.

[33] l.c., 54 (1872), 45.

[34] All of V. Solovyev's works are published in a critical German edition by Erich Wewel Verlag, Freiburg-München, 1955-1978.

[35] An abundant bibliography on the history of moral theology and a list of the most used manuals of moral theology is to be found in my earlier work, *The Law of Christ*, I, 53-59. There can be found a more complete sketch of the history. For further bibliography and information, see G. Angelini, A. Valsecchi, *Disegno Storico della teologia morale*, Bologna, 1972; P. Tillich, *A History of Christian Thought from the Judaic and Hellenistic Origins to Existentialism*, edited by C.E. Braaten, New York, 1972; H.R. Niebuhr, *Christian Ethics. Sources of Living Tradition*, edited with introduction by W. Beach and H.R. Niebuhr, 2nd ed., New York, 1973. The most complete and reliable information and bibliography on the history of moral theology can be found in L. Vereecke, *History of Moral Theology*, lectures given at the Academia Alfonsiana, Rome (mimeographed copies are available); Id., *Histoire et morale*, in *Studia Moralia*, 12 (1974), 81-95; for the latest development of moral theology, esp. in Germany, see the well documented study of J.G. Ziegler, *Die Moraltheologie des 20. Jahrhunderts*, in H. Vorgrimler, *Bilanz der Theologie des 20. Jahrhunderts*, vol. III, Freiburg, 1970, 316-360.

Chapter Three

Creative liberty and fidelity in responsibility

I. FOR A BETTER UNDERSTANDING OF KEY CONCEPTS, PATTERNS AND SYMBOLS

It is not at all my intention to present a comprehensive moral theology as a rigid system in which everything is presented as flowing from a single concept or idea. We are not dealing with abstract ideas but with discipleship in Jesus Christ. He is always the centre, origin and purpose of our life. This does not, however, prevent us from looking for a leitmotif and for key concepts that would help today's Christians to understand what it means to live one's moral life as witness to Christ.

The choice of a leitmotif must not be an arbitrary decision. It should be made only after having carefully studied the biblical patterns and after discerning, in view of those patterns, the special signs of God's present action and call in history.

As the title of this book implies, there is special emphasis on a life in Christ marked by liberty and fidelity. Since our life can be understood only in view of God's initiative, we exercise and develop our creative freedom and fidelity by listening and responding. It is therefore a distinctively Christian approach to emphasize *responsibility* as a leitmotif, but in a way that shows it as expression of creative freedom and fidelity.

Vatican II has given a very helpful analysis for this particular approach. "In every group or nation, there is an ever increasing number of men and women who are conscious that they themselves are the artisans and the authors of the culture of their community. Throughout the world, there is a similar growth in the combined sense of independence and responsibility. Such a development is of paramount importance for the spiritual and moral maturity of the human race. This truth grows clearer if we consider how the world is becoming unified and how we have the duty to build a better world based on truth and justice. Thus, we are witnesses of the birth of a new humanism, one in which man is defined, first of all, by his responsibility towards his brothers and towards history".[1]

In reaction to all kinds of faulty obedience under authoritarian rules and manipulation, people today emphasize the words "independence" and "liberty". But our leitmotif is not just a reaction. Far beyond protest, it seeks a balanced vision. Therefore, in this effort to describe a morality of response and responsibility, I insist as much on creative fidelity as on creative liberty.

An abstract concept, even if well chosen, cannot inspire action or increase the psychodynamics and noödynamics of persons or communities. People are more effectively influenced and brought to common action by symbols than by abstract concepts.[2] Neither the word "freedom", nor "fidelity", nor "responsibility", of itself, nor all of them together, would be a sufficiently unifying symbol. They receive, in this moral theology, their basic force and dynamics in Christ.

II. CHRIST, THE UNIFYING SYMBOL AND REALITY

Only by knowing Jesus Christ, the Incarnate Word of God, do we come to a specific and dynamic understanding of responsibility. "The point of departure for Christian ethics is not the reality of one's own self, nor is it the reality of standards and values. It is the reality of God as he has revealed himself in Jesus Christ".[3]

Christ is revealed as the Word Incarnate through whom the

Father speaks out all his love and wisdom. In him, God gives to humankind, in infinite freedom, his greatest and undeserved gift. Jesus is his final Word, in whom he gives himself.

In an absolutely unique sense, Jesus of Nazareth lives by the Word that comes from the mouth of the Father (cf. Mt 4:3). He is not only the One who speaks the truth but, even more fundamentally, is the One who listens and can give the consoling and healing message. "The Lord God has given me the tongue of a disciple, that I may know how to sustain, with a word, him who is weary. Morning after morning, he awakens my ear to hear, as those who are disciples. The Lord God has opened my ear and I did not turn away" (Is 50:4-5).

Jesus is both the Word who calls and the One who is called and sent. In him who is the hypostatic covenant between the eternal Word of the Father and the word of humanity, God and humanity have found the perfect listener.

Jesus of Nazareth is the Christ, anointed by the power of the Holy Spirit for a response in life and in death, a response in which he gives not only words but himself, in the blood of the covenant. Always his response is directed both to the Father who has called and sent him and to those to whom he is sent, his brothers and sisters. His response is one of absolute fidelity to the Father. It is not fidelity to a defence morality but the fidelity of one who listens and responds creatively and in utter freedom. Thus his response truly creates something new, the new earth and the new heaven.

"Freedom of the Son of God is that in which and by which the free response to God is effected. The freedom of the Son of God has its source in itself and in him, but the whole generation of Adam is in the Son of God".[4] In this vision of Nicolas Berdyaev we can see our own responsibility to share in Christ's infinite capacity to listen and to respond, to answer to God and to man. And we are to do so in a freedom analogous to Christ's.

While we choose as paradigms or symbols those perspectives and key concepts that respond to the passionate interests of today's world, we bring them into the all-inclusive vision of our central and real symbol, Christ. There we see the word "responsibility" in the light of the One who died for us, is risen for us and acknowledged by the Father as Lord over all, the One who is the Word, the Calling, and the Response in the name of all of us.

The broader Christological vision includes also a Christian anthropology which gives a distinctively monotheistic and Christian understanding of man. We know that we are created in the Word who became man for us, and that we are called in him, through him and for him. And we know that, as believers, we can give a valid response to God the Father through the power of the Spirit sent us by Jesus. "The Christian knows that while he is called, he is called as the one who already is elected from eternity even before he is formed in his mother's womb".[5]

The Christian is aware that he is, from the beginning, called from God and for God, and that he finds his truthful existence in a total answer to God's grace. In the light of the Word Incarnate who calls us all together, we see our whole existence as a word spoken and confirmed by God, and realize that we gain our own identity by making our whole life a response in Jesus Christ.

In modern literature and philosophical ethics, the word "responsibility" sometimes has the limited meaning of accountability before one's self or before others. But for us who are believers, it has a much deeper meaning. "God does not only impute responsibility, he imparts responsibility".[6] And this creative and redemptive gift is given in the Word Incarnate and by the grace of the Holy Spirit.

III. THE SACRED AND THE GOOD: RESPONSE AND RESPONSIBILITY

Discussions on a distinctively Christian ethics frequently centre around some specific norms. I think that James Gustafson has pointed the right course in centering, first of all, on the basic structures of ethics itself and confronting it with Christ.[7] The question that concerns us here is whether the whole pattern of moral theology follows the basic structure of Christian faith.[8]

The greatest fault of most of the manuals of moral theology written in the last two centuries was that they presented a morality that did not at all manifest the dialogical dynamics and structure of faith. The distinctive and truthful way of responding with all one's being is by faith, hope, love and adoration. A distinctively Christian morality is and must be characterized by the same responsorial dialogical structure.

1. Religion as response and obedience of faith

It is self-evident that the content of faith — God's revealing himself in Jesus Christ whom he gave us as Saviour and Lord — must direct our whole life. Here I focus on faith as it is lived.

A genuine faith-response is quite different from just following the pattern of an organized religion without personal choice and interiorization. In faith, we freely entrust ourselves to God in a joyous, grateful and humble response to his self-revelation.

Genuine faith, as the Bible presents it, includes faith-experience. This is something quite different from all other human experiences. It transcends them and gives them meaning by its character of *wholeness*. In faith, we experience God as the Life of our life and the Lord of all our being. Faith-experience is not just in the intellect or the will alone. It seizes one's whole being and gives a sense of completion, of wholeness and salvation.[9]

The experience is quite different from conceptualization, although it does not exclude it. Whoever tries to communicate faith to others through dry concepts only will fail dismally. There will always be faith looking for deeper understanding of itself, *fides quaerens intellectum;* but faith, as it is lived, is not produced by concepts and norms. It is far more than subscribing to a code of dogmas.

For a Christian, it should be easy to understand that believers are not faced just with a system of teachings but, above all, with Jesus Christ, the living and most real symbol of God's love for humankind. This central and most real symbol, and the symbols used in Christ's teaching, touch our intellect, our intuition, imagination, our affectivity, and thus also, more deeply, our will. "Symbols are not signs or images apart from the mind; they are dominant patterns in the imagination that mediate experience and create the world to which we belong. It is certainly possible that the symbols that rule the imagination are in fact symbols that reveal the hidden structure of reality, and thus lead people into a reconciled life and make them build a world in keeping with the deepest inclination of their being".[10]

God speaks in many ways to awaken, deepen and strengthen faith, hope, love, and the spirit of adoration. We are believers to the extent that, in all of reality and in all events that touch us, we perceive a gift and call from God. "Responsibility affirms: God is acting in all actions upon you, so respond to actions upon you as you respond to his action".[11]

Our response in faith is to the reality that is at its heart, the Word Incarnate, in whom all things are made. Since God speaks in all his words and works, the truly religious person gives a trusting response to him in all events. "The radical faith becomes incarnate insofar as every reaction to every event becomes a response in loyalty and confidence to the One who is present in all such events".[12]

The God of love speaks to us, most of all, through loving people, since by the quality of their life they are truly an image and likeness of God who is love. If we open ourselves to all that is genuine love, and readily respond to others as persons who love or who need love, we are always on the way of faith, even if only in the form of "analogy of faith". The God of love calls us also through all that he creates, and through his personal love for all people. He, the living and loving God, calls us especially through those who share his love, "and all human activity is essentially response to his call".[13]

Our response is truly a part of the total faith-experience if, confronted with people, we know that they must never be disregarded and are to be honoured and loved. Thus our response is integrated into the sovereign freedom of God who has created us all, not for any utility but as a sacred image and special sign of his presence.

God's word is almighty; but as a word that reaches us, it is spoken as if it were a finite word, a word of man. Yet this finite word turns us to the almighty Word of God if we have learned absolute reverence for every human person. "The original relation to God is the love of neighbour".[14]

2. Responsibility in a distinctively Christian vision

Whenever we synthesize our moral value system in categories unrelated to faith-response, we cause a split between religion and our everyday life. Responsibility, seen in a distinctively Christian way, is our God-given capacity to make all of our moral aspirations and decisions, indeed, all of our conscious life, a response to God, and thus to integrate it within the obedience of faith.

I have no difficulty in accepting Karl Barth's key concept of "obedience of faith" if it is understood in the original meaning of obedience, *ob-audire*. That means a rapt listening, a hearkening with all our being, so that we may respond totally. This radical obedience of faith is truthful only if our life follows the same pattern and it thereby becomes an integrated part of us. Barth also strongly emphasizes our accountability before God, the final judge, who does not allow us to make any derogating judgment of our brothers and sisters.

"It is the idea of responsibility which gives us the most exact definition of the human situation in the face of the absolute transcendence of the divine judgment".[15] However, in Barth's thought there is much more. The final issue is whether we respond in our whole life in all our attitudes, decisions and actions, in a way that makes us witnesses to God's grace. When we do so, we already experience, to some degree, the final saving judgment. We come to know our true self to whatever extent we respond with all our being. "I am invited and made responsible and enabled to fulfil my responsibility as this particular man, this one beloved by God, and therefore a responsible partner in the divine covenant".[16]

In faith-obedience — that is, in the radical hearkening to God's word, gift and action — we experience the divine command as a gift that is lost when, lacking gratitude, we refuse that total readiness to respond which is at the heart of faith. "The claim of the divine command is concerned with decisions, both as a whole and in detail. It is in these decisions that we give our witness to the fact that we belong to God. And he is our Lord by reason of his command, he is also the law by which we stand and fall".[17]

When self-fulfilment or self-perfection becomes the leitmotif and key concept of morality, then God is seen simply as a means to it. The Holy God remains foreign to this "business" of self-actualization. Quite different is an understanding of morality as a radical and all-embracing response to God, who calls each of us in our uniqueness and all of us together. Christ, the Word of God, who came for our salvation, is truly our Saviour when we receive him as our Lord, in readiness to follow him and respond to him, witnessing to his grace.

Our effort to dethrone our selfish self and even to remove from the centre our legitimate desire for self-fulfilment (self-actualization, self-perfection) does not at all threaten our inner, real self. On the contrary, it is precisely when we entrust our whole being to God that we experience the joy and peace of having, at last, found our true selves.

Because our own being is entrusted to us by the Father and identified with Christ Jesus, our brother, we must never disparage its worth. "The person who inwardly feels worthless is the one who must build himself up by selfish aggrandizement; but the person who has a sound experience of his own worth, that is, who loves himself, has the basis for acting generously towards his neighbour".[18]

An ethics of responsibility in Christ, the Word Incarnate, requires careful attention to appropriate *interpretation*. This is possible only if we "let Christ shine upon us" (Eph 5:16) by bringing all of our life into the light of faith in him who is our Light. As we grow in religious and moral maturity, we become ever more conscious of the presence of the One who calls us. And as we become more able to respond in gratitude and trust, we also become increasingly aware that our response to God, the giver of all good gifts, is authentic only if we are fully responsive also to the needs of our fellowmen in view of his gifts.

For genuine deliberation, evaluation and interpretation of God's call and our own tentative response, we need the support of a faith community. There, in that profound openness of conscience that unites us with all people of good will in the search for what is good and right, we find the truthful solutions to the many problems that arise in our individual life and social relationships.[19]

As followers of Christ, we can never limit our attention to how our response affects our own life. We must also, and most carefully, consider how it affects all our fellow travellers on this earthly journey. "Because of its objective embodiment, every free act produces a change in the sphere of freedom shared by all".[20] Hence we will give particular attention to how our own desires, decisions and actions affect our relationships with others and, indeed, the very lives of others.

Since each free act changes our own selves, our relationships, and even the lives and reality of others, interpretation never ends. From the very beginning, responsibility means the capacity to evaluate the foreseeable effects of our decisions. Not infrequently we realize that our assessment of a situation was less than complete. We therefore come back to our decision to seek new and possibly better evaluation and interpretation.

A vital condition for responsibility is "purity of heart", which means purity of motives and intentions. This purity is present in a distinctively Christian way when we discern whether we can offer this decision to our Lord who is crucified for us, and can do so in a genuine spirit of thanksgiving for his grace.

If we envision a Christian morality in this perspective then we shall have no doubt about the paramount importance of prayer, or about what genuinely Christian prayer is. We shall see it as total openness and listening to God in all the ways he decides to speak to us, inviting us and challenging us with the graced readiness to respond with all of our heart, our mind, our will, and all of our life.[21]

IV. RESPONSIBILITY IN CREATIVE LIBERTY

While we shall give great attention throughout this book to the nature and dynamics of freedom, my intention here is to show that creative freedom is a main trait of a Christian ethics of responsibility. Indeed, no genuine ethics can be understood without explaining clearly what freedom means and does not mean. "The negative forms of freedom confused freedom with licence and overlooked the fact that freedom is never the opposite of responsibility".[22] If we speak of creative freedom then we always mean freedom faithful to its divine origin.

Nicolas Berdyaev expresses well my own vision of freedom. "I do indeed love freedom above all else. Man came forth out of freedom and issues into freedom. I have put Freedom rather than Being at the basis of my philosophy".[23]

This means that I see God essentially as Freedom, the freedom to love, to create, to redeem. "Freedom has brought me to Christ and I know of no other path leading to him".[24] To be called by God in freedom and for freedom gives us a share in his creative purpose. "The word of God addresses man in his personal existence and thereby gives him freedom".[25]

1. *Responding to Christ and in Christ, the Liberator*

We can be creative in freedom only because we are called and liberated by Love Incarnate, Jesus Christ, our Redeemer. In his creative love, he calls us to make us sharers and co-revealers in his ongoing work of creation and redemption. I think of God's creative and redemptive love as the super-abundance of his own freedom. But if this is so, he wants us to be co-creators, co-artists, and not just spiritless executors of his will.

"Characteristically, Bultmann understands love as the goal of freedom, as the law of freedom. The servitude which the Christian finds in his freedom is also serving one another".[26] The law of Christ is, therefore, essentially a law of perfect liberty. To be free through that freedom by which God manifests his infinite love is to be totally free for genuine love.[27] Surely, God does not need us; but in his infinite freedom he created us to be co-creators throughout history. In Christ he has chosen us to be partners in the ongoing work of redemption. As parable for this understanding, perhaps we could take the work of a great artist whose genius reaches its peak in company with loving and co-creative disciples.

To affirm man's creativity or creative freedom, in view of God's infinitely creative and redeeming word, does not infer arrogance on man's part. Rather, it is gratitude for the way God calls us. It is "devotion to Being itself. It is the service of the Infinite in and through finite man's part in God's own work of promoting and expending his presence among men".[28]

In and through his own creativity, God has shown us that he does not want mechanical application of his laws or weary, stereotyped responses. He grants to us and requires from us a creative response in generosity beyond general norms. The relationship is dialogic. A genuine dialogue is quite different from reciting a learned text. If we truly listen to the other, something new is born in our mind. So, while we keep firmly in mind that everything is God's gift and deserves gratitude, this does not mean that God in any way determines our response.[29] Through his very gift, he enables and wants man to enrich the history of salvation in a creative way.

That history is one of interaction between God and his people and between person and person, in which all the partners are engaged in the co-creative dialogue. The outcome of our response is not something that is already fixed. "It is something which God does not reveal directly to man but he looks to man to complete the revelation himself".[30] This does not mean, of course, that the revelation is man's invention. The creative perception that goes on through history is indeed God's work, yet man's work too, in co-creativity. So great is this gift that comes from God's innermost freedom!

2. Uncreative freedom

God does not give his gifts to no purpose. He expects us to use them in his redemptive work. Whoever wastes, neglects or refuses his gift of creativity thereby impairs the work of redemption, and is culpable. This lack of creativity is strikingly visible in a legalism that creates nothing new, that never brings forth the newness of Christian morality beyond the letter of the law. It is a sin against the Lord of history who wants always to manifest his own creative love and liberty, through our participation.

Only in sin is man's freedom — although still freedom — thoroughly uncreative. Whenever a person fails to do the good he could and should do, or does the evil he could have avoided, he not only diminishes his own freedom but also impoverishes the whole of salvation history by the unproductive or destructive use of his freedom.

Yet, it has to be clearly seen that we can speak of personal sin only because there is freedom. The human person "has the power of contradicting himself and his essential nature. Man is free even from his freedom; that is, he can surrender his humanity".[31] By that very freedom which is our title to the human dignity granted by God, the sinner gradually destroys his freedom to choose the good. He freely decides to ignore the truth that "the freedom of the Christian is a freedom for Jesus: to be free for a divine purpose that is from the beginning".[32]

3. Creative mutuality

Creativity in freedom is manifested mainly in interpersonal relations. Great thinkers like Tillich and Berdyaev have indicated that, for them, the Trinitarian dogma is a source of joy. Through the relationship of the Father and the Son in the love of the Holy Spirit, they understand better the overflowing freedom of God in his innermost life, and realize that love is at its most creative when it brings forth healthy mutual relationships, "to the image and likeness of God".

In his important book, Insight and Responsibility, Erik Erikson writes, "I would call mutuality a relationship in which partners depend on each other for the development of their respective strengths".[33] In an authentic mutual relationship of fidelity, reverence and trust, the partners help each other to develop one of the most important aspects of creative liberty, the capacity to discover within themselves their own inner resources for greater love, fidelity and creativity.

Although personal relations take first place, we should not minimize our relationship with our total environment. If we tend to see what is positive in all that is around us, we will be able to enrich our whole environment with the harvest of creative liberty. If, however, we tend to look on culture, language and structures chiefly as hindrances or obstacles to our freedom, then we lose much of our creative potential. "Fitting action is action that fits into a total interaction as response and anticipation of further response".[34] A creative anticipation of reciprocal response is always filled with trust. Trust helps us to discover, in those around us, their inner core of goodness. We give credit to them, and thus can hope to solicit a positive and creative response.

4. Creativity of all our energies

If one's upbringing stresses only the naked energy of the will or the power of the intellect, one's creativity and freedom are greatly impaired. This is especially so in a success-oriented society. Only if we give ourselves to the service of God and neighbour, with imagination, sensitivity, passions and affectivity can we fully develop our freedom.

Creativity arises from a tentative wholeness and leads to an ever more authentic wholeness. It grows with the fostering of imagination and intuition. In this growth, we should not disregard the symbols that can tell us more than abstract concepts can convey. They appeal to our whole being. On this point I fully agree with Gregory Baum who has worked out a sociology and theology of symbols in his book, *Religion and Alienation*. "According to a sociological view, experience involves the creativity of the mind. Experience has a structure in which the symbols governing the imagination have a creative part. Symbols guide people in their encounter with the world, as well as their response to it".[35]

It is true that our world of experience, including symbols, is substantially moulded by the total economic, social and cultural structure, but it is also true that our response to the world can be creative and renewing if vital and truthful symbols are operating in our minds.

It is almost impossible to realize, or even to imagine, what great harm was done to freedom and creativity by various thought-patterns which degraded the body, the emotions, passions and all human affectivities. Max Scheler is right when he insists throughout his books that, divorced from the spirit, human instinct — all of the body-soul drives and impulses — runs wild and becomes destructive; and that it is equally true that, divorced from emotions, passions, and affectivity the spirit is powerless and absolutely uncreative.[36] "We know that all activity of man, action as well as neglect of action, his genuine love as well as his worst excesses, are linked with instinctive forces of passion".[37]

The creativity seems to be in proportion to the capacity to rejoice, to sorrow with the sorrowful, to bear a part of another's anguish, and to abound in hope, as well as the capacity to be gentle and wrathful at the proper times, in order to forcefully withstand the evil.

The greatest source of creativity is a faith that abounds in joy and peace. I am not speaking here of "instant happiness", the desire for immediate and easy success and happiness without earning them. All this ends in frustration and is inimical to creativity. "Joy, rather than happiness, is the goal of life, for joy is the emotion which accompanies the fulfilment of our nature as human beings. It is based upon the experience of one's own identity as a being of worth and dignity".[38] Whoever truly follows Christ knows that joy comes, above all, from the creative love that gives us the desire and the courage to be with and for others. Joy is not only the final harvest of being totally free for others; it is also a most heartening source of creativity on the road to self-actualization.

5. *Redeeming response in a sinful world*

God has called us to share in his creativity and freedom, but he has also endowed us with the kind of freedom that, while it calls for a "Yes", makes possible also a "No" before God. But wherever a person utters this "No", refusing himself to him who calls us to co-create with him in freedom, the whole structure of creation is so ordered that the "No" receives a strong rebuke. Jesus has given a severe rebuke to the evil spirits, to the arrogance and stubbornness of the Pharisees, to Peter when he tried to tempt him to be unfaithful to his mission as Servant.

An essential part of our response to God is the very freedom and creativity of a firm commitment to withstand the sinful world. An effective dialogue with our fellowmen and our culture is never "simply an adaptation to a new cultural consciousness or to new social conditions of life; it is, or ought to be, at the same time, a creative response to the sinful world".[39] The truly imaginative response, as we find it in Jesus Christ, is

not merely a "No" set against the "No" of a sinful world.
His firm negative in the context of his positive message is
redeeming. It uncovers and brings into full light the misery
of sin. Only through that creative faith that helps us to discover
our own and our fellowman's God-given inner resources can we
give a creative and redeeming response. We can throw a helpful,
saving light on the twilight of the world around us only if we
allow God to take hold of us and free all our energies for the
great task to which he has called us.[40]

6. *Creative freedom as gift of the Spirit*

It is the Spirit of God who renews the face of the earth
and the hearts of the faithful. The central symbol of renewed,
creative and faithful freedom on earth is the Risen Lord. In
the power of the Spirit he has fulfilled his mission, and it is
he who sends us from the Father the Spirit to enable us to
walk in his steps. Those who are guided by the Spirit recognize
every good thing and, above all, their freedom as an undeserved
gift of God. "There is no freedom of spirit without God as its
original source".[41] Only to the extent that the Church and
all the faithful truly believe in the Holy Spirit, giving God the
honour for all that he has done and given to us, can they make
a creative use of all their capacities and respond generously to
the various charisms. Thus they adore the Spirit together with
the Father and the Son and become a sign of creative and faithful
liberty for the world.

Trust in the Spirit makes us sensitive for the cry of other
people for a share in the freedom of the children of God and
gives us also the courage to become involved in the sometimes
painful process of liberation in the world. This is not possible
without being ready to give ourselves as Christ did, in the very
power of the Holy Spirit. But since we are, unlike Christ, weak
human beings we also need trust in view of our shortcomings.
Dietrich Bonhoeffer explained this involvement and died for it.
"The meaning of free responsibility depends on a God who
demands bold action as the free response of faith, and who
promises forgiveness and consolation to the man who becomes
a sinner in the process".[42] It is the Spirit who has ever given
the spirit of boldness and frankness to the prophets, and has

anointed Christ, *the* Prophet, to speak truth to the godless world and especially to those who misuse religion. And it is also the Spirit who gives consolation in midst of turmoil.

V. RESPONSIBILITY IN CREATIVE FIDELITY

A distinctively Christian ethics of responsibility entails as much creative fidelity as creative liberty. We give particular attention to this in view of an existentialism that is so obsessed with self-affirmation that it loses the sense of continuity and commitment. Where there is arbitrariness and total discontinuity, there is neither responsibility nor creativity. As soon as one loses a sense of history, he loses also a sense of commitment, and all the new creations of self-affirmation fall into the abyss of nothingness.

1. *Commitment to the covenant*

By its very nature, our response in faith is a firm commitment to Christ, the Covenant, and to the people of his covenant. Christ is the faithful One. We can have no share in his creative liberty unless we follow him in fidelity. Even from a merely human interest in the development of freedom in the life of individuals and society, "we must also have the courage to affirm the need for commitment".[43] To be free for any great purpose, and even more, to be free for Christ and his kingdom, requires "ultimately the freedom of the subject to commit himself".[44]

The New Testament presents redemption that comes from Christ as freedom for commitment of self to another; this freedom shares in the redemptive and creative power of Christ.[45] Since we receive our freedom from Christ and in Christ, we can rejoice in it only insofar as we are committed to him and have discovered our true selves in that commitment. "Man achieves self-control only as he lets go of himself".[46] It is not so much that freedom is in a person as a possession as that the redeemed person is free when he is in Christ. Fidelity to Christ and to the people of the covenant creates a sphere of freedom in which we can live creatively in dialogue and mutuality.

2. *Fidelity to freedom*

"It is for freedom that Christ has set us free" (Gal 5:1). We are committed to the covenant in Christ only when we are equally committed to the freedom of all. Christ has called us together in the covenant to grow in co-responsibility and thus in personal and social freedom.

Christians will never choose false security at the price of freedom. Fidelity to Christ, who makes us free, obliges us not to restrict the sphere of freedom for anything except freedom itself. Therefore, we will never betray the Lord of history by trying to impose our preferences, rules or convictions on others against their own convictions. Our own freedom and the sharing of our free convictions should always serve the growth of freedom in all and for all.

Our commitment to responsibility in creative freedom and fidelity requires education for freedom. That includes growth in that love "which patiently accepts those restrictions without which so many who are to be loved can no longer exist today".[17]

3. *Commitment to the goal commandments*

Attention too exclusively focused on the prohibitive laws can divert Christians from the great law which Christ has proclaimed by the Paschal Mystery, in the Beatitudes and in all his teachings.

Christ gave us a clear and positive direction by his authoritative words, repeated six times, "But I tell you . . ." (Mt 5). Through the law of the covenant, Jesus sets us on the path to an ever more liberated and creative love. He liberates us *from* defence morality *for* covenant morality.

All the goal commandments of covenant morality can be synthesized in Jesus' words, "Love each other as I have loved you" (Jn 15:12) and "There must be no limit to your goodness, as your heavenly Father's goodness knows no bounds" (Mt 5:48). Luke gives the same message in other words. "Be compassionate as your Father is compassionate" (Lk 6:36).

One of the most uncreative approaches in the Church is to stress fidelity to certain negative commandments to such an extent that fidelity to Christ and his great affirmative commandments of justice, love and mercy is seriously neglected. Rudolf Bultmann speaks on obedience of faith, or simply obedience, when he directs our attention to these great commandments of the Lord that are written in our innermost being as the law of the Lord. "Freedom is obedience to a law of which the validity is recognized and accepted when man recognizes it as the law of his own being".[48]

VI. CREATIVE CO-RESPONSIBILITY

Christ is the rallying call. His fidelity to the mission entrusted to him by the Father creates a community of disciples. He calls together men and women of different backgrounds, temperaments and education, to be one in his name, thus liberating them from isolation, aloofness and imprisonment in self-centred groups and tribes. Hence, for a Christian moral theology, it is essential to reflect on freedom and fidelity in a perspective of co-responsibility.

1. *From defence morality to covenant morality*

Unredeemed man is tempted from within by his own selfishness and from without by the pressure of self-centred organizations and societies. All this works in the direction of a defence morality, where the individual and the collectivity are defending their own separate rights and advantages.

Christ calls us, instead, into the covenant which he himself lives with the Father in the Holy Spirit. It is a relationship of fidelity in freedom: one for all and all for one. Christ is the "man for all others", and those who have found life in him cannot seek their selfish advantage. "The love of Christ leaves us no choice when once we have reached the conclusion that one man died for all and therefore all mankind has died. His purpose in dying for all was that men, while still in life, should cease to live for themselves and should live for him who, for their sake, died and was raised to life" (2 Cor 5:14-15).

Those who are reconciled in Christ know that there can be no genuine creativity and no creative fidelity outside the covenant. Even such an existentialist theologian as Rudolf

Bultmann stresses this point. "Christian freedom exists only in community, and the Christian comes to himself in the fellowship of the Church, within the community of the saints created by God's election and call".[49] Karl Barth is at his very best when he speaks on both freedom and fidelity in a long chapter entitled "Freedom in Fellowship".[50] Similarly Berdyaev, whose central message is always creative freedom and fidelity, reaches its most profound perspective when he speaks on the fellowship in the Holy Spirit.[51]

The great breakthrough of Vatican II coincided with increased attention to the grace of the Spirit who creates community through all the gifts that manifest creative and faithful liberty. Speaking on co-responsibility, the Council turns our attention to the promptings of the Spirit. "The faithful in their turn should enthusiastically lend their cooperative assistance to their pastors and teachers. Thus the very diversity of graces, ministries and works gathers the children of God into one, because 'all these things are the work of one and the same Spirit'" (1 Cor 12:11).[52]

All our creativity in co-responsibility, which is always a gift of the Holy Spirit, seems to be mediated through the various forms of fellowship, and especially through the Church. The Church, in turn, enriched by these same gifts, becomes ever more a visible sign of fidelity and creativity in genuine co-responsibility. Thus, in Church and society there exists an ever enlivened investment of all the wisdom, inventiveness and faithfulness that is prompted by the Holy Spirit and by Christ's rallying call throughout the ages.

2. Co-humanity

One of the essential words and concepts of today's German theology and culture is *Mitmenschlichkeit*, which could be translated as "co-humanity". We realize our full humanity in all its dimensions and potentialities insofar as we honour and promote the same humanity in our fellowmen.

The Eternal Word assumed the humanity of Jesus Christ for all of us: so Jesus is the embodiment of co-humanity. He is truly human and is united with the Divine Word as "the man for the others" (Dietrich Bonhoeffer). Those who honour only the rich and powerful or only members of their own clan, class, race or colour, and not the poor, the alien, the disinherited, have not yet discovered their own humanity, their dignity and freedom as persons. We become fully human only in the fellowship of people who respect each other, love each other and bear each other's burdens. This is an essential part of reconciliation and forgiveness.

To express the message of reconciliation and forgiveness, Karl Barth frequently uses the German word *Freispruch*, which not only means acquittal that frees us from the court but also conveys the basic message that we are sent into the free realm of mutuality, co-humanity. People who, by the grace of the Spirit, know themselves as reconciled, know that God accepts them and their fellowmen, seeking them where they are. These people are free in self-acceptance which, before God, can never be separated from freedom for others. And this freedom is constituted by the *Freispruch* of God's reconciling action.

We can live this liberating mutuality only in reciprocal acceptance and trust. And in that same acceptance and trust, we develop our best creativity. This can be exemplified by a community that prays together. People can easily recite cursing psalms, stereotyped songs and other prayers without being reconciled with each other; but only where there is mutual trust, love and encouragement will everyone follow the inspiration of the Spirit, will pray freely and share faith experiences. The same holds true in all our human relationships.

3. *Freedom in community and society*

Since F. Toennies,[53] the distinction between person-oriented *community* and success-oriented *society* has been common. It has to be seen, however, that there are qualitative as well as quantitative transitions.

What really distinguishes a community from a merely utilitarian organization is the level of liberty, fidelity and creative co-responsibility. On the one hand there is a community — perhaps a family or basic Christian community — where persons are committed to each other not only in a Thou-I relationship of reverence and love but also in a common dedication to the community. On the other hand, there is massification, where the driving force is psychic contagion. "For the process of infection, no spiritual creativity is required. Still, that contagion which affects attitudes of the minds and leads to mental orientations always presupposes some degree of intellectual life".[54] In a success-oriented organization, the individual does not count as a person with a unique individuality, and all one's creativity is not exercised on the level of personal freedom and covenant fidelity but only on the level of that reliability which is measured by success.

The mere pursuit of common interest does not constitute a genuine community. Neither is organization the main cohesive force. Community is expression of the individual persons in their co-humanity. It is deeply rooted in human nature. Our most creative relationships are those which follow the Thou-I-We pattern, whose chief characteristic is mutual fidelity.

The experiences of fidelity, respect and love in families and other communities humanize and enrich societies, nations and the family of nations. To the extent that there are shared values, ideas, ideals and commitments to the common good, beyond economic success or political power, the larger society can contribute to the protection of people's freedom and dignity. But a society cannot promote human dignity, freedom or fidelity if organization and success are so constantly and onesidedly stressed that massification and manipulation prevail in the form of psychic contagion and conditioning by external rewards and punishments.

Society should receive from the Church not only prophetic protest wherever manipulation or plain injustices are stifling people's freedom. The Church should also contribute to the whole society by building up model communities. This was one of the main purposes of ancient monachism as ideally planned by St Basil, St Benedict and others. They wanted their communities to be integrated within the Church and within society, not separated, as the sect of Qumram was, from the broader society.

4. *Models of the Church*

The contribution of the Church for the growth of creative freedom and fidelity depends greatly on her self-understanding.[55]

If the Church is governed and looked upon as if she were a "perfect society", as were the national states of the last century and early twentieth century, there will be a strong emphasis on centralism, on unified common law, on administration, control and penal sanctions. To the extent that all these elements are over-developed and over-emphasized, there will not be enough space for creative co-responsibility. Where, on the contrary, the Church is understood, above all, as a *koinonia*, as a "fellowship in the Holy Spirit", and where this kind of self-understanding takes hold of people's minds and of the whole evangelization, worship and style of government, there will prevail collegiality, subsidiarity and special appreciation of the charisms of the Holy Spirit who works in all, through all and for all. There the sphere of creative liberty and fidelity will grow.

The Church is called by the liberating love of Jesus Christ to be and to become ever more a sacrament of unity in diversity, a sacrament of creative freedom, fidelity and covenant morality. At the present time, however, we live in an almost unavoidable conflict. Many of the structures of the Church, and partially the exercise of authority, are still impregnated by a self-understanding of the Church as a "perfect society": a view that dates back to the Constantinian era with its "sacred alliance" between the Pope, as emperor of the Church-state, and other emperors. On the other hand, the self-understanding of the Church, strongly proposed by Vatican II and by Pope John's charismatic approach, is of a Pilgrim Church, a sacrament of creative liberty and fidelity, a "fellowship in the Holy Spirit". Thus there can arise a dangerous split and harmful tensions in people's minds when the divinely revealed symbols of Christ the Prophet, who embodies creativity in fidelity, are contradicted by authoritarian tendencies and by controls that aim mainly for conformity.[56]

5. Radical monotheism

The covenant morality that expresses the "fellowship in the Holy Spirit" contradicts not only individual selfishness but also and especially group egotism. Anyone who truly believes in the one God and Father, the one Liberator and Saviour Jesus

Christ, and the one Holy Spirit, cannot escape the call to that solidarity which Richard Niebuhr rightly calls "radical monotheism".[57] He means monotheism, not as an abstract affirmation of one God, but monotheism lived truthfully, with firm purpose.

The final decision in human history is between a saving solidarity in Jesus Christ, and the enslaving solidarity of selfish people, groups and collectivities. There are only two choices for human freedom: either to live in and with Christ in courageous and generous co-responsibility, or to remain imprisoned in the sin-of-the-world, the solidarity of perdition.

In this perspective, "original sin" is not explained by or based upon monogenism, the singularity of the racial element in human history, but on monotheism. Since there is but one God, one Saviour, one holy Spirit, all humanity is unavoidably under the law of solidarity, and God's offer, grace and calling is to free and faithful co-responsibility in his creative work. Those who freely decide to renounce the freedom of the children of God in saving solidarity condemn themselves, of necessity, to solidarity in collective egotism, in frustration and alienation.[58]

6. Collective guilt?

Enemies in power struggles, in wars, and especially the victors in wars, tend to consider all citizens of the opposing nation as collectively accountable, and not only in view of injustices committed and injuries inflicted. In a moralist self-righteousness, they tend also to accuse them of collective guilt. This very tendency is a sign and harvest of the "sin of the world": that sin-solidarity that radically contradicts monotheism.

However, simply to refuse to follow these trends in power struggles, and this self-righteousness, does not prove us innocent. As individuals and as members of the community, we all have to examine our consciences about whether we have any share in the oppression, manipulation and violence that persist around us. This terrifying share can fall to us not only through direct participation in criminal misuse of authority or of power, but also because of uncreative use of our freedom, a lack of commitment to the common good, or lack of initiative and creativity. One of the main causes of so many evils in society and Church is surely a legalistic morality that stifles the positive energies of liberty.

VII. LEITMOTIF AND NORMATIVE PATTERNS

To be responsible, free, creative and faithful in Jesus Christ is a leitmotif, but it is also a normative pattern. It can be an effective theme for our lives only if it permeates and elucidates all our norms, ideals and goals. Hence, in a work on moral theology, it does not suffice to explain, in an introductory chapter, what responsibility means. The theme and the normative patterns must be everywhere effectively present.

1. Normative pattern

I use "normative pattern" for the frequently used German word *Zielgebot*, or "goal commandments". Responsibility is more than just an ideal. To act in all circumstances as a responsible person, and to move on the paths that lead to responsible personhood and responsible community and society, is truly a normative value. The unifying leitmotif is of enormous relevance for the strength and coherence of moral and religious life: but if it is to be effective and unifying, all our life has to be tested in its light.

This is something quite different from systematizing in such a way that we deduce all secondary principles from one highest principle. We take all the values in their own right and dignity. But we feel obliged to give special attention to the scale of values and the urgency of values, so that we may make a faithful and creative response in view of the needs of others and in view of the particular gifts God has given us.

2. A relational and salvational approach

Our leitmotif, "free and faithful in Christ", calls not so much for a metaphysical approach in view of the abstract "being" as for a personalistic and communal approach. One of the main perspectives, therefore, is *healthy relationships* with God, with fellowmen, with one's self and with all of creation. The whole of doctrine is to be seen explicitly in view of salvation, wholeness of persons and of fostering families, communities and societies of responsible persons.

Our leitmotif is a commitment to a responsible Church and society and to the promotion of wholesome relationships everywhere. It calls for careful deliberation and presentation of role expectations, of rules or norms for dialogue and for structures that help to inspire in those around us responsibility in creative fidelity. It also requests concern for the relation between freedom and norms in Church and society.

3. *An option for a certain kind of deontology and teleology*

Responsibility in creative liberty and fidelity does not mean simply a new application of all the rules worked out in a static society and in a static self-understanding of the Church. It also means a careful new approach to the whole realm of norms, criteria, discernment, and so forth.

Our leitmotif is also, unavoidably, an option for special emphasis on teleology without, however, excluding all kinds of deontology. To know Jesus Christ, and to make this knowledge a central purpose, leads us to the knowledge of the countenance and true meaning of redeemed and redeeming love. That is for me the very substance of deontology. Our emphasis on responsibility in a specifically Christian sense does not allow an unprincipled ethics of an unstructured "love" as, for instance, that of Joseph Fletcher. We look on love as manifestation of God's overflowing love and liberty and as a call to love in discerning and generous freedom. In the chapter on norms and laws (Chapter Seven) special attention will be given to these problems.

When I stress teleology, it means something quite different from the utilitarian consequentialism of a naive and unintelligent situation ethics. Priority is always given to the inner *telos*, the inner calling of the person and to the inner needs that arise from God's design. The *telos* is the law inborn in us that urges us to grow into maturity as responsible persons, with wholesome relationships, and to promote a responsible society with the broadest possible sphere for creative freedom and fidelity. But teleology calls also for a continuing effort to acquire greater competence, to know life better in its complexity, in order to evaluate the foreseeable consequences of our plans, our words, our actions.

It is also clear, as we have already emphasized, that great attention must be given to the goal that has to be attained and towards which we must constantly strive. The prohibitive laws will then be seen more in a perspective of criteria for discernment. We shall see in them clear indications of what always and essentially contradicts the kingdom of God, the kingdom of redeemed and redeeming freedom and fidelity.

Having chosen this normative pattern, it follows that we will give preference to the biblical, eschatological virtues such as hope, gratitude, vigilance, rather than to the Hellenistic cardinal virtues. This does not exclude attention to Greek or other virtues on which a given ethos can be built when people come into contact with the gospel message. In such an approach we do not only speak on right and wrong, for instance, for or against the theory of just war. The creative approach compels us above all to spend our energies in finding ways by which humankind can finally free itself from the age-old slavery of war.[59]

4. Basic rules of dialogue

The very choice of our leitmotif and normative pattern calls for special attention to basic rules of dialogue. The first of these rules is that we honour God's initiative by listening to him, accepting ourselves with our capacities and limitations, and using to the full the present opportunities he offers us. Thus we also learn how to listen to each other and how to interpret the events and situations in our own conscience standing before God and in the reciprocity of consciences.

Here again we are clearly faced with a personalistic approach. The rules for dialogue will always give first place to persons in communities and communities of persons, in view of redeeming relationships. We will ponder God's grace which calls us, and the mission he bestows on us. And since God gives us his gifts so lavishly in view of fellowship, and especially in view of the needs of our fellowmen, one of the basic rules in this normative pattern is to allow the poor, and everyone who is in need, to impose on us, and to respond to them

according to the gifts God has given us. We see the "other",
who cannot remunerate us, as one who is coming from below
but is sent from above.[60]

Our leitmotif also clearly indicates a common commitment
to salvation truth. It therefore never allows knowledge of
dominion or abstract philosophy to take first place over and
against salvation truth. Those who have chosen this leitmotif
find it intolerable to look for "certainties" when they should
look, courageously and patiently, for truth. We believe that
truth makes us free. And if we are committed to Christ who
is Truth and, therefore, committed to act in truth, we cannot
allow ourselves a neurotic search for "certainties" that are not
in accordance with God's vocation for his people. After all,
our leitmotif obliges us to become responsible, creative persons
and to help our fellowmen towards the same goal.

VIII. THE RESPONSIBLE AND CREATIVE PERSON

Moral theology is interested not only in decisions and
actions. It raises the question, "What ought I to do?" but
asks, first of all, "What ought I to be: what kind of person
does the Lord want me to be?" Our view is that we have
to become responsible and creative persons in the discipleship
of Jesus Christ. So we ask ourselves the basic question, "What
is the makeup of a responsible, creative person?"

1. *The new person in Christ*

Those who want to live creative freedom and fidelity in
Christ ought to understand themselves, above all, in relationship
with God, with fellowmen, themselves and all of creation. It is
not so much new ideas as new relationships that change people,
communities and societies. Only one who understands his or
her self in a relationship of response and dialogue with God
and fellowmen can reach that selfhood that is truly free to
love and to be faithful in a creative way. The highest ideal
of the disciple of Christ is to be conformed with the loving
will of God. "Be conformed to Jesus Christ . . . To conform

with the action of Christ is to do for others and to be for others what Christ has done and been to us and for us".[61]

If we look to Christ, we do not ask first what his actions were but, rather, who he was. We want to know his relationship to God and to people.

This dialogical perspective requires a dialogic character in the person. We can express it in the best traditional understanding of faith, hope, love, adoration. I do not see faith primarily as a quality of our mind and will, but much more fundamentally as that relationship between God revealing himself as saving truth, as Father, as love and compassion, and ourselves, opened by and for the grace of the Holy Spirit and responding freely with our whole being. Similarly, I see hope not only as *my* purpose and expectation but, above all, as God's promise and my/our trustful response to it. As disciples, we are formed by God's own love. He invites us in Christ to love him in return and thus to become sharers of his love. And because it is a covenant between the all-holy God and us lowly creatures, faith, hope and love are unthinkable without an adoring response.

Modern humanists, therapists and psychologists have made profound statements about the "true self" and "ego strength". For us, the true self, or the ego in its surest strength is the person called by God and responding with all his heart, mind, will and energy. Thus it makes sense to me what Erik Erikson writes, "The ego thus is the guardian of meaningful experience, that is, of experience individual enough to guard the unity of the person".[62] It also makes sense when he distinguishes the "I", the totally conscious, responding person, from the "ego", the person in his or her unconscious depth, already determined by the essential relationships in which one finds one's own ego strength and identity.

2. *The wholeness of the person*

By faith we know that all our being is a word that expresses God's love and calling. Therefore, we also realize that we come to our full identity and wholeness only when our whole being becomes a grateful, trustful and loving response to his love and his call.

A Polish socialist who is not very fond of the hierarchy said to me, "However, Cardinal Wyszynsky is a man of one piece. If he says 'yes' he means 'yes', and if he means 'no', it is a plain 'no'". To me that suggests a person who is "whole".

To be free and faithful in Jesus Christ — that is, to be a believer who is responsible and creative — entails, above all, having the character of wholeness. We can be responsible and creative only to the extent of our wholeness, our inner integrity, the integration of all our energies. This means that our leitmotif and our fundamental option take flesh and blood in our life and so transform our desires, our intuitions, our imagination, that fundamental intentions become also fundamental attitudes. This is what the traditional expression, "virtue" means.

I believe that Eric Osborn has rightly interpreted the best of our tradition when he says, "Virtues are neither value-terms like good and bad, nor are they normative terms like right and wrong. A distinct category, virtues are traits of character. They are relevant to choice-situations in which the good of some being is at stake. They enable a choice to be made without the obscuring or blurring effect of passion".[63]

Erik Erikson comes to the same conclusion. He sees the virtues' inner strength as subjective forces that are the product of successful integration of the various dimensions at the given stage of development. "In this first attempt to name the basic properties of these 'strong' persons — matters so far left to moralists and theologians — I have given these properties their everyday name: this is what they look like when observed in others; this is what they feel like when possessed, and this, above all, seems absent when 'virtue goes out' of a person".[64]

Generally, however, modern ethicists, moralists and psychologists avoid the word "virtue" because many misunderstand it as character traits of the all too tamed, too quiet, too submissive person. Or it is understood as a trait of the "virtuous" person who is all too conscious of his own importance and moral value. Therefore, they are seeking other words that best express what good tradition meant by "virtue".

What gives coherence and vitality to the ethical thought

and orientation is sometimes called "pattern" or "posture" or "character". James Gustafson speaks of a "posture" that determines, from within, the manner, bearing, consistent behaviour. A pattern — or posture, or character — does not issue from abstract concepts but from a symbol, a myth or a picture that appeals to a person in his or her wholeness. It is an artistic design that shines through the person's whole being.

The pattern that makes people responsible and creative is, above all, a felt security in thought, word and action, a fundamental trust that allows them to be neither too scrupulous nor too self-defensive, but always to be sincere. Without this character there cannot be prophetic boldness or *parrhesia*.

3. *The spirit of a person: fundamental dispositions*

When one's fundamental option so permeates one's inner self that it becomes a fundamental attitude, new perspectives, new intuitions and new dispositions arise. There develops a lasting tendency to think, desire and act in such a way that the person becomes trustworthy, and there can be no doubt about his or her identity or character.

Dispositions frequently have deeper roots than intentions. The totality of a person's dispositions can be called the "spirit" of the person; and this spirit will give life and direction to one's conduct. In this light we can understand St Paul's words, "Let your bearing towards one another arise out of your life in Christ Jesus" (Phil 2:5).

When one is marked by the pattern of Christ, who humbled himself to become a servant, and made God's love for us visible even on the cross, then this perspective, this faith and this personal relationship with Christ will give one the freedom and readiness to act in a certain way. Conduct which, according to Paul, contradicts the kingdom of God and is the fruit of deeply rooted selfishness (cf. Gal 5:19-21) then has no appeal. Rather, the harvest of the Spirit comes forth: "love, joy, peace, patience, continence, goodness, fidelity, gentleness and self-control" (Gal 5:22). These are the signs of a fundamental attitude for Christ and a profound relationship with him.

James Gustafson notes well the dispositions that are basic

for becoming a sign of freedom in Christ and of fidelity to him. Those who believe in Christ and trust in the gift of the Spirit "are to have lasting dispositions of hope and trust; they are to have a willingness to be bold".[65] Faith and trust in Jesus Christ make his disciples inwardly free from unhealthy concern for the self, from any crippling anxiety about displeasing others, from excessive scrupulosity, and free "to give oneself in love for the neighbour, to seek the other's good rather than one's own, to identify with the oppressed and the anxious. This freedom is part of the Christian's readiness; it is a persisting tendency in the Christian moral life".[66]

Cowardice, uncritical submissiveness, excessive scrupulosity stem from fear and lack of purpose. People with these dispositions might well be in the state of grace, but reconciliation, faith and hope have not yet transformed their psycho-dynamics, their character and disposition. Their relationships are less than healthy. Where a vibrant faith and trust create a person's integrity and wholeness, there is courage to accept one's own finiteness, courage to be for others, courage to be thoroughly involved for justice and peace, even if this entails the risk of making mistakes. And the courage to make mistakes includes equally the courage to aknowledge the mistakes and to correct them.

Courage arises from trust in God's kindness and patient love, trust that he has given us inner resources, and from trust in people's fundamental goodness. "Courage is the basis of any creative relationship".[67] It is a vital disposition or virtue for spiritual growth. "Strange as it sounds, steady, patient growth in freedom is probably the most difficult task, requiring the greatest courage".[68]

Often it requires greater freedom to preserve inner peace in the search for truth and growth in maturity than to stand defiantly for outer freedom. The courage most characteristic for creative freedom and fidelity to Christ is the courage not so much to assert one's self as to give oneself for the cause of God and fellowmen. And there is no greater courage, inner freedom and fidelity than the readiness to be so committed to God's kingdom, to justice and peace, as to risk one's own life or one's outer freedom.

4. The heart of man (The value-person)

An ethics that wants to serve the formation of responsible and creative persons will give great attention to emotions, affectivity and the whole realm of sensitivity to values that lie deep in man's being and are particularly expressive of the human longing for inner wholeness, for integrity and integration.

The German school of ethics of value and particularly those ethicists from the phenomenological school of Husserl — for instance, Dietrich Hildebrand, Max Scheler, Alexander Pfänder, Edith Stein — have given enormous attention to what is called, in German language, Gesinnung and Gemüt. It is very difficult to translate these concepts into English. Perhaps at no other point does the different genius of the two cultures and languages become more evident. The meaning of both words comes closest to the biblical word "the heart of the human person".

"Heart" points to the person in his or her wholeness, building bridges to others, grasping the unique value of each one as a person and the manifold values embodied by persons, and thus calling for an ever new embodiment of these values in one's own life.

The fundamental attitude (Gesinnung) is the person's overall disposition to respond to the dignity and appeal of values in a characteristic, persistent way. The particular attitudes (Gesinnungen) are dispositions to respond to certain sets or spheres of values and to kinds of human behaviour or to events in a specific manner.

Gesinnungen entail emotions and sentiments as part of the value response, especially when it is a matter of relations to persons. They are, therefore, quite different from mere moods which may be caused by biological pressures but not evoked by values perceived. Gesinnungen are sentiments enlightened by a kind of intuition.

Rudolf Otto speaks of Intentionales Fühlen, which entails the manifestation of sensitivity for values that attract and can enrich the person. These responsive sentiments precede and transcend particular actions. They are richer and more profound than mere conceptual understanding, and go far beyond the realm of usefulness, beyond pragmatic decision-making and even consciousness of duty. This dimension is very important in overcoming an ethics centred on obedience or an ethics of dry duty. It also helps to unmask all kinds of utilitarian ethics characterized by emotional starvation because of lack of the capacity to admire, to rejoice, to contemplate, to repose before God and to be truly with the other as a person.

In Chapter Five we shall return to the same theme insofar as the fundamental option gives unity, integration and final firmness to attitudes, sentiments and emotions.

When the ethical sphere is reduced to a bare "must", a mere consciousness of duty, it can form a duty-bound citizen, one submissive to law. It can stress categorical imperatives and general, always valid norms and principles. But it cannot form the creative, responsible person.

An integrated affectivity brings quite different emotional responses from those aroused by mere purposive intentions. If educational and ethical systems call only for dispositions that make people ready for purposive action, they mobilize energies for common purposes, but there is danger that the purposes will serve only selfish concerns of individuals and groups. But if we want to form a purposive person who is also creative and responsive, we have to give attention to those *Gesinnungen* or value responses that re-echo in the heart of man beyond any particular purpose. "Sometimes love, affection, friendliness are entirely quiescent. At home in man's heart, they find their object without any desire to possess it or to make a purpose about it".[69]

When we speak of responses re-echoing in the innermost being of the person, we do not at all mean that value-filled emotions tend to lock themselves up in the psychic enclosure of man. On the contrary, precisely because they are value-responses and not directly purposive, these emotions, by their very nature, can transform our intentions and purposes into genuine responses to persons and to the whole realm of values. We speak of those dispositions of heart, mind and will that strike the most intimate core of one's heart. As in the case of the genuine experience of conscience, the whole of our being participates. The whole psychodynamics is affected and lends its energies to the most valuable and creative noödynamics.

Spirited emotions and dispositions are an intimate "Yes" to persons embodying attractive values, and to the values embodied in lovable persons. It is a sort of confirmation of their worth, acknowledged simply as such, and not for any particular purpose.

Emotions make up the very "heart of man" from which come both good and evil. We are not speaking, of course, about emotions that are scattered or are mere moods under the pressure of biological reality, or emotions which neither express the depth of the person nor are approved by the free will. We speak rather of the emotional mindset of that affectivity that expresses the person's basic relationship to the Other, the others and to one's self.

Gesinnungen are emotions that express the inner and profound capacity of a person to value, to discern, to respond beyond the biological pressure. They are manifestation of the person's ego strength, of the inner depth of the person. Very different are the emotions set in motion by the super-ego, by the constant need to conform to how others may judge, evaluate, remunerate or punish.

The health, wholeness, responsiveness and creativity of the person depend greatly on whether positive or negative emotions prevail. The prophets are prototypes of the responsive person. Having a deep experience of God's holiness and mercy, they are marked by an equal compassion for the poor, the oppressed, and by concern for all others. Thus their wrath, although pyschologically a negative emotion, is thoroughly integrated into their positive value responses. It is as much a part of their commitment to the holy and merciful God and to their fellowmen as are their hymns and songs of joy and peace.

When negative emotions and reactions in one's heart (becoming visible in words and deeds) are not integrated into a positive commitment and disposition, they are a sign of emotional starvation, a sign of one's loss of responsiveness to positive values, insofar as they tend to occupy one's inner life. This kind of disintegrated negative emotion makes one destructive, first against one's self and then also against others.[70]

These are persons who always need someone or something to fight against. They can gather only against a common enemy. Similarly, power systems that cannot unite people for a common purpose or good, for peace and justice, need a constant mobilization of hatred or mistrust against other ideologies, other nations, other systems. Nothing creative comes from such groups and persons.

The ethos of responsive and creative people is positive. There is an inner need to contemplate, to admire, to adore, a rejoicing because of the goodness of others, a capacity to discover the inner resources of themselves and of others. It includes a healthy rhythm between the Sabbath and creative work, between contemplation, reposing before God, rejoicing with and about others, and a commitment to common purposes and tasks.

I am convinced that a proper understanding and worthy celebration of the Eucharist, and of worship in all its forms can transform persons, can produce genuine holiness and integration that makes them ready for profound value experiences and value responses, without the temptation to withdraw from commitment. But again, we must be warned never to celebrate the Eucharist just to gain our own integration and wholeness. First of all, we celebrate to praise the Lord, to acknowledge him as the Lord, to respond to his goodness. But if we do so in truth, all of our life will become a response, and we shall recognize the mission for common commitment.

5. The purposeful person

An ethics of responsibility in action could be as one-dimensional as an ethics of obedience, of the "must" if it were only an ethics of ends and means. We need a configuration of an "ethics of the heart" in which the value-response that re-echoes in the depths of our hearts and minds with all the accompanying emotions is seen as the first and fundamental response to God's sharing his love with us in infinite freedom. But then follows even more strongly the capacity to respond in praise and thanksgiving and not less in commitment to godly purposes. And the main purpose is to be servants to the gospel, to the kingdom of God and to our fellowmen.

The foundation of a Christian morality is life in Christ Jesus: "to be in Christ". In such a life there is no place for a naked ethics of do's and dont's, nor for an ethics of external imitation or of discrete purposes. Christ's farewell discourses give us the right and essential vision: "Dwell in me as I in you. No branch can bear fruit by itself, but only if it remains united to the vine; no more can you bear fruit unless you remain united with me . . . This is my Father's glory, that you may bear fruit in plenty and so be my disciples . . . I appointed you to go on and bear fruit, fruit that shall last" (Jn 15:3-16).

The value-response in faith, hope, love, all that can be synthesized in praise, thanksgiving and adoration, and human relationships marked by the same direct value-response: all this is what makes the tree good, the roots without which we cannot bear fruit.

However, we must not push this important paradigm to the point of slighting fully conscious intentions and purposefulness. Intentions and commitment to specific purposes may have a greater degree of self-consciousness and rationale than dispositions, patterns or emotions.[71] But they will be weak and uncreative if they lack the spiritual outpouring of the total value-response that re-echoes in the human heart and will.

A person becomes ever more responsive and creative in commitment and faithfulness as his or her purposes take shape by listening and responding. We listen to the nature of things and to the message of the whole creation, but most of all to the inner needs and inner resources of persons. Our intentions and our purposefulness must remain in the responsorial structure of a truly Christian ethics. We shall never commit ourselves to things, natures, purposes or means without thereby manifesting our spontaneous response and our purposeful commitment to God's history of salvation.

6. The leitmotif and the particular motives

What determines the ethical value of our actions is never the materiality of the external act but strictly the "heart", the

basic dispositions and value-responses which can be the source
of ethical good as well as evil. The decisive question here is
whether we are just pursuing purposes alien to our leitmotif
or purposes inspired and moved by our basic dispositions and
our value-responses.

The psychology of motives does not consider so much the
purposes that determine our conscious intention as the hidden
and unconscious motivations and dispositions. Even in mature
people, the fully conscious motives are frequently only the
tip of the iceberg. However, what is partially unconscious can
be a tremendous wealth of value-responses. It can be the sum
of all the positive experiences and appropriate value-responses,
a fundamental option insofar as it is fully transformed in fundamental attitudes.

These motives, prompting our best actions from the depth
of the heart, have no reason to hide themselves in the unconscious; it is, rather, that the person who is truly value-oriented,
responsive to God's liberty, fidelity, love, does not need constantly to turn his or her attention explicitly to this profound
motivation. They are a source of spontaneity and creativity.
Nevertheless, from time to time, we all have to look and to
discern sharply what does motivate our desires, words, decisions,
actions.

The inimical motives that responsive, creative persons
should watch for are those that have every reason to hide
themselves: a basic selfishness, a powerful super-ego whose
pattern is mainly shaped by the desire to be socially acknowledged or not to be penalized. These motives and forces cause
anxieties, security complexes, destructiveness and inner misery
as a result of bad experiences and/or an unfitting response to
all of this. These distorted and distorting motives will prevail
less, the more one's heart is filled with the re-echoing value-
responses of faith, trust, joy, peace, gratitude, admiration. But
watchfulness over our motives makes sense only in the process
of conversion. It can be effective only in a new context of openness for personal values, in a new commitment of genuine
fidelity.

Unless we gain healthy relationships with God, our fellowmen, ourselves and all creation in a creative pattern and a

responsive disposition, the many motives that consciously or unconsciously move us will be neither united nor purified. To become creative and responsive, we should choose the best possible leitmotif that corresponds with our fundamental option and disposition. It should be broad and deep enough to give integration to all the particular motives, while eliminating all those that do nor correspond to the leitmotif and the fundamental option.

IX. HISTORICITY AND CREATIVE RESPONSIBILITY

1. *A courageous Yes to our history*

A distinctively Christian ethics of responsibility must never forget that historicity is an essential dimension of human existence. Man has a history; he himself is a history in which he directs his destiny and shapes his history and that of his fellowmen. Human experience is always a mediation of the past into the future. The present moment is truly our presence before God and with each other when we give creative direction to what we have received from the past as our common heritage. If, in view of it, we accept the challenge of the present and the expectation of the future, we act responsibly and are creative.

To cling to the status quo and its false securities is to obstruct the history of salvation. There is no way to begin our moral and religious existence outside of our common history and our present history. We do not live in abstraction. As moral beings, we have received the capacity to meet history consciously, gratefully and critically.[72] Only in grateful acceptance of history and in creative response to its challenge does man reach eternity. By faith we are inserted into the history of liberation and salvation made possible by Jesus Christ. In openness to the present, we come creatively in contact with eternity, which reaches us out of the past and leads us into the future. In no other way can we reach out for eternity except through the mediation of destiny and that creativity which is the precious gift of the Lord of the history.[73]

2. A grateful memory

The achievements and failures of the past come to us through culture and through the whole configuration of the collective memory. As persons and as communities, we gain our creativity and freedom through our memory of the past. By it, we can come to an overview of the conditionings and obstacles on the way to freedom and also can inherit the achievements which creative liberty and fidelity have invested in the past.

Memory and discernment together are those forces of creativity "which conduct a constant battle against the mortal principle of time".[74] When a grateful memory reaches into the past, it can give to many aspects of our life a new meaning, a new direction. To the extent that we see the here and now in the light of what has been, and in openness for new encounters, we discover the dimensions of our own self.

A memory that scrutinizes the broader traditions will neither cling to the latest "tradition" — which so frequently becomes absolutized — nor accept stereotyped interpretations of the past that issue from anxiety and insecurity complexes characteristic of a defence ethics. To live creatively and responsibly on the level and in the perspectives of the memorial of the Lord's Supper, we need a discerning knowledge of past history that liberates us. Then, entering into the history that is Christ's, we are freed to compare our traditions with those of others, and to compare the latest traditions with earlier configurations of history.

3. The future has already begun

Memory is a source of our creativity. The more it is receptive to the whole of prophetic history, the more it finds its centre and summit in Jesus Christ. We never celebrate the memorial of the Lord fruitfully unless we open ourselves to the prophetic vision that inspires a hopeful and creative response. The prophetic spirit of Christ guides the people to discover the meaning of history and the challenge of the present moment.

The grateful memory, which unites us with the redemptive events of the past and the promises given by Christ, gives us the hope and the courage to face the uncertainties of the future.

"Hope, in its creative self, can and should be an energizing attitude, the bringing of part of the joy about some future event into the present so that, by anticipation, we are more alive and more able to act in the present".[76]

4. The gift of the present moment

The past and the future are precious. They provoke creativity because and insofar as we see them as part of the present. The past lights up the present and the future makes it all the more challenging. One who hopes for the future will use the present opportunities to the full, knowing that the future is formed and born of the present.[77] Eternity comes into the present moment as a quality of existence through a grateful memory and courageous responsibility for our own and our fellowmen's future.

Nicolai Berdyaev says that existential time — that is, the intensity of the present moment — is emerging from cosmic and historical time through the very intensity of experience.[78] This points in the same direction as Paul's warning to superficial Christians: "Awake, sleeper, rise from the dead, and Christ will shine upon you. Be most careful, then, how you conduct yourselves: like sensible people, not like simpletons. Use the present opportunity (kairós) to the full" (Eph 5:14-16).

If, in faith, we turn our eyes and hearts towards Jesus Christ and experience his love, then we discover the wealth of the present moment. "The man of faith is free for love which opens the eyes to what God requires from him in the moment."[79] We are free and creative whenever, conformed with the loving will of God, we accept the gift and the challenge of the present and sincerely make the best response to the present opportunities, always with gratitude for what comes from God and with openness to the needs of our fellowmen.

Obedience to the kairós concerns not only the individual believer and the believing community but also, and particularly, the Christian ethician. Willingly or unwillingly, he is part of the present culture, with its best and, to some extent, its worst.

Christian ethics was always at its best when persons with prophetic vision, fully alive in their moment, tried to express the Christian message in view of those who had to live in a

certain culture in a certain era. Today we are vulnerable. We
have the cold wind of the spirit of this era on our backs if
we do not face it consciously and creatively. Only by redeeming
the best, entering into a dialogue and expressing ourselves in
the language of the day can we avoid an unconscious and false
adaptation.

We should bring to our critical consciousness the fact that
our symbolic mindset and all our philosophical reflections on
ethical problems are not created by religious traditions or by
pure faith alone. To a considerable extent — but not to the
extent that Karl Marx supposed — they depend on the material
conditions of life and the totality of cultural expressions. We
are able to take critical positions. However, we cannot do so
as if we were not living in a certain culture and a certain era.[80]

In the process of evangelization of non-Christian groups,
and in meeting new generations, it is a logical necessity to use
non-Christian patterns of ethical thought.[81] No one is completely a beginner in ethical argument. "There is some choice
to be made and it is better to be aware of our philosophical
framework than to adopt one without examination".[82]

Because of the unavoidable risk involved, Karl Rahner gives
a pointed warning to those who reject this approach just
because it involves risk. "The Christian's historical action in
society, state and Church bears inevitably the character of risk,
of uncertainty, of walking in the dark, for we know not what
to ask; we must beg for gracious guidance from above and
beyond what can be calculated and foreseen. If, because of
this risk, a Christian thinks himself dispensed from making
individual decisions, he sins against the historicity of his
existence and becomes all the more guilty. For he must not
only proclaim the ever valid principles but must also risk the
concrete future, trusting in God".[83]

X. RESPONSIBILITY IN AND FOR THE WORLD

Set free from the solidarity of sin and lust for power that is
in the world and in alienated religion, the disciples of Christ
can face the world with a discerning, prophetic word. They will

not allow themselves an unconscious or easy adaptation. Rather, in the light of faith, they discover the presence of Christ in the world and in the age they live in, just as they have discovered his presence in their innermost being.

The Christian gains this liberating distance from the world around him by a deep solidarity in Christ in the fellowship of the Holy Spirit. And this becomes also a new experience of solidarity with all of humankind. Thus, discovering Christ in their own depths, in the world and in every person, the disciples of Christ become free for expressing themselves creatively in and for the world.

One of the greatest dangers is the radical separation of the realm of the sacred and that of the profane, which leads to profound estrangement and deceptive ideologies. Those who believe in the living God, the Lord of history, experience God not only as the voice from above that calls one away from the world to a higher level, but, also and quite as much, as a transcendent mystery present in the world and in life itself. This kind of God experience enables the disciples of Christ to assume responsibilities for their world and to move forward into the future.[84]

The whole mental structure and pattern of radical separation between the sacred and the profane made it impossible for legalistic manuals of moral theology to see rightly the role of Christians in the world. In the context of a too defensive attitude of a besieged Church, whose image for the world was largely shaped by the presence of the Inquisition, the world in which Christians lived was considered mainly as "proximate occasion to sin". All this led to a one-sided defence morality. The renewed self-understanding of the Church, as it emerges in the Second Vatican Council, calls for a covenant morality in and for the world. For the Church herself recognizes herself as a servant in the world.

"Theology today understands man in terms of his capacity, vocation and power to achieve his own existence and to better the world in which he lives. Man's life does not come to him as a completed whole but, rather, man has the task and vocation of becoming more of a man and making more human the world in which he lives".[85] If we want to be loyal to the Church that gave us *The Constitution on the Church in the Modern World*, this is the only way to present ethics. The same mission and vocation is presented in the *Decree on Priestly Formation*. There the Council speaks on the necessary renewal of moral theology. "It should show the loftiness of the vocation of the faithful in Christ and their mission to bring forth fruit in love for the life of the world".[86]

NOTES

1 *Gaudium et spes,* 55
2 Cf. G. Baum, *Religion and Alienation,* New York, Paramus, Toronto, 1975, 242: "Experience has a structure in which symbols governing the imagination have a creative part... Man's response to the world is also determined by the symbols operative in their imagination... Symbols guide people in their encounter with the world as well as their response to it".
3 D. Bonhoeffer, *Ethics,* New York, 1955, 8.
4 N. Berdyaev, *The Destiny of Man,* New York, 1960, 137.
5 R.T. Osborn, *Freedom in Modern Theology,* Philadelphia, 1967, 127. The author synthesizes here the vision of Karl Barth about freedom and responsibility. My own vision of respensibility does, theologically, not fully coincide with that of Karl Barth.
6 A. Jonsen, *Responsibility in Modern Religious Ethics,* Washington-Cleveland, 1968, 183.
7 Cf. J.M. Gustafson, *Can Ethics Be Christian?,* Chicago/London; and *Christ and the Moral Life,* New York, 1968; J. Fuchs, *Existe-t-il une morale chrétienne?,* Gembloux, 1973.
8 B. Häring, *Das Heilige und das Gute,* Krailing vor München, 1950; P. Baelz, *Ethics and Beliefs,* London, 1977.
9 R. Otto, *The Sacred,* calls religious experience sometimes "irrational" not in the sense of contradicting reason, but transcending a conceptualization or a merely rational approach.
10 G. Baum, l.c., 243.
11 R. Niebuhr, *The Responsible Self,* New York, 1963, 126.
12 R. Niebuhr, *Radical Monotheism and Western Culture,* New York, 1960, 48.
13 Cf. K. Rahner, *Grace in Freedom,* New York, 1969, 217.
14 l.c., 218.
15 K. Barth, *Church Dogmatics,* Edinburgh, 1957, II/2, 641.
16 l.c., 655.
17 l.c., 632f.
18 R. May, *Man's Search for Himself,* New York, 7th printing, 101.
19 Cf. *Gaudium et spes,* 16.
20 K. Rahner, l.c., 233.
21 Cf. my book *Prayer: Integration of Faith and Life,* Slough and Notre Dame, 1975.
22 R. May, l.c., 157.
23 N. Berdyaev, *Dream and reality,* New York, 1950, 46.
24 N. Berdyaev, *Freedom and the Spirit,* New York, 1935, X.
25 R. Bultmann, *Jesus Christ and Mythology,* New York, 1958, 40.
26 R.T. Osborn, *Freedom in Modern Theology,* 26.

27 Cf. l.c., 28.
28 Robert O. Johann, Philosopher's Notebook, in America, Aug. 1964, 111.
29 Cf. Enda McDonagh, Invitation and Response, New York, 1972; Id., Gift and Call, St. Mainrad/Ind., 1975.
30 N. Berdyaev, Truth and Revelation, Coller Books, 1963.
31 P. Tillich, Systematic Theology, 3 vols, Chicago, 1951, 1957, 1963, II, 32.
32 R.T. Osborn, Freedom in Modern Theology, 125.
33 E. Erikson, Insights and Responsibility, New York, 1964, 231.
34 R. Niebuhr, The Responsible Self, 61.
35 G. Baum l c. 747; cf. E. Osborn, Ethical Patterns in Early Christian Thought, 5: "Clement (of Alexandria) valued symbolic language because it could say more than one thing at a time".
36 In his later years Max Scheler unfortunately made strange applications of this thought to the understanding of God as if he, too, would be an embodiment of both of passion and spirit in the sense of Panentheism; cf. particularly his book Man's Place in Nature, New York, 1971.
37 P. Siebeck, "Wissen und Glauben in der Medizin", Universitas 5 (1950) 42.
38 R. May, Man's Search for Himself, 96.
39 G. Baum, l.c., 189.
40 Cf. K. Rahner, l.c., 218f.
41 N. Berdyaev, Realm of Spirit and the Realm of Caesar, London, 1952, 32.
42 D. Bonhoeffer, Letters and Papers From Prison, London, 1953, 138.
43 K. Rahner, l.c., 243.
44 l.c., 257.
45 R.T. Osborn, l.c., 14.
46 H. Schlier, Eleutheros, in Theol. W.z. NT II (1935), 492.
47 K. Rahner, l.c., 250.
48 R. Bultmann, Jesus Christ and Mythology, 57.
49 R. Bultmann, Essays, New York, 1955, 126.
50 K. Barth, Church Dogmatics III/4, 127-366.
51 See above all N. Berdyaev, Freedom and Spirit, New York, 1935; and Spirit and Reality, London, 1939.
52 Lumen gentium, 32.
53 F. Toennies, Gemeinschaft und Gesellschaft, 5, Auflage, 1922.
54 E. Stein, "Individuum und Gemeinschaft", in Jahrbuch für Philosophie und phänomenologische Forshung V (1922), 224.
55 Cf. A. Dulles, Models of the Church, Garden City, N.Y., 1974; and my book The Sacraments and Your Everyday Life, Liguori, 1976, The Sacraments in a Secular Age, Slough, 1976.
56 Cf. G. Baum, l.c., 249.
57 R. Niebuhr, Radical Monotheism and Western Culture and Responsible Self, 73.
58 Cf. my book Sin in a Secular Age, Slough and New York, 1974.
59 Cf. A. Jonsen, l.c., 192ff.
60 Cf. E. Levinas, Totality and Infinity: An Essay on Exteriority, english tr., Pittsburg, 1969.
61 J.M. Gustafson, Christ and the Moral Life, 153.
62 E. Erikson, Insight and Responsibility, 148.
63 E. Osborn, Ethical Patterns in Early Christian Thought, 2.
64 E. Erikson, l.c., 139; cf. his Essay "The Role of Virtue", in J. Huxley (ed.), The Humanist Frame, New York, 1961, 145-165.
65 J.M. Gustafson, l.c., 249.
66 l.c., 253.
67 R. May, l.c., 226.
68 l.c., 230.
69 A. Pfänder, "Zur Psychologie der Gesinnungen", in Jahrbuch für Philosophie und phänomenlogische Forschung I (1913), 1-80; III (1916); 1-124; quote III, 52.

70 Cf. E. Fromm, *The Anatomy of Human Destructiveness*, New York, 1973.
71 J.M. Gustafson, l.c., 249.
72 Cf. R. Niebuhr, *The Responsible Self*, 112 and 124.
73 Cf. P. Tillich, *The Religious Situation*, Meridian Books, 1960, 32f.
74 N. Berdyaev, *Meaning of History*, Magnolia, 1973, 73.
75 N. Berdyaev, *Solitude and Society*, New York, 1938, 52.
76 R. May, l.c., 262.
77 Cf. l.c., 268.
78 Cf. P. Klein, *Die "kreative" Freiheit nach Nikolaj Berdjajew*, Regensburg, 1976, 148-159.
79 R. Bultmann, *Existence and Faith*, New York, 1960, 182.
80 Cf. G. Baum, l.c., 248f.
81 Cf. E.L. Long, *Survey of Christian Ethics*, Oxford, 1967; the author gives special attention to the problem of encounter of Christian ethics with contemporary thought patterns.
82 E. Osborn, l.c., 201; an example of a most conscious choice is St. Ambrose's *De officiis*, following the title and thought patterns of Cicero without renouncing to a specific Christian reflection.
83 K. Rahner, l.c., 234.
84 Cf. G. Baum, 188.
85 Ch. Curran, "Responsibility in Moral Thought: Centrality, Foundations and Implications for Ecclesiology", in *Jurist*, 31 (1971), 122.
86 *Optatam Totius*, 16.

Chapter Four

Created and recreated by freedom and for freedom in Christ

For a Christian ethics understood as an ethics of responsibility, freedom must be a key concept, for by faith we know that God has created us in freedom and for freedom's sake. And this very freedom, in which he creates us and all things, indicates also the purpose and the shape of his creation. In God is infinite freedom of infinite love, and he wants sharers of his own freedom, love and bliss. So perfect is his love that, because of his own name, he wills to restore true freedom to those who freely have turned away from him.

Since, together with creative love and fidelity, creative freedom is a key-concept and leitmotif of Christian ethics, we have, first of all, to explore the main dimensions and the limits of this freedom.

The point of departure is God's creation in his Word, which gives us the liberating power of the Word and the response to it (Section I).

God's design comes to its fulfilment in the incarnation of his Son, his final word to us and the revelation of the infinity of his freedom. We know liberation and liberty by knowing and loving Jesus, the Liberator and the embodiment of freedom (Section II).

Discipleship in and for creative freedom raises the fundamental question, "From what did Christ liberate us, and for what kind of freedom did he set us free? (Section III).

Christology leads us to pneumatology. What does it mean for Christian freedom when we profess, "We believe in the Holy Spirit"? (Section IV).

Freedom as a gift of the Spirit bestowed on us by the Word Incarnate disallows any kind of flight and spiritualism. The freedom that comes from the Spirit is task and capacity to embody it in our whole life and in the world around us (Section V).

All this points towards moral psychology and pedagogy. How do we educate each other to become ever more visible signs of God's creation, called forth in love and liberty, and redeemed for the liberty to love? (Section VI).

The central role of the freedom for which Christ has set us free should also determine our understanding of the Church as a great sacrament of evangelical freedom and of her ministry to promote creative freedom everywhere. How far and in what dimensions do we see her liberating presence in the world? (Section VII).

I. CREATION AS EVENT OF FREEDOM AND FOR FREEDOM

To perceive the real newness of the paschal message of freedom transmitted to us in the Bible in the Greek language, we should see it beyond the concept of freedom (*eleutheria*) that prevailed within the Greek culture. There, freedom was chiefly a prerogative and concern of Greek males, who were a minority in the Greek free cities. It did not apply to women, Greek or not, or to slaves or aliens ("barbarians"). Consequently freedom was fundamentally a matter of self-exaltation and exclusiveness for a single group in an already exclusive culture, although there were some hopeful signs of a broadening understanding in the time of Jesus and the Apostles. Its moral purpose was mainly self-perfection, self-fulfilment.[1]

Greek thinking was impregnated by the concept of causality, God being the "prime causality". Therefore, freedom confronts an almost insoluble problem: how can a world made by and for causality provide room for personal freedom, even true freedom for a small privileged class? The paradox was equally insoluble in the Roman Empire which divided people into two radically different classes, free Roman citizens and colonized people.

The totally different biblical message is one of God who creates the world in his Word, setting free the energies by his Spirit and creating a family of humankind united in the same dignity, and calling them all in freedom and for freedom.

1. In the beginning was the Word

"Before the world was, the Word was. The Word was sharing in God, and the Word was God. He then was with God at the beginning" (Jn 1:1-2).

All things arise from that eternal inner event in God. He is sharing his very self in a Word; and it is God's solemn, joyous and free decision to share with creatures, in and through that Word, his own love and freedom.

All things are made in the Word and, therefore, are a message, a gift. However, God's sharing in the Word comes to its summit and purpose when he creates the human person in his image and likeness. "Then God said, 'let us make man in our image, after our likeness'; so God created man in his own image, in the image of God he created them; male and female he created them, and God blessed them" (Gen 1:26-28).

Man is a word and he can find the Word who calls him, and thus understand himself as an embodied word spoken by God and as a calling to respond in freedom and gratitude.

When John speaks of the Word that was in the beginning with God, he does not follow gnostic speculations. His interest is centred on the Word that God spoke from the beginning, before the world was: the Word that is sharing Godhood with the Father and that in the fullness of time became flesh. All creation expects him, and all that is spoken by that Word in whom the Father shares his freedom, love and wisdom is directed towards the coming of Jesus Christ. "So the Word became flesh; he came to dwell among us, and we saw his glory, such glory as befits the Father's only Son, full of grace and truth"

(Jn 1:14). He is the Word that was from the beginning, and the Word through whom God speaks to us in the midst of the times. "In him everything in heaven and on earth was created, not only things visible but also the invisible, orders of thrones, sovereignties, authorities and powers; the whole universe has been created through him and for him. And he exists before everything, and all things are held together in him (Col 1:16-17).

Creation, and particularly the creation of human persons, is not just acting by causality; it is sharing in the Word and thus expressing the infinite freedom of love that is in God. God's creation, directed towards his perfect visible image, the Word Incarnate, and in him and through him to every person, is for communion, for sharing. The word "communion" comes from the Latin *cum* and *munus*, "with", "gift". It is the free self-bestowal through which God wants to be with us, to share with us his own freedom to love, to understand and to respond. It is because of this fundamental event that persons can reveal their selfhood to others in a word in which they share their love, their respect, their nearness and reverence.

The person created in the Word is gifted by the Word. He remains in the Word who shares with the Father and he cannot exist one moment without that Word. It is in and through him that man comes to selfhood and comes also to the consciousness that others, too, have a selfhood, have the same dignity, and are called to share in the same freedom. It is thus that man is an image of God, *imago Dei*.[²]

a) The gift of language in creation

"Out of the ground the Lord formed every beast of the field and every bird of the air and brought them to man to see what he would call them; and whatever man called every living creature, that was his name" (Gen 2:19).

The gift of word, of language, makes man free in comparison with the animals. He can discover meaning, a message in all created realities and especially in the animals. For the human person they are not just numbers. Each species has a special message and meaning. Through language, man communicates, and communication gives all mankind greater freedom.

Man needs the word to fulfil his vocation as *imago Dei* in the created world, as steward over all the created things, the plants and the animals. He grows in freedom by sharing his insights, discovering meanings, and is truly a sharer of God's freedom, an image and likeness of his Creator, if, amidst all the created "words", he never forgets the One who calls all these things into being by his Word and thus speaks to man of his goodness and wisdom. Man has the freedom to impress his own understanding, his own wisdom on his works, in his art and in all the ordering of his total environment. He becomes ever more an image and likeness of his Creator if he uses language not only in ordering things and sharing this task with others, but especially if he himself is a responsive word before God.

b) The liberating word before God

Since all things are created in the Word and *are* words — revelation, message and gift — for man, it is in man's very nature to understand himself as one who is called and who finds his truth and meaning by responding to the divine Word by words and deeds which he can share with others. All that he does in the world is faithful and creative insofar as he can offer it to God as grateful response. According to the Scriptures, it is the distinctive nature of man that he, and he alone, stands freely before God as a partner, as a creature who can decide what kind of word and action he offers to God as a response.[3]

It is the mystery of God's freedom that he invites man to stand before him, the Creator, to repose *(Shabbat)* and rejoice, and to give his word of praise for all created things to the One who called everything into being and made it a message and gift for him. Therefore, it is most essential for man's dignity and freedom to celebrate and rejoice before God, knowing that God listens to him and responds to his adoring word. (Later we shall explore more deeply how much adoration is a part and condition of man's true freedom before God).[4]

All the works of man and his name-giving decay if he refuses to make proper use of the gift of word and to make all his action a response before God. "For all that may be known by men lies plain before their eyes; indeed, God himself has disclosed it to them. His invisible attributes, that is to say, his everlasting power and deity have been visible ever since the world began, to the eye of reason in the things he made. There is, therefore, no possible defence for their conduct: knowing God, they have refused to honour him as God or to render him thanks; hence all their thinking has ended in futility" (Rom 1:19-21).

Man is truly at home in God's creation and finds his own true self-consciousness there: that is, he is truly free to the extent that he is responsive to God. The Bible sees the fundamental decision of man in his readiness to respond to God, to recognize that he is called by him in all his being. He emerges from nature into personhood in the fullest sense when he freely decides to understand himself as the one who is called in liberty and freely responds.

c) Intersubjectivity

Man is not able to express himself freely before God or to emerge into self-consciousness without attention to the word that is in the world. And for us the most helpful word of God is our fellowman, with whom we share the same dignity and the same freedom to express ourselves. Our subjectivity, our emerging selfhood, depends upon the word that others give us in a way that reveals also their freedom to love. Then we recognize our true personhood, dignity and freedom as equally reflected in ourselves and in the other.

Creaturely freedom is conditioned by the level of dialogue. Insofar as people express to each other their deepest word that is a free gift of themselves, revealing their being for each other, freedom is born. It grows in encounter with the other's freedom.[5] An individual person emerges into freedom in reflection and communication only when he finds himself in a community of persons. For him, this givenness is involuntary until he decides for voluntary communion, for free sharing in word and love.

He finds his inner word in an objective realm of freedom that comprises, above all, language, the various cultural and political structures and all the liberating arrangements that manifest mutual respect and co-responsibility.[6] Freedom is actualized objectively in the family, society and state, insofar as all this is sharing of past and present wisdom and freedom. The given social world does not cause interpersonal relationships but influences them in the sense of providing the context that permits and limits the depth and breadth of liberating dialogue. Each communicating word and action shapes and reshapes this realm of freedom.

Hegel defines the capacity to be free as the capacity to be with one's self; but being and becoming one's self is related to the other's freedom. "Each has real universality in the shape of reciprocity, insofar as each self knows itself recognized in the other freeman and is aware of this insofar as it recognizes the other and knows him to be free".[7] Freedom has this "inner law" that it cannot disclose itself without reciprocity, without that total word in which people recognize and affirm each other in the same dignity. This is the deep meaning of Kant's categorical imperative. "Act only on the maxim which will enable you at the same time to will that it be a universal law". This is the communion that is free sharing and full recognition of the other's word.

The liberating power of the word is much greater on the level of "we" relationships than on that of "they" relationships. The word that reveals the quality of the we-thou-I relationships can become a truly free self-revelation in mutuality. But the word is different when the other is recognized only in a certain function or service as, for instance, a bank employee, a postman, a store clerk. While we cannot be with them on the same wavelength as with our friends and family, we can recognize them respectfully, appreciate the quality of their service and greet them in such a way that they feel recognized as persons. Thus the world around us becomes humanized and transfigured by the deeper meaning of the free gift of word.[8]

d) To know the good and to be free

The dimension and strength of freedom depends upon the quality of the word expressed in the we-they relationships, in social conventions, traditions, laws, and so on. The most meaningful question is always whether and how the person receives the message by which others reveal and share themselves and how one responds and shares himself, in analogy to God's self-revealing and self-giving Word.

The child has a basic knowledge of the good, knowing it not only by precepts and prohibitions but also by "faith" in the parents' goodness as he has experienced it. If this trust is shaken or undermined then the child's moral knowledge is also shaken. Since the growing person has to live in a world that is both good and bad, more or less, parents have to help the child to discern what can be approved and accepted as valid in their own, in the child's and in other people's word and deed. There is great danger to their growth in freedom if an enormous amount of knowledge of things, concepts, laws and prohibitions is imposed upon them before they sufficiently experience the live word in which persons reveal and share their own inner moral values.

The breakdown of moral knowledge is near if there is mere communication of concepts, laws and precepts formulated by an alien will, without sharing that self-giving word of wisdom and love that allows the person to interiorize the command and the value inherent in it. Values that appeal to freedom are those embodied in persons or understood as relevant to the growth of persons in their own identity and in healthy relationships with God, with fellowmen and the created universe. They are values relevant for a fully personalized being-with and being-for each other, values expressive of creative freedom, fidelity and truthfulness. Always they are "we-values", manifestations of solidarity in freedom and in the word. These are what Abraham Maslow calls "B-values": the values that arise as inner needs of persons in their growing experience of *being-with*, of being a realized self in communion with the other.

For our understanding of freedom it is important to discern between merely conceptual knowledge of ethical norms, laws and values, on one hand, and value-experience on the other. Value experience arises from that mutuality in which we become more and more able to speak a live word that is genuinely self-revealing and sharing, receiving and giving on the level of the "we-values". Liberty grows in the we-dialogue, in the experienced participation, in grateful grasp of the word and the love which comes from others, and in readiness to respond creatively, generously. Thus true moral knowledge is born, embodying freedom and inviting greater freedom.

Conceptual knowledge should not be discarded as unimportant but should be seen as a carrier of liberating energy, if it is based upon or conducive to personal experience. Max Scheler rightly says, "There are more persons who grasp God existentially through love than there are people who are able to conceptualize their knowledge of God".[9]

Life-giving and liberating knowledge of the good is rooted in knowing "value-persons", and can be followed by genuine conceptualization. This enables a person to promote the cause of human liberty by relating all these values not to the blue sky of abstract values but to value-persons in their genuine relationships that manifest the word of love that speaks to the heart. All elaboration of moral norms must be related to this basic experience. And if it is a matter of Christian ethics, then it has to be related to that great event of freedom in which God speaks his creative Word, the Word Incarnate, as a sharing of his wisdom and love. This, in turn, is related to the inner sharing of the Father with and by his Word and in the Holy Spirit.

Liberating ethical knowledge contains moral intuition in the same sense in which Scripture speaks about "knowing". It arises from the word in which a person reveals and shares himself or herself. "The unloving know nothing about God" (1 Jn 4:8). Analogously, we can say that the unloving know nothing about the good. If a person suffers under isolation, or under the many words that do not reveal another's love, then growth in freedom is greatly handicapped. It is a matter of reciprocating the word of love, receiving it and returning it, and always a matter of a live word that comes from inner freedom, the freedom to love and to share.

"If a man says, 'I love God', while hating his brother, he is a liar. If he does not love the brother whom he sees, it cannot be that he loves God whom he has not seen" (1 Jn 4:20). In the Bible, especially in the writings of John, the word "seeing" has the same profound meaning as the word "knowing". The introduction of John's First Letter speaks of this experience of seeing and knowing the Word of God, the embodiment of the free love of the Father.

Knowledge of the higher, enriching and more demanding moral values depends essentially upon the increasing connaturality with the good. That has to be created and ever re-created in personal relationships by people who live in the image and likeness of God. "Absolute condition for a profound experience of value is the endorsement of a clear intuition, but this is not a sufficient guarantee to preserve it; an inner competence of the subject must be added in order to make possible the interiorization of value".[10]

One's inner competence arises from reciprocation of that "word" which is free manifestation of love and a gift of self. It is enriched by a healthy order in the realm of they-relationships, conventions, traditions and laws, and the social, economic and political structures. But for freedom's sake, for a human person to become increasingly an image and likeness of God's free Word, it is important to test all they-relationships and all structures of life, as to whether they genuinely serve the essential word that is sharing love, justice and goodness. Therefore, the understanding of natural law as the law written into the hearts of persons and communities of persons can never stress enough the importance of shared experience and reflection.

The full experience of sharing that leads to ideal moral knowledge and to freedom is a matter of development. Partial blindness and limitedness arise from the imperfection of the persons with whom one lives and from the embodiment of value-blindness — ideologies, taboos — in the total environment, in the culture and finally in language. We can never determine accurately what part is personal guilt. However, the knowledge about how much our own level of freedom relates to that of others and to the culture is not for excusing one's self. It is necessary for prevention of over-scrupulosity and guilt complexes but it does call clearly for co-humanity and co-responsibility.

2. *The original gift and burden of freedom*

The free will is, from the beginning, a gift born of God's free self-manifestation and sharing. From the beginning it is a gift in the Word and in view of the Word that takes the flesh of our humanity. Therefore, it is freedom for giving one's self in return and, as a result, for being an image and likeness of God in the realm of creative activity, of personal communion in the world and in the realm of celebration and adoration.

This free will, understood as gift of the Word, is not indifferent, not equally attuned to evil and to good. It is, by its very essence, a gift for the good, for the capacity to speak out one's self for the others, to share and to receive the genuine word of love and goodness. It is, however, a created, limited freedom that entails the possibility of refusing freedom for the good and of incapacitating it by a "no": a "no" which refuses one's self to God and refuses to discover the Word that has called us.

Man's greatness as image and likeness of God is visible in that freedom which allows him to be co-creator, to become capable of that selfhood which overflows in genuine sharing and self-revelation. Each authentic expression of freedom "enlarges the circumference of the circle of one's self".[11] However, this does not allow, but rather discourages, a selfish outlook. Our freedom depends upon sharing the loving word that images God's free word of creation in love.

It is a profound mystery how a creature who has received everything from God and cannot live one moment without his life-giving word, can contradict the very meaning of his life. "This act of freedom that denies God is thus the absolute contradiction in which God is affirmed and denied simultaneously".[12]

The person who, in his basic option, refuses God, refuses the good for which he is created but does not lose the energy of his free will. However, he gradually destroys his capacities to love and to do the good. Indeed, only through a new divine gracious gift can the sinner regain his freedom for the good and his freedom for God.

II. CHRIST, THE FREE GIFT OF THE FATHER

Before we ask from what and for what Christ has freed us, we should first realize that Christ himself is the great event of freedom. Only to the extent that we know him as the free gift of the Father to humankind, anointed by the Spirit for self-giving love even unto the cross, can we appreciate the freedom he offers us.

1. *The Trinitarian dimension of freedom in Christ*

In the Synoptics, and even in the Acts of the Apostles, we find little conceptualized liberty and liberation. However, the whole New Testament presents Christ to us as the great gift of freedom, the embodiment and personification of freedom for love. He is the gift of the Father's own infinite freedom and love.

This is seen in Paul's theology on justification by grace. Humankind, in its bondage of sin, has no claim before God. It is only because of his name as Father that God freely decides not to abandon his creatures who have perverted the gift of freedom into rebellion and other forms of bondage. He owes it to his own name, to his overflowing love, not to abandon us. The Incarnation reveals for us, insofar as we can perceive it, what God truly is.

Berdyaev rightly says that freedom is a Trinitarian event. "The kingdom of love in freedom is the kingdom of the Trinity".[13] In the same freedom that the Father gives himself to his Word, with all his wisdom, love and might, and in the same freedom that the Word shares with the Father, comes to us the Redeemer. It is the absolute gratuity, the splendour, the glory of God that appears in the incarnation and in all that Christ is, does and says for us. As the Father has given everything to his Word, so, in his infinite freedom, he gives everything to us by sending us his only begotten Son to be our Saviour and our brother.

The unique glory that shines through in Jesus Christ is the freedom of the Son. "The Word became flesh; he came to dwell among us, and we saw his glory, such glory as befits the Father's only Son, full of grace and truth" (Jn 1:14). Some biblical scholars suggest that, without betraying the meaning, we could translate this, " . . . and we saw his freedom, such freedom as befits the Father's only Son". Only in Jesus does the full graciousness and truth of freedom appear.[14] Even if he never would have used such a word as freedom, all that Jesus is, says and does, manifests the truth and fullness of freedom, and spells out an event of freedom.

As gift of the Father's freedom, the Son is radically free to give himself for us.[15] He is filled by the Holy Spirit who has anointed him to give us a message that is Spirit and truth, a liberating word. And more, he is anointed by the Spirit to be the servant to all mankind in absolute freedom, and to give himself for the salvation of us all.

In the freedom-event of the incarnation, life, death and resurrection of Jesus Christ, the Holy Trinity is present on earth; and this event reveals to us that God is love. Freedom is an essential dimension of love. The co-humanity of Christ, Emmanuel, his total being-with-us and for us, is the glory of God's infinite freedom to love. It is, therefore, natural for Jesus, in his freedom, to remove the obstacles to human freedom and love. He is the saving conflict against everything that contradicts them, for even "piety that stands in the way of love, stands in the way of God himself".[16]

As Son of the eternal Father and bearer of the Spirit, Jesus has no need to seek his own glory or to do his own will. Filled by the Spirit, he gives himself freely to the glory of the Father, in full manifestation of the Father's self-giving love. And the Father glorifies him, making visible his liberating freedom.

The power of the Holy Spirit in Christ becomes fully apparent in the resurrection. "Where the Spirit of the Lord is, there is liberty" (2 Cor 3:17). But even before the resurrection the glory of the Father and the power of the Spirit shine through in Christ's life, in his radical personal freedom and his total openness to the Father in a new co-humanity. In this way he announces and enacts the gospel of liberation from a piety enslaved by laws. He was executed because he was perceived as a blasphemer against law, tradition and priestly authority, and denounced as an agitator against the *Pax Romana*.[17]

2. Jesus, The Prophet

The history of the prophets in the Old Testament and of the great prophetic saints of the Church is a history of the freedom that is given by the Holy Spirit. Christ is *the* Prophet. He belongs to no priestly class or tribe but receives his mission and authority directly from the Father. His *parrhesia* comes from the trust in the Father and from the Spirit by whom he is anointed.

Jesus manifests his prophetic freedom, above all, in his total availability for sinners, the sick, the poor, the oppressed and the marginal people. It is especially here that the gratuitous character of his love is seen and the infinite love and freedom of God become visible.[18]

Jesus does not follow the rules of the priestly tradition in his interpretation of the Bible. His use of the Old Testament is creative.[19] His teaching about the Sabbath and the law, his opposition to meaningless traditions that hinder freedom for God, and especially his protest against a religion that would attribute such pettiness to God, is in itself manifestation of God's gratuitous freedom, an undeserved gift of himself.

3. *Jesus is the New Covenant*

The covenant of God with Israel intended to make her a servant among the nations and thus a witness to the Fatherhood of the one God. Israel, however, became arrogant and, in her pride, her witness was concealed. Jesus is the New Covenant, the Servant, the man for all people. In his saving solidarity, and as the Prophet and the Covenant, he tears down all the barriers between Jews and Gentiles, Jews and Samaritans, between the various priestly classes and the people of God. In this freedom, manifesting the power of the Holy Spirit, Christ brings the old covenant to fulfilment; but he also abrogates it where it failed through man's sinfulness. "Only in Christ is the old covenant abrogated" (2 Cor 3:14).

The covenant idea is rooted in the Trinitarian freedom. Again and again Jesus speaks of his being one with the Father and, therefore, one with his disciples. His prayer that all may be one, as he is one with the Father, is manifestation of the divine life. In the gospel of St John a key concept is Life. It is Jesus who, as bread of life, gives life to all; and those who have life in him overcome divisions and are free for each other, to the glory of the Father of all.

4. The embodiment of the kingdom of God

The Synoptics present the eruption of freedom, above all, under the paradigm of God's kingdom. It is the new freedom under God's rightful rule, a rule to save the oppressed, to heal the sinners, a rule of goodness that can be accepted and fulfilled only in that freedom which responds to God's undeserved gifrs.

Christ embodies this kingdom, since he did not come to seek his own glory or power but acted under the reign of the Holy Spirit, to the glory of the Father. Those who belong to the kingdom of God are guided by God's gifts perceived in their absolute gratuity and honoured by gratitude and generosity.[20] Jesus contrasts all the established powers with the radical freedom of the kingdom of God, of which his own freedom is forever the foretaste and fulfilment. He is wholly guided by the Spirit, and his life is totally open to the Father. Whoever comes to him is led to the Father. "Who believes in me believes in him who sent me rather than in me; seeing me he sees him who sent me" (Jn 12:44-45).

The idea expressed in the Synoptics comes to its final and most powerful formulation in Paul: the end comes when Jesus delivers up the kingdom of God to the Father after abolishing every kind of dominion, authority and power. "And when all things are thus subject to him, then the Son himself will also be made subordinate to God who made all things subject to him, and thus God will be all in all" (1 Cor 15:24-28).

Jesus' total freedom for the Father, as the real symbol of the kingdom of God, becomes strikingly apparent in the Synoptics: Jesus saw the political concept of messiahship as the most terrifying temptation. It is the age-old temptation of those revolutionaries who want to impose their will on others by violence and manipulation, and therefore can never free themselves and their fellowmen. Christ proclaims the kingdom of God by the power of the Spirit and the power of his word and, finally, by the powerlessness of the cross.[22]

5. The freedom of Jesus on the cross

The Carmen Christi (Phil 2:6-11), praising the freedom and power of God's love as revealed in Jesus Christ, puts the emphasis on the *kenosis:* "For the divine nature was his from the first; yet he did not prize his equality with God; but made himself nothing, assuming the nature of a slave, bearing the human likeness revealed in human shape, he humbled himself, and in obedience accepted even death". The obedience of Christ is the event of our liberation but it is also the manifestation of God's own freedom beyond all human concepts.[23]

There is a temptation to explain Jesus' obedience in a philosophical way instead of in the biblical understanding. Philosophy invented a divine decree that determined the Jews to kill Jesus and imposed upon Jesus the acceptance of the outcome of this decree. But in the Bible, God, in his freedom and his love, enters into human history through Jesus Christ, the liberator and bearer of our human burden. Jesus, guided by the Spirit, wanted to convert Israel to God's design. It was not under a divine decree but under a rebellious spirit that the Jews decided to crucify Jesus. The mission the Father had given him was to manifest the full extent of his love and that of the Father. And this he did, under circumstances that were not decreed by God but were rather the climax of man's rebellion. Jesus transformed all this into the most dramatic revelation of love, in the giving of himself. Even his prayer for those who crucified him and for all who are crucified by the power-lust of sinful mankind manifested, in that hour, Jesus' creative and faithful freedom.

Moltmann rightly says that the cross of Christ forces us to review our concept of God in view of this incomparable event that a "crucified God" overcomes the power of death.[24] Only because God is almighty and absolute freedom can he, in the incarnation, enter into the human history of freedom and bondage and transform the most horrifying event of abused freedom into the revelation of the infinite freedom of love.

Against a one-sided theology of glorification, Ernst Käsemann insists on the centrality of the cross, without which we cannot celebrate resurrection and freedom. "It is only from the cross of Jesus that we can recover the necessary freedom of movement in life and thought".[25]

Christ's cross also reveals him as embodied freedom. He does not throw away the body as something useless, as the Gnostics would have done. He offers his body as the supreme sign of freedom. "Destroy this temple and in three days I will raise it again. But he spoke of the temple of his body" (Jn 2:19-21). Thus, in Christ's death the human body becomes the real temple in which man is to worship.

"The Incarnate Word has made all temples of religion, at best, preparatory. Jesus' body as temple means temples are significant only in relation to the human body. What counts is to act in the body, in the totality of our being, in response to God's unconcealment".[26] Christ is free in his body, as in all of his being, since he receives everything as a free gift of the Father, given for all. "Sacrifice and offering thou didst not desire but thou hast prepared a body for me. Then I said, 'Here I am; I have come, O God, to do thy will' " (Heb 10:5-7).

However, Jesus becomes fully visible as the Father's free gift to humankind for the liberation of all people only in the resurrection. Now he is no longer just the Father's gift but the fully accepted response in a wholly free self-giving love. It is significant that Jesus not only points to the resurrection as a future event, he says, "I am the resurrection and I am the life" (Jn 11:25). The reality that becomes apparent in his resurrection and that will finally become visible in our resurrection is already given in Jesus Christ. He has the fullness of life; he *is* the life, and, therefore, he can so freely give himself on the cross.

6. *Faith as grateful acceptance of the free gift of the Father*

Moral theology can never begin with a code or even with the details of what Christ wants us to do. The roots and foundation of salvation and of true Christian freedom are faith.

We understand faith here as joyous and grateful acceptance of him who is the Truth, the Way, the Life: grateful acceptance of our Father's free gift to us. Therefore, before all other reflections on the purposes for which Christ has freed us, we turn to him in order to know him as the Father's gift of love, and thus to know the Father himself.

The basis of a distinctively Christian anthropology is Christology. In Christology, we surely cannot separate what Christ is from what he has done, but the primary concern is always *who* he is: that he is the man for others.[27] As free gift of the Father, his own freedom is always directed towards our freedom. Hence, on the basis of Jesus' personal freedom we try to construct a description of human freedom as portrayed by the symbolics of Christian faith.[28]

III. FROM BONDAGE TO FREEDOM IN CHRIST

Now we face the question, "For what kind of freedom has Christ set us free?" And to understand thoroughly the positive content and direction of freedom in Christ, we have also to face the other question, "From what kind of unfreedom or bondage are we liberated?"

We speak of the "bondage of sin" in its various species and aspects only in the context of liberation. In any other context all talk on sin is sinful because it does not acknowledge God's mercy or render thanks to him and, therefore, leads to despair.

We have to face not only the finiteness that limits our human freedom, we have also to concentrate on the bondage that arises from sin and leads to sin, disallowing any kind of metaphysical explanation for sin that would excuse us. We can rightly speak of sin — personal sin and the sin of the world and in the world (original sin) — only insofar as a person or mankind refuses, in freedom, to be free for God, for true love and for fullness of truth.

This liberation in Christ is the focus of profound reflection in the theology of Paul and John. For both, salvation understood as a liberation is a central concept. However, their emphasis and conceptualization are quite different. While Paul emphasizes redemption from the bondage of selfishness and for a self-giving love, John stresses more the bondage of falsehood and liberation in and for truth. For Paul, freedom is an intensely personal matter. He himself has experienced the liberating power of the risen Lord and he has a special prophetic mission to free early Christianity from all those misinterpretations of law that would keep the gospel in bondage.[29]

Christ has set us free *from* a stolen freedom — freedom as theft — and *for* freedom gratefully received as gift (1). He has freed us from falsehood, deception and delusion, and for the truth of life in him (2). We are freed from bondage under law and the injustices that arise from it, and liberated for the law of Christ, the law of the Spirit that alone can free both man and law (3). Christ has delivered us from sin-solidarity, and given us covenant-liberty (4). He has freed us from enmity, and given us the reign of love (5). He has liberated us from anguish, overscrupulosity and guilt complexes, and brought us trust and confidence (6). Christ sets us free from sloth, flight, alienation, and leads us to creativity, inner freedom and peace (7). In Christ is freedom from the powers of oppression, greed, racism, sexism, cult of violence and liberation for authority that is service (8). And, finally, Christ has set us free from the fear of death, and given us the joy of life (9).

1. *From freedom as theft to freedom as gift*

Even where the New Testament gives a shocking picture of man's enslavement to sin, the formal freedom of will is always supposed. However, the only freedom that truly deserves the name — the freedom that comes from God and returns to God — is lacking in the sinner.[30] He cannot excuse himself simply by saying that he is not free to do the good and to avoid the evil, for God's gracious gift of conversion is never lacking.

The sinner is under bondage. He experiences his lack of the right kind of freedom but it is still he who sins. He is, as it were, split into two selves. He stands against himself, stands in his own way; yet, it is not another who sins but himself. This is his very misery: that sin is not something outside of himself; it is *in* him, it dwells in him (Rom 7:17).

The one who sins still has some freedom to see the good and to know, somehow, that there is a law that is just and holy; but he is a stranger to himself. Whatever the power of sin, it is in the sinner and he has to give account of it (cf. Rom 7:7-25).[31] Insofar as he is sinning, his freedom is asserting itself selfishly while refusing gratitude to God. He does not want to accept his freedom as a gift of God to be used in response to God. Thus, God's very gift of true freedom is misused through a kind of radical theft.[32]

From this bondage of thievery, that introduces such contradiction into man's innermost being, liberation is possible

because of Christ's death. While Adam wanted to use his freedom
for his own self-exaltation (wanting to be like God), Jesus
Christ honours his freedom as a gift and surrenders himself
totally to the Father (cf. Gen 3:5 with Ph 2:5-11). By freely
giving himself, Christ manifests the fullness and truth of freedom. Through his Holy Spirit, Christ teaches us that we, too,
can be truly free when we render thanks always and everywhere,
and honour our freedom as gift of the Father by surrendering
ourselves to him in the service of our brothers and sisters as
he has done.

The transition from bondage to freedom is one from self-
centredness and stubbornness to conformity with the loving will
of God. "And this was the result, that I willed not to do what
I willed, and willed to do what thou willest".[33] This is
St Augustine's experience of the new freedom as a gift of God,
and thus freedom through God, for God, and for love of
fellowmen with God. Quite different is Paul Sartre's view of his
freedom. "If existence really precedes essence, there is no
explaining things away by reference to a fixed or given human
nature. In other words, there is no determinism. Man is free,
man is freedom. We are alone, with no excuses".[34] Sartre is
right in rejecting an overall determinism, but wrong in asserting
unlimited freedom.

If we accept our limited freedom as God's gift, and gratefully use all its potentialities, we can say, with Käsemann,
"The power of Christ's resurrection becomes a reality here and
now in the form of Christian freedom, and only in that. That
reality is opposed on earth by anything that stands in the way
of Christian freedom".[35] But we can never forget that we can
share in the risen Lord's freedom only if we also accept the
task to "put to death your selfish self". In other words, we
renounce freedom by theft and accept it as God's gift of love.

In his fight against Pelagianism, Augustine stresses the
gratuity of Christian freedom and makes clear that only thus
can we truly preach freedom. "Therefore, we do not undermine in any way the free choice of human will when we do not
deny with ungrateful mind, but affirm with grateful devotion
that grace of God by which free will is helped".[36] My point is
that we speak not only of an added grace but of a definite

conversion by which all our freedom is understood, acknowledged and realized as a gift of God.

Freedom as Christ's gift can only survive through faith understood as grateful, humble, joyous acceptance of him who is truth, saviour and source of genuine freedom. The greater the element of gratitude in faith, the greater will be the creative power of response. By the power of the Holy Spirit, the divine indicative gives meaning and dynamics to the genuine imperative; it arises from within us: Live by the freedom for which Christ has freed you.

To live creatively and faithfully the new life and liberty in Jesus Christ, we must never forget that these are not only the gift of the Creator but also the harvest of Christ's death and resurrection. Therefore, we can abide in this freedom only if we celebrate and live gratefully the mystery of the cross and resurrection.

2. From falsehood to freedom in true life

The Gospel of St John presents the bondage of sin especially as man's being under the power of deception, self-deception, embodied lies and darkness. Liberation is, therefore, understood as entering into the realm of truth and life in Jesus Christ. The forthrightness of truth in the very person of Jesus Christ unmasks the arrogance and the delusion of those who think they can be their own selves by living for themselves. Whoever thus deludes himself is "godless world" in the sense of John's gospel. Jesus speaks about truth, is Truth in person, and fulfils truth in his total surrender to the Father. He reveals the truth that can liberate us again for God so that we can find our true self.[37]

John does not directly confront the problem of bondage under the law, as Paul does. It is inferred, however, in a rather solemn way in the prologue: "While the law was given through Moses, grace and truth came through Jesus Christ" (Jn 1:17). It is mainly in this perspective of grace and truth, as revealed in Jesus Christ, that the gospel of St John treats of freedom. Most explicitly, it speaks in chapter 8:31-36 of freedom coming from Christ: "Jesus said, 'If you dwell within the revelation

I have brought, you are indeed my disciples; you shall know the truth and the truth will set you free'. They replied, 'We are Abraham's descendants, we have never been in slavery to any man. What do you mean by saying 'You will become free men'? 'In very truth I tell you', said Jesus, 'that everyone who commits sin is a slave. The slave has no permanent standing in the household but the Son belongs to it forever. If then the Son sets you free, you will indeed be free' ".

Here we find a magnificent theology on freedom. The freedom comes through Jesus Christ, the Son, who manifests the freedom and truth that come from the Father in his infinite and all-embracing love. Those who, in living faith, know him as the truth and act as his disciples, and thus become, in Jesus Christ, sons and daughters of God, experience the liberating power of this truth.

When unbelieving Jews put their trust in their kinship with Abraham, Jesus tells them that they are not truly offspring of Abraham by faith. "If you were Abraham's children you would do as Abraham did" (Jn 8:39). Those who live in contradiction to the gift of the covenant are offspring of the liar, Satan, and "You are doing your own father's work" (Jn 8:41).

Those who stubbornly refuse to acknowledge Christ as the revealer of truth are in bondage to falsehood. The Pharisees looked to religion as a guarantee of status and of vainglory, and therefore do not come to faith. Jesus, the shining light of liberating truth, does not look for status or self-assertion; his whole life and purpose is to reflect the love of the Father. "Jesus replied, 'If I glorify myself, that glory of mine is worthless. It is the Father who glorifies me; he of whom you say, 'He is our God'. Though you do not know him; but I know him. If I said that I did not know him, I should be a liar like you, but in truth I know him and do his word' " (Jn 8:54-55). "Some Pharisees in his company asked, 'Do you mean that we are blind'? Jesus said, 'You would not be guilty, but because you say 'We see', your guilt remains' " (Jn 9:40-41).

What, then, of churchmen, careerists, status seekers, who act as if they knew everything and tell others, "we see"? They know so many things indeed but not salvation truth. If only they would renounce the selfish use of their freedom and knowledge, they could recognize Jesus. They are not without guilt when faced with the forthrightness of liberating truth which they stubbornly resist.

The truth which Jesus speaks out with his total being is the truth of divine love manifest in the humility of the Son, the Servant of God. One can "know" this truth which breathes love only by renouncing pride and arrogance. It is liberation only if one sees that the truth of life is in doing what divine love makes possible in us, and that is to love one another as Jesus has loved us (Jn 15:12).

There are numerous texts in John's gospel that indicate that Jesus' word has a divine power to liberate (Jn 8:28,38-43; 14:10; 15:22; 17:8,14), that it gives true life (5:24; 6:68; 8:51), that it cleanses from sin (15:3), and is also a power of judgment (12:47f). Hence Jesus, in person, is Truth, Life and the Way (14:6).

The central truth of John's gospel is that the Word that breathes love became flesh, and we can be free only by receiving him and putting our faith in him. Illumined by the unconceal-ment of God's truth in Jesus Christ, we know that we can live genuine freedom only as "final liberty in truth and goodness".[38] After the revelation of God's love in Jesus Christ, it is no longer a problem of God's hiddenness but of men's blindness when faced with him who is the light and the truth. "And man's blindness is the problem, especially in the confidence that he sees what ought to be and what the criteria are for being human",[39] while at the same time refusing to live radically in the light of Christ.

Even Christians must constantly be challenged in their thoughts and words about freedom. They are in need of libera-tion from their own selfishness and from the world around them, from which comes the constant temptation of falsehood. A classical example of this challenge to Christian talk of freedom is Paul's response to those who say, "We are free to do anything". "Yes, but is everything good for us? We are free to do anything, but does everything help the building of the community? Each of you must regard not his own interest but other people's" (1 Cor 10:23-24).

3. *From bondage under law to the law of the Spirit*

The passionate concern of the Apostle of the Gentiles is liberation from bondage under law, a liberation which in no way makes us lawless but brings us, rather, into the law of the Spirit in which man is freed from the bondage of a depersonalized and depersonalizing law.

Paul himself feels that before Christ threw him from his horse he had been an idolater. He had given so great a cult to the law of Moses and man-made traditions that he had been blind to the kingdom that had come in Jesus Christ. Paul experienced the power of liberation from that cult. For him it was not just questions about whether circumcision and other laws might be imposed on the Gentile Christians. He saw, in the fanaticism of those "sham Christians, interlopers, who had stolen in to spy upon the liberty we all enjoy in the fellowship of Jesus Christ" (Gal 2:4), men who were honouring more the written law than Jesus, the Saviour. They saw Jesus as only a reinforcer of the law, while, for Paul, the first and most essential thing was to receive Jesus Christ in faith, in gratitude, as the undeserved gift of the Father.

It is, then, a matter of living by the undeserved justice of God that gives us a justice quite different from that of the Pharisees and the doctors of the law (cf. Mt 5:20). Christ is not servant to the law. He has not come to reinforce a law beyond himself. He has shown that the Son of Man is Lord over the law of the Sabbath. As Christ is free for the Father and free for sinners and the sick, so, through faith, we should become free to give ourselves wholeheartedly to the service of our fellowmen.[40]

When Peter yielded to the pressure of the legalists, Paul saw it not only as a hindrance to evangelization but also as danger for the very identity of the gospel he preached. He, therefore, dared to oppose Peter (Cephas) publicly "because he was clearly in the wrong. When I saw that their conduct did not square with the truth of the gospel, I said to Cephas, before the whole congregation, 'If you, a Jew born and bred, live like a Gentile and not like a Jew, how can you insist that Gentiles must live like Jews?' " (Gal 2:11-14).

Wherever man does not live by faith and trust in God, he is tempted to hide behind the observance of external laws. He considers even salvation truth as something like a code of dogmas and is ready to fight for them without longing for the true knowledge of Christ. There can even be a formal obedience and devotion to the law in such a way that a person refuses to surrender himself totally to God and to his saving justice (cf. Gal 6:2; Ph 3:9). There can be an obedience towards law and authority, a performance of religious acts that in reality are self-seeking, a stubborn self-assertion in many forms, manifesting a lack of openness to the Spirit.[41]

The solemn words of Jesus on the Mount of the Beatitudes, "But I tell . . . ", that lead to the summit of the new formulation of the law, "Let your goodness have no limits, just as the goodness of the heavenly Father knows no bounds" (Mt 5:17-48), are not just a quantitative sharpening of the Torah of Moses. They make clear that the main content of gospel morality is an unreserved surrender to God and to his kingdom of freedom and love.

People must not be so submitted to the many laws that they lose sight of the all-embracing law of liberty of the children of God. The priest and Levite were not free to serve the man who lay bleeding on the road, but Jesus is free to receive, to love and to console the sinners who by breaking their laws have become unacceptable to the rigid exponents of organized religion. In his goodness and graciousness, he receives the public sinner, so that she, too, may become able to love (cf. Lk 7:36f). In the eyes of the legalists, Jesus frequently sinned against the law; but for him it was not a matter simply of transgressing an obsolete law; it was a matter of freeing us from the strictures of law behind which the unbeliever hides by a kind of cult.

Liberation happens when, by the power of the Holy Spirit, we become humble, poor, recognizing that all that we are and have is a gift of God, and thereby find our true selves in surrender to him and in openness to others. This is the law of the Spirit which, in Jesus Christ, gives life and sets us free from law and death (Rom 8:2). Far from making people lawless, it makes them holy. "You are no longer under the law but under grace" (Rom 6:14). Under grace, and freed from legalism, they find their full freedom and law in Christ (1 Cor 9:20f). Believers do not stand before a meaningless law that threatens them; they are not slaves of the letter of a written law. The liberating reality is the new law of the new covenant, "written into their minds and upon their hearts" (Heb 8:10).

Thomas Aquinas gives the following commentary on this new reality of the law of the Spirit. "The Old Testament was written in a book with a sprinkling of blood (Heb 9); thus the Old Testament is a covenant in the letter. The New Testament, on the contrary, is a covenant in the Holy Spirit through whom love is poured forth into our hearts (Rom 5). And so, the Holy Spirit, insofar as he effects love in us which is the fulfilment of the law, is the new covenant".[42] For Aquinas, the law and the dogmas written in a book are only the secondary aspect that receives strength through and from the covenant aspect. "What is most characteristic in the law of the new covenant, and what gives it its entire efficacy, is the grace of the Holy Spirit which is given through faith in Christ, and so the new law is fundamentally the grace of the Holy Spirit himself".[43]

The Father not only gives us his own liberating Word in Jesus Christ; he also sends us the Holy Spirit so that we can respond to the self-giving love of Jesus with all our hearts, our minds and with all our energies.

4. *From sin-solidarity to saving solidarity*

Greek culture offered the word "liberty" (*eleutheria*), but for a long time liberty was meant only for Greek male freemen as against the non-liberty of women, slaves and barbarians. In Stoic ethics, then, the ideal of liberty is privatized, a matter of one's own mind and one's own quietude and uninvolvement.

Freedom in Jesus Christ is quite the opposite. It is offered to all for involvement by all. Christ wants us to be freed from that egotism that ties us together in the "sin of the world", with its cumulative investment of falsehood, injustice and violence. He is the New Covenant, and he makes it clear that only two choices are given us: either we turn in discipleship to him who is the covenant with the people, the embodiment of saving solidarity, or we remain enslaved in collective selfishness, arrogance, falsehood and malice.

In the Bible, the "sin of the world" is a threatening reality, infinitely more than just a stain on a soul that can easily be washed away by a ritual. For Jesus Christ, to be baptized meant absolute solidarity in bearing the burden of all. He is finally baptized in the blood of the new and everlasting covenant, to draw all men together in his love and in the new justice. This is all an undeserved gift to us in the covenant, and whoever refuses to live the covenant morality remains in the slavery of individual and collective selfishness, pride, arrogance and alienation.

For me, as for many of today's theologians, the essence of the doctrine on original sin lies in this absolute choice that we have to make: we are unavoidably under the law of solidarity, since we are all created by the one God and Father of all. Either we honour him together, by unity and common commitment to justice and peace, or we wilfully stay under the threat, the influence and the bondage of all the sinfulness that has been spawned by the various forms of selfishness.[44]

Each time we refuse the grace of God and do the evil we could avoid and omit the good we could do through God's gifts and grace, we are Adam or Eve, bringing into the world an increase of the powers of darkness, deception and oppression. There is no true liberation from all this except by turning to Christ and committing ourselves to the kingdom of God in justice and peace, in response to God's gifts.

It is clear, then, that anyone who wants only to save his own soul cannot be freed from the bondage of sin-solidarity. Christ's act of redemption is the supreme manifestation of the heavenly Father's concern for all. He who is the very embodiment of solidarity has redeemed us all for freedom, and we cannot receive this gift without being concerned for the same freedom for all, in union with Christ. "For the love of Christ leaves us no choice, when once we have reached the conclusion that one man died for all and therefore all mankind has died to selfishness. His purpose in dying for all was that all people while still in life, should cease to live for themselves and should live for him who for their sake died and was raised to life" (2 Cor 5:14-15). It is impossible to live for Jesus Christ "the covenant of the people" without being committed to the increase of redeemed freedom on all levels of human history.

5. *From the bondage of enmity to the reign of love*

In his utter freedom to love sinners, to die for those who had offended him, and to pray for those who drove the nails into his hands and feet, Jesus has shown us the kind of freedom for which he sets us free. It is the freedom to love one another in Christ, with Christ and in the manner of Christ, whose self-giving love brought him even to death on the cross. The foundation of this freedom is faith in God who is Love, and in him who reveals for us the full extent of the Father's love. Jesus not only calls us to his freedom — "Love each other as I have loved you" — but sets us free to receive his love and to love with him.

The sickness of sinful man is very deep. He sees in God a threat to his autonomy; and since he is chiefly concerned with his own rights and freedom, he is in constant conflict with his fellowmen. The bondage of both law and lawlessness is rooted in this self-centred, self-concerned existence. Liberation through Christ, however, lets us see all creation as a gift of God, and we know that we are given to each other. Then, in this perspective, we find genuine loving relationships in a saving solidarity with Christ. "For though everything belongs to you, Paul, Apollos and Cephas — the world, life and death, the present and the future, all of them belong to you — yet you belong to Christ as Christ to God" (1 Cor 3:22-23). When, by faith, we respond with our hearts, our minds and all our energies to Christ, the great conversion and liberation has happened. We join Christ in his love for our fellowmen and for ourselves, and in this we find the new freedom.

Living faith is filled with gratitude, and it gives a grateful memory. "Christ died for us while we were yet sinners, and this is God's own proof of his love for us" (Rom 5:8). The hope to be free in Christ's love is no vain dream, "because God's love has flooded our inmost heart through the Spirit he has given us" (Rom 5:5). And thus the promises of the

Old Testament are fulfilled, that God will give us a new covenant and a new law, a law written in our inmost heart (cf. Jer 31:31-38). "A new heart I will give you and a new spirit I will put within you, and I will take out of your flesh the heart of stone and give you a sensible heart. Indeed, I will put my own spirit within you" (Ez 36:26-27).

By the Spirit of Christ, the believer understands that this is the commandment that binds and frees us from the beginning; but in Christ it is given in a new and wonderful way: "Love each other as I have loved you" (Jn 15:12). Now it is Christ's special gift to us, interiorized by faith and the grace of the Holy Spirit. Conversion and liberation happen to the extent that we see all this no longer as only a commandment but as a liberating gift which we can share with each other in the eschatological covenant community. When, in the light of Christ who is our free gift of love from the Father, we recognize and honour each other as gift instead of threat, we are freed from the bondage of enmity and are free to be with each other and for each other.

In this light we also look differently at the matter of human rights and of our own freedoms. The believer now understands a "right" as what is "good for each other".[47] The same is true of law. We understand that there is no freedom without law in a human community and society. But only if people have come to understand the one great gift of Christ and his law of mutual love, to "love as I have loved you", can they see all laws, all rights and all freedoms in the truly Christian perspective.

Christian freedom is, fundamentally, not just encounter with observance of objective norms, important as they may be. In the love for which Christ has freed us, we realize that the binding moral norms express the very structure of the human person. All other things below the level of persons are relevant only in view of persons and their relationships. We may transform things and structures below ourselves as we think best, for we are their masters, not their servants. "The only ultimate structure of the person which adequately expresses it is the basic power of love, and this without measure".[48]

Sin and bondage are then seen as the choice of a lesser or

pseudo love, because if it refuses to become greater it is no longer love. We are truly free if our measure is now the immeasurable love of Christ for us. We can also say that our love for our neighbour is the measure of our freedom. To love them as Christ loves us makes us totally free for each other and for the Lord.

The gospel of Christian liberty, given in the letter to the Galatians, explains that "the freedom to which they are called is, in its meaning and purpose, the freedom to love. The true nature and purpose of the freedom becomes visible in the mutual love of the disciples".[49] Liberty as gift and law in Christ can be summed up in selfless love. "For love cannot wrong a neighbour" (Rom 13:10). This is what we mean by the perfect law of liberty when we say with St Augustine, "Have true love and do what love wills".

6. *Free from anguish, free for trust*

Joyous and creative freedom is frequently blocked by anguish, fear, useless worry, scrupulosity, blame, guilt feeling and guilt complexes. Only God knows how much of this is caused by personal sin and how much by the investment of sinfulness in the world around us. Some of this can also be the product of biological pressure. But if the Lord has set us free from sin and from slavery under the law, then that part of anguish and fear that still remains as frustration can and does receive a new meaning. It is no longer poisoned. It can enter into the dimensions of Christ's sufferings. Freed from selfish worries, we can bear the daily cross and take responsibility for each other.

Jesus did not promise to keep us free from all anxiety, suffering and frustration. However, he wants us freed from all those forms of anxiety that arise from selfishness and alienation. "I bid you put away anxious thoughts. Set your mind on God's kingdom and his justice before everything else, and the rest will come to you as well. So do not be anxious about tomorrow; tomorrow will look after itself. Each day has troubles enough of its own" (Mt 6:25-34).

Through faith, trust and gratitude for all that the Lord has given us, especially for our lofty vocation of discipleship, there happens a wonderful liberation from useless worries, from pressing fears and uncreative anger. This message is very central in Christ's teaching: "Let your troubled hearts be at rest and banish your fears" (Jn 14:27). This is not just an imperative; it is Christ offering his peace that will accomplish this liberation if we are grateful for his peace and remember that it is not just for ourselves but a gift to be shared with others. So we create an atmosphere, an environment in which peace and trust can allow us a still more creative expression of our liberty.

It is not just a matter of being set free from some concrete fears but, rather, liberation from a system of religion that is built too much on sanctions, laws, controls: a system that unavoidably creates fearfulneses, scrupulosity and lack of loving trust. It is against this kind of religion that Karl Marx fought. B.F. Skinner, too, accuses organized religion of using chiefly negative "reinforcers" and so having produced frightened people.

Creative fidelity to Christ means constant effort in faith education, in renewal of authority structures and in building up mutual relationships that form communities of believers at peace with themselves and with each other. Christian parents, teachers and office holders should be ashamed if those under their care find out, from the psychoanalysts to whom they go for help, that their troubles are caused by an oppressive use of authority. Confessors, pastors, and everyone in authority should learn to distinguish between sin and needless guilt complexes. Freedom cannot grow and become creative if such complexes are allowed to stifle the joy and the energy that we should find in the following of Christ.

In the Christian context, liberation from fearfulness and useless worry means freedom for grateful and generous love. We cannot enjoy the inner peace of this liberty as the gift of the one Lord if we are not concerned with helping others to enjoy the same peace. Only when the believer finds the synthesis between grateful love of God and zealous love of fellowmen will this love liberate him from anguish and fear. "There is no room for fear in love; perfect love banishes fear. For fear brings with it the pains of judgment, and anyone who is afraid has not yet attained to love in its perfection" (1 Jn 4:18).

Paul's appeal not to fall back into a spirit of slavery and fear is coupled with an appeal to be sensitive to the desire of all creation to be freed from corruption. "All who are moved by the Spirit of God are children of God. The Spirit you have received is not a spirit of slavery leading you back into a life of fear but a Spirit of adoption that makes you children of God, enabling you to cry, 'Abba, Father' " (Rom 8:15) As heirs of God, with Christ, we cannot forget that all creation groans in all its parts, "and even those to whom the Spirit is given, as first fruits of the harvest to come, are groaning inwardly while we wait for God to make us his children and to set our whole body free" (Rom 8:18-23).

Those who, like the Stoics, want to be passionless — and therefore without compassion — for the sake of their own self-fulfilment, can never experience this liberty. Christ, who set us free, took upon himself the deepest anguish of us sinners: "My God, my God, why have you forsaken me?" (Mk 15:34). In his compassionate love he shows us the way to the final trust, with his last words on the cross, "Father, into your hands I commit my spirit" (Lk 23:46).

Jesus' utter trust in the Father gives him the boldness to speak out the truth to the hypocrites and to those who misused their authority. He embodies *parrhesia,* and speaks the truth that can open the way to true life and freedom. He gives hope and trust to the sinner by loving him, so that he, too, may gain the freedom to love. When he speaks boldly to the priests and Pharisees, it is because he believes that they can be freed from their stubbornness and arrogance. In our own times, Mahatma Gandhi has given witness to the same charism, the same trust in God, by conveying the message that not only the downtrodden can be freed from oppression, but the oppressors themselves can be freed from their lust for power. When our hearts turn to God in trust we, too, gain the freedom to speak frankly to our fellowmen, but always with equal concern for them.

Many enmities and even wars are caused chiefly by unhealthy fear and anguish. My numerous encounters with the white people in South Africa and Rhodesia convinced me that the main obstacle to reconciliation is no longer racism, as such, but rather the mentality of the besieged. While racism is, in itself, a terrible enslavement, its power comes from this mentality which refuses to trust the "other". So if we want to work for peace, we must look for ways gradually to liberate people who are oppressive and defensive because they have not yet found peace in their hearts or trust in others. They still rely only on negative self-defence and oppressive power.

To participate creatively in liberation from anguish, we should understand the interdependence between trust in God and trustful relationships with fellowmen. It is from faith and trust in God, that new trustful human relations arise. But it is also from crediting each other, manifesting trust and exercising authority in a trust-inspiring way that we learn trust in God, and thus become free from slavish fears and scrupulosity.

7. Free from sloth, free for responsibility

Freedom, as the saving intervention of God, happens between God and man in the history of salvation. While it is totally God's gift, it is equally man's response. Therefore, the gift of freedom is also an urgent call to active participation. Sloth and flight from active involvement are great sins against the Lord of the history of salvation and his people.

The two evils that lead to oppression and discouragement are pride and arrogance on the side of the oppressors and, on the other, sloth or apathy that frequently arises from fear and from selfish concern for one's own tranquillity. Whoever refuses his share in co-responsibility becomes accountable for the persisting injustice and many other evils in the world.

The freedom for which Christ has set us free entails "the courage to risk the unforeseeable future. The freedom of responsible decision certainly demands knowledge, circumspection, reflection".[50] We should know to what we are committing ourselves. However, there must be the courage to cope with the difficulties that are not foreseen as well as those which arise again and again in the course of our involvement.

Sloth and apathy are frequently the product of perfectionism. But a Christian who knows about God's power and forgiveness and his own finiteness will not dare to stay idle in order to avoid the burden of risk.

8. *Free from the powers, free for service of salvation*

In the Old Testament, and even more in the New Testament, the dialectic between redemption and emancipation becomes visible. Full liberation from sin and deception implies also liberation from oppressive structures and from sinful alienations ꟸꟸꟸꟸ ꟸꟸꟸ ꟸꟸꟸꟸꟸ ꟸꟸ ꟸꟸꟸ ꟸꟸꟸꟸꟸ ꟸꟸꟸꟸꟸꟸ himself. Jesus, in his radical freedom, not only preached liberation from sin but also confronted the powers of legalism, ritualism and abuse of authority that contradicted the freedom of the kingdom of God. He might never have been put to death if his preaching had centred solely on peace of soul. He died his redemptive death because of his battle against the powers, and especially against the abuse of power in organized religion.

Believers who, in faith, open themselves to the energizing powers of Christ, the risen Lord, whom the powers of earth can no longer keep in bondage, will become agents of redemption and emancipation from unjust powers and potentates. Where the reign of God is accepted in faith, the poor and the weak will be no longer oppressed. Anyone who calls himself a Christian and continues to take part in any kind of exploitation or oppression should know that he is no longer or not yet truly a believer. And it is not enough simply to refrain from active participation in oppression. As disciples of Christ we must join with all other people of good will to bring about reforms of authority structures at all levels of secular and religious life which will foster freedom for all people.

When the Apostle of the Gentiles tells us that our fight is not only against human weakness but also against "cosmic powers, authorities and potentates of this dark world" (Eph 6:12), he is not thinking only or mainly about disembodied spirits or devils. The evil spirits exercise their darkening powers through the authorities and potentates of this world who misuse this precious gift of God called authority. If, then, we truly want to be free and to see our fellowmen free from manipulation and exploitation, we, as followers of Christ, will seize every opportunity to work for healthy authority relationships and structures necessary for that end.

In the political field, for instance, authorities "must dispose the energies of the whole citizenry toward the common good, not mechanically or despotically, but primarily as a moral force which depends on freedom and conscientious discharge of the burden of any office which has been undertaken".[31] Where office-holders or legislators overstep their competence and oppress or exploit people, citizens should obey only in what is for the common good and observe laws only insofar as they foster the common good. "It is lawful for them to defend their own rights and those of their fellow citizens against abuse of this authority, provided that in so doing they observe the limits imposed by natural law and the gospel".[52] Conscientious objection to unjust and harmful laws and precepts is not only a defence of one's own conscience but also a necessary service for the good of all people. Both in the secular world and in the Church, a ministry of dissent is sometimes necessary, if it arises from a felt co-responsibility and careful reflection in the sight of God.

The inimical power called "mammon" by Jesus is the unjustly acquired wealth and the unjust use of possessions, privileges or one's own capacities if used selfishly. Jesus is clearly on the side of the poor and oppressed, but he is equally concerned that the powerful and wealthy should not become or remains slaves to the lust for power and possessions. Those who truly believe in one God and Father and one Lord Jesus Christ know that all earthly goods and all our capacities are gifts of the one God for the benefit of all. If we do not make generous use of the little things — our material goods — how can we be trusted in great things? "The man who is dishonest in little things is dishonest also in great things. If, then, you have not proved trustworthy with wealth of this world, who will trust you with the wealth that is real?" (Lk 16:10-12).

The rich young man (Mk 10:17-22) is called simultaneously to discipleship and to liberty from the bondage of wealth. Since he is still under the reign of a defence morality that does not see that all things become unjust unless they are put to the service of the neighbour, he remains unfree. The house of the rich man was filled with earthly goods while his brothers and sisters, the children of Abraham were dying of starvation. While boasting that he observed the prohibitive commandments, he was breaking the one law that keeps them all together: the law to love one's fellowmen as one's self.

Christ warns his followers to make their choice between the two lords, God, who liberates, or power and wealth, that enslave. "Do not store up for yourselves treasure on earth where it grows rusty and moth-eaten, and thieves break in to steal it. No servant can be the slave of two masters; for either he will hate the first and love the second or he will be devoted to the first and think nothing of the second. You cannot serve God and Money" (Mt 6:19-24).

A most harmful power in the world is male power, *sexism*. As early as in the book of Genesis we are shown that the domineering attitude of man over woman is a result of sin and alienation and continues to embody sinfulness in this world (cf. Gen 3:16). As servant to all, Christ frees humankind from male predominance. If someone would argue that humankind could be saved only by the incarnation of the Word in maleness, although I could not accept the argument, I would still find some meaning in it, since throughout history men have far outstripped women in domineering attitudes. Hence, it might be appropriate, according to our own limited human thinking, that Christ became a man to break the fetters of sexism by his absolute humility and liberty for the others. Surely, anyone who wants to overemphasize Christ's maleness in order to establish prerogatives of males ("priests") over females has not understood Jesus as the liberator of all people, men and women, and has not understood the way he liberated us.

In his own life, Jesus scandalized the representatives of organized religion by his availability to women and his reverence for them. As Hodgson notes, "Given the social realities of that religious and cultural milieu, perhaps only a male could have attained even the relative freedom and following that Jesus did in carrying forward a ministry of liberation".[53]

Jesus welcomed women in his company and treated each one not in terms of the cultural stereotype but as a unique person. In his sight, the difference between man and woman faded to insignificance. What remains is their complementarity, their being for each other (cf. Mk 3:35; 7:24-30; 12:41-44; 14:3-9; Lk 7:36-50; 8:1-3; 10:38-42; 13:10-17; 23:55;

Jn 4:7-30; 11:1-44; 12:1-3; 19:25-27; 21:18). Therefore, every man should realize that he cannot represent Christ, the prophetic priest, unless he has a natural and supernatural resemblance to Christ, the Servant, and therefore renounces all kinds of sexism. Women as well as men should be able to affirm Christ's sonship while "keeping from their minds the idolatrous idea as if Jesus would have been a kind of male offspring of a male deity. He, the Son of God and Son of Man, was radically free because he lived in liberated openness to God, to the God of freedom and to all people".[54]

The Church cannot look to the future in creative freedom without confessing, humbly and frankly, the contamination of her theology and authority structures by a prevailing sexism, and hence favouring the male power in the societies in which she exercised her ministry and in which she should have exercised a more prophetic role.

Another dangerous power that keeps people in bondage is that of *ideologies*, those collective and individual ideas and half-truths used for group or collective advantage. All the misuse of half-truth for one's own self-enhancement, for the sake of possession and power, coalesces and becomes a collective bondage in ideologies.[55] It is not enough to oppose arrogance, abuse of power, unwholesome authority structures and oppressive socio-economic relationships unless we also unmask the ideologies that are on the side of the powers. We can do this only in a genuine conversion and a courageous commitment to renewal of Church and society.

Vatican II shows such an approach. "The Church does not lodge her hope in privileges conferred by civil authority. Indeed, she stands ready to renounce the exercise of certain legitimately acquired rights if it becomes clear that their use raises doubt about the sincerity of her witness or that new conditions of life demand some other arrangement".[56]

A particularly dangerous ideology that strengthens the powers hostile to man's freedom is that of violence. It is an ideology of those who have power over others whom they keep submitted by a system of oppression, punitive sanctions and violent reactions against any effort towards liberation. Often revolutionaries are contaminated by the ideology itself and remain in the same vicious circle, hoping for qualitative changes in society through the very use of violence against violence. While I do not favour any legalism that forbids all use of force against evildoers, I am convinced that one of the most important questions for the future of humanity is a theology and psychology of non-violence, in the vein of the concept of patience which, for St. Thomas Aquinas and the best of our tradition, is the most noble part of fortitude and endurance. It is that power of inner and outer freedom that does not allow violent explosions and loss of energy but uses, rather, one's collected energies for justice, peace and love.

Non-violence must never be confused with passivity, sloth or inactivity. It is a liberating event only when it is, at the same time, most active and creative. Only non-violent attitudes and actions can bring a truly qualitative change in the hearts of men and in society.

9. *Free from the bondage of death, free for true life*

In one exultant hymn, Paul speaks of a liberation from sin and from death. "The life-giving law of the Spirit in Christ Jesus has set you free from the law of sin and death" (Rom 8:2). He develops this theme more explicitly in the First Letter to the Corinthians. "At the end, when he delivers up the kingdom to God the Father, after abolishing every kind of domination, authority and power, the last enemy, death, will be abolished, for he (Christ) is destined to reign until God has put all enemies under his feet" (1 Cor 15:24-26).

At the very heart of salvation history is our faith in Christ's victory over death, which can become our victory if we put all our trust in him and follow him. Jesus, living totally for his brethren to the honour of the Father and dying on the cross, brings all this to the summit and reveals it. Thus, death cannot imprison him. He is the Gift accepted by the Father and raised to life. He is Lord over all, in view of the victory over death on the cross. "In him was life, and life was the light of man" (Jn 1:4).

The life Jesus embodies in his death and resurrection is freedom from death in many ways. Although he dies for us, death has no power over him. He gives it a totally new meaning.

What was, because of sin, the most miserable event on earth becomes the greatest event of inner freedom through Christ's life-giving love and the power of the Holy Spirit who raised Jesus from death. His death and resurrection are one and the same event of freedom, an event which, for the followers of Christ, gives meaning and freedom to every person's life.[57]

If we believe and gratefully celebrate the mystery of Christ's death and resurrection, then the meaning of our death is totally transformed for us. As it happens among men, death is the most ambiguous phenomenon, but accepted with Christ and for the sake of Christ's death and resurrection it gives new significance to all our life. When one discovers the meaning of Christ's death and of one's own death, the deepest meaning of life is revealed to him.

No one, of course, chooses death in itself except the one who totally fails to find the sense of life and death and commits suicide. But whoever, in the spirit of Christ, accepts death in all its reality, although it is not planned, reaches a summit of liberty.[58]

In Christ's death, God suffers, as it were, with the death of his crucified Son and with our death. In all its freedom, his compassionate love flows into our death if we believe. "Only that which is suffered and undergone can also be overcome. God suffers death — not to let death prevail, but to prevail over it, to liberate from it".[59] This is a part of the message of faith in resurrection. God is the giver of life "who gives life to the dead and calls into existence the things that do not exist" (Rom 4:17).

One who believes in Christ who is the Resurrection, who died for us and lives for us, is not only free from fear of death; he is, above all, free for that life which we share with the Father, Son and Holy Spirit, free also for the life of those around him and of all people. Through faith in Christ, and in that fraternal unity that arises from faith and frees from disunity and rivalry, we know that Jesus comes from the Father and returns to the Father; and thus we are taken up into the same life. "So if the Son liberates you, you will be free indeed" (Jn 8:36). A Protestant theologian tells us, "this is the core thought for our age".[60]

If we believe in the death and resurrection of Christ who is Lord of the world, we then see that sin is, above all, privatism that denies corporate life. The result is that man leads a meaningless life and suffers a senseless death. He leaves behind a world which he has not enriched but rather impoverished, since he has acted as if death were the end of everything.

"Eternal life", given by the risen Lord, is life not free from the bondage of meaningless death. Our belief in Christ, the risen Lord, gives us a share in his eternal life (cf. Jn 3:16). This means not only life in fullness after death; it means also authentic life as a human person on earth, liberated for service of the brethren and the courage to give this earthly life for the sake of faith, justice and peace.[61]

The bondage of death manifests itself in flight from responsibility, in flight from life and corporate freedom, while liberation by Christ means commitment for the life of all people now, in view of life everlasting. The ethics of the Stoics glorified suicide as a liberation from the prison of body and of the world. It was indeed a kind of murder of the world, a sign of radical flight from responsibility for the life of the particular time and age. Faith in the death and resurrection of Christ makes this kind of worldview impossible.[62] Freedom is an irreducible dimension of the Christian experience, even in death or, indeed, especially in death. For the last word is Jesus, the name above every name. He died in the fullness of freedom and lives everlasting life.[63]

IV. WE BELIEVE IN THE HOLY SPIRIT

A theology that focuses mainly on creative freedom and fidelity must be both Christological and pneumatological. What is vital is to know Christ as the One anointed and filled by the Holy Spirit and the One in whom we are children of God by his Spirit. "The Spirit is the empowering source and eschatological norm of the new birth of freedom".[64]

Only by the Spirit can we be born anew (Jn 3:3-7) to a Christlike life, a life as sons or daughters of God. To be sanctified by the Spirit is also to be called to that freedom and fidelity that befits the children of God. Christ's freedom, in which he lived and for which he suffered, is for him and for us the prompting of the Holy Spirit. He is the embodiment of freedom and the Liberator because he is filled by the Spirit. "Now the Lord is the Spirit, and where the Spirit of the Lord is, there is freedom" (2 Cor 3:17).

1. The freedom of the children of God

The true and perfect freedom is that of the Son of God. The Son does not speak from his own freedom, he does not consider anything his own; everything is given him by the Father. Therefore, when he makes himself the servant of all, he manifests that the greatest and purest freedom arises from gratitude and the power of love.

The freedom of the Son is expression of his being one with the Father (Jn 10:30) who is infinite freedom for love; and his sharing everything with the Father breathes the power of the Holy Spirit who is the sharing, in person. He shares the Father's freedom while giving himself up for us, and thus returns to the Father. In his human nature Jesus is remedy for the fall of the first Adam. He dies for us in freedom and arises for eternal freedom for himself and for his brothers and sisters. For him and for us it is freedom in the Holy Spirit. The new birth that frees us to love our brothers and sisters is the newness of life that comes from the Spirit (cf. Rom 7:6), the same Spirit through whose power Jesus fulfilled his task of manifesting his creative liberty and fidelity and our liberation.

Our adoption as sons and daughters of God is thoroughly marked by the Spirit. "He destined us — such was his will and pleasure — to be accepted as his children through Jesus Christ, in order that the glory of his gift, so graciously bestowed on us in his Beloved, might redound to his praise" (Eph 1:5-6). This text is one of the most classical expressions of what it means to live on the level of the Spirit. Everything is perceived as gift and accepted in the profound gratitude that marks all attitudes, desires and decisions of true disciples of Christ; and all this is a response directed to the glorification of God who has loved us so graciously in Christ.

The fundamental expression of the liberty enjoyed by the

children of God in the Holy Spirit is dedication to the glory of God's graciousness, so that, united with the Beloved Son, all our life can become thanksgiving that "redounds to the praise of God". Thus our life enters into the perspective of the Eucharist, where Jesus is present in the same power of the Holy Spirit by which he gave himself up for us and gives himself to us. And when, by the same power of the Holy Spirit, we are united with him, our life does indeed redound to the praise of the Father. In this gratitude we are united with Jesus; we are becoming "one body and one spirit", manifesting the glory of the graciousness of God, praising his name (cf. Eph 1:10).

Gratitude, the first and basic sign of a life in the Spirit, produces also the other eschatological virtues such as hope, vigilance, joy and discernment. Whoever lives on the level of the Spirit sees all the gifts of God, the one Father, as given to us in view of the needs of all people and in view of building up the one body of Christ. "Thus in their diversity all bear witness to the admirable unity of the body of Christ. This very diversity of graces, ministries and works gathers the children of God into one, because 'all these things are the work of the one and the same Spirit' " (1 Cor 12:11).[65]

In the lives of those who are moved by the Spirit, there is no separation between natural and supernatural: everything is sacred, a sacred gift, a message and appeal coming from the one God and Father. Thus all that we call "natural" enters into the realm of redemption. And the first reality that has to enter into this realm is our very freedom. "God's grace, which ultimately means himself, must set freedom free for God. It can, therefore, perform its very own deed to which it is called, namely, to receive God from God through God only in this way".[66] Thus all of mankind's truth and freedom proclaims that God is gracious, and becomes praise to the glory of God in the Holy Spirit.

For freedom to be creative and faithful in the new creation, it is essential that we see it always as a gracious gift and recognize also that only through the blood of the Redeemer and the power of the Holy Spirit are we freed for this vision and its liberating power. This dimension of our freedom can truly mark our life only when we view all that we are, all that we have and what others mean for us in the same perspective of praise and thanksgiving.

All genuine God experience is marked by this vision. The reality of God, on which one's subjectivity and trans-subjectivity depend, is encountered only when the person "receives himself as a gift in the experience of freedom".[67] One who accepts the new freedom chooses Christ because he knows himself chosen by him; he prays to God with confidence and thanksgiving because, before he prays, he knows himself called and elected by God.

The new justice that comes through justification by mere grace can be lived only in the eucharistic spirit of wholehearted thanksgiving and praise. This, however, cannot be severed from life. It must manifest itself in every facet of our life, in grateful acknowledgement of the other, in helping one another to discover our inner resources, the gifts of the Spirit, and in mutual relationships marked by generosity, all to the praise and glory of the gracious goodness of God.

Although we are most active and creative when guided by the Spirit, we no longer consider our decision, works and achievements first of all as our own merit, but see them rather in the new dimension of God's undeserved love that calls us and empowers us to give a creative and generous response.[68] Where praise and thanksgiving take hold of all our life, we can, in a certain sense, say that in the Holy Spirit the freedom of Christ becomes our freedom. Then God's commandments and our special calling — whether to the work of evangelization, service to the poor or family and civic responsibilities — are no longer merely a "must"; they become gifts for us to share with all. A life under the law of grace, under the law of the Spirit, becomes a life in truth. We no longer, then, appropriate to ourselves what is God's free gift; we are free for sharing everything.

This same truth is quite clearly expressed by Gutierrez, the most balanced of Latin America's liberation theologians. "Without liberating historical events there would be no growth of the Kingdom. But the process of liberation will not have conquered the very roots of oppression and the exploitation of man by man without the coming of the Kingdom, which is, above all, a gift".[69]

The human plan and the gifts of God imply each other, so that all our planning is conceived and carried out in view of God's gifts and people's needs. This vision of history, and above all the history of freedom and liberation, comes to its full truth when we realize that Christ has prepared this gift for us by suffering on the cross, by giving himself. Hence, our gratitude will include the suffering entailed in a life of service for others, for we know that God is present in all events and especially in "the event of suffering, as liberating love".[70]

While I contradict any theology that presents predestination in a way that seems to make God exclude a part of humanity from his salvific, long-suffering love, I would insist that we must not discard the truth of predestination. In Jesus Christ, God has predestined all people to become his children. However, this plan addresses man's own freedom. It is carried out by those who live gratefully on the level of gratuitous predestination and election, in the firm faith and hope that God reaches out to all. Our abiding fidelity unto the hour of our death is undeserved grace, but it will be given to all who pray unceasingly. By prayer, I mean that total, joyous acknowledgement that everything is gift of the one God and given for all. Christian prayer can never be severed from zeal for the salvation of all people.

2. Freedom in the Spirit and openness to mission

Christ is sent by the Spirit to proclaim Good News to the poor and to act as liberator of the oppressed. His dedication to his brothers and sisters arises from the overflowing gratitude in which he lives by and in the Word coming from the Father. He is totally driven by the Spirit, who is the sharing between the Father and the Son.

Those who live by the Spirit, and are guided by the Spirit, have a new existence. They no longer belong selfishly to themselves; they are free for the others, sent to make known the abundant gifts of the one Spirit, which are destined for all. Whoever is filled by the indwelling Holy Spirit knows that he does not belong to himself. Nor will he throw himself away as worthless: he learns to glorify God in his body by a genuine expression of love (cf. 1 Cor 6:20).

It is only by the gift of the Spirit that we realize what death and resurrection mean for our life with Christ and with our fellowmen. "The love of Christ leaves us no choice, when once we have reached the conclusion that one man died for all and therefore all of mankind has died. His purpose in dying for all was that men, while still in life, should cease to live for themselves and should live for him who for their sake died and was raised to life" (2 Cor 5:14-15). In this experience the Apostle of the Gentiles offers himself for the ministry of reconciliation (cf. 2 Cor 5:18-21). And since he acts in gratitude, considering all his service a gracious gift, he appeals to all, "You have received that grace of God; do not let it go for nothing" (2 Cor 6:1).

The law of the Spirit, who gives us life in Christ Jesus while freeing us from the slavery of sin and law, sets us free for mutual service, for a new order in the "law of faith", the "law of grace". Paul is set free, and indeed sent for his ministry by a "spiritual bond". Through the Spirit who gives life, he is a free servant of the new covenant (2 Cor 3:6). Filled with hope, it is in this Spirit that he can speak out boldly (2 Cor 3:12). The fruitfulness of evangelization and of Christian witness comes from the Spirit. Under his influence we can be transfigured, able to give valid witness. He sets us truly free, for "where the Spirit of the Lord is, there is liberty" (2 Cor 3:18).

Openness to the Spirit gives us an ever deeper experience of the gift character of all our life and especially of the Gospel, and makes us ready to accept our responsibility for the world around us. These are co-constitutive structures of the freedom that comes from Christ through the Spirit.[71]

The locus of the Spirit's activity is a community of believers who are free for each other and altogether free for their mission to be light to the world and salt for the earth. Guided by the Spirit, they do only what is good and helpful to the others, so that whatever they do brings blessing to those who hear and see them.

The eschatological hope of final liberation does not allow us to grieve the Spirit by failing to do the good we can do, "for that Spirit is the seal with which you were marked for the day of our final liberation" (Eph 4:30). The more a believer is seized by the Spirit and transfigured by the experience of God's graciousness, the more he will be a free and responsible instrument of the Spirit in the world around him. To live in the Spirit means that we are truly ourselves by fulfilling our mission for the others.[72]

At this point we see the striking opposition between the Christian view and Marxism. For the Christian, freedom is not a movement emerging from within a given system or ideology. "It is, rather, the insertion of a new reality into history, in such a way that the closed present is broken open for the new".[73] It is through the very experience of God's undeserved grace that the spiritual person is sensitive to the groaning of the world that is in travail and expects deliverance. The experience of the freedom of the children of God cannot be separated from its dynamics towards responsible activity in and for the world.[74]

3. *The conflict between the Spirit and embodied selfishness*

Paul's letter to the Galatians speaks forcefully of the freedom in and by the Holy Spirit, in view of the conflict that arises from ingrown selfishness and legalism. The good news of the freedom of the children of God as gift of the Spirit is a powerful warning not to "turn your freedom into licence for your selfish self, but be servants to one another in love" (Gal 5:13).

The appeal to live on the level of the Spirit, totally free for God and for witness to justice and love, would be absurd without the faith that God truly gives us the freedom to which he calls us.[75] Throughout the whole New Testament, and already in the prophetic intervention of the Old Testament, there resounds the indicative that God grants us everything necessary to live a new life, to live on the level of the Spirit. "If you are guided by the Spirit you will not fulfil the desires of incarnate selfishness. That selfishness sets its desires against the Spirit while the Spirit fights against it" (Gal 5:16-17). The indicative becomes imperative because, although nothing is lacking to those who trust in God, there remains in us and in the world around us a terrifying embodiment of selfishness.

The Spirit is more powerful than all the powers of the world. Paul tells of its harvest: "Love, joy, peace, patience, kindness, goodness, fidelity, gentleness and self control" (Gal 5:22). If, under the influence of the Holy Spirit, we truly believe in the death and resurrection of Christ, we are assured of the final victory. "Those who belong to Christ Jesus have crucified the selfish self with its passions and desires. If the Spirit is the source of our life, let the Spirit also direct our course" (Gal 5:24-25).

The harvest of the Spirit is not produced automatically, however. Whether we, or rather the Spirit, will produce in us the fruits of the new life depends on the gratitude and strength of our faith. As Christians we must learn to discern between what comes from the Spirit and what arises from the selfishness in us and around us. Paul warned the legalists of this danger when they tried to seduce the Galatians, and warned also those Corinthians who were boasting of their own freedom because they had not yet learned what true freedom in the Spirit is (cf. 1 Cor 9-10). The Spirit moves us in a way congenial to our human dignity and our responsibility for others. He helps our weakness (cf. Rom 8:26) moving us from within.

While the warning against misunderstanding, and especially against empty boasting, is necessary, there is even more need to joyously proclaim the good news that those who believe and trust in the Lord, and render thanks to him, are moved and helped by the Spirit from within. The emphasis on warnings can be so great that gratitude for the gift of the Holy Spirit is concealed. To fall back into timidity and legalistic search for self-assurance is, in Paul's eyes, an injustice to the Spirit and to the lofty vocation bestowed on us (cf. Gal 5:4; 1 Cor 6:2). It is an enormous injustice to the Holy Spirit to limit the Christian outlook to the bare minimum of negative laws or to look only at the many laws instead of at the one law of life in the Spirit in grateful, joyous faith that brings forth the harvest of love, peace and joy.[78]

As Christ reaches out to all people, so too is his Spirit

active beyond the realm of the visible Church. "In every free act God is present, though not explicitly grasped as its fundamental impulse and final goal".[79] But from those who believe in Christ and profess their faith in the Holy Spirit, there should be expected a superabundant witness to the presence of the Holy Spirit. "Whoever believes in me, let him drink. As Scripture says, 'streams of living water shall flow out from within him'. He was speaking of the Spirit which believers in him would receive later; for the Spirit had not yet been given because Jesus had not yet been glorified" (Jn 7:37-39).

Christian life should manifest a profound knowledge of that truth that breathes love. "When he comes who is the Spirit of truth, he will guide you into all the truth" (Jn 16:13; cf. Jn 15:26). Those who believe in the Spirit and live on the level of the Spirit in constant thanksgiving will be witnesses to Christ (cf. Jn 15:27).

V. EMBODIED LIBERTY

1. *In the light of the Mystery of the Incarnation*

Whoever wants liberty and peace only of soul, or liberty for the inward journey alone, will have no liberty. The Word of God has created man as an embodied spirit in a visible world, and it took the flesh of this world to free us from sin. We can be free only if, together, we embody freedom in all of our personal life and in the structures of life in the world around us.

All our good thoughts and decisions inscribe themselves in our cerebral cortex, in our memory. Thus, they are embodiments of goodness and freedom. But it is also true that every time we fail to think, to desire, to decide the right things, we have missed an embodiment of freedom for the good. And every evil thought or decision increases the already existing negative informations in our cerebral cortex and diminishes our radiance for the world around us. Abuse of liberty is alienation, and this alienation becomes rooted and demonically intensified in the social involuntary which "surrounds the individual, rendering unfaulted human existence impossible".[80]

The world we live in has been infected by sloth, flight,

idolatry and guilt. The originally individual acts have, as it were, become institutionalized and constantly reinforced through our mutual relationships. The conclusion is evident: freedom itself, rightly understood, must be embodied in all our life and objectified, "institutionalized" in the structures that influence people's decisions, thoughts and desires.

As we have already seen, each sin is a self-imposed bondage, incarnated not only in the psychic but also in the social world. The good and the bad that we think and do is objectified in the physical and social involuntary, "taking on the aspect of inevitability or fate, but still distinguishable from the involuntary as such".[81] It is essential to see, then, that the evil cannot be undone simply by a new "purpose"; it can only be countered by a purposeful embodiment of the good we can do, and by giving all our burdens and difficulties a new meaning in this perspective.

Freedom, too, needs its own sphere, its own realm. As we purposefully embody freedom for God, for adoration and for all people, we must never overlook the interplay between genuine freedom that comes from God and the fraudulent "freedom" that embodies all the pride, sloth, collective selfishness, deception and manipulation which constantly reinforce the bondage of people in unfreedom.

In the Christian understanding, freedom is the gift of the Word Incarnate and becomes reality through the Spirit that renews the hearts of people and the face of the earth. Hence, we cannot realistically expect the final kingdom of freedom without proving our commitment on earth to that freedom that will be perfected in heaven.[82] Believers are meant to unite, to build up a "kingdom of freedom" as their true abode. "The system of right is the kingdom of freedom actualized, the word of the Spirit brought forth out of itself like a second nature".[83]

Just as our freedom in the image of God belongs to our very nature and vocation, so does our bond with the earth in the realm of family, culture, politics, economic relations and processes. Freedom must be creative in its purpose as well as in its use. But the creations of freedom never stand for themselves: they can solicit the right response from us or their alienations can tempt us. The responsible person, however, is the one who again and again tries to overcome the alienations by focusing on inner freedom and the various forms in which genuine freedom can be embodied or invested.

The social involuntary resulting from previous uses of freedom does not coerce interpersonal relations, but it does provide a framework, incentives, appeals or bondages that both permit and limit the dimensions of our freedom.[84] The realization of human freedom is a problem of one's inner strength but also a problem of one's relations to oneself, to God and to fellowship within the concrete context. There is no absolute freedom except God's because there is always a limited consciousness, limited strength and a limited sphere of freedom.

If we truly want to be free, we respect the freedom of others. Only a solipsistic denial of other free subjects would think in terms of oneself alone. Genuine freedom is realized in a social sphere and therefore demands that everyone's rights and freedom should be respected. Besides cooperating in establishing a genuine atmosphere of freedom, we all should be aware that, in its objective embodiment, every free act produces a change in the sphere of freedom that belongs to all.[85]

The behavioural sciences have taught us that it is not possible to provide a genuine atmosphere of freedom without embodying other fundamental values like truthfulness, justice, peace. These values cannot, all and at once, be embodied in laws; but everyone can enrich the world by his own life, his own witness to these values and by his effort to promote public concern for them.

2. *Personal freedom and societal structures*

Freedom is endangered whenever laws and the various societal structures are preserved for themselves without attention to how they influence human relationships. In this perspective we can think also of Paul's gospel of liberation from ritualistic and juridical conditions, remembering how frequently, in the Church's history, rituals and laws were kept when they could no longer serve the growth of personal freedom or benefit interpersonal relations.[86]

Each interpretation and consequent action changes the sphere of freedom by making a positive or negative investment.

Great openness is, therefore, necessary in interpretation and planning if we are to embody freedom, justice, peace and truth in the world around us. We should always be "open further, beyond every experience and beyond every given situation."[87] It is a matter of creative fidelity to embody freedom in our life and our world, and to do so we need to be vigilant, attentive and flexible in our responses.

There is important interplay between the identity of the individual and the upbuilding of a healthy community and society. All the patterns of cooperation that foster love, and everything that provides grounds for fidelity and creative freedom, enrich our total milieu and strengthen our good dispositions. In a similar context, Erik Erikson reminds us that motherhood is one of the basic realities that strengthens the milieu and the disposition for fidelity and love.[88] Our age needs such a reminder. If only for its own sake, our society should come to a better understanding and appreciation of genuine motherhood and, indeed, of responsible fatherhood too. It is a matter of witness, a total structure of life in fidelity and love, through which those qualities become embodied in the world around us.

We are repeatedly faced with the basic question: which comes first, the embodiment of creative liberty and fidelity in people or liberation through liberating structures? "Which is more basic, psychic or social reality?"[89]

It seems to me that both the teaching of Christ and daily experience indicate that the priority is in conversion of the human heart — but not understood in a spiritualistic way. The "heart" is where bridges are built and integration is found, where the person reaches wholeness. But one should never forget that the two goals — conversion of the heart and embodiment of the new spirit in the total environment — constitute an inseparable unity. There can be no abiding conversion of the heart where there is not at least a cooperative effort to renew the face of the earth.

The kingdom of God includes a transfigured earth. I believe, however, that authors like Cullman are right when they say that "the social question would actually be already solved in our time if every individual would become as radically converted as Jesus demands".[90] This makes perfect sense to anyone who understands that conversion of the heart "as Jesus demands" includes commitment to the whole "kingdom of God", and that infers a response to the longing of all creation to share in the liberty of the children of God.

Genuine repentance and conversion of the individual lead to that investment of justice, peace and truthfulness in all life's conditions that can overcome the demonic objectivations of bondage. I agree with Moltmann that, "personal inner change without change in circumstances and structures is an idealist illusion, as though man were only a soul and not a body as well. But a change in external circumstances without inner renewal is materialist illusion, as though man were only a product of his social circumstances and nothing else".[92]

Our strong emphasis on the embodiment of liberty does not mean that we approve all kinds of liberation movements. Only those who know and manifest true freedom contribute to the cause of freedom. Wherever there is fanaticism, intolerance, inclination to use violence, or where people are used as tools, there will be no valid objectivation of freedom, no matter what changes of structures may be made. Therefore, our partnership in liberation movements cannot be other than discerning or critical.[93] Nevertheless, a clear awareness of the ambiguity of history does not allow us to stay on the sidelines. There are historical moments where non-involvement can mean a tragic failure. When history offers the possibility for truly noble projects, sloth and flight can be great sins against the embodiment of freedom.[94]

Liberation is an ever unfinished task. Our best efforts are frequently marked by unsuccess. Yet, as Christians, we will never give up our efforts to live according to the gift of freedom and to embody it in the economic, cultural and political structures as well as in our Church. We know by faith that, in the end, God's love will bring a total victory of freedom in the new heaven and the new earth. However, this hope allows us no passivity, flight or docetism. It is truthful and convincing only through our contribution for the growth of this freedom in societal structures as well as in our personal life. Our hope asks not for looking lazily to heaven but for watchfulness for the present opportunities. Gratitude for redemption that took the flesh of this world and our hope for the final liberation and salvation give us courage, patience and endurance.

3. Liberty and education

Whoever is future-oriented in the Christian sense of history will be concerned with the whole area of education and the effort to embody in it our faith in freedom and liberation. The new generation should learn how greatly our freedom is conditioned by the past; but they should also learn that, while we are somehow "created" by each other, we have also the capacity to experience and to create ourselves while making the best possible contribution to shaping the future.

Education is an ongoing process of becoming aware of one's own potentialities and vocation. It is also a process of discovering one's own freedom and its purpose and of helping others in the same direction. Education is the best medium for embodying freedom in psychic and social life.

B.F. Skinner has been keenly aware that the educational processs is decisive; yet the very purpose of his educational endeavour is to deprive people of freedom or, as he would say, "to free people from the illusion of freedom". To do so he focuses, in education, on what man has in common with animals. The whole educational process is manipulative, guided by the twin masters "pain and pleasure". This process, as well as the environment that plays the main role, is embodied materialism.

Without mentioning Skinner's name, Rollo May gives an acute analysis of the foreseeable results of such an education in "Skinner's box". Where persons, groups and nations are deprived of freedom, they go through various stages of protest, hatred, resentment. Some arrive at the point of self-pity, a "reserved" form of hatred and resentment that deprives the person of any form of initiative or creative liberty. Once the person is no longer able to protest and to hate the slavery, there is little hope for healing or for restoring liberty. Dictators who have deprived a nation of its freedom and have tried to do so mainly through manipulation, a system of threats and material promises, have also tried to channel resentment and hatred against others, the scapegoats. This system is most evident in the Kremlin's communist imperialism.[95]

Educators and psychologists have shown us how important is the sense of self-esteem, a healthy faith in one's own inner goodness, a growing experience of one's freedom for the good. But alien over-control creates a lasting propensity for doubt and shame that can easily be absorbed by guilt complexes and resentment.[96]

While Skinner's system of manipulation is based on radical pessimism about any freedom beyond what is motivated by pain and pleasure, other educators and therapists can convey a sense of trust and faith in the human capacity for creative liberty and fidelity. Erikson writes confidently, "There is little that cannot be remedied later, there is much than can be prevented from happening at all".[97]

This faith in man's fundamental goodness and the capacity for renewed freedom should permeate all of education, in the family and in the school, in adult education and in the whole area of public opinion. Recognizing, however, that everyone senses the limitations of his freedom, we should also learn together that "acceptance of limitations need not at all be giving up, but can and should be a constructive act of freedom; and it may well be that such a choice will have more creative results for the person than if he did not have to struggle against any limitation whatever".[98]

The child, the adolescent and, indeed, all people and all institutions need limitations of the exercise of freedom. These limitations can be to a certain extent stifling, but if they are motivated by concern for yet more genuine and widespread freedom, then the very limitation can contribute towards a growing fidelity to the cause of freedom. There one can see "that the sphere of freedom is limited for the sake of freedom itself and not by an alien element".[99]

Freedom is like the mustard seed. If the ground in which it is sown is favourable, it can grow. But it does so only if there is a sustained effort by all to contribute to its growth, and an increasing public consciousness that true freedom cannot exist without mutuality, without human relationships in which everyone is respected and honoured.

VI. THE CHURCH AS EMBODIMENT OF CREATIVE FREEDOM AND FIDELITY

I rejoice that the Church is called to be and to become an ever better embodiment of the freedom and fidelity for which Christ has set us free. The Lord has called her out of nothingness by his very freedom to love and to create new things.

The Church must never appear as a slavewoman whose children are under bondage. She is the freeborn woman, the spouse of Christ who is the Liberator, Freedom Incarnate. "It is written there that Abraham had two sons, one by his slave and the other by his freeborn wife. The slavewoman's son was born in the course of nature; the free woman's through God's promise. This is an allegory. The women stand for two covenants ... The one bearing children into slavery ... But the heavenly Jerusalem is the free woman; she is our mother" (Gal 4:21-24).

. It is both easier and more difficult to love the Church when we see her in this fundamental vocation. We appreciate everything in the Church that is faithful to this calling, and we suffer whenever we see her falling short. However, if we say "Church", we must look first at ourselves and judge whether we are making an embodied contribution to the Church's progress in her vocation to be the free and embodied response to Christ, the Liberator.

The Church ought to be a community of liberated people committed to the liberation of all, in response to the longing of all creation to share in the liberty of the children of God. She ought to be a sacrament of the history of liberation, celebrating in liturgy and life God's liberating love, remembering all the events in which she truly responded to her vocation, and remembering also, in repentance and humility, the many instances when she has fallen short. It is her vocation to be a community that develops a prophetic vision for all the present opportunities to serve the cause of freedom, in fidelity to the Lord of history: a community that celebrates, in the memorial of the Lord, the hope of final liberation, and thus commits herself ever more to her task.[100]

The basic attitude that should shine through in all the life of the Church, and especially in her celebration, should be a grateful memory that praises and gives thanks to God who has sent us Jesus Christ, the Liberator, and the Holy Spirit through whom we are enabled to live creatively in freedom and fidelity. However, although the Church is created out of nothingness, she is called out of a world with many conditionings and bondages. She is called in freedom but is composed of people whose freedom is frequently concealed and blocked by the bondage of power and falsehood.

All these realities, and especially the effects of distorted authority structures, and unfaithfulness of officeholders and members, have created within the Church many embodiments of unfreedom and false understandings of both freedom and law. All too often, in her liturgy, her canon law, her inflated administration and defensive, intolerant attitude towards others, she has evidenced that "Christians have not always been tolerant and freedom-minded, often committing dreadful atrocities, and have often canonized forms of society that were anything but free". Among other things, Karl Rahner recalls the principle that princes could determine the religion of their subjects, and the *Bulla* of Leo X, *Exsurge Domine*, directed against Martin Luther, condemning his view that torturing and burning heretics was a sin against the Holy Spirit. There was also, of course, the deeply rooted ideology of the completely ecclesiastical state.[101]

Recalling to mind these historical truths is not useless breast-beating. There is no way to freedom in the future without repentance. The past has ingrained itself in the total reality, and it is an act of freedom to bring all this to consciousness and to test our present ideas, teaching, canon law and authority structures to find if there still resides in them a partial investment of the sins and unfavourable conditionings of the past.

Respect for everyone's upright conscience, religious freedom, tolerance, must not be a matter of tactics in the life of the Church; they ought to be understood as an essential demand of the Church, so that she may stand among all people and nations as a luminous sign of embodied freedom and a call to fidelity and creativity in working towards ever increasing freedom in the world.

The Church's educational effort ought to be especially directed to the right understanding and embodiment of freedom, fidelity and creative action. In this difficult time of transition from the Constantinian era to a Christianity by free choice of faith, Christians should learn, in their disputes and diversities, that a common profound devotion to responsible freedom and unconditional respect for the dignity and conscience of all people help more than anything else to lead us to Christ the Liberator.[102]

To this end, the Church should give much more attention to the prophetic ministry, along with the priestly ministry. And we should realize that God can call prophets not only from the ranks of office holders but equally from among the faithful and even from among the saints outside the boundaries of the Church. The Church's own embodiment of freedom and fidelity and the prophetic role of believers in the secular world, for growth in freedom and in discernment between true freedom and fidelity and their counterfeits, are "a testing ground of the kingdom of God".[103]

The Church's attitude towards freedom within her own life and structures, and her commitment to it in the secular world, are a test of her faith in Christ, who came to free us, and of her trust in the promptings of the Holy Spirit. The temptation to build up too many fences and controls, to give too much emphasis to a system of sanctions and rewards, comes from a lack of faith and of trust in the Holy Spirit. Whenever the Church imposes limits to creative liberty and fidelity, she should be able to prove that this is done solely for the sake of freedom itself: to create favourable conditions for its growth everywhere and for all people.

To the extent that the Church is able to celebrate gratefully a past history of fidelity and liberation, to bring into the open her past faults and accomplishments in a spirit of thanksgiving for God's renewing power, and to discover the present opportunities in responsive fidelity and creativity, she is "an eschatological community pioneering the future of all mankind".[104]

Being open to the Spirit, she will be open to the voice of the prophets, giving equal attention to both the challenging prophetic voices and her own prophetic vocation. She will, then, be able to provide criteria for distinguishing between true and false liberation.[105] Words alone will never suffice. Freedom must be embodied; creative liberty and fidelity must take flesh in all the structures of the Church, in all her vision and her teaching, including her liturgy.

Here I see a serious responsibility for theology: to mobilize all the resources in the Church so that the people of God can contribute to the actualization of this vision and be witnesses to it.

NOTES

1 P.C. Hodgson, *New Birth of Freedom. A Theology of Bondage and Liberation*, Philadelphia, 1976, 216.
2 Cf. F. Herzog, *Liberation Theology: Liberation in the Fourth Gospel*, New York, 1972, 25-44; H. Kessler, *Erlösung und Befreiung*, Düsseldorf, 1972.
3 Cf. K. Niederwimmer, *Der Begriff der Freiheit im Neuen Testament*, Berlin, 1966, 93; Q. Quesnell, *The Gospel of Christian Freedom*, New York, 1969.
4 Cf. J.W. Mödlhammer, *Anbetung und Freiheit. Theologisch-anthropologische Reflexionen zur Theologie Dietrich Bonhoeffers*, Salzburg, 1976.
5 Cf. K. Rahner, *Grace in Freedom*, New York, 1969, 219-222.
6 Cf. Hodgson, l.c., 14off.
7 Hegel, *Encyclopedia*, §436f, §385.
8 Cf. P. Ricoeur, *History and Truth*, Evanston, Ill., 1963, 103-109.
9 M. Scheler, *Der Formalismus in der Ethik und die materiale Wertethik*, 3rd ed., Halle, 1927, 305.
10 E. Stein, "Beitrag zur Begründung der Psychologie und Geisteswissenschaften", 2. Teil: "Individuum und Geneinschaft", *Jahrbuch für Philosophie und phänomenologische Forschung* 5 (1922), 145.
11 R. May, *Man's Quest for Himself*, New York, 1953, 162.
12 K. Rahner, l.c., 208.
13 N. Berdyaev, *Freedom and the Spirit*, London, 4th ed., 1948, 139.
14 Cf. Hodgson, l.c., 261ff.
15 H. Schlier, *W.z.NT* II, 495.
16 E. Käsemann, *Jesus Means Freedom*, Philadelphia, 1970, 25.
17 Hodgson, l.c., 214.
18 Cf. K. Niederwimmer, l.c., 157.
19 Cf. E. Käsemann, l.c., 24-25.
20 Cf. Niederwimmer, l.c., 151.
21 Hodgson, l.c., 241.
22 Cf. O. Cullmann, *Jesus and the Revolutionaries*, New York, 1976, 39-42; M. Hengel, *War Jesus ein Revolutionar?*, Stuttgart, 1970.
23 Cf. Niederwimmer, l.c. 171f.
24 J. Moltmann, *The Crucified God: The Cross of Christ as the Foundation and Criticism of Christian Theology*, New York, 1974, 147-153.
25 E. Käsemann, l.c., 76
26 F. Herzog, l.c., 59.
27 Hodgson, l.c., 273.

28 Cf. R. Pesch, "Jesus, a Free Man", in *Jesus Christ and Human Freedom*, *Concilium*, New York, 1974, 56-70.
29 Hodgson, l.c., 253.
30 Niederwimmer, l.c., 89.
31 Cf. l.c., 94 and 115f.
32 Cf. K. Rahner, l.c., 224.
33 Augustine, *Confessions*, Book 7, ch. 1, PL32, 763.
34 P. Sartre, *Existentialism*, New York, 1947, 27.
35 E. Käsemann, l.c., 154.
36 Augustine *On Widowhood*, 17.21, PL 40, 443.
37 R. Bultmann, *Theologie des Neuen Testaments*, 4th ed., 1961, 379.
38 N. Berdyaev, *Freedom and the Spirit*, 147.
39 F. Herzog, l.c., 134.
40 This will be treated explicitly in Chapter VI.
41 K. Rahner, l.c., 224.
42 Thomas Aquinas, *Commentary on 2 Cor., III*, Lectio II.
43 Thomas Aquinas, *Commentary on Hebrews VIII*, Lectio II last lines.
44 Cf. my book *Sin in the Secular Age*, Slough and New York, 1974.
45 Cf. E. Osborn, l.c., 3o.
46 Cf. Hodgson, l.c., 259.
47 Cf. Niebuhr, *Radical Monotheism and the Western Culture*, New York, 1960, 108.
48 K. Rahner, l.c., 216.
49 H. Schlier, *Der Brief an die Galater*, 10th ed., Göttingen, 1949, 176.
50 K. Rahner, l.c., 257.
51 *Gaudium et spes*, 74.
52 l.c., 74.
53 Hodgson, l.c., 221.
54 l.c., 222.
55 Cf. my book *Sin in the Secular Age*, Slough and New York, 1974.
56 *Gaudium et spes*, 76.
57 Cf. F. Herzog, l.c., 13of.
58 Cf. P. Ricoeur, *Freedom and Nature. The Voluntary and the Involuntary*, Evanston, Ill., 1966, 355-443.
59 Hodgson, l.c., 252; cf. J. Moltmann, *The Crucified God*, 147-153.
60 Cf. Herzog, l.c., 127f. The author insists that this should be at the heart of the Christian message, and no longer "justification by faith alone".
61 Herzog, l.c., 46 and 208.
62 Cf. Niederwimmer, l.c., 52f.
63 Cf. R. Osborn, *Freedom in Modern Theology*, 209.
64 Hodgson, l.c., 326.
65 *Lumen gentium*, 32.
66 K. Rahner, l.c., 229.
67 W. Pannenberg, *The Idea of God and Human Freedom*, Philadelphia, 1973, 96.
68 Cf. Niederwimmer, l.c., 182. The following pages are greatly indebted to this author, especially what he writes on "Freedom in the Holy Spirit", l.c., 168-218.
69 G. Gutierrez, *A Theology of Liberation*, Maryknoll, N.Y., 1973, 177.
70 J. Moltmann, *The Crucified God*, 252.
71 Cf. Hodgson, l.c., 222.
72 Cf. Niederwimmer, l.c., 185.
73 R.A. Alves, *A Theology of Human Hope*, Washington, 1969, 105.
74 Cf. R. Osborn, l.c., 272.
75 Cf. Niederwimmer, l.c., 91 and 191
76 D.M. Stanley, *Boasting in the Lord*, New York, 1973, 124.
77 Niederwimmer, l.c., 176.
78 Cf. F. Böckle, *Law and Conscience*, New York, 1966, 43.

[79] K. Rahner, l.c., 206.
[80] Hodgson, l.c., 147.
[81] l.c., 168.
[82] E. Käsemann, l.c., 155.
[83] Hegel, *Philosophy of Right*, §4.
[84] Cf. Hodgson, l.c., 443.
[85] Cf. K. Rahner, l.c., 233.
[86] E. Käsemann, *Perspectives on Paul*, Philadelphia, 1971, 42-45
[87] W. Pannenberg, *What is Man? Contemporary Anthropology in Theology*, Philadelphia, 1970, 8.
[88] E. Erikson, *Insight and Responsibility*, New York, 1964, 142.
[89] Hodgson, l.c., 308.
[90] O. Cullmann, *Jesus and the Revolutionaries*, 28.
[91] Cf. Hodgson, l.c., 239; on this point I disagree with Hodgson to whom otherwise I am greatly indebted.
[92] J. Moltmann, *The Crucified God*, 23. This prophetic word of a great theologian is illustrated by the publications of a great sociologist who does not less emphatically believe in freedom than the theologian: George D. Gurwitch. See, above all, his book *Déterminismes sociaux et liberté humaine; vers l'étude sociolologique des cheminements de la liberté*, Paris, 1955.
[93] Hodgson, l.c., 317.
[94] Cf. P. Ricoeur, "Christianity and the Meaning of History", in *History and Truth*, Evanston, Ill., 1965, 81-97.
[95] Cf. R. May, *Man's Quest for Himself*, 145-151.
[96] Cf. E. Erikson, *Identity: Youth and Crisis*, New York, 1968, 113.
[97] E. Erikson with Joan Erikson, "Growth and Crisis in the Healthy Personality", in *Symposium on the Healthy Personality* (edited by Hilton Senn), New York, 1950, 104.
[98] R. May, l.c., 261.
[99] K. Rahner, l.c., 230f.
[100] Cf. J.B. Metz, *Glaube in Geschichte und Gesellschaft*, Mainz, 1977, 87-119.
[101] K. Rahner, l.c., 238. It is sad to be reminded of the terrible *Liber Bomorrhianus* of Pier Damiani and the introductory letter to it by Leo IX, twice referred to as witness of a long-standing tradition by the Doctrinal Congregation in its declaration on some matters of sexual morality; cf. B. Häring, Reflexionen zur Erklärung der Glaubenskongregation über einige Fragen der Sexualethik, in *Linzer Theol. prakt. Quartalshcrift*, 124 (1976), 115-126.
[102] K. Rahner, l.c., 256.
[103] J. Moltmann, *Theology of Play*, New York, 1972, 58-61.
[104] W. Pannenberg, *Theology of the Kingdom*, Philadelphia, 1969-75, 75.
[105] J. Moltmann, l.c., 22.

Chapter Five

Fundamental option

New psychological knowledge and new theological thought bring to the foreground the matter of the fundamental option. How it is approached has far-reaching consequences for an understanding of the first and the ongoing conversion, the distinction between mortal and venial sin and, indeed, for almost all aspects of moral theology. There exist some excellent studies on this subject.[1] However, the textbooks of moral theology have not yet integrated the results of these reflections. It is imperative that this be done.

I. BLENDING OLD AND NEW THINGS TOGETHER

Traditional moral theology, especially the Thomist branch, gave proper attention to the basic decision for the ultimate end (finis ultimus). All the individual decisions and the quality of one's freedom depend on this choice. Leaving aside for the moment the problems of the psychological understanding of fundamental option and, indeed, the total neglect of psychology in this area, I want to stress the abiding value of the traditional treatise on the ultimate end and man's necessity to make this decision. Man is thoroughly seen in dependence on God, the ultimate origin, and called to give his response to God by the whole orientation of his/her life towards God as the ultimate end. In biblical terms this means: God calls us to himself. The basic decision is whether our life will be one of listening and responding to him in and through all our attitudes and decisions. In secular language it is a question of giving ultimate meaning to existence and expressing that meaning in every facet of our lives and throughout our entire lifetime.

Although, today, we are particularly attentive to the total context of this basic decision, it has always been known that it has to be worked out in the midst of conflict. We are not born indifferent beings. Our life means being called by God's infinite love; and this is deeply written in our innermost being. However, we are also born into a sinful world that has idols, perverted societal structures, false gods, in other words, ultimate ends that contradict our very origin and the orientation written into our hearts.

In this respect we are faced with two opposed trends: one optimistic, the other pessimistic and frequently rigoristic. Building on tradition we have to make our choice. As in so many other dimensions and questions of moral theology, the understanding of the fundamental option will greatly depend on how we evaluate the relationship between our being created to the image and likeness of God and our being born into a sinful world in a mysterious solidarity with the "sin of the world". My choice is surely not an easygoing optimism, but one of hope and trust. We are more marked by the fact that we are the "handiwork" of God who is love for us; we are born into a history which is infinitely more affected by redemption than by sin solidarity.

However, on the practical level, a great deal depends on the quality of the milieu or community into which the child is born, and whether the evil in the environment is sufficiently counteracted by a genuine faith community and holy people. If the young person is exposed to a perverted milieu that is in no way qualified by good elements, then it might well be that the noisy voices of the idols could conceal the tiny voices of a remote culture of the good and stifle the innate desires for righteousness. We have at least to raise the theological question whether in such a case a young person may at all have enough freedom to be accountable if he/she never reaches a fundamental option for God and good.

Today, the traditional theme of the choice of the ultimate end has to be approached in view of psychological studies and insights. The fundamental option is studied above all in the light of a psychology of development. As a consequence, a much more dynamic vision prevails which better meets the biblical perspectives.

In spite of a common concern, psychologists and theologians, and the latter among themselves, have not yet found a common language; they may sometimes use the same words but differ in the understanding of them. Joseph Fuchs, who as theologian did pioneering work, understands the fundamental option or "basic decision" as "a mature act of self-determination".[2] As we shall see later, he comes close to Erik Erikson's vision of the quest of identity and integrity. Others, for instance Piet Fransen, understand it more as a "preliminary and as yet immature groundwork". It seems to me that the difference can somehow be bridged by emphasizing both, the indispensable depth and at the same time the constant need of deepening the basic choice and translating it into all of life. Unless it grows in depth and breadth, it can be blunted and even turned into the opposite.[3]

Karl Rahner describes the fundamental option as "the total self-understanding and the radical self-expression", while, however, acknowledging that "it remains first frequently empty and unfulfilled".[4] These two qualifications can, in my eyes, be harmonized only if the first part is understood in the light of Rahner's transcendental philosophy, while the second part comes closer to psychological experience. Instead of using "total self-expression", I propose to speak rather of the profound dynamics directed towards total self-understanding and self-expression. The dimension of totality has, however, to be stressed. Throughout this and the next chapter we shall see how both, the fundamental option for the good and a profound experience of conscience, are distinguished by the dimension of totality; it is an experience that one's wholeness and all the basic relationships are at stake.

It may be useful to alert the reader, at the outset of this

chapter, to pay special attention to the way in which the fundamental option and the wholeness and maturity of conscience are interrelated.

Close to the concept of fundamental option is that of "basic intention".[5] This is more than just a pious intention concerning certain works. It is an intention that has at least the dynamics of being all-pervasive in the orientation and quality of all one's free decisions and actions. From the basic intention, then, the ever increasing basic attitudes gradually arise. The basic intention is not valid if it does not show the dynamics which permeate and transform all attitudes and patterns and the very character of the person.

One of my special interests is to examine whether the fundamental option, as expression of "basic freedom", is at the same time an option for creative freedom and creative fidelity. Under this perspective the very fundamental option, although conceptually directed towards the good, can be abortive if, for instance, the "good" is understood in a legalistic and static way.

Richard Niebuhr has challenged our way of life which, while seeming to be an expression of faith in God, is frequently more a kind of polytheism. Although in the creed we profess faith in one God, our life venerates many other gods. The fundamental option or basic intention truly reaches out to the ultimate end in the one God if all our life gradually becomes adoration of God in spirit and in truth.[6] The healthy fundamental option is openness to the Other and the others. It includes cooperative relationship in trust and self-transcending love. Otherwise it is a wrong or an abortive fundamental option.

While we can purposefully and explicitly make a basic intention, for instance, to serve God with all our being, the fundamental option of which we speak here is, by its very nature, more than a single act set into our life. Rather, it includes a continuing free activation that is inherent in all our important choices, or at least tends to give all of them the character of basic freedom. "If moral life follows the line of the basic free option, this is further developed and strengthened".[7] It can, however, be contradicted by superficial inconsistencies, which, although they do not reverse, can still weaken the fundamental option for the good. It can also be contradicted by free actions of a depth and relevance that can point the very basic freedom and fundamental option in the opposite direction. The least we can say here is that a fundamental option is the activation of a deep knowledge of self and of basic freedom by which a person commits himself. It is not thinkable that the fundamental option is fully activated by committing oneself to a mere idea, for a person is more than an idea. Fundamental option is confirmed in its essence only when the person, as a person, commits himself to the Other, to the value person. In the fundamental option, human freedom manifests itself as "the capacity for the eternal".[8] This does not exclude, however, that a profound commitment to fellowmen in self-transcendent love can implicitly be commitment to the Eternal, to a personal God.

II. CONTRIBUTION OF THE BEHAVIOURAL SCIENCES AND PHILOSOPHY

I rely, in this section, especially on those thinkers and therapists like Erik Erikson, Edward Spranger, Soren Kierkegaard, Abraham Maslow and Viktor Frankl who have an outstanding grasp of wholeness, a profound understanding of ethical values and a particular interest in the ethical dimension of the growth of the person. I consider them as eminent "common sense philosophers". I do not try to enter into a critical analysis of their whole thought but choose those insights with which I can readily identify myself, even though I might, here and there, give them a somewhat different place in my own philosophical approach.[9] While I do not explicitly refer here to the work of Erich Fromm, I did learn a great deal from the ethical vision which characterizes all his works.[10] Much that is said about Erikson's reflections on identity and integrity can be found also in Fromm under other headings.

1. Erik Erikson's life-cycle

Perhaps no modern psychologist, therapist or philosopher comes closer to our problem than Erik Erikson who, throughout a long life, has addressed himself so creatively to the subject of identity and integrity. Therefore, I try here to explore what we can learn from him for our specific theme.

Like other great psychologists, for instance Abraham Maslow, Erik Erikson discovers inborn dynamics, the inborn need to unfold while seeking the ultimate meaning. "Anything that grows has a ground plan, and out of this ground plan the parts arise, each having its time of special ascendancy, until all parts have arisen to form a functioning whole".[11] Erikson sees the individual person in a continuing development, but also faced with constantly threatening decay.[12] And he gives great attention to the personal dimension, personal relationships and the interdependence between the individual and his environment. I find particularly helpful what he says about the stages or cycles of life. The stages are dynamic configurations having certain contours, so that, while redefining the inner and outer limits, they spell out change within a larger sense of continuity.

While Erikson does compare the stages of life with the biological laws of unfolding, he stresses equally the creative and adaptive power of the individual and his capacity to create his own way of life. He also vividly presents a personalistic vision without falling into individualism. Personal development and growth is activated through interaction with others, and its extent is measurable by its inter-personal dimensions. Each stage opens new horizons of creativity if the person keeps a clear direction. Erikson thinks of life "as a series of steps, with plateaux and precipices that do far more than reveal the directions set by the first few steps.[13]

Erikson himself stresses creativity while giving special attention to continuity. The focal point of his description of the life cycles is the gradual affirmation of identity and, then, integrity as the basis of a fruitful life. I hope that the reader, especially one familiar with the writings of Erikson, will at the end see how the unfolding of identity comes very close to what theologians call fundamental option or basic intention. He helps us to come to a more vital understanding of the growth process as the unfolding of life's great decision. "Man is not organized like an archaeological mound, in layers. As he grows, he makes the past a part of the future, and every environment he once experienced is a part of the present environment".[14]

This last quote also indicates how Erikson integrates the social dimension in his psychology of development.

As a therapist, Erikson is also quite aware that goodness is never achieved to such a degree that it is impervious to all possible conflict.[15] The continued presence of the lower stages, their successes and failures, explain the phenomena of regression. Man's development is always precarious. He is condemned to regression as much as society is, if there is not a clear purpose of growth and conversion.[16]

Erikson comes especially close to our search for a better understanding of fundamental option when he shows how, at various critical moments in life, achievements are won or failures occur in a way that the future is either better or worse for it.[17] He describes important moments or crises as "a turning point for better or for worse, a critical period in which a decisive turn one way or the other is unavoidable".[18] He sharply distinguishes between neurotic or psychotic crises and the normative crises that mark man's life in its growth. The normative crises represent "a normal phase of increased conflict characterized by a seeming fluctuation in ego strength as well as by a high growth potential".[19] A crisis in a developmental sense that calls for a fundamental option or, rather, for its deepening, is "a crucial period of increased vulnerability and heightened potential, and therefore the ontogenetic source of strength and maladjustment."[20]

Erikson presents eight stages with their specific crises and the basic decisions that have to be worked out if the person is to succeed.

1. Basic trust versus mistrust.
2. Autonomy versus shame and doubt.
3. Initiative versus guilt.
4. Industry versus inferiority.
5. Identity versus role confusion.
6. Intimacy versus isolation.
7. Generativity versus stagnation.
8. Ego integrity versus despair.[21]

Erikson speaks about "sense of basic trust", basic initiative and so on, pointing towards attitudes, directions and patterns that gradually pervade surface and depth, the conscious and the unconscious.[22] Even in normal development there remains after each stage a healthy tension that can dynamize the next stage.

(1) Basic trust versus mistrust

In the first stage as baby or toddler, if the child has the good fortune to receive genuine love from trustworthy parents, there will be the groundwork for basic trust. This does not exclude, however, a healthy capacity for distrust, so necessary for discernment. It is always a matter of a synthesis in a delicate balance. "Unless the high in a man somehow includes and reinstates the low, the high is weak, *anaemic* and unstable".[23]

Although the basic trust depends greatly on the quality of the mother-child relationship, the child's inner resources are so great that later positive experiences can restore this sense if it is lacking. Basic trust always gives the capacity to hope. Once established as a basic experience and response, hope allows the person in the following stages to discover his inner resources and to grasp and cherish present opportunities.[24] The development in each of the following stages depends on whether and how the basic trust is deepened and reaffirmed, and the tendencies to basic mistrust are overcome.

(2) Autonomy versus shame and doubt

Just as the groundwork for basic trust is laid in infancy, so is the foundation of autonomy, self-determination, laid in early childhood. The child manifests an inborn tendency to affirm his selfhood, his own will. This has to be seen in a perspective of the individual's *vocation* to live his own life, to act according to his own conscience. "Will is the unbroken determination to exercise free choice as well as self-restraint, in spite of the unavoidable experience of shame and doubt in infancy".[25]

The child has also to learn that his will is confronted with the will and autonomy of others. It is one of life's greatest tasks to learn about this mutuality and to accept it. One's own autonomy is worthless if the autonomy of the other is not acknowledged and honoured. Parents make a great mistake if they try to break the will of the infant instead of helping him to understand this interaction. The "behind", the small being's dark continent, is all too frequently the seat of a painful experience of invasion by those who deny the child his own will. If shame and doubt are the prevailing experience at this stage, they will greatly block the development of freedom.

(3) Initiative versus guilt

The play age is decisive for setting free or inhibiting the creative energies. Initiative adds to the search for autonomy, the capacity for undertaking, planning, attacking a task with imagination. Over-protective parents greatly hinder the development of the child at this stage. A mother who constantly burdens the child with do's and don'ts, while over-watching and over-feeding, does almost irreparable harm to her child. It is also important that the play age lasts long enough to develop a sense of play, of imagination and creativity. In this stage a new dimension of consciousness appears. If things go wrong, the child now is not only afraid of being found out and blamed but also learns to hear the "inner voice" that approves or disapproves from within.[26] He has to be helped to harmonize this inner voice with the approval or disapproval of the environment. There must not be an emphasis on guilt but, rather, on the happy discovery of his roles and of his own capabilities and inner resources.

(4) Industry versus inferiority

The school age lays the groundwork for the virtue of *competence.* The delicate problem is task identification without confusing one's own identity with the task and success in life. However, the person, as a social being, cannot reach his identity without dedication to a common task. Much depends on whether this industry and task identification receive the meaning of vocation, that is, a service for the common good. If work and task are not understood, not fulfilling because of lack of meaning, then the sense of futility arises and greatly blocks the further development of the person as a person.

(5) Identity versus identity confusion

Erikson's main concern in describing the life cycles is identity. This will not be reached without a creative crisis.

The identity crisis predominates in adolescence, but its influence is felt throughout the whole life.[27] One's identity arises gradually from selective acceptances and repudiations and partial assimilation of childhood identifications. These must receive their total meaning in a new configuration in which the ego strength prevails over the super ego, if the identity crisis is to be resolved. Much depends on how society and those closest to the individual identify the young person, how they recognize him as somebody, and to what extent they accept him as he is.[28] The adolescent tends to "depict some meaningful resemblance between what he has come to see in himself and what his sharpened awareness tells him others judge him and expect him to be".[29]

The final identity includes all the significant identifications of the past, but they are transformed in a way that they can make a unique and reasonable coherent whole for the person's total outlook.[30] To the extent identity is somehow accomplished, the focus of attention changes from self-development and self-assurance to an active inter-relationship of the person with his environment.[31]

It is impossible to describe identity without focusing on fidelity. A person not yet committed to a cause worthy of him, and especially a person not yet able to commit himself to other persons without losing selfhood, has not yet reached the core of his identity. Fidelity encompasses sincerity, authenticity, devotion, "a freely given but binding vow, with fateful implications of a curse befalling the undedicated".[32]

At this point it becomes clear how near Erikson's concept of identity is to what theologians call fundamental option. It does not arise all at once. The groundwork is laid, however, when it comes to the self-commitment of a person in the very discovery of identity. And this, in turn, is dependent on fidelity which itself entails courage and trust expressed in self-commitment. The search for identity coincides with the search for inner coherence and a durable set of values. "Fidelity is the ability to sustain loyalties freely pledged in spite of the inevitable contradictions of value systems".[33]

The young person cannot come to a firm identity without pledging loyalty to a world image convincing enough to support his sense of individual and collective identity.[34] Especially those who have rich potentialities that entail complexities sometimes need more time to resolve the identity crisis. Erikson has shown this, for instance, in the lives of Mahatma Gandhi and of young Martin Luther.[35] Both somehow exemplify the difficulty of freeing themselves from identification with a powerful father-image. "The adolescent or the young person sometimes needs a moratorium, a span of time after they have ceased being children, but before their deeds and works can count towards a future identity".[36]

Erikson's reflections on the moratorium seem to be important for understanding both self-commitment and creative fidelity. The moratorium does not need to be consciously experienced as such. On the contrary, the young person may feel deeply committed, and may find out much later that what he took so seriously was only a period of transition.[37] These insights seem to be extremely important in relating fundamental option to the great decisions of life such as the reception of the sacrament of confirmation, the marriage vows, religious vows and the choice of priesthood.

Following Erikson, we have given here most of our attention to the positive solution of the identity crisis, since this is indispensable in a Christian ethic presented as a theology of life. It is understandable that a moral theology written mainly for confessors would focus mostly on sin and failure, but even in that case it must be said that the aborted fundamental option cannot be understood without a prior understanding of the successful fundamental option or identity.

The Old Testament frequently conceived sin as "missing the mark".[38] A disastrous "sin" is a negative solution of the identity crisis although a positive solution was possible. Identity confusion or an "identity" that affirms one's own self against the Other, and the others, is the basic failure. However, we cannot judge whether identity confusion in others is more a psychological or more a moral reality. A severe form of identity confusion can arise from a deliberate choice of a negative identity that could also be called a "protest identity" of young persons, "an identity perversely based on all those identifications and roles which, at critical stages of development, have been presented to them as most undesirable and dangerous and yet also most real".[39] "The negative identity is the sum of all those identifications and identity fragments which the individual had to submerge in himself as undesirable or irreconcilable".[40]

This might well be the result of an education based mainly on prohibitions or a reaction against a domineering authority that was unacceptable to the developing person. The history of such a choice reveals a set of conditions in which it is easier for the person to derive a sense of identity from total identification with that which he is least supposed to be, than to struggle to attain an acceptable role,[41] since acceptable roles were never presented in an attractive or realistic way. Or else the now confused person may have freely "missed the point". One of these "pathological identity confusions" occurs when a person's problems are a constant evasion into "if only": life and strength seem to exist only where one is not, while decay and danger threaten wherever one happens to be.[42]

(6) Intimacy versus isolation

The sixth stage of the life cycle is characterized by the fundamental choice between intimacy and isolation. The young adult who has not reached a genuine identity is always afraid of losing his selfhood, yet is not able to enter into a covenant like friendship or marriage. He tends to retire into highly stereotyped and formal relationships which lack real spontaneity and creativity.

In a successful solution of the identity crisis, the person realizes that he can give himself to the other without losing himself: that self-realization comes with self-transcendence.[43] His own sufficient identity allows mutuality, and the other is then perceived as a gift. One's true selfhood "permits the person the capacity to commit himself to concrete affiliations and partnerships, and to develop the ethical strength to abide by such commitments".[44] The self-commitment of a young person strong enough to commit himself not only to a good cause but also to a person guarantees identity, basic freedom and creative fidelity in shared intimacy.

(7) Generativity versus stagnation

Stage seven in the life cycle coincides with adulthood.

Those who have found their identity, and therefore also the readiness for mutuality, are creative in many ways. Erikson takes generativity as paradigm. In a society in which the child is no longer necessary as life support or as status symbol, the responsible transmission of life depends on how deeply one has found meaning in life and committed oneself to it. But nor only procreativity manifests generativity; even more it is the overall readiness to take responsibility, to take the time to discover creative solutions and to contribute to the life of the present and future generations. A person's creative fidelity and liberty, spirit of openness and co-responsibility depend on how he or she has resolved the decisive crises of the previous life cycles. Stagnation reveals an abortive fundamental option from which only a profound conversion can free the person.

(8) Ego integrity versus despair

The eighth and final stage of the life cycle, coinciding with adulthood and old age, brings to culmination the achievements and challenges of the previous stages. "In the ageing person who has taken care of things and people and has adapted himself to the trials, triumphs and disappointments of being: only in him, the fruit of the seven stages gradually ripens. I know of no better word for it than integrity".[45] Integrity marks the ego in which has accrued the assurance of a sense of meaning and meaningful ordering of life. It includes "emotional integration, faithful to the image-bearers of the past and ready to take, and eventually to renounce, leadership in the present. It is the person's acceptance of his one-and-only life cycle and of those people who have become significant and meaningful to it".[46]

This integrity entails and allows a renewed love of one's parents and acceptance of others and of ourselves, free of the senseless wish that everyone and everything should have been different. It is in this way that we accept and realize our true responsibility. Integrity is the inner strength to face, with a certain detachment and at the same time active concern, life and death. It is wisdom in its many connotations, "mature judgment and inclusive understanding".[47]

The danger in this stage or, rather, the sign of a previous abortion of the fundamental option, of life's meaning, is despair, bitterness, fear of death, panic and a general displeasure that frequently manifests itself in discontent with situations and persons.

One can easily see that Erikson does not provide us with a readily made definition of fundamental option, but he offers a framework and many lively insights for better understanding the underlying dynamics that we might call fundamental option. We cannot simply equate our notion of fundamental option with Erikson's vision of identity, but they have much in common. It is identity that gives the ego strength so necessary for a total commitment. It is, again, identity that allows the development of generativity and integrity. The description given by Erikson allows us to recognize in them what we call basic dispositions and attitudes insofar as they draw their direction and strength from the fundamental option. Furthermore, we can find in Erikson's overall vision of the life cycles an original synthesis between creativity and continuity.

2. *Edward Spranger's fundamental choices and types of men*

Half a century ago, Edward Spranger, a psychologist and philosopher, and, as the author of this book experienced, an inspiring teacher, devoted much effort to describing the fundamental choices made throughout life within various social and cultural contexts.[48]

Spranger opens our eyes to the enormous influence of the cultural environment on the shape of the fundamental orientation. He not only describes fundamental dispositions which we might identify with our traditional concept of "virtues", but he also shows us how choices of the ultimate goal and values are incarnate in cultures that can greatly influence the content and colour of the individual's fundamental choice. He asks what sphere of value occupies the principal place in people's emotions, sentiments and basic choices. Concerned with the interdependence between the value types of a culture and the corresponding ethos of dispositional orientation, he lists the following value types:

(1) Economic value type: it gives priority to the economic utility, profit, success. Its positive ethos is devotion to work, to one's profession.

(2) Aesthetic value type: its predominant value is in the beautiful, in harmony, noble enjoyment. The positive ethos is devotion to cultural activity and the nurturing of harmonious and balanced personality.

(3) Political value type: its first values are power, heroism, sometimes racial supremacy. The positive ethos is the cult of courage and self-mastery. Its shade is lust for power.

(4) Theoretical value type: its dedication is to science, research and reflection. The ethos is devotion to search for truth, objectivity, truthfulness.

(5) Social value type: dedication is to the good of community. The prevalent ethos is devotion to the "thou", to the common good, the cult of altruism.

(6) Religious value type: it gives first place to God, searches for union with God and for salvation not only of souls but of people. The ethos is devotion to God, detachment from everything that opposes the kingdom of God's love.

It is quite apparent that each of these value types contains positive dispositional orientations and ethos rich in values. But every person of a type that gives first choice to secondary values, such as the economic type of life, is always in danger of betraying the higher values in the ultimate decisions and purposes. This is a danger inherent in many cultures today. For while none of these types exists in a pure and unmixed state — they are only more or less predominant tendencies and inclinations — it should be evident how great the loss is if they become mutually exclusive.

The knowledge and recognition of the religious values as supreme is, by its very nature, open to the social and all the other values so long as they are not claiming first place. To give to God the absolute first place is the religious fundamental option that should guarantee the order of love and the proper scale of values.

The great danger for religious values comes from the imbalance of those value types that tend to be so fundamental and encompassing that ethical, social and even religious values are used as a means or instrument to serve the predominant value. We see the shocking example in the businessman or political leader who attends Church services and even receives the sacraments for the sake of "public relations". How many times religion has been used as a trump card in the game of power politics!

3. *Kierkegaard's "Stages on Life's Way"*

As the title of Kierkegaard's book [49] indicates, the dynamic element in the four stages has to be kept in mind above all. Each stage, if the development is healthy, opens the horizons for the next. In this perspective he is closer to Erikson than to Spranger. But he is grasping a dimension that neither in Erikson nor in Spranger receives explicit attention. His contribution can broaden our vision of the fundamental option. The four stages on life's way present predominant dispositions responding to a predominant scale of value. But Kierkegaard presents these dispositions with the conviction that each stage calls for the next. This underlying dynamics has a certain affinity with our understanding of fundamental option.

(1) The aesthetic stage implies the sense and search for beauty, the capacity to admire, to be filled with awe, to rejoice, and a dedication to the values of harmony and to art. Once we realize that beauty is the splendour of the good and of truth, we can agree with Kierkegaard who sees the aesthetic stage and dimension as indispensable for the growth of personhood. Whoever has truly grasped what beauty is and knows how to admire it, and dedicates himself to harmony, will open himself to the next stage.

(2) The ethical stage on life's way. The person realizes the majesty of the good, the dignity of each person, and gives priority to the art of loving.

(3) The anthropocentric-religious stage on life's way. Here the focus is on the horizontal level. Religion is approached in view of man's wholeness and salvation. God is sought and thought of as necessary for man's own perfection. This stage can have all shades of an imperfect horizontal vision while

reaching a deeper understanding of God the Father and of Our Lord Jesus Christ who reveals himself as God for all mankind.

(4) The theocentric religious stage on life's way. Life is understood as adoration of God in spirit and truth. God is radically at the centre. The ethical is then viewed as sharing in God's own love for man, as adoring response to his love and justice.

Kierkegaard does not see these stages as final or static but, rather, as stages of development tending towards integration and dynamic harmony. The economic value type which in the capitalistic work ethos and in the Marxist ideology tends to subordinate all other values has, of course, no place in the stages of life presented by Kierkegaard. It rather constitutes a supreme peril to personal value even where it manifests positive ethos and inculcates a certain order of moral life.

4. *The contribution of Maslow and Frankl*

I think that the moral theological understanding of fundamental option could gain immensely from Abraham Maslow's description of peak experience and from Viktor Frankl's "Search for Meaning". The peak experience is, for Maslow, an expression that reaches the depth of the person and entails a profound realization that this is the right direction in life. It is an experience of wholeness and of gratitude, a new way of knowing that self-realization is possible only in self-transcendence. It is a "Yes" to the scale of values, arising from the depth and giving direction to the whole of life.[50]

Viktor Frankl not only has discovered the noögenic neurosis that befalls people who, in spite of their great potential, have radically failed to search for life's ultimate meaning, and thus have completely "missed the point"; he also offers help, through his logotherapy, to those who come to realize their existential emptiness but are still yearning for the freedom to give meaning to their life. He believes that there are inner resources that can be awakened so that the person can find his or her identity through a new dedication to truth and the will to make a firm commitment to it. In this wholehearted search there is already a contact, although unconscious, with the "hidden God". The fundamental option is gradually unfolding to a fully conscious union with the ultimate ground of meaning.

The fundamental option brings forth a great spontaneity in individual ethical decisions. A person who has firmly dedicated himself to that freedom for truth and final meaning does not need long reflection and pain before making decisions coherent with his dedication. Rather, the choice arises spontaneously and creatively from the inner depth where the unseen God is present.[51]

III. BASIC FREEDOM AND BASIC KNOWLEDGE

The basic option, as realization of basic freedom, can be considered only in indivisible unity with profound knowledge of the good. Basic knowledge and basic freedom are interrelated. Where the person has reached his or her identity and has made the total self-commitment to the good and finally to God, there is given a new way of knowing the good and knowing God.

Man's freedom is patterned on the divine, since it is sharing in divine freedom. God's freedom is light, truthfulness, lucidity. It belongs to the splendour of his glory and manifests itself in his glory. The loftiest level of divine likeness in man is his knowledge of love, penetrated with love and engendering more and better love; for God is Love. The Second Person of the Holy Trinity "is not just any word, but the Word breathing forth love".[52] The Word spoken out by the Father, in his infinite freedom of love, is filled with the same *élan vital* and, therefore, together with the Father, breathes forth the Spirit of love.

True moral and religious knowledge, knowledge of wholeness and salvation, can be a profound assimilation with God and is participation in his freedom, his knowledge, his love. This is a knowledge far superior to all scientific achievements in the realm of technology and economy. A simple peasant saint with loving knowledge of God and of good is closer to divine wisdom and freedom than the greatest scientist and most learned theologian, if these are lacking the same kind of existential knowledge or do not reach the same level of depth and wholeness.

In the Trinity, the Word is the Second Person, the Spirit (Love) is the Third. The Holy Spirit proceeds from the Father and the Son. From this divine pattern, we sense that basic moral knowledge on the level of basic freedom issues from love and breeds love. Without this kind of knowledge we have not reached the level of basic freedom or transcendental freedom or of free option. Basic knowledge is that kind of grasping of the good which is inseparable from commitment and calls to an ever deeper commitment. Basic knowledge about good (not necessarily conceptual knowledge but existential) contains all the dynamics of creative freedom and fidelity. Without this kind of knowledge, the fundamental option of which we are speaking is not yet fully given.

Even though in the Trinity, the Word is the Second Person and Love is the Third Person, nevertheless in the intimate divine life *(perichoresis)*, love is not in any way just a conclusion or the term; it is also the source and the centre of the *perichoresis* (compenetration of the divine Persons). In love, from love and to love, the Father speaks his consubstantial Word. The more one is an image of God, the more dynamic is the inter-action and synthesis between the knowledge of good and total commitment to it. Only insofar as knowledge of the good is sustained by the actual goodness of the person (by the self-commitment in basic freedom) can it provide effective impulse to virtues and to good deeds.

Clear and attractive perception and the depth of moral understanding (wisdom) reveal the good in us, manifest our basic freedom and self-commitment to love God and neighbour. A selfish life is unthinkable in a person who "knows" God with mind and heart. "No one who sins has seen him or has known him" (1 Jn 3:6).

The observance of the all-embracing commandment of love of neighbour is a sign not only that we love God but also that we "know" him. "He who says that he knows him and does not keep his commandments is a liar and the truth is not in him" (1 Jn 2:3f). The commandments of which John speaks are fundamentally faith as joyous, grateful, humble reception of God and self-surrender to him, and love of neighbour. And "the truth" here seems to be what we call basic knowledge.

existential knowledge of the good in the depths of our being.
There is no contradiction in John's statements. On the one
hand he is saying that we cannot love what we do not know,
nor can we do the good before we know it. On the other hand
he is telling us that we cannot know what we do not already
deeply love.

We understand this synthesis when we consider the different levels of knowledge and commitment. The knowledge of
which John's First Letter speaks is that given in and with the
fundamental option, the self-commitment of the whole person
to God, commitment to love of God and neighbour.

All particulars of morally relevant values and of all types
of value rest in the basic value, in the *good*: ultimately in God
who is the fullness of all love. A perfect and comprehensive
grasp of the basic value of the good would include within it the
full knowledge of all values, since they are contained in it. But
it does not follow that the knowledge of basic value necessary
for the fundamental option (basic freedom in one's commitment
to the good) always guarantees the right understanding, with
heart and mind, of all types of value.

One may possess a general knowledge of the good in a
vital awareness of good and evil, and some understanding of
significant types of value, yet have only a meagre knowledge
and appreciation of certain virtues. There are many people,
for example, who understand and appreciate legal justice and
honesty in exchange. They also have a knowledge and a sense
of the evil of injustice and are willing to promote justice and
order. But it can happen that they do not grasp the depth and
breadth of social justice and of the commandment, "Be compassionate as your Heavenly Father is compassionate (Lk 6:30).
This does not mean that they are ignorant of this divine command; but they cannot truly grasp it because they have not
yet fully integrated into their life the necessary basic knowledge
and freedom. If, however, the fundamental option is genuine,
their basic freedom puts them on the road to better understanding and realization of all values.

Corresponding to the main objects of moral knowledge
(basic value, type of value, particular value) there are three
kinds of value-blindness possible: (1) all-pervasive blindness

to value, (2) partial blindness to value, and (3) blindness in the concrete application of a type of value. The first, the all-pervasive blindness to value, is found in varying degrees in those persons who have "missed the mark", who have made a wrong fundamental option and thus have failed to find their true identity. Because they do not realize basic value, their knowledge lacks vital perception and attraction. There is no intuition. But, happily, during this life on earth, there is never absolute blindness as long as moral freedom and responsibility can still be awakened.

Partial blindness extends to a particular type of value or even to a group of values. The loftier and more demanding values are more likely to be affected where there is no profound and continued effort to obtain the good. But we should realize that even the lack of such vital effort in some field does not necessarily mean that the very basic knowledge of good and the knowledge of the precepts necessary for the potential fulfilment of good are absent, as long as the person is still on the way to working out the fundamental option.

The third kind of blindness is concerned with the subsumption of concrete instances under the general value or principle. One recognizes moral value and the types of value in general but fails to discern the particular application when a value challenges him in opposition to the still unconquered selfishness or pride. This type of blindness is not necessarily incompatible with an incipient good will.

Blindness to value is overcome to the extent that one makes a profound conversion until all one's energies are awakened and ready for the good. Unless we deny that a person can and must convert, we ought to concede that he is responsible for many sorts of blindness to value, even though the forces that blind man's heart and mind operate mostly on the level of the unconscious and subconscious.

Everything depends on how a person is orientated in that innermost centre which energizes the unconscious and subconscious. It is in man's heart that basic knowledge and freedom are indivisible and, on the other hand, where blindness and partial lack of freedom coincide.[53]

IV. THE HEART OF MAN

Some theologians relate the concept of fundamental option to the biblical vision of "the heart of man".[54] In the Bible the "heart of man" does not at all mean a person withdrawn into interiority. Rather, it draws our attention to that inmost focal point where the person is sensitive and open to the other. It is where the bridges of the thou-I-we relationships are built and man in his wholeness commits himself to the Other and the others. Or it can be where man is gradually destroying himself, becoming void and empty, blind and wicked. When he loses the capacity to love genuinely, he loses the best part of his "heart".

When there is a firm fundamental option for the good, man's heart is filled with the *pneuma*, filled with the Holy Spirit (Eph 5:18). An ethics that focuses on responsibility, the capacity to respond to God with all one's being and life, is of necessity an ethics of the heart. One who wants good fruit must make the tree and its roots good. In his magnificent letter on Christian liberty, the Apostle to the Gentiles makes clear that the only alternatives are between the Spirit and the selfish self. "You, my friends, were called to be free persons; only do not turn your freedom into licence for the selfish self, but be servants to one another in love, for the whole law can be summed up in a single commandment, love your neighbour as yourself. But if you go on fighting one another tooth and nail, all you can expect is mutual destruction. It means that if you are guided by the Spirit you will not fulfil the desires of the selfish self. The incarnate selfishness sets its desire against the Spirit, while the Spirit fights against it. They are in conflict with one another so that what you will to do you cannot do. But if you are led by the Spirit you are no longer slave of law".

"Anyone can see the kind of behaviour that belongs to incarnate selfishness: fornication, impurity, indecency, idolatry, sorcery, quarrels, a contentious temper, envy, fits of rage, selfish ambition, dissension, party intrigues and jealousies, drinking bouts, orgies and the like. I warn you, as I warned you before, that those who behave in such ways will never inherit the kingdom of God. But the harvest of the Spirit is love, joy, peace, patience, goodness, kindness, fidelity, gentleness and self-control" (Gal 5:13-22).

God does not want only external deeds. True morality arises from basic freedom, that fundamental commitment of self that becomes a transcendental freedom giving ultimate meaning and direction to one's free choice in the concrete situation. "My son, give me your heart" (Prov 23:26). A good decision and the right deed express morality in the full sense only when the act comes from one's heart where the fundamental option is for God and good, and reaches into that depth where one turns in the right direction.

The heart of man is determined by the value centre. "For where your treasure is, there will be your heart also" (Mt 6:21). He who, in basic freedom, has chosen the kingdom of God will have light for his whole life and will choose the good with a certain instinct of heart.

Yahweh does not complain so much about the perverted actions of the Israelites as about their "hardened hearts", their adulterous and perverted dispositions (Is 6:9f; 29:13; Mk 6:52; 8:17f; 16:14; Jn 12:39f). The summit of the great messianic prophecies is reached in God's promise to give his people a "new heart" and instil fear of him and love for him in their hearts (Jer 32:40; 31-33; Is 51:77; Ez 36:26). "And I will give them a new heart and will put a new spirit in their innermost being; I will take away the stony heart out of their flesh and will give them a sensitive heart" (Ez 11:19). God wants a total conversion, a total commitment to him, not only ritual penances. "Rend your hearts and not your garments" (Joel 2:13). Whereas the Pharisees severely condemn external infractions of petty human regulations, the Lord castigates the "evil heart", the base dispositions from which, as from a polluted spring, all evil flows (Mt 5:18; Mk 7:20f).

The most challenging reproach is in Peter's accusation of Simon Magus: "Thy heart is not right before God" (Acts 8:21). Both Stephen and the converted Saul, Paul, charged the legalistic Jews with being "uncircumcised in heart", a fact which accounts for their resistance to the Holy Spirit (Acts 7:51). The summary of the Lord's proclamation of the

Good News calls for "a new heart" (Mk 1:15). *Metanoein*, frequently translated as "repent", means more literally and accurately, "Live with a new heart and in a new spirit".

The call to conversion comes in the context of God's promises, now fulfilled, that he will give us a new heart. And our response is total self-commitment made in our heart so that all our actions will be marked by this fundamental option for him. The circumcised heart means an inner disposition of radical conversion and a profound change of life, arising from within (Rom 2:5; 2:29). A "pure conscience" and a basic option for God and good are as inseparable as two sides of the same coin (Rom 1:5). The very essence of conversion is to assume the inner spirit of Christ. From that will flow new conduct. "Let your bearing towards one another arise out of your life in Christ Jesus" (Phil 2:5). The new orientation of the disciples of Christ is made possible not merely by conformity with the example of Christ but, above all, by the indwelling of Christ in us (Rom 8:10; Eph 4:17-24). If, through faith and grace, we allow Christ to dwell in us, and if his words also dwell in us, we shall bear fruit in plenty and show ourselves to be disciples of Christ (Jn 15:7-9).

Faith as joyous acceptance of Christ, the saving truth, and firm commitment to him is the same as to "put on Christ" (Gal 3:27). Our fundamental option in faith becomes an inner force and voice calling us to act as Christ would. "Let Christ Jesus himself be the armour that you wear; give no more thought to satisfying the selfish appetites" (Rom 13:14). This new way of living is expressed both in Paul and John as "life in Christ Jesus", as "abiding in his love". From this disposition of the heart arises the new dynamic of the life of discipleship as co-worker and co-revealer of God's own love in Christ Jesus.

The theology of St. Augustine, where he treats of the grateful memory and of the heart of man, follows the biblical patterns. He calls for a firm and wholehearted commitment of self, and is convinced that freedom for good action is then guaranteed. "Change your heart and your work will be changed".[55] The fundamental option is either for self-giving love (*dilectio*) or for selfish, disordered love. "The right will is good love; perverted will is an evil love".[56]

For Thomas Aquinas, the basic or "first" spiritual act of man is a weighty act, a total self-disposal.[57] It does not follow from this, however, that a little child of five or six could make this basic self-disposal against good and God, although one should not exclude the possibility that in a child who awakens to spiritual and moral activity there is present the basic freedom and knowledge for the good that gives moral value to his or her choices. The presence of the Spirit who awakens us for the good is one thing, but quite another is to have so much awareness and freedom that one could be accountable for the basic grievous act of separation from God. For such a grievous act, one must have acquired the possibility of basic identity through experience, reflection, knowledge and freedom.

From all this it becomes clear that freedom in its "basic depth" is not just a matter of saying "Yes" or "No" to a specific decision; it is the power to mould and create ourselves, to become what we truly are.[58] The fundamental option decides about one's "heart" which can overflow with love and goodness but can also harbour deeply rooted selfishness. "Self-realization in openness towards others — love — is the true moral commitment of a person's basic freedom. Withdrawal into oneself is the negative self-commitment".[59]

These insights lead us to the conclusion that a firm self-commitment to others in a covenant such as marriage or religious vows is only possible on a level of fundamental option. That is, if a person has reached this level, the fundamental option arises from and leads to one's authentic identity, or else it is a matter of accountable loss of one's chances to reach a genuine identity. "The free self-commitment of ourselves as persons is more than any particular action or actions, and more than the sum of them. It underlies them, permeates them and goes far beyond them".[60]

However, there can be particular decisions made with such a profound awareness that they entail the radical affirmation or the change of one's own orientation. There can be such a peak experience, such an act of faith, hope and love of God, that a person knows which direction he has been given and has freely and gratefully accepted. There can also be negative acts of profound awareness and free decision by which the person changes direction and knows it in his heart, in the depth and wholeness of his being.

V. FUNDAMENTAL OPTION AND THE GREAT DECISIONS OF LIFE

In the past few decades, a whole branch of psychology has focused attention on decisions methodology [61] and has explored the various dimensions of the great decisions of life and everyday decisions.[62] If we want to say anything relevant for today's critical society about fundamental option and freedom of choice in relation to it, we cannot ignore the contribution of the behavioural sciences. The moral revelance of human acts cannot be severed from their psychological structure, as they cannot be separated from their meaning in the context. "Just as not everything that is presented in the form of a sentence can claim to be a statement or judgment in a psychological sense, not all events in which something is chosen are truly decisions or human choices".[63]

The great decisions that manifest or deeply affect the fundamental option are mainly decisions in which we commit ourselves in a covenant to a community or to a particular person. Only if such a decision is taken with that depth of basic knowledge and freedom that realistically allows fidelity to the commitment can we speak on decision in the full moral and psychological sense.

Without any claim to completeness, I want to point to such fundamental decisions as personal choice of faith in Jesus Christ and in the role and mission of the Church, made by an adult or an adolescent who already has reached the necessary stage of identity. I would list among such choices: adult baptism as sign of personal commitment to Christ and covenant with the Church — and since adult baptism is the exception in the West, I would note confirmation as a mature ratification of what God offers us in baptism; marriage vows; the vows of celibacy for the kingdom of God; a decision that is the test of deep and true friendship or of self-giving love; the deliberate choice of a profession such as that of a physician or of a politician with a firm commitment to the positive ethos.

A better understanding of the relation between a decision of great relevance and the fundamental option can shed light not only on the troubled question of the validity of a marriage initiated with insufficient preparation and without maturity. It can contribute also to our effort to help people to prepare themselves better for the choice of the future spouse, and is indispensable for the catechumenate in preparation for such an important self-commitment. Marriage would be much better understood as a weighty decision related to the fundamental option if it were presented not as canon law presents it — as a contractual duty regarding certain "acts open to procreation" — but, rather, as mutual self-bestowal, a "covenant" of persons to be with each other and for each other, as the Vatican Council preferred to express it after long discussions.[64] We have to explore all dimensions of a self-commitment insofar as it allows and fosters lifelong creative fidelity. The great choices of life are promising to the extent that they arise from and penetrate into the depth of the person's heart.

The validity of the fundamental option is never affirmed, weakened or changed without relation to the basic decisions about our covenant with fellowmen, our commitment to professional integrity or to responsibility to the world around us. If the great decisions are made soundly, and not precipitously or defiantly, they can change the direction in which unconscious forces push. They can reorganize our pyschic energies in the proper direction. "It seems that there are potentialities within us which are not released until we make a conscious decision".[66] Things are quite different if decisions are made too quickly, before a person is truly ready on all levels of his personality. This does not mean that a decision is valid and fruitful only if it is the decision of "a completely unified person".[67] However, we have at least to allow people to take time so that they can make their great decisions in full identity and with the best dynamics towards greater integration of their conscious and unconscious life.

These great decisions should not be seen as unrelated to everyday life. A person should always act and love as much as he can on his present level of freedom, so that his basic freedom increases. "Courage is required not only in a person's crucial vocational decision for his own freedom, but in the little hour-to-hour decisions which place the bricks in the structure of his building himself into a person who acts with freedom and responsibility".[68]

The crucial decisions should be prepared for by a period in which the person is most careful to live and act faithfully and creatively while making every day's ordinary choices in view of maturing for the decision that is already envisioned. If, for instance, a priest or religious comes to me for counsel regarding a change of status such as a possible dispensation in order to live a married life, or if spouses come regarding the awful decision of divorce, I urge them to live for a certain period a more intensive life of prayer and to examine their life every day to see whether they are reaching out for that level of fidelity and openness to God that will allow them to make their decision as a faithful response to the present opportunity and God's calling. One must never try to dissociate the great decisions from one's total moral life, and especially from every day's decisions to be faithful to God's grace and open to the needs of fellowmen.

It seems to me that in this time and age, when Christianity by birth is yielding to Christianity by personal choice of faith, confirmation should be postponed until the young person realizes, in his or her personal identity, the *importance* of a renewed, solemn self-commitment to Christ and his Church. In the period of preparation, a most thorough understanding of the meaning of our life as response to God's calling us to life in Jesus Christ should be developed. It would be especially fitting if confirmation could be celebrated at a time when the person also faces the great decisions about vocation and profession.[69] At this time, one should learn to see the choice of his or her profession not only in view of self-fulfilment and personal growth, but equally and even more in view of response to God by commitment to the common good, the service of fellowmen.

The choice of one's vocation, whether in religion, marriage, or unmarried service, whether in the service of the Gospel or of the poor and sick, or in a profession as journalist, politician, artist, homemaker or whatever, should be made with that profound reflection and consciousness of self-commitment that reaches the same level as a profoundly confirmed fundamental option. Life's great decisions will release the energies of creative freedom and fidelity to the extent that one has reached the level of responsibility to oneself and is able to mould and create and, at the same time, to commit oneself in a covenant for the common good in the sight of God.

In these great decisions that relate to our fundamental option, and affirm and strengthen it, we must be keenly aware that they are not automatically once-and-forever; they have to be nurtured. It is a kind of psychological suicide to live one's life, and especially one's life-commitment, in a tentative or escapist attitude. We might well say with Goethe's Faust: "The last result of wisdom stamps it true: he only earns his freedom who daily conquers it anew".

The fundamental option and the self-commitment made by the great decisions cannot be lived faithfully and creatively unless moral life is understood more in the light of the goal-commandments (as expressed in the Sermon on the Mount, in the "Farewell Discourses" and in the whole New Testament) than on the level of defence morality. Whoever wants to live only the minimal requirements of prohibitive and limitative laws will not be able to live according to his self-commitment. What is needed is prime attention to the positive realities and opportunities that, day by day, allow a creative fidelity to one's commitment.

Each celebration of a sacrament should be viewed and realized on the level of our fundamental option and the basic decisions of our life.

The Eucharistic celebration is meant to deepen our covenant relationship with Christ and the Church, to lift us up to that profound gratitude that recommits us ever more deeply to the law of grace, faith and love. The whole community celebration and the personal participation should have those qualities that enable us, in the depths of our basic freedom, to transform our fundamental intentions into more vital orientations and attitudes.

Not only in the case of a reconversion "from death to life" but in each celebration of the *sacrament of penance*, our repentance and purpose should be on the level of a profound decision. The sacrament is somehow aborted if our fundamental option is not strengthened by a firm purpose that helps us to translate it into a new dimension of our inward journey and more concrete planning of our future, as manifestation of our reconciliation with God, with ourselves, our fellowmen and all of creation. Our particular purposes do not truly affect our lives unless they are integrated in the overall purpose or fundamental orientation. It is not so much a matter of a discrete or isolated decision but, rather, the whole outline of life that pre-plans the particular decisions and one's future progress.

Our examination of conscience in preparation for a profound act of repentance and purpose, especially in the sacrament of penance, should not only look at the individual sins but should try to discern how they were pre-decided by conditionings, wrong choices and desires and by lack of firm overall decision.[71] With each sacramental celebration, our essential purpose to love God above all else and to love, in him and with him, all of his creatures, should become more vital, deeper and more effectively concrete.

VI. THE EMBODIMENT OF THE FUNDAMENTAL OPTION IN FUNDAMENTAL ATTITUDES

1. *Act, virtue and life-style*

As we have seen, there are basic decisions that arise from or reach into that same depth in which the fundamental option and basic knowledge are united. A fully human act is the person's self-expression and self-commitment; but not each free act is a full expression of the person, for mainly two reasons. First, many decisions of life — the daily desires, deeds, words spoken with deliberation and freedom — do not appear to one's consciousness so important as to awaken one's full freedom. The person, in his or her development and concrete circumstances, does not see them as relevant enough to radically affect one's whole life plan; they are peripheral. Secondly, even after a sincere and valid fundamental intention, there remain in the person various areas and tendencies not yet illumined or fully transformed by the fundamental option. Therefore, a possibility exists that on a peripheral level the person is inconsistent with the fundamental intention. It needs a lifetime to come to full identity, integrity and integration. And this process of integration and complete consistency is frequently impeded by the contradictions encountered in the world around us.

I have no difficulty in seeing, with Thomas Aquinas, that before a full activation of basic knowledge and freedom in the child there can, and indeed does, exist an intentionality or orientation towards the good and towards God. But the question arises immediately whether a child can posit free acts of self-expression of such depth and intensity as to effectively reverse the inborn orientation towards God. In other words, I am convinced that the child can grow in goodness, but I cannot conceive that a child of seven or eight can commit a mortal sin, as a certain Thomistic tradition, restated again by Maritain,[73] wanted to assert. While the fundamental orientation inscribed in the child's heart by the Creator and Redeemer can be gradually confirmed or weakened, there is not yet that self-expression in freedom of choice that would pervert the very depth in which the presence of God's Spirit is orienting the child to the good.

It seems to me that Maritain's opinion contradicts the psychology of child development when he thinks that a rather irrelevant act like eating on the sly could activate a fundamental option against God and good. Such an act is not normally commensurate with full self-expression and self-commitment even in the life of an average adult, much less in the life of a child. The child is not yet so fully developed that even an important act of stubborn resistance to the parents can inscribe a fundamental intention against God and good.

To assume such an easy change from good to evil on the occasion of a peripheral and relatively irrelevant act is not only against good child psychology but also manifests a pessimism about the depth and strength of the inborn orientation of the human person towards the good. God saw that his creation, especially that of the human person, was "very good". This would not be the case if the inborn goodness of the child could change to evil on the occasion of a relatively superficial act. This perspective has to be kept present in our treatise on sin, especially on the distinction between mortal and venial sin.

In a "divine milieu", an environment with a full embodiment of all the good, the inborn goodness of the human person — especially if once ratified by a fundamental option — would easily shine through in the person's whole life-style, character and posture, and in all his individual acts. But in the concrete situation of most human beings, marked by poor genetic heritage and constantly pulled in different directions by a disturbed environment, the fundamental option cannot fully exercise its influence on all human acts. It needs long and patient striving, attention and continuing conversion until that fundamental option is so embodied in fundamental attitudes, in virtues, that the whole life-style is a coherent and true expression of the unique self as God created it to be.

Surely, it can be said that a person is known by his "style", "the unique pattern which gives unity and distinctiveness to his activities".[74] But this presupposes a whole process of development and activation of the basic freedom and the many free choices which clearly establish the person's identity and integration.

A fundamental option for God and good is a response to God's good creation and to his order of redemption which is everywhere present. Through this affirmation man becomes, in a profound sense, a co-creator with God. But the work of this creation requests ongoing attention and alertness. Where God's wonderful work and design are accepted with the profound freedom which we mean by "fundamental option and intention", there is a dynamic of growth, integrity and maturity which cannot be easily overthrown. All free acts, but particularly decisions marked by creative freedom and fidelity, inscribe themselves in the person's psychodynamics and thus further strengthen the spirit. It is not just a matter of embodiment of the fundamental option in the whole person but also a task of reaching greater depths of firmness and clarity in the fundamental option itself.[75]

2. *Human virtues*

Virtues are a part of the wonderful creation of the fully

human person in which God and his human partner cooperate. This new creation shows essentially two dimensions: first, it takes roots and shape in all the human faculties, activating ever more the will in its inborn longing. It brightens the intellect with a more profound intuition of the good, and gives greater strength and clearer shape to one's emotions and sensitivities. Thus the unity between will and intellect is promoted. Hand in hand with this inner creation of unity and strength comes unification with the world of values, openness to the Other and co-humanity with the others.

While Plato considered virtues primarily in view of one's inner faculties, Aristotle and the main Catholic tradition consider equally the spheres of values with which one enters into an ever-growing relationship as if into a covenant. The creation of the inner person brings with it openness to God's creation and participation in it through creative relationships.

Virtue is genuine to the extent that freedom is basic to it. Through freedom of choice we build up a growing capacity to respond to whole spheres of values, and particularly to the values of persons and their needs. The actual value of a moral act depends upon the freely chosen basic self-commitment (fundamental option) and the free and joyful response to those values that give breadth, depth and a clear countenance to that option. But it is always chiefly the activation of the basic freedom and knowledge that gives moral value to the act.[76]

Virtue is not built up by mere repetition but, rather, through the unifying power of the leitmotif and the authenticity of those motifs that correspond to the various spheres of values. Immanuel Kant expresses this well, "Virtue is moral strength in pursuit of its duty which should never become a habit but always spring from the spirit as entirely fresh and creative".[77] It is kept alive and brought to ever more life by each value response in everyday life, but above all through those value realizations that reach into one's depths and into the depths of human relationships. "Virtue is neither stoic indifference (apatheia) or mechanical habit but a spiritual strength in joyful achievement. Nor is it superficial virtuosity. It draws its life from profound decision, while it is a permanent disposition for the good. It is constantly animated by joyful acceptance of the value which is embodied in it. Consequently, virtue is possible only where there is true insight into value and love of it".[78] Max Scheler has superbly shown that misunderstanding of virtue as mere habit or as response to superimposed duties would deprive virtue of all its creativity.[79]

3. Integration of faith and life

Christians become salt of the earth and light of the world to the extent that their faith and life are thoroughly integrated. We are on the road to this integration when the basic decision of faith (fundamental option) permeates and unifies all of one's energies and faculties in an ongoing effort to gain more light and to give an ever more embodied response to God's gifts and people's needs. This brings with it a constant readiness to share in God's creative and redemptive action in our own innermost being and in the world.

We can conceive virtues as specific attitudes in response to particular spheres of values. These virtues manifest and promote wholeness and salvation to the extent that they are rooted in the fundamental option of faith. Faith is a joyous, grateful acceptance of God's saving truth and liberating love; and this very acceptance entails profound gratitude and willingness to respond to these gifts with our whole being. Faith is a trustful and loving self-commitment to God, the source and goal of all good; and Christian life is the creative and faithful concretization of the basic act of faith.

Faith means wholeness and salvation to the extent that it is filled with hope and trust and bears fruit in love for the life of the world. If it is active in love, faith is truly a fundamental option. Hope and love do not belong only to the later unfolding of faith; they are an essential part of faith as a fundamental option. The unfolding of these three virtues — faith, hope and love — understood as integration of faith and life, occurs in the choir of virtues.[80]

With his love, God gives us everything as a sign of the very freedom of his love and as a gracious and simultaneous appeal to join with him in his love for all creatures. Therefore we can describe the shape of the Christian fundamental option ·as love of God above all things and love of our fellowmen according to the measure and mode in which God has shown his love for us in Jesus Christ.

The integration of faith and life through the various virtues was treated in the scholastic tradition under the heading, "Charity as form of all virtues". This traditional approach can be better understood and will gain depth if it is seen in the spectrum of the fundamental option and, at the same time, in the perspective of integration of faith and life.

G. Gilleman has made an important contribution to this better understanding in the perspective of redeemed and redeeming love.[81] While he does not use our key concept of fundamental option, he does stress some identical points: that faith as loving response is wholly a gift of God; that love is not only added as a new quality but is already inborn in man's heart and unfolds under God's grace; that the influence of charity goes far beyond conceptual knowledge and explicit reflection; that, where there is recognition that everything arises from the depths of the human heart, the virtues are understood as mediation of the one basic and all-embracing power of love.[82] Thus, all the virtues are an unfolding of the total beautiful picture of life in Christ, with Christ in our midst, and with his love as the basic and unifying force.

Love is not structureless. It is not mere sentiment nor a vague option. It has a countenance, and it is through the unified diversity of all the Christian virtues that love gives witness and integration to faith and life.

Love is not in the first place a commandment. Faith that bears fruit in love for the life of the world is a gift. It is the innermost shape of the redeemed person; it is Christ's sharing his love with his disciples and thus writing his all-embracing love in their hearts. Thus, love is not one commandment among many others; it is the great commandment, the one that gives light and life to all the virtues that respond to God's various commands.[83] One cannot know the countenance of love as it is revealed in Jesus Christ without knowing the virtues that respond to various spheres of values; and one cannot know the virtues and spheres of values without seeing them in the one great order of love, as St. Augustine emphasized so consistently.

Another traditional way of approaching the matter of integration of faith and life was to advise frequent renewal not only of the good purpose but also of the "pious intention" such as "Everything for the love of God, everything to the glory of God". Good spiritual theology has always understood that constant renewal of the good purpose and intention must not be just an addition to our daily actions, and that repetition does not suffice for a true synthesis of life. Not only should there be renewal of the individual motifs and the unifying leitmotifs but also vigilance to keep the fundamental intention alive and to relate it vitally to one's activities and decisions.[84] The renewal of the all-embracing intention and of particular good purposes should go hand in hand with watchfulness over our mixed motives. It is an ongoing effort to reach the beatitude of those who are pure in heart.[85]

We should bring the unconscious and semi-conscious motives into the full light of our faith. Alphonse Auer who, in all his writings, gives particular attention to the integration of faith and life, understands the renewal of the good intention as a purposeful meditation in view of the various situations and activities of our life.[86]

What counts is not the number of repetitions of the good intention but the depth and intensity with which we bring our daily life into the sphere of the fundamental option.[87] Although a meaningful renewal of our intention, along with renewal of concrete purposes, might be useful and frequently necessary, the moral and religious value of our acts can reach the highest level only when the fundamental option so pervades our vision and our energies that the pure motives and important decisions arise spontaneously from the depth in which the Spirit moulds and guides us.

Viktor Frankl, who has given great attention to the unifying force of ultimate meaning in our lives, speaks of the unconscious God in us, especially in view of the interaction between the spiritual and existential centre of our life and the transformation of all the layers of our psychic life.[88] It is on this level of integration and depth that the exercise of both liberty and fidelity displays the quality of creativity.

The transformation of the whole of life, where redeemed love finds its true countenance, and our heart, touched to its

depths by the Holy Spirit, yields its abundant fruit, is what
St. Augustine envisioned. The Holy Spirit works, above all,
through the power of our fundamental option, and thus our
life bears the harvest of the Spirit in "love, joy, peace, patience,
kindness, goodness, fidelity, gentleness and self-control" (Gal
5:22).

4. Praise of virtue

Max Scheler, presenting the image of virtue in his personalistic value ethics, is convinced that he can show that virtue
is not a "toothless and loveless old spinster".[89] The truly virtuous
person does not gaze at his own perfection, nor does he make
his individual happiness his main purpose. While Scheler sees
that man has to struggle for his synthesis and wholeness, he
gives special attention to the person who loves virtue — loves
the good — not so much in order to grow richer in goodness
but, rather, because of his inner wealth of goodness. He blames
Immanuel Kant not only for his emphasis on duty instead of
response to the attractive good but also for giving preference
to the difficult decisions where man has to labour and struggle.
"Only vice or the lack of virtue renders the doing of good
difficult or toilsome, whereas strength of virtue imparts to every
good action a certain sweetness of life and light which calls to
mind the blithesomeness and beauty of a lovely bird fluttering
in the sunlight".[90]

It is true that the acquisition of virtue in a sinful world
presupposes the sweat and toil of ongoing effort, but the pain
and the effort do not constitute the virtue. They cannot produce
it for it is, above all else, "a free gift of grace for whose joyful
acceptance all effort and strain of will are only the necessary
preparation".[91]

Abraham Maslow discovers in the spiritually healthy person
who has had "peak experience" a vision of gratitude, a perception of the gift character of all life.[92] Such a person is one
who perceives life in the light of a good and deeply rooted
fundamental option. What makes that person most creative is
the glad acceptance of the gift. He knows that within him there
is a dynamic "towards unity of personality, towards spontaneous
expressiveness, towards full individuality and identity, towards

seeing the truth rather than being blind, towards being creative, towards being good and a lot else; that is, the human being is so constructed that he presses towards fuller and fuller being; and this means pressing towards what most people would call good values, towards serenity, kindness, courage, knowledge, honesty, love, unselfishness and goodness".[93]

Equally, Confucius, the great pedagogue, presents the loftiest virtues as the gift of Tao, a gift of heaven. "The four greatest gifts heaven has bestowed on the wise people are benevolence, gentleness, justice and prudence".[94]

What scholastic theology has taught about the virtues as infused by the Holy Spirit and acquired by human endeavour might be seen in a new light. The person who is truly open to the Spirit sees everything in the dimension of gratuitousness and graciousness. He does not appropriate virtue to his own glory but renders thanks. He is careful not to desire, to say or to do anything that he cannot offer to the Lord as a part and sign of his gratitude. The dimension in which we especially see the promptings of the Holy Spirit is the fundamental option. Through vital faith in the Spirit who renews the hearts of people and the face of the earth, the person's whole inner and outer life comes truly under the influence of the Spirit. Everything is perceived and honoured as gift, and no gift is lost where a person or a community lives truly on the level of the Spirit. Hence, at that focal point where the Spirit draws the whole person to himself creativity and fidelity gain their strength.[95]

VII. THE FUNDAMENTAL OPTION AND THE ESCHATOLOGICAL VIRTUES

The four cardinal virtues are by no means characteristic of biblical ethics. They are taken from the Greek culture in a creative effort by the evangelizing Church to be faithful to the promptings of the Lord of history in that culture. The purpose was to bring home the valuable ethos of those who turned to Christ.[96] However, the emphasis of the Bible is on the eschatological virtues. Revelation understands man as a partner of God in the ongoing history of creation and redemption. My intention, here, is to show that a return to the biblical vision can generate and release energies of creative liberty and fidelity in today's world.

1. Gratitude — Humility

At the centre of Christian life is the Eucharist in which we join our Redeemer, Christ, in thanksgiving and praise to the Father when we celebrate together the memorial of the Lord's incarnation, life, death and resurrection, looking forward to his coming. As believers, we perceive all the past history, including God's promise for the present and the future, as undeserved gift. The Christian outlook, therefore, combines the two inseparable attitudes of gratitude and humility. We look to God from whom we have received everything, and while we praise him for his *agape* we come to share in his divine self-giving love towards those who "come from below".

Christian humility is "an inner spiritual sharing of the grand and unique movement of God in Christ, in which he freely renounces the splendour of his majesty in order to dwell among men as one of them, manifesting himself as the free and blessed servant of every human person and all creatures".[97] Humility is, therefore, the virtue not only of the creature-and-sinner status; it also belongs to the status of the Son who is the Man for all people and of those who share in the mission of the Master. It is, as it were, the fundamental option of Christ, Servant of God and of men, to free humankind from pride and arrogance by being the Servant of all; and this becomes grace and norm for our fundamental option.

Our bearing should arise from our life in Christ Jesus, "for the divine nature was his from the first; yet he did not prize his equality with God but made himself nothing, assuming the nature of a slave, bearing the human likeness, revealed in human shape, he humbled himself and in obedience accepted even death, death on a cross" (Phil 2:5-8).

Christ's humility does not spring from baseness or inferiority but flows from the heights above, from the inner wealth and freedom of God's love for us. In the words of St. Augustine, it is God "who descends from heaven by the weight of his love".[98] God does not fear or suffer loss if, in his love, he stoops down to his creatures. Only a miserable creature in arrogant pride seeks presumptuous superiority. "All pride is beggar's pride".[99] Whoever, in profound gratitude, knows the wealth of God's love in us follows the bold way of love for the little and the least. No bolder event of love is possible than the incarnation of the Word of God and the Lord's total freedom for sinners.

Christian humility is sustained by a grateful memory of what the Lord has done for us. That is why the believer allows the poor who "comes from below but is sent from above" to impose on him, according to the gifts God has bestowed on him and the needs of the poor. Those whose lives are shaped by the memorial of the Lord in the Eucharistic celebration remember, in the concrete realities of their life, that the Lord did not come to be served but to serve. "I am in your midst as he who serves" (Lk 22:27).

Humility in gratitude is at the heart of the basic beatitude. "How blessed are those who, by the Spirit, know their dependence on God; the kingdom of heaven is theirs" (Mt 5:3). Receiving everything as gift of the one Father to be shared with all his children according to their needs, they share gratefully, empowered by the Holy Spirit. The life-song of Mary, praising this mystery of divine humility revealed in the incarnation of Christ, is the response of the faithful one. "So tenderly has he looked upon his servant, lowly as she is, for from this day forth all generations will count me blessed, so wonderfully has he dealt with me, the Lord, the mighty One . . . The arrogant of heart and mind, he has put to rout but the humble have been lifted high" (Lk 1:38-52).

In his first address following his election, Pope John XXIII touched the hearts of many believers when he voiced the programme of his Petrine ministry in view of Christ the Servant: "The cardinal virtue and the precept that draws all the others after it is the Lord's word, 'Learn from me for I am gentle and humble-hearted' " (Mt 11:29).[100] Humility in gratitude opens us to the grace and truth of Christ. Insofar as we humbly open our hearts to him, we learn from him, the Servant of God and man, and share in his wisdom, truth and grace.

Humility before God is praise of his mercy: I, a sinner, have been lifted up by God; God has stooped down in incomprehensible love to me. Thus, humility turns our eyes away from our sinfulness to blissful contemplation of the goodness and mercy of God. In the basic "knowing" that permeates all our moral and religious knowledge, we rejoice in our total dependence upon God. And in this total dependence, the most profound and lofty freedom is born. We see that freedom itself, and all that we have and are comes from God, inviting us to use everything faithfully and creatively for the building up of his kingdom on earth.

A sinful fundamental option for pride and arrogance is followed by disintegration and emptiness. Gradually, it draws all one's faculties into the same alienation. "The proud person comes to exalt himself by perpetually gazing into the depths in order to feel he is towering in the heights over and above others. He actually sinks lower into the abyss while he over-compensates for the loss by looking down on others, so that he must fancy himself actually rising higher, though he is constantly falling. He does not realize that the abyss, with its fatal fascination, is gradually drawing him down as he continues his gaze, and in his illusion fancies that he is rising ever higher above it. Thus, gradually, the angel falls, lured into the pit by the pride of his gaze".[101]

St. Augustine praises God because he comes down from heaven to earth for our salvation; the Incarnate Word of God makes himself freest servant and thus raises up humanity to the heights. "It is an essential element of humility that it directs the heart to what is above, but it is an essential element of self-exaltation that it depresses the heart. It is, indeed, para-doxical that pride is directed to that which is below us, humility to that which is exalted above us".[102]

In his utter humility and gratitude, Jesus is free to fulfil the will of the Father under all circumstances, even unto death on a cross. The humble disciple of Christ will never be a slave to others for the sake of honours. He will not bow in cowardice, for he is willing to bear scorn in the following of the crucified. Thus, he upholds self-respect and keeps that honour which is essential for effective labour in the kingdom of Christ.

Humility is a fundamental gift of the Holy Spirit, the giver of life. "It is the motion of a constantly inward dying in ourselves so that Christ may live in us".[103] Through humility, one's heart is free for the value, beauty and strength of divine truth, whereas pride shuts itself off from every truth which does not serve its own self-enhancement. Without gratitude and humility, there is no liberation for life and truth in Jesus Christ. "I praise you Father, Lord of heaven and earth, for these things that remain hidden from the learned and the wise, you have revealed them to the simple. Yes, Father, I thank you that such was your choice" (Lk 10:21-22; cf. Mt 11:25-26).

Pride produces an unhealthy memory, forgetful of all the good. It also prevents man's heart from a saving sorrow for sins while it constantly uncovers what is wrong with others. A grateful humility helps us to discover in ourselves and in others the inner resources that come from the Spirit. Pastoral experience frequently notes that while pride gradually takes hold of all of man's energies, blocking and distorting them, humility and gratitude gradually foster all those attitudes that embody the right fundamental option.

2. The creativity of hope

While gratitude and humility exploit all the wealth of the past through a grateful memory, hope opens the horizons of the future. It brings us into contact with Christ who is the Way, and is the One who was, who is and will come.[104] Hope gives us clear orientation and purpose as co-actors in the ongoing creation and redemption. It turns our eyes to the absolute and abiding future in God and makes us clearsighted about the proximate steps to take.

In hope we not only can dare to dream dreams and allow imagination to picture utopias. Christian hope is realistic, since it unites us with the Lord of history, with Christ who is our open future. It guarantees continuity in our fundamental option for ultimate meaning and the ultimate goal. The direction is visible in Christ's passion, death, resurrection and ascension, and in the mission of the Holy Spirit. Hope frees us from a static clinging to the past or to the present moment. By inscribing in us the dynamics of God's promises and the goal-commandments, it inspires our engagement in the world. It gives also a new meaning to the limitative laws and commandments, since we see them now as criteria for what would block our way into the future and our configuration with Christ.

Hope makes us eager for growth and for ongoing conversion. It never says, "This is enough", for it bears in itself the energies of divine love and the dynamics of faith. "There is nothing love cannot face, there is no limit to its faith, its hope and its endurance" (1 Cor 13:7).

Hope is faithful. As our past is marked by God's fidelity in all its vicissitudes, so hope turns our heart and will to his promises. It makes of the believer a living gospel, a prophecy for the better world and the better future that will come when all people will unite their energies through the same hope in Christ. It is inseparably wedded to saving solidarity, since Christ is our Hope, our incarnate solidarity, the covenant of the people. Therefore, my hope is your hope and our hope is the hope of all our brothers and sisters in Christ Jesus. Through hope and its essential mark of solidarity, Christ unites us as his co-workers and co-artists for a better future.

3. Vigilance

Through vigilance, the believer is creatively involved in the present history of salvation and redemption. As harvest of gratitude for the past and consequent hope for the future, vigilance sets him free from distraction, superficiality and wishful thinking, and gives him a prophetic vision in which he discovers the present opportunity. Thus, he embodies the prophet's prayer, "Lord, here I am, call me; Lord, here I am, send me".

The virtue of vigilance corresponds to the biblical key concept of kairos, hora, "signs of the times".[105] Its specifically Christian dynamic is beautifully synthesized in Paul's Epistle to the Ephesians. "Awake sleeper, rise from the dead and Christ will shine upon you. Be most careful then how to conduct yourselves: like sensible people, not like simpletons; make fullest use of the present opportunity, for these are evil days. So do not be fools but try to discern what the will of the Lord is. Do not give way to drunkenness and the dissipation that goes with it, but let the Holy Spirit fill you" (Eph 5:14-18).

In vigilance we will not waste our time complaining about bad days or wishfully thinking "if only". We will always discover first what the Lord's handwriting is, before we turn our attention to the crooked lines on which he writes. We will grate-fully discover the signs of the times that are positive and helpful; then we can also face the challenging signs.[106]

Through the virtue of vigilance we see the present moment in the light of the great moments of past and future history, in the light of the incarnation, of the great hour when Christ redeemed us, of the Paschal Mystery, and in the hope of the final coming of Christ. If we see our great decisions and everyday decisions in this perspective of the history of salvation, then they will more easily reach the core of our basic freedom and basic intention. This will give us greater openness for creativity and, at the same time, guarantee the continuity which responds to God's fidelity in the past and the firmness of his promises.

Vigilance gives us discernment about priorities but it also directs our attention to the little steps and the temporary dif-ficulties, the necessary hiatuses that prepare for more important future steps and decisions.

The ability to see the present moment in the light of the great moments of salvation history enables one to enter into that history as co-creator, freed from that individualism that enslaves one in sloth and collective sinfulness. We can grasp the meaning and enter into the dynamics of the present moment only if we are living on the level of Christ, the covenant of the people, the incarnate solidarity. Only in communion and saving solidarity can we decipher the signs of the times and respond to them.

The eschatological virtue of vigilance discovers also the profound meaning of temporary frustrations and of suffering. If we are willing to share in Christ's suffering, then everything is a means in the hands of the divine artist to transform us into his true image and likeness.

4. *Serenity and joy*

Through the eschatological virtues our fundamental option for God and good enter more fully into the light and life of the Paschal Mystery. If the death of Christ is operative in us, then his resurrection and the power of his Spirit are also operating. Then, in the midst of distress we can say with the priest and prophet Esdras, "The joy of the Lord is our strength" (Neh 8:10). Through these virtues we accept the joys and the burden of each moment without anguish for the future (cf. Mt 6:25). Only those who lose sight of the horizon and the perspectives of the history of salvation can be worried about petty things. Serenity and joy, the harvest of the other eschatological virtues and the gift of the Spirit, keep us free from anguish and useless worry, from slavish fear and misdirected scrupulosity.[107]

The gift of the fullness of time is peace, reconciliation. If we are grateful for these gifts we can joyfully commit ourselves to the work of reconciliation, peace and justice. "Whoever, in obedience to Christ, seeks first the kingdom of God will, as a consequence, receive a stronger and purer love for helping all his brothers and for perfecting the work of justice under the inspiration of charity".[108]

The eschatological virtues must, of necessity, be seen as gifts of the Holy Spirit and as harvest of the Spirit. They mean openness to the promptings of the Spirit, and thus join us with God's own creative liberty and fidelity in the work of creation and redemption.

In view of all this, it seems evident that a genuine biblical renewal of moral theology and our mission in the world requires more thorough attention to the eschatological virtues, not only in separate contexts but in the whole vision and synthesis.

VIII. ABORTIVE FUNDAMENTAL OPTIONS

A moral theology that stresses creative liberty and fidelity cannot avoid warning against some fundamental intentions or leitmotifs which, in spite of their pious appearance, can in reality be abortive choices. Although I realize that all of us need further liberation from the bondage of falsehood, there can be a kind of fundamental option that is so definitely under that bondage that a healthy development of fundamental attitudes is almost impossible.

1. Individualism: "Save your soul"

A conversion from sinfulness to the search for ultimate meaning should not neglect the legitimate self-interest of the individual. Our conscience is a cry for personal wholeness and, thus, for our salvation. Moreover, it would be an illusion to think that the most lofty and pure motives would necessarily be the most effective for an initial conversion. Therefore, it is not false to preach, "Save your soul".

However, it must be clear from the very beginning that our concern is not with disembodied souls or with individual salvation alone. It has to be understood that our own wholeness and salvation are included in the greater reality of wholeness and salvation of all of humankind. One cannot find one's own salvation, freedom, dignity and final friendship with God without equal concern for the salvation of all. Furthermore, salvation can never be severed from the all-embracing reality of God's glory. The legitimate self-interest must, therefore, be appealed to in such a way that the person learns from the outset to adore God in Spirit and truth.

As we have seen earlier, self-perfection is not a fitting leit-motif nor a fitting fundamental option in a religious and especially in a distinctively Christian ethics. Self-realization or self-perfection is indeed a legitimate interest and a great good, as long as it is seen in the proper perspective; but in the progress towards maturity, a person gains an ever clearer intuition that self-actualization means, above all, self-transcendence. Our innate desire for happiness, and even more for joy and beatitude, does assist our progress in love of God and neighbour. However, the initial option must be not only deepened but also purified.

St. Bernard describes this journey very profoundly: "In the first place, the individual loves himself for his own sake ... However, when he finds that he cannot subsist by himself alone, he begins the search for God by faith and love, as necessary for himself. Thereby, on the second level, he loves God for his own sake but not so fully for God's sake ... But once having tested how sweet God is, he passes on to the third degree where he loves God not just on account of himself but truly for God's own sake. On this level of love of God he finds stability, and I doubt if anyone can be found in this life who has attained the fourth degree of love so that he loves himself only on account of God".[109]

The religious educator must know this dynamic of development. If it is ignored or stifled, the fundamental option will be easily aborted. It must also be realized that to love God for his own sake means to join him in his fatherly love for all people. Our genuine and distinctively Christian option is for Christ, the Covenant of the people, and thus for the one God and Father of all.

2. A static misinterpretation of the fundamental option

When a person truly turns to God in adoration, he not only outgrows the danger of individualism and self-centredness but also the equally great danger of a static concern. We have seen repeatedly that religion, under the patronage of knowledge of dominion and control, greatly endangers its wholeness and dynamics.

There can be in religion so much concern for social status or for the status quo that the good is identified with the external order and with inner and outer security. In this approach the image of God becomes immobile, impersonal, even boring. The clinging to the past and the present situation creates security complexes of all kinds. People seek certainty or, rather, assurance over and against truth, over and against sincerity and freedom in the search for ever better knowledge of God and man. Thus, they are never freed from anguish and fear. In spite of the religious appearance, their adherence to the Church and her faith for security's sake can betray an unwillingness to believe in the God of history, the living God who is love and life.

3. A choice of false images of freedom and fidelity

The above mentioned types of abortive fundamental option have much to do with faulty understanding of freedom and fidelity. The "fundamental option" can become an option for security under law that leads to an idolatrous cult of laws and leads away from the all-embracing law of grace, faith and love. It may become a choice of external fidelity to the powers — including religious powers — whereby fidelity towards the living God is gradually stifled and eliminated.

IX. FUNDAMENTAL OPTION AGAINST GOD AND THE GOOD

1. *Mortal and grave sin*

After having considered abortive fundamental options or those doomed to failure if they are not purified and deepened, we now consider the horrifying possibility that man can, with sufficient freedom, choose false gods against the true God. Such a fundamental option coincides with the theological concept of mortal sin. This does not mean that all grave sins are a fundamental option against God and the good, just as not all grave ailments bring death. But one who has committed a mortal sin and perseveres in it is in a state of death.

I want to repeat my conviction that small children or even pre-adolescents, although truly able to move in the direction which, through God the Creator and through the Holy Spirit, is written into their hearts, cannot normally be able to commit a mortal sin: that is, to turn away from God and good in the very depth of their hearts and with so great freedom that they deserve not only the death penalty but everlasting death.

We are not speaking here of the many sins but of *the sin* that underlies the many sins. Paul, in Romans 5-7 and frequently elsewhere, makes a distinction between *hamartia* (sin in the singular) and *hamartiai* (the many sins).

Sin, in its fully malicious sense, is turning away from God, and it destroys the fundamental option for the good self-commitment to the service of God and love of neighbour. We have to keep in mind that it is impossible simply to distinguish between serious and non-serious sins. By its very nature, sin is always serious. The venial sins that gradually lead to the extreme danger of a mortal sin (fundamental option against God) are to be considered as very serious.

There is again an important difference between the grave venial sin of a person who is still in the state of grace and any grave sin of one who has already abandoned God's friendship. In the enemy of God there is that utter poison of his inimical fundamental option affecting each sin, whereas the person whose fundamental option is for friendship with God does not have this mark of enmity in the depth of his being. However, if there is sickness in a person and he does not care for healing, that very carelessness can become the cause of his final ruin. So it is with venial sin, especially the grave venial sins.

2. Gradual or sudden loss of God's friendship

By now it should be clear that the fundamental option has not the same firmness and strength in all individuals. An option that is already articulated in fundamental attitudes, in a coherent chorus of virtues, cannot easily be removed. In this case we can only agree with Thomas Aquinas' assertion that the state of grace cannot so easily be lost.[110] According to St. Thomas, habitual grace gives so strong a basic inclination to the good that one act cannot easily destroy it. However, he also acknowledges that it is finally through one act that the friendship of God can be lost.

The manuals of moral theology that did not consider the fundamental option or give close attention to the way God's grace operates within us frequently gave the impression that an average Christian can fall seven times a day into mortal sin and rise from it. This is psychologically almost unthinkable. However, the fundamental option can be reversed, and all the more easily when it is not yet affirmed in all the layers of our being by corresponding attitudes (virtues).[111]

Even though essentially sincere, the fundamental option can also be in danger of reversal if it has those negative qualities which we considered "abortive". Such a reversal of the basic commitment from God to idols, from genuine love to an inverted self-love, is a weighty act. Normally, the way is prepared by many imperfections and venial sins, acts that do not fully respond to God's grace, and failures to do the good that is within one's reach. Venial sins, which can be less or more grave, may first weaken some of the important virtues or fundamental attitudes, but they also indirectly weaken the rootedness of the fundamental option.

We may consider two extreme types of how one loses the friendship of God. In one case it can be through the mortal sin committed by a person who is still clear-sighted, has a sharp awareness that a certain act contradicts the friendship of God, and nevertheless decides in favour of the act that reaches into the depth of his heart and shapes his whole being. The other extreme could be the result of many venial sins: through frequent abuse of God's grace, and an increasing laxity that deadens more and more the person's sensibility for the good, his gratitude to God, and responsibility for the needs of others, there finally comes the point where the fundamental option is reversed through a free act of choice, although without great sensitivity; as if a slight wind had blown out a candle that was already burnt down. Therefore, we should not see the fundamental option in a stationary frame or as automatically self-sustaining. All decisions set in motion a certain process of development either for the good or for evil. But it should not be denied that there are moments in a person's history when a concrete act may reverse the fundamental option.[112]

Once the basic sin that involves a fundamental option is committed, all the sins share in this underlying misery and malice. They partially flow from it and partially confirm and solidify it.[113]

3. Can a relatively small matter be occasion of mortal sin?

St. Augustine initiated a long-lasting dispute among theologians by asking whether an ordinary lie that does not damage anyone can be a mortal sin, if it is the lie of a perfect man. He left the question open.

Moral theology for the use of controllers denied such a possibility because the theologians thought they could objectively determine the border-line between mortal and venial sin, according to the gravity of the matter. Some moralists, however, asserted that in sexual morality, everything is a grave matter. They did not take into account the enormous diversity of levels of development and moral sensitivity.

My conviction is that an objective border-line, valid for all, between mortal and venial sin can never be determined. We can, however, say that a relatively small matter normally cannot be the object of a mortal sin. The emphasis is on *relative*, which means in proportion to the moral level, the maturity, awareness and full use of freedom of the individual person. What one person does not consider as a grave matter can, for a very sensitive person, appear to be absolutely irreconcilable with God's friendship.[114] A relatively small act of goodness will normally not turn a bad fundamental option into a good one, although it can be a first step in that direction. Similarly, each sin, if not soon repented, has the frightening possibility of being a first or next step towards downfall.

4. *Can sin committed by mere weakness entail a fundamental option?*

Our response to this question greatly depends on how we define the sin committed by weakness. If we understand it as a grave sin by a fundamentally good person who, taken by surprise, did not withstand the temptation but will continue in his good intention,[115] then I would simply say that mortal sin is excluded because this definition of "sin of weakness" infers the very persistence of the good fundamental option. If our whole understanding of fundamental option is right, then we can simply say that where the option for good and for God is not uprooted, there is no mortal sin even though there can be a grave venial sin.

Quite different is the problem if we define as "sin of weakness" all sins that are not committed in direct rebellion against God. In this hypothesis, the full malice would exist only if the person has directly and explicitly the intention to turn away from God or to seek his ultimate goal in evil. If only these sins were mortal, then there would not be many of them. However, a person can fully realize the malice of one's sin — that it contradicts the honour of God and the solidarity of people — yet *regretfully* commits it because such a sinner freely prefers his own arbitrariness, egotism, pride or satisfaction. Sins of weakness understood in this way can well be mortal because they can truly entail a fundamental option for evil, in basic freedom.

For a reasonable approach to this problem, a less punctual understanding of great decisions for good or evil seems to be necessary. These decisions are not momentary happenings. Everything that prepares such a "sin of weakness" and results from it should be taken into consideration. If the momentary failure, even in grave matters, is not preceded by a series of offences of infidelity to God's grace, and not followed by a substantial weakening of the good direction, then there is at least a high probability that the sin of weakness was not mortal, although it might have been a *grave* venial sin.

H. Reiners warns, however, against an oversimplification in this kind of reasoning. The fundamental option that has formed fundamental dispositions for the good, as response to the various spheres of virtue, could cease even though the dispositions or attitudes continue somehow.[116] However, where the fundamental intention turns to evil, the all-embracing disposition for the good cannot remain.

No human being can give an accurate definition of how much freedom and awareness is necessary for a mortal sin that always means a sin proportionate to eternal damnation by an all-holy and all-merciful God. It is my conviction that there can be no mortal sin without a fundamental option or intention that turns one's basic freedom towards evil. And we have at least approximate criteria for determining whether a person lives with a fundamental option against God. That is, to presume that the person has no such option if, soon after the fall, he or she has genuine sorrow for the sin and continues to strive to please God and to do what is right.

X. CONVERSION IN THE LIGHT OF THE FUNDAMENTAL OPTION

The human person is not born with a basic indifference or neutrality towards good and evil. It is true that we are born into a sinful world from which many temptations and bad influences arise, but it is a more basic truth that we are the good creation of the all-holy God and are more deeply marked by the reality of redemption than of sin. The child is, from the beginning, under the influence of the Holy Spirit who renews the face of the earth and the hearts of people. Nevertheless, each human being, except Jesus in his humanity, and his mother, is in profound need of purification from evil tendencies. Only those who, by a fundamental option, have turned away from God and from good are in need of radical conversion — a change in their basic freedom and knowledge, in their fundamental intention — but everyone is constantly in need of God's gracious gifts, of the promptings of the Holy Spirit, and of grateful acceptance of these gifts in view of an ongoing conversion.

1. *Basic conversion and justification*

The change of the fundamental option from evil to good is a weighty act and is, in a unique way, both a gift of God and a free acceptance of his gift by the person. Justification happens through the attractive power of God's love, who draws the person to himself. Sanctifying grace or justification "occurs in that centre of the person in which he is totally present to himself, in undivided self-awareness and freedom".[117] But the preparation for the final acceptance of the attractive love of God is also the work of God's grace. It always builds on the gifts of God that are still present in the person, even though he has made a fundamental intention against true love. There is always an inner core where the image of God is present even though it may be terribly distorted. And there are always some good inclinations although there may not be truly affirmed good dispositions. Again and again, the saving grace of God reaches into the depth of the human heart to find acceptance in the person's basic freedom, and from there to work the transfiguration, the transformation of the whole person.[118]

There are many ways by which God's attractive love and graciousness can touch man's innermost being. One way could be by the fear of punishment; but only if one's heart allows God to attract it by his love can the great revision happen, the transformation of all of one's attitudes and their unification through one's new fundamental option. There can be a kind of "fear of God" that means that the person indeed already fears nothing more than to lose the friendship of God. However, a mere slavish fear is not yet the sign of justification and of an effective fundamental option for God and good.

2. *Continuing conversion*

The ongoing conversion which is necessary for all of us is the effective radiation of the fundamental option or, rather, of

the "justification by grace" into all our faculties and attitudes.
God wants us whole and wholly, in full integrity and integration,
with all our energies and faculties drawn into his love. Although
the fundamental option is, in its intention, a total self-surrender
to God and to the kingdom of good, in its realization it is
"not a complete self-commitment of the whole person" [119] until
our whole being is transformed and unified by divine love. We
could easily deceive ourselves into thinking that we are already
"a completely unified person". [120] There remains always the need
to struggle against the concupiscent ego, the selfish self that
remains hidden in some corners of our being. The fundamental
intention is proven genuine in the deepening awareness that we
are in need of further growth, integration and purification.

We are not pure spirits. The Holy Spirit touches and reaches
us in our innermost being, but he calls us as we are, with all
our life history which has left us with an inner wealth but also
with scars and wounds, distortions and idiosyncracies. The actual
realization of the fundamental option is, time and again, an
open-ended compromise of the basic option with our past
history. [121] I insist on "open-ended". It is a sign of God's
presence in us if we are never satisfied with anything less than
the total transfiguration of our life for the love of God and of
fellowmen.

3. *The experience or knowledge about the state of grace*

There are two quite different questions. The first is about
a concrete act: was it a mortal or a venial sin? The second,
which we face here, is a more important and wholesome question:
Am I in the friendship of God? Am I in the right direction?
It has to do with whether we can know that we are in the "state
of grace", a question which played a major role in the past
history of theology. A better understanding of the fundamental
option may shed some light on this.

The Council of Trent gives an important warning for those
who want to assert absolute knowledge and certainty about
their being in the state of grace. [122] This doctrine excludes, above
all, self-righteousness and complacency. We can approach the
existential question only while we are in the process of ongoing
conversion, for the question of our salvation can never be posed

outside of this dynamic process. But, while searching for God with all our heart, and expecting everything from his gracious mercy, we may sometimes reach a profound transcendental self-awareness, not for self-complacency but for the praise of God and in view of a more unified and complete response to all his gifts.

A person's own state of conscience can never be so completely and directly the object of his knowledge that he can judge, as it were, from outside. There is never a certainty comparable to scientific proof. However, there can be a profound existential knowledge that is not posed but "given" in the act of love for God and neighbour.[123] It is in the peak experiences of contemplation and action, in that contemplation that leads to action for justice and peace, and that kind of action that leads to a deeper contemplation, that we come to "know" in the depth of our heart that the Lord is gracious to us and to all who seek him. It is a transcendental knowledge, a profound religious experience which far from tempting us to self-complaisance, urges us on to yet more fervent action and contemplation in deepened humility, gratitude and love.

Beyond these special peak experiences in the midst of our striving towards God, there can be some kind of conjecture based on concrete signs, such as the fidelity of our life of prayer, our greater sensitivity to the needs of others and readiness to allow the poor to impose on us, through which we come somehow to a reflexive judgment about ourselves.[124]

But we never allow ourselves any judgment about whether or not another person is in the state of grace, for we can never know his inner disposition or the kind of compromise he can make between good will and the idiosyncracies and conditionings of his life. The very desire to make ourselves judge about another's inner disposition can only diminish our self-awareness of salvation. We experience salvation in gratitude for God's mercy and in action that helps our fellowmen to discover their own inner goodness and resources, the signs of God's saving presence.

NOTES

1 Besides works later repeatedly referred to, I mention books of theologians who take the newer insights of psychology, esp. that of development, into account: H. Kramer, *Die sittliche Vorentscheidung*. Würzburg, 1970; Id., *Unwiderrufliche Entscheidungen im Leben des Christen. Ihre moralanthropologischen und moraltheologischen Voraussetzungen*, Paderborn, 1974; F. Furger, *Sittliche Praxis. Vorentscheidung - Vorsatz - Wollen*, Augsburg, 1975; K. Demmer, *Die Lebensentscheidung. Ihre moraltheologischen Grundlagen*, Paderborn, 1974; Id., *Entscheidung und Verhängnis*, Paderborn, 1976; the latest and most comprehensive treatment offered by F. Herràes Vegas, *La opción fundamental*, Salamanca, 1978 (I have greatly profited by directing this dissertation presented to the Academia Alfonsiana, Rome, 1977); J.B. Libanio, *Peccato e opzione fondamentale*, Assisi, 1977. For the traditional treatment of the choice of the ultimate end see: J. Maritain, *Raison et raisons*, Paris, 1947, 131-165 ("La dialectique immanente du premier act de liberté"); S. Dianich, *L'opzione fondamentale nel pensiero di S. Tommaso*, Brescia, 1968.

2 J. Fuchs, *Human Values*, 94.

3 Already here we can see the connection between the understanding of the fundamental option and the role ascribed to ongoing conversion.

4 K. Rahner, *Grace in Freedom*, 213.

5 Cf. Reiners, *Grundintention und sittliches Tun*, Freiburg/Br., 1966.

6 R. Niebuhr, *Radical Monotheism and Western Culture*, New York, 1960.

7 Fuchs, l.c., 97.

8 Rahner, l.c., 214.

9 The vision offered in this chapter will be broadened in chapter VI through the insights of Lawrence Kohlberg, Rollo May and others. There are notable differences among the authors to whom I refer but it is more a matter of complementarity than contradiction. Each has his own "see-level", according to his cultural background, education, experience and expectation, but all have such a broad vision that they can share with Christians and all other humanists. My own effort is to bring these insights home into a distinctively Christian vision of the ultimate goal of our life and the corresponding fundamental option.

10 Cf. E. Fromm, *Man for Himself*, Greenwich, 1969; *The Art of Loving*, New York, 1956; *The Heart of Man: Its Genius for Good and Evil*, New York, 1964.

11 E. Erikson, *Identity: Youth and Crisis*, New York, 1969, 65.

12 E. Erikson, *Childhood and Society*, New York, 2nd ed., 1963, 34.

13 R. Coles, *Erik H. Erikson. The Growth of His Work*, Boston, 1970, 132.

14 Erikson, *Young Man Luther*, New York, 1958, 117/8.

15 Erikson, *Identity*, 91/2.

16 *Young Man Luther*, 253.

17 Cf. esp. *Young Man Luther* and *Gandhi's Truth*, New York, 1969.

18 *Insight and Responsibility*, New York, 1964, 138.

19 *Identity*, 163.

20 *Identity*, 96.

21 *Childhood and Society*, 273; *Identity*, 94.

22 Cf. *Childhood and Society*, 251.

23 D.S. Browning, *Generative Man: Psychoanalytic Perspectives*, Philadelphia, 1973, 65.

24 Cf. *Identity*, 85.

25 *Insight and Responsibility*, 119.

26 *Identity*, 110.

27 Erikson, "Psychological Identity", in *International Encyclopedia of the Social Sciences* 7 (1968), 62.

28 Cf. *Identity*, 159.

[29] *Young Man Luther*. 16.
[30] Cf. *Identity*, 161.
[31] Cf. "Psychological Identity", 61.
[32] *Identity*, 158.
[33] *Insight and Responsibility*, 125.
[34] Cf. "Psychological Identity", 62.
[35] *Young Man Luther*, 242: "In Luther a partially unsuccessful and fragmentary solution of the identity crisis of youth aggravated the crisis of manhood"; cf. also *Gandhi's Truth*.
[36] Cf. *Young Man Luther*.
[37] *Identity*, 257/8.
[38] Cf. Robert Koch C.Ss.R., *Peccato nel Vecchio Testamento*, Rome, 1975.
[39] *Identity*, 174.
[40] Autobiographic Notes, in *The Twentieth Century Sciences*, edited by G. Holton, New York, 1970, 6.
[41] *Identity*, 176.
[42] l.c., 173.
[43] This is a central thesis of A. Maslow. Cf. his book, *Religions, Values and Peak Experiences*, Columbus, Ohio, 1964.
[44] *Childhood and Society*, 263.
[45] Cf. *Insight and Responsibility*, 128.
[46] *Identity*, 139.
[47] *Childhood and Society*, 269; *Identity*, 140.
[48] Cf. E. Spranger, *Types of Men: The Psychology and Ethics of Personality*, Halle, 1925.
[49] S.A. Kierkegaard, *Stages on Life's Way*, New York, 1967. See, in chapter VII, my critique of Kierkegaard's misunderstanding of the intended sacrifice of Isaac by Abraham, an error that led him to the idea that the religious value can request the sacrifice of the highest ethical values.
[50] A. Maslow, *The Farther Reaches of Human Nature*, New York, 1973.
[51] Cf. Viktor Frankl, *Der unbewusste Gott*, Wien, 1948, 28f; *The Doctor of the Soul*, New York, 1965; *Man's Search for Meaning: An Introduction to Logotherapy*, London, 1964.
[52] S.Th., I., q 43, a 5 ad 2: "Verbum spirans amorem".
[53] Cf. J. Fuchs, *Human Values*, 102.
[54] Cf. K. Rahner, *Grace in Freedom*, 213; J.B. Metz, "Befindlichkeit", *L.Th.K.* II (1958), 103.
[55] Augustine, *Sermo* 72, 4 PL 38, 468.
[56] Augustine, *De civitate Dei*, lib 14, c. 7 PL 41, 410.
[57] S.Th., I II, q 89, a 6. Cf. A. Zychinski, "Der wichtigste Akt im Menschenleben, Bemerkungen zu S.Th. I II, q 89 a 6, in *DTh* 31 (1953), 315-327; J. Maritain, "La dialectique du premier acte de liberté", *Nova et Vetera* 20 (1945), 218-235; H. Reiners, *Grundintention und sittliches Tun*, Freiburg/Br., 1966, 15-37. According to Maritain (l.c., 219), the fullness and depth of the first act is so great that in later life it will be reached only seldom, "à des rares et miraculeuses occasions". For us, under the influence of today's psychology, it is difficult to view the first moral act of a child in this way.
[58] R. May, *Man's Quest for Himself*, 165.
[59] J. Fuchs, l.c., 95.
[60] l.c., 96.
[61] Cf. D.J. White, *Decision Methodology. A Formalization of the OR Process*, London-New York, 1975 (with abundant bibliography).
[62] One of the most illumining books on this question is H. Thomae, *Der Mensch in der Entscheidung*, München, 1960 (with much bibliography in English and German language); cf. also J.B. Metz, "Zur kategorialen Differenzierung des Freiheitsvollzugs", in *Gott in Welt* (Festschrift für K. Rahner), Freiburg, 1964, I, 312-414; E. Rothhacker, *Schichten der Persönlichkeit*, Leipzig, 1938.

[63] H. Thomae, *Persönlichkeit. Eine dynamische Interpretation*, 2nd ed., Bonn, 1955, 198.

[64] *Gaudium et spes*, 49-51.

[65] Cf. Fuchs, l.c., 98/99.

[66] R. May, l.c., 220.

[67] l.c., 220.

[68] l.c., 229.

[69] Cf. P. Ernst, "Option vitale. Contribution à une psychologie ascétique de la vocation", *N D Th* 69 (1947), 731-747; 1065-1084; K. Rahner, "über die religiöse Weihe", in *Glaube und Leben* 21 (1948), 407-448.

[70] R. May, l.c., 173.

[71] Cf. J. Gründel, "Vorsatz", in *LThK* 10 (1965), 882; Id., "Vorentscheidung", in *LThK*, 879.

[72] Cf. H. Reiners, *Grundintention und sittliches Tun*, Freiburg, 1966, 52f; S. Dianich, "La corruzione della natura e la grazia nelle opzioni fondamentali", *Scuola catt.* 9 (1964), 209.

[73] For J. Maritain the fundamental intention (option) coincides with the first free rational (moral) act of the child; this is the way he interprets Thomas Aquinas, S.Th., I II, q 89, a 6; cf. J. Maritain, "La dialectique immanente du premier acte de liberté", in *Nova et vetera* 20 (1945), 218-235; Id., *Raison et raisons*, Paris, 1947, 131-165; Id., *Neuf leçons sur les notions premières de la philosophie morale*, Paris, 1949, 119-128. H. Reiners, in his valuable book, *Grundintention und sittliches Tun*, refers frequently to Maritain, without ever taking position regarding his out-dated child-psychology, although all the psychological insights of the author seem to demand it (cf. especially Reiners, 45).

[74] R. May, *Man's Search for Himself*, 67.

[75] Reiners, l.c., 67.

[76] Cf. Fuchs, l.c., 99.

[77] I. Kant, *Anthropologie in pragmatischer Sicht*, ed. Cassierer VIII, 32 (English translation by M.J. Gregor: *Anthropology from a Pragmatic Point of View*, The Hague, 1974). This is one of the most readable books of Kant.

[78] Th. Steinbüchel, *Philosophische Grundlagen der katholischen Sittenlehre*, 4th ed., Düsseldorf, 1950, II, 136.

[79] M. Scheler, "Zur Rehabilitierung der Tugend", in *Vom Umsturz der Werte*, Leipzig, 1919, I, 14.

[80] Cf. H. Reiners, l.c., 143-168; A.J. Falanga, *Charity Form of the Virtues According to Saint Thomas*, Washington, 1948; J. Fuchs, "Die Liebe als Aufbauprinzip der Moraltheologie. Ein Bericht", in *Scholastik* 29 (1954), 79-87; G. Gilleman, *Le primat de la charité en théologie morale. Essai méthodologique*, Bruxelles/Bruges, 2nd ed., 1954; O. Lottin, *Au coeur de la morale chrétienne*, Tournai, 1957, 129-133; R.W. Gleason, *Charity* as the Form of the Virtues, *Irish Th. Q.* 24 (1957), 144-153.

[81] G. Gilleman, l.c., 77-92.

[82] l.c., 100-110.

[83] Cf. K. Rahner, "Das 'Gebot' der Liebe unter den andern Geboten", in *Schriften zur Theologie* V, 494-517.

[84] Cf. K. Rahner, "Gute Meinung", *Schriften zur Theologie* III, 127-154.

[85] Cf. my book *Blessed are the Pure in Heart: Beatitudes*, New York, 1977, *The Beatitudes: Their Personal and Social Implications*, Slough, 1976.

[86] A. Auer, *Weltoffener Christ*, Düsseldorf, 1960, 207. This is also a main concern of my book *Prayer: Integration of Faith and Life*, Notre Dame and Slough, 1975.

[87] Cf. P. Fransen, *Gnade und Auftrag*, Wien-Freiburg-Basel, 161, 104.

[88] Cf. V. Frankl, *Der unbewusste Gott*, Wien, 1948, 28f.

[89] M. Scheler, *Umsturz der Werte*, I, 13.

[90] l.c. 14.

[91] l.c., 18.

[92] Cf. A.H. Maslow, *The Farther Reaches of Human Nature*, New York, 1973, 41-80.

[93] A.H. Maslow, "Psychological Data and Value Theory", in Maslow (ed.), *New Knowledge in Human Values*, Chicago, 1970, 125-126.

[94] *The Four Holy Books of Confucius*, French and Latin translation by S. Coureur S.J., *Les quatre livres*, Ho Kien Fou, 1895, esp. p. 616.

[95] Cf. W.W. Maissner S.J., *Foundation for a Psychology of Grace*, Glen Rock N.J., 1966, 196-222.

[96] Cf. ch. II, Historical sketch of moral theology.

[97] M. Scheler, l.c., I, 18.

[98] *De sancta virginitate* 37f, PL 40, 117: "qui de caelo descendit pondere caritatis".

[99] M. Scheler, l.c., I, 25.

[100] John XXIII, Speech delivered on Nov. 4, 1958 at his installation AAS 50 (1958), 887.

[101] M. Scheler, l.c., I, 22.

[102] Aug., *De civitate Dei*, lib. 14, c. 13, 1 PL 41, 420.

[103] D.v. Hildebrand, *Transformation in Christ*, New York, 1948, 151.

[104] Cf. my book *Hope is the Remedy*, New York and Slough, 1974.

[105] P. Tillich was one of the first to see in *kairos* a key-concept. M.D. Chenu, *L'Evangile dans le temps*, Paris, 1964; Id., Les signes des temps, *Nouv. R. Theol.*, 1965, 29-44.

[106] Cf. my book *Evangelization Today*, Notre Dame/Ind. and Slough, 1974, 7-24. This is a main theme and over-all perspective of the book.

[107] Cf. chapter IV: "The Freedom for which Christ has freed us".

[108] *Gaudium et spes*, 72.

[109] Saint Bernard, *Liber de diligendo Deo*, c. XV, PL 182, 998.

[110] Thomas, *De Veritate*, q 27 a 1 ad 9.

[111] Cf. J. Fuchs, l.c., 102f, 110.

[112] Cf. *Declaration on Certain Questions Concerning Sexual Ethics* of Jan. 15, 1976, by the Congregation for the Doctrine of Faith; text in *Catholic Mind* 74, N. 1302 (April 1976), 52-65; Articles in response cf. R. McCormick S.J., "Notes on Moral Theology", *Theol. Studies* 38 (1977), 147-164.

[113] H. Reiners, l.c., 68.

[114] Cf. my Book *Sin in the Secular Age*, ch. V.

[115] Thus H. Ernst, "De zonde uit swakheid", *Jaarbook* 1958, 18-30; Ernst does not, however, exclude the possibility that sins committed in weakness and because of weakness might be sometimes mortal; he does still equate mortal and serious (grave) sins, while I consider the more frequent situation in which serious sins are still venial sins, just as grave sickness is not the same as death. Cf. also H. Reiners, l.c., 126-135.

[116] H. Reiners, l.c., 135; J. Fuchs, l.c., 110.

[117] J. Fuchs, l.c., 108.

[118] Cf. P. Fransen, *Gnade und Auftrag*, 128.

[119] Fuchs, l.c., 96.

[120] R. May, l.c., 220.

[121] May, l.c.; cf. H. Thomae, *Persönlichkeit*, p 70.

[122] Denz-Sch. 1534f.

[123] Cf. J.B. Metz, "Befindlichkeit", in *LThK* II, 104.

[124] Cf. J. Fuchs, l.c., 108.

Chapter Six

Conscience: the sanctuary of creative fidelity and liberty

The Second Vatican Council makes a programmatic and profound statement on our understanding of conscience. "In the depths of his conscience, the human person detects a law which he does not impose on himself but which holds him to obedience. Always summoning him to love good and avoid evil, the voice of conscience can, when necessary, speak to his heart more specifically: do this, shun that. For man has in his heart a law written by God. To obey it is the very dignity of the person; according to it he will be judged (cf. Rom 2:15-16). Conscience is the most secret core and sanctuary of a person. There he is alone with God whose voice re-echoes in his depths. In a wonderful manner conscience reveals that law which is fulfilled by love of God and neighbour (cf. Mt 22:37-40; Gal 5:14). In fidelity to conscience, Christians are joined with the rest of men in search for truth and for the genuine solution to the numerous problems which arise in the life of individuals and from social relationships. Hence, the more a correct conscience holds sway, the more persons and groups turn aside from blind choice and strive to be guided by objective norms of morality".[1]

I. CONSCIENCE AND DISCIPLESHIP

1. *To know together and be free for each other*

The word 'conscience' derives from the Latin *cum* (together) and *scientia, scire* (to know). Conscience is the person's moral faculty, the inner core and sanctuary where one knows oneself in confrontation with God and with fellowmen. We can confront ourselves reflexively only to the extent that we genuinely encounter the Other and the others.

Within us re-echoes the call of the Word in whom we are created, the call of the Master who invites us to be with him. Our conscience comes to life through this Word that has called us into being and now calls us to be with him as his disciples, through the power of the Holy Spirit, the giver of life.

In the depth of our being, conscience makes us aware that our true self is linked with Christ, and that we can find our unique name only by listening and responding to the One who calls us by this name. The sensitivity and truthfulness of our conscience grow in the light of the divine Master who teaches us not only from without but also from within by sending us the Spirit of truth.

Although conscience has a voice of its own, the word is not its own. It comes through the Word in whom all things are made, the Word who became flesh to be with us. And this Word speaks through the inner voice which presupposes our capacity to listen with all our being. Of itself, conscience is a candle without a flame. It receives its truth from Christ who is Truth and Light; and through him it shines forth with his brightness and warmth.

In the search for truth, man's conscience is the focal point for sharing experience and reflection in a reciprocity of consciences. There is a truthful encounter of consciences to the extent that we are free for each other, free to receive and to give not only some knowledge but to give, along with the knowledge and experience, ourselves. When we know each other in the sight of God, and accept each other as belonging to one another in the divine Word, then our consciences are fully alive and creative.

2. *The biblical vision of conscience*

a) Conscience in the Old Testament

If we were to study the problem of conscience in the Old Testament, relying only on the vocabulary and seeking Hebrew or Greek concepts for our word "conscience", we would be greatly disappointed. Only in the late Book of Wisdom (17:10f) do we find the Greek word *syneidesis*, which indicates the unquiet or bad conscience. But the Old Testament knows the reality to which we refer when we speak of conscience in a profound way.

As in other cultures, so in Hebrew thought, there is a development. We can see from the older parts of the Bible that the Israelites looked upon the experience of good and evil in an extrinsic, objective and sometimes collective perspective. God's will is mediated by traditions and religious leaders. However, they experience God's voice also as calling them from within. This understanding of conscience as internalized was one of the great contributions of Israel's prophets. It is a person's innermost being, called to fidelity to God and to the people of the covenant. It is the spirit within the person who guides him if he is willing to open himself to it.

So we turn our attention, above all, to the great biblical vision of "the heart" of man. We have spoken of it in relation to the fundamental option. Through the Spirit of God, man receives, in his whole being, an inner disposition and call to do good, to search honestly for God's will, in readiness to do it. His "heart", his innermost being, is shaken if he has disobeyed that inner voice of his best self. "For the Semites, the heart was the seat of thoughts, desires and emotions, and also of moral judgment".[2]

The believer in Israel knows that God "searches the heart and reins". He believes that there the Spirit of God can touch him and call him. Therefore, the heart praises or blames one's deeds. "My heart does not reprehend me in all my life" (Job 27:6). When King David begins to show his own and Israel's power by a census, his "heart struck him after the people were numbered" (2 Sam 24:10). The evildoer knows in his heart that he has done wrong against God and his fellowmen. It is not just an intellectual knowing; it is a deep pain of heart. And in this pain the person still stands before God although he has turned his face away from him as Cain did. "Cain said to the Lord, 'My punishment is too great to bear ... From your face I shall be hidden. And I shall be a fugitive and a wanderer on the earth' " (Gen 4:13f).

We do not find in the Old Testament any reflection like that of modern theologians and psychologists on "antecedent" and "following" conscience; but the reality is most evident in the inspired writers. The heart can do more than accuse the person after he has done the evil. It can also listen to the prompting of the Spirit that illumines him, guides him to righteousness and, if he has done wrong, calls him to meet God again. "You with sad hearts, cry aloud, groan in the heaviness of your spirits" (Is 65:14). From his inmost being, shaken by the spirit, the Psalmist prays, "Create in me a clean heart, O God, and put a new and right spirit within me. Cast me not away from your presence, and take not your holy Spirit from me" (Ps 51:12-13). Conversion begins with the affliction of one's heart (cf. 1 Kgs 8:38).

The profound vision of man's heart, where he is touched and moved by the Spirit, overcomes all merely extrinsic morality. It is the great message of the prophets that God will write his law into the person's heart, in his innermost being (cf. Jer 31:29-34; Ez 14:1-3 and 36:26). "The sin is engraved in the tablet of their hearts" (Jer 17:1). Man's heart can be hardened; but the message of the prophets is that God can renew even the hardened hearts and give them a new sensitivity and openness to God's loving will and to their fellowmen's burdens.

b) Conscience in the New Testament

The reality of experience of conscience in the New Testament should be seen in the light of the Old Testament which is brought to completion. The Gospel message is that now the time has come when God takes away the hardened heart and gives sinners a new heart so that they can live a life renewed in heart and spirit: the time when God gives them not only a new spirit but his own Spirit. If they do not respond with a renewed heart, it is their own fault. The light shines with new brilliance on them and they can be light in the Lord. But they can, instead, be lacking in docility and can become stubborn. "If the light that is in you becomes darkness, how great will the darkness itself be?" (Mt 6:23; Lk 11:33f).

What we have said earlier about liberation from falsehood and for the truth in Christ infers that inner renewal, the experience of a new heart and a new spirit. God's calling that resounds in our heart is at the same time a religious experience and an experience of conscience. It is always marked with wholeness. The whole person is called by God, for God and for the good.[3] We can be at peace only if we respond with our whole heart to this call. This is the law of love of God and of neighbour that is written into the human heart.

As apostle, Paul brought to his ministry the vision of the Old Testament and the experience of the Lord calling him and renewing his heart. "His sensitivity in dealing with the consciences of others springs from the delicacy of his own conscience (2 Cor 1:12), from his constant awareness of divine mercy for himself and God's presence (2 Cor 4:1-2), and from the fear of the Lord (2 Cor 5:11)".[4] Paul conveys this message to the Gentiles in their own language, building upon their own experience of conscience and religiousness, while trying at the same time to bring them into the full light of Christ. He not only accepts and approves "all that is lovable and gracious, whatever is excellent and admirable" (Phil 4:8; cf. 1 Thess 5:21), he also takes up a key concept of the Stoic ethics, *syneidesis.*

Biblical scholars and historians discuss how much Paul actually took over from the Stoic tradition. Surely, he was not ignorant about what this concept meant to his audience.[5] And, surely, he did focus on what he found acceptable and positive in the Greek concept of *syneidesis.*[6] "Even if Paul actually did borrow the term from the philosophical language of his time, he fortified it with the whole biblical tradition on the role of the 'heart' and further enriched it with the dynamic presence of the divine Pneuma".[7] What he thinks, preaches and writes is deeply rooted in the biblical tradition of Israel, yet he is able to bring the message home in the language of his listeners.

It is highly probable that, until the time of Paul, the Stoic ethics used the concept *syneidesis* exclusively for the consciousness of the evil that followed the decision; but even so, it is understood as a cry of the innermost being for wholeness and for existential knowledge of oneself confronted with good and evil. Several times Paul uses *syneidesis* for the conscience that accuses the sinner, which fits into both the biblical and the Greek traditions. However, even in direct dialogue with the Gentiles, he explicitly broadens the understanding of conscience in the light of the prophetic tradition. Perhaps no other text shows better than Romans 2:14-15 how Paul can blend together the old and the new: "When Gentiles, who do not possess the written law, carry out its precepts by the light of nature, then, although they have no law, they are their own law, for they display the effects of the law inscribed in their hearts. Their conscience is called as witness, and their own thoughts argue the case on either side against them or even for them".

While using the concept *syneidesis*, Paul intends to convey the message of the prophets about the heart of man wherein God makes known his law of love. *Syneidesis* is brought explicitly into the context of the essential message that God writes his law into man's heart. It is not only a question of remorse or of an accusing conscience; the heart or *syneidesis* argues the case "on either side". Today it is more and more agreed among biblical theologians that Paul uses the word *syneidesis* also to point out the constructive, creative quality of the human heart to grasp what is good and right. "He also uses it to cover decisions in advance of what should be done".[8]

For Paul, the question is not only whether the heart speaks out only as a wounded conscience after sin or speaks also while the decision is being worked out; his special concern is about the integrity of conscience. He notes that the good conscience is expressive of one's wholeness; and his core message is always that the Spirit renews the heart of man, that there is repentance and conversion which includes a rebirth of the "heart". Clearly, he means what we mean when we speak of "conscience".

Paul describes the split in one's innermost self if one professes to acknowledge God but withstands the grace and calling of faith. "Nothing is pure to the tainted minds of disbelievers, tainted alike in reason and conscience. They profess to acknowledge God but deny him by their actions. Their detestable obstinacy disqualifies them for any good work" (Titus 1:15-16).

Redemption includes not only liberation from falsehood in the mind and reasoning but reaches deeper, even into the person's conscience. If we believe in Christ and trust in him, then "his blood will cleanse our conscience from the deadness of our former ways and fit us for the service of the living God" (Heb 9:14). The conscience also gives witness to the believer about the sincerity of faith and life. "We are convinced that our conscience is clear; our one desire is always to do what is right" (Heb 13:18; cf. 2 Tim 1:3). A good conscience, however, is not self-assurance or self-affirmation. The apostle stands before God, his divine Saviour and Judge (cf. 1 Cor 4:4). And a person who truly lives before the Lord never judges his conscience individualistically. Rather, he lives the reciprocity of consciences in constant concern for the integrity of the other (cf. 1 Cor 10:25-29). All this accords with Paul's insistence that the law of mutual love is inscribed in our "hearts" (consciences).

II. ANTHROPOLOGICAL AND THEOLOGICAL REFLEXION

1. *The act of conscience and the abiding endowment of conscience*

The Apostle of the Gentiles could fulfil his role as messenger of the Good News and of the moral message only by entering into dialogue with the respective cultures. The basis of our understanding of conscience is always Holy Scripture, read, understood and reflected on, however, in the community of believers. This makes the dialogue with each culture and each era imperative.

A history of moral theology could well be written in the main perspective of how conscience was understood, presented, and how the whole life manifested a concrete understanding of conscience. Helmut Thielicke is right when he asserts that the understanding of conscience mirrors always a concrete anthropology.[9] Therefore, we can never simply repeat the formulations of previous theologians, and cannot even understand their purpose without being aware of their different context.

The theological reflections of Scholastic theology and later moral theology are grealy influenced by a sharp distinction between *conscientia* (corresponding etymologically to our "conscience") and *synteresis* or *synderesis*. Conscience was treated only as the judgment or the act by which man reaches the conclusion that this or that is good or evil. *Synteresis*, however, meant the abiding endowment that urges man to seek truth and to put it into practice, to do the good and avoid evil. This word came into theological reflection probably through the commentary of St. Jerome to Ezekiel, by a corruption of *syneidesis*.[10]

The Scholastic tradition took from Jerome *synteresis* as that profound quality which makes man have conscience and qualifies him to perceive the moral order and moral values as his obligation. Thomas Aquinas sees it as the most profound inborn disposition (*primus habitus*) of the practical intelligence.[11] All Scholastics agreed that it is that unique and most relevant endowment or inborn disposition that makes man a moral being.

2. *Incomplete theories regarding conscience*

a) Emphasis on the practical intellect

For Albert the Great and Thomas Aquinas, the *synteresis* is the practical intellect's inborn endowment with the highest moral principles, insofar as they are immediately perceived as binding one's self and every human being. The moral principles are not abstractions, good only for drawing conclusions, although they enter as the main subjects into all moral reflection. *Synteresis* tells the person that "the good is to be done", or "love your neighbour as yourself".

The judgment of conscience is an actual conclusion from the *synderesis* and from a concrete moral judgment about what is actually the good or right expression of love of neighbour, justice and so on. Later, Thomists and moralists, who did not know Thomas Aquinas, conceived this theory in a merely intellectual way and, in practice, frequently combined it with "knowledge of dominion". Thus, the uniqueness of the person and the depth of the person's heart were no longer seen.

However, this was not Thomas Aquinas' doctrine. His vision

put great emphasis on knowledge of the good, but in the sense of the biblical understanding of "knowing". It is a knowledge that comes from the depth of the heart, a knowledge of salvation, of wholeness. "We must bear in mind that, according to Thomas, the natural inclination of the will is always bound up with the knowledge of the practical reason. Thus, by the very nature with which it is created, there is in the will a profound disposition that urges it, of itself, to strive for the good conceived by reason ... It presses towards the good as known by reason (*bonum rationis*)".[12]

Moreover, it should not be forgotten that, for St. Thomas, a right moral reasoning and weighing of the values requests the virtue of prudence. So the outcome of a sincere judgment of conscience is the harvest of the inborn disposition called "synderesis", and the virtue of prudence which, for its very being and functioning, presupposes the fundamental option for the good. As theologian, Thomas Aquinas does not forget that the gifts of the Holy Spirit can give a kind of connaturality to the loving will of God and permit an intuitive grasp of the good.

b) Emphasis on the inborn disposition of the will

Alexander of Hales, St. Bonaventure, Henry of Ghent, and many others, see in the *synderesis* the inborn disposition of the will to love and to desire what is known as the good. The mystics understood it as the *scintilla animae*, the spark of the soul, the passionate love that sets man's innermost being on fire for the good. Thus, what is recognized as corresponding to right reason receives its dynamic force in each particular instance from the profound and inborn tendency of the will to love and to do what is understood, here and now, as the good. Through the *synderesis*, the human will is a little spark of love kindled by the divine love. The will, in its innermost disposition, is touched by God, the source of all love. Here, the religious depth of this theory of conscience becomes manifest.

St. Bonaventure has no intention of devaluating the intellectual aspect so strongly emphasized by St. Thomas Aquinas, for the will is never conceived as a blind force but as a power drawn to the known good. It seems to me that the two theories, when proposed by the great teachers Thomas and Bonaventure, are not opposed but complete each other. Or, let us say that they manifest the same vision but from different angles. However, as soon as the two schools became antagonistic, there was a militant emphasis on one aspect as against the other, and thus the wholeness was shattered.

c) Sociological and psychological reductionism

The fascination of half-truths is one of the greatest enemies of truth. This is especially so in the matter of conscience, because by its very nature, a healthy conscience is experience of wholeness and requires openness to all dimensions.

B.F. Skinner is fascinated by what men have in common with his Norway rats and his apes. He knows men insofar as they can be trained like animals by reward and punishment, by "reinforcers".[13] In Skinnerian behaviourism there is no place for a word about conscience. As soon as people discard freedom and dignity as illusions, the word "conscience" has no relevance anymore. Then follows a new way of socialization that is nothing more than a "training for socially acceptable behaviour".

A.S. Neill tells teachers to forget completely about moral concepts and about appeal to conscience: the only thing is adjustment to the school, loyalty to the school, preparing thus for loyalty to society.[14] These radical views are somehow prepared by a great sociologist, Emile Durkheim, who is fascinated by the interdependence between social institutions and processes on the one hand and man's consciousness on the other.[15] He, therefore, relates conscience totally to the upholding of the institution, and has no regrets when man is thoroughly guided by the law and order concept. "Durkheim is perhaps the greatest explicit defender of the concept of obligation as directed to the group or institution rather than to the welfare and claims of its members".[16] He still would leave a corner for privacy, but morality is for discipline, for order, and arises through adjustment to society rather than through the love and freedom experienced in the family.

Some sociologists have gone far beyond Durkheim's thesis. Their fascination centres on their statistics. With all their special determinisms, they can find no place for genuine freedom and, therefore, no place for conscience.[17]

I know no sociologist more clear-sighted or more competent than George Gurvitch in unmasking this reductionism. He believes in the human conscience, and sees how life in community and society is, by its very nature, an appeal to embody in it the creative freedom that manifests man's conscience. "Society as a whole, the social classes, the various groups, and all the individual persons create their own 'fate' by the different ways in which, in every situation, in every context, with every structure, they deal with the forces opposing them, bend them, overcome them, take them in hand and make use of them. People create their own character and pattern by giving shape to their milieu. Demiurges of the social structure and their social determinisms, they are also the creative artisans of human freedom which is an active part of the whole life".[18] It makes all the difference whether a sociologist is interested in the human person and the community of persons or more with the mechanisms and determinisms in social life.

The same can be said about psychologists: are they chiefly analyzers of functions and determinisms or do they believe in the inner resources of the person? It cannot be denied that in the social processes and relationships, and in the psychic realm, there are dimensions that somehow escape that profound freedom that arises from the depth of man's conscience.

Sigmund Freud discovered within his patients' egos "a special agency" through which the person is kept dependent on the parents and on the milieu. He called this agency "superego". "The parents' influence naturally includes not only the personality of the parents themselves but also the racial, national and family traditions handed on through them, as well as the demands of the immediate social milieu which they represent".[19]

It was the great concern of psychologists and therapists like Erik Erikson, Erich Fromm and many others, to assign to the *superego* its proper role, but also to warn against the danger of a false education that builds only on the superego.[20] The superego gains overpowering strength through the emotions caused by fear of the authority and by an education that uses chiefly the pain-and-pleasure principles for training, while the conscience, as such, is overlooked.[21] "The superego performs well within a given set of limits . . .; but its legitimate function deals with the more primitive levels of psychic life".[22]

There are psychoanalysts who know only the primitive levels and those psychic functions that can be understood without freedom and without the inner resources of conscience. But they are not the only ones who sin by reductionism. They have unconscious allies in those educators and moralists who are unable to transcend the conventional morals that are concerned with external rules, with order, and who put their trust mainly in sanctions and rewards. "The person who is dominated by his superego has the accuser, judge and tormentor all wrapped up in one, built into his own psychic make-up. When such a person hears the Christian message given with an accent on God as Judge, he can project his superego on this divinity and use religion as an instrument to subject himself to this court and, unknown to himself, to promote his own unconscious self-hatred".[23] But where the Gospel is rightly preached and education is based on it, the superego is not reinforced and the person is gradually freed from its domination.[24] It can become an ally of social consciousness.

3. *The holistic understanding of conscience*

a) The innermost yearning for wholeness and integrity

Most moral theologians today agree with outstanding psychologists and therapists who insist that conscience is not just one faculty. It is not more in the will than in the intellect, and it is a dynamic force in both because of their belonging together in the deepest reaches of our psychic and spiritual life.

The dynamic of our conscience is "the reaction of our total personality to its proper functioning and disfunctioning, not to the functioning of this or that capacity but to the capacities which constitute our human and individual existence".[25] We are created for wholeness biologically, psychologically and spiritually. The deepest part of our being is keenly sensitive to what can promote and what can threaten our wholeness and integrity.

The concrete judgment of prudence, accepted as judgment of the conscience, depends on many conditions. But what gives urgency and attractive appeal to the judgment of prudence is conscience's own longing for wholeness. Being created for wholeness, we can dynamically decipher and experience the good to which God calls us in the particular situation. One's conscience is healthy only when the whole person — the emotional as well as the intellectual elements and the energies of the will — is functioning in a profound harmony in the depth of one's being. This innermost depth is the locus where we are touched by the creative Spirit and brought to ever greater wholeness. It is "the pivotal personal centre of man's total response to the dynamics, direction and personal thrust of the divine claim on him".[26] Conscience has to do with man's total selfhood as a moral agent.[27] The intellectual, volitional and emotional dynamics are not separated; they mutually compenetrate in the very depth where the person is person to himself.

This view is not alien to the great tradition of the Church; it relates to a great deal of theological reflection about man as image and likeness of God. I refer particularly to the thought of the Augustinian school. God the Father who is the source of knowledge and love, the Son, his Word who speaks out all his love, and the Holy Spirit who is the sharing of the love and the Word, are united in one and the same essence, three persons in one nature. The human person in his or her totality — intellect and will, with their affectivity united in the substance — is the most profound image of the divine Trinity.

In the wholeness and openness of our conscience we are a real sign of the promptings of the Spirit who renews our heart and, through us, the earth. Even though in the depths of the human spirit, intellect and will are somehow distinct, they cannot really thrive without each other. It is, however, the mark of their finite nature that intellect and will can oppose each other, although not without unleashing profound grief in the innermost depths in which they are united. The rift that is created is painfully perceived. It is in this wound that the soul cries out for healing; and this cry is itself a sign of the presence of the Spirit who summons the person to close the dreadful gap of dissension through restoration of that unity and harmony which makes him or her a true image and likeness of God.

Because of the profound integration of intellect, will and

affectivity in our very nature, the intellect's longing for truth and goodness is shaken when, out of sinister motives, the will struggles against it. And the will, in its turn, must agonize when it tries to withstand the intellect's yearning for better knowledge and realization of the good. The person suffers in his whole being if there arises a kind of split into different selves, the true self that longs for wholeness and truth and the selfish self that seeks a mere image of the good. As root and source of unity of all one's powers, the depth of the soul is tortured, torn by the dissension.

Here is the profound reason for the first elemental agony of conscience, a spontaneous unreflected pain. Theologically, we might dare to say that the image of the Trinity within us recoils in horror at the distortion of the divine likeness in us.

b) Wholeness and openness for truth and solidarity

The call to unity and wholeness pervades our conscience. It is a longing for integration of all the powers of our being that, at the same time, guides us towards the Other and the others. The covenant reality is inscribed in our heart.[28]

There cannot be peace in our heart (or conscience) unless our whole being accepts the longing of the intellect and reason to be one with the truth. Since our very substance unites these powers with the will and with all our being, there can be genuine inner wholeness only in that openness to the light that is in the world from the beginning. This includes openness also to our fellowmen, since our self-understanding and growth in the knowledge of the good depend greatly on the symbols created by the interaction of many minds in mutual human relationships. We come to know ourselves in our depths and wholeness in that interaction which responds to the same longing for dignity and wholeness in everyone else. We need, from those around us, love and respect as persons with consciences, and we can explore the depth and dynamics of our conscience only if we respond to that love in a creative way.

The covenant dimension of the conscience is solemnly proclaimed in the great messianic prophecy of Jeremiah to which the Pauline Letters refer. " 'Behold the days are coming' says the Lord, 'when I will make a new covenant with the house of

Israel and the house of Judah ... I will put my law within them, and I will write it upon their hearts; and I will be their God and they shall be my people' " (Jer 31:31-33; see also Heb 8:8-12).

The law that re-echoes in our being is the golden rule that simply deserves the name "law". "Love your neighbour as yourself": this is the sum of the law. "Treat others as you would like them to treat you: that is the law and the prophets" (Mt 7:12; Lk 6:31). It is the distinctive quality of the mature Christian that he understands the inner law in the light of Christ who manifested for us the all-embracing law of the covenant, "Love one another as I have loved you" (Jn 15:12). We are sealed with this understanding of the law, written in our hearts, when we receive the Spirit and are open to him. We celebrate it each time we take the cup of salvation. What Jesus proclaims re-echoes in our hearts, "This is the blood of the New Covenant" (Lk 22:20). If the Eucharist, which is at the centre of our faith, becomes also the rule of our life, then we will reach wholeness in our conscience and unity with our fellowmen.

As we have seen in the chapter on fundamental option, our conscience has only two basic choices, either for solidarity of salvation in authentic covenant morality or for solidarity in collective sinfulness. At this point, we can relate the theological insight on solidarity to the findings of psychology about the functioning of the superego.

In childhood and early adolescence, the temporary strength of the superego is a normal phase of transition. It can play an important role in the process of socialization. And if, at the proper time, the person works out a deeply rooted fundamental option for solidarity in the good, the energies of the superego are directed into the same course. The result is a mature, peaceful conscience, the integration of the person in his inner core and integrity in covenant morality.

However, if the education tactics are wrong, if they distort the dynamics of the superego for the mere enforcement of obedience, it can become a prepotent agent of all the dark powers that draw persons eventually into collective sinfulness, hypocrisy, belligerent group egotism and the slavery of falsehood. Even at best, superego morality tends to be sterile, repetitive, degrading, whereas covenant morality opens one to ever new and creative responses to God and neighbour.

c) Conscience in its creative fidelity and liberty

The way we have approached the problems of conscience shows that our main concern is to make the tree good so that the fruits may be good. We are, indeed, interested in the mature and right judgement of conscience but then we have to give our attention to its conditions.

The creative judgment of conscience, with its strong tendency towards living in the truth and acting on it, depends on several conditions: first, on the God-given dynamics of the conscience, the inborn yearning for wholeness and openness; second, on the firmness and clarity of the fundamental option which confirms the natural yearning for those qualities but which should be honoured as the harvest of the Spirit; third, on the strength of the dispositions towards vigilance and prudence and all the other dispositions that embody a deep and good fundamental option; fourth, on the mutuality of consciences in a milieu where creative freedom and fidelity are embodied and there is active and grateful dedication to them; fifth, on the actual fidelity, creativity and generosity in the search for truth in readiness to "act on the word".[29]

Many theologians who have reflected on the creative quality of the conscience have especially noted Thomas Aquinas' teaching on intuitive knowledge of the good, made possible by connaturality with the good.[30] This is always the work of the Holy Spirit, who enables us to bear fruit in abundance according to our openness. "An unspirited person refuses what belongs to the Spirit of God; it is folly to him; he cannot grasp it because it needs to be judged in the light of the Spirit. A person gifted with the Spirit can judge the worth of everything" (1 Cor 2:14-15). This is the main theme of Paul's theology and of John's. "You are among the initiated; this is the gift of the Holy One, and by it you all have knowledge . . . As for you, you need no other teacher, but learn all you need to know from his initiation, which is real and no illusion. As he taught you, then, dwell in him" (1 Jn 2:20 and 2:27).

Reflecting on the dynamic element in the Church, Karl

Rahner gives particular attention to intuitive knowledge.[31] His description of it reminds us of Abraham Maslow's theme of "peak experience".[32] Bernard Lonergan also speaks of this dimension: "Faith is the knowledge form of religious love. First, then, there is a knowledge born of love. Of it Pascal spoke when he remarked that 'the heart has reasons which reason does not know'. The meaning of Pascal's remark would be that, besides the factual knowledge reached by experiencing, understanding and verifying, there is another kind of knowledge reached in love".[33]

A moral theology that sees creative fidelity and liberty as key concepts can never neglect this dimension. "It is precisely a growing awareness of the fact and nature of such knowledge that prompts a number of theologians to see abstract and systematic knowledge as a secondary and derived form of knowledge".[34]

An aspect of the creativity of conscience becomes evident in the growth of one's conscience into new dimensions. It is conscience itself that teaches the person to overcome the present stage of development and to integrate it into a higher one. In other words, the openness manifested in intuitive knowledge is also the process of the person's self-realization in his or her conscience.

4. *Wholeness and the erring conscience*

Vatican II has reaffirmed a classical Catholic tradition regarding an erring judgment of conscience. "Conscience frequently errs from invincible ignorance without losing its dignity. The same cannot be said of a person who cares but little for truth and goodness, or of a conscience which by degrees grows practically sightless as a result of habitual sin".[35]

As far as objective truth and values are concerned, the human conscience is surely not infallible. The Council acknowledges that error in evaluation happens rather frequently. But more important is the acknowledgement that it happens frequently without personal guilt, without conscience losing its dignity. This is so whenever the intentions are right and the conscience is sincerely seeking the best solution. By "best solution", I do not mean the abstract best, but what is for the person here and now, in this particular situation, the most fitting step in the right direction.

There is something unique — one might even say "untouchable" — about the conscience, because it is the judgment of a person on his or her journey towards ever fuller light. To err in one's judgment of conscience in an important matter can be a great misfortune; but it is much worse, a moral evil, if the conscience errs because of lack of sincerity. The greatest evil is when the conscience becomes dull and sightless. The Council speaks sharply of this happening when a person "cares but little for truth and goodness", is careless in the very search for moral knowledge, careless especially in situations that are morally relevant, and finally becomes practically blind as a result of habitual, unrepented sins.

When a person is truly looking for what is good and right, there is a kind of indefectibility in the conscience. With unwavering certainty, it orders the will to conform with the intellect, following its light, as the two are rooted together at the core of one's being. This imperative, written in the heart, has moral majesty even though it may have a background of defective moral knowledge, indeed even if it makes a fully erroneous judgment. If the error in evaluation is in no way due to negligence or ill will, there is nothing in the faculty of conscience itself which would murmur against acting on the ground of that erroneous judgment. Rather, it is sustained by the whole sound dynamic of conscience.

An inculpably erroneous dictate of conscience obliges in the same way as a correct conscience, just as a servant feels obliged to carry out the order of his master as he has understood it after listening attentively, even though the order was actually different. If we really seek to discover the Lord's will in a sincere search for truth and with the intention to act on the truth, then the Lord sees into our heart. Hence, Cardinal Newman is correct in his famous statement, "I have always contended that obedience even to an erring conscience was the way to gain light".[36]

On this point, we find the same emphasis in the moral and pastoral theology of St. Alphonsus de Liguori.[37] He speaks of the invincibly erring conscience, where a sincere conscience cannot internalize a positive law of the Church or of the secular authorities, or even a valid aspect of natural law teaching. From an existential point of view, it might not be so much an erroneous assessment as an impossibility to take the third step before the second in one's progress towards a more profound knowledge of the good. From an objective, abstract point of view, we might, as outsiders, say that the person's conscience is erring, but existentially it might indicate the best possible step in the direction towards more light. It would be a most serious fault against the dignity of the conscience if a pastor, a confessor, or anyone else were to press the person to act against his sincere conscience, or indiscreetly try to inculcate the objective norm if this would disturb the person who simply cannot accept a particular precept or norm.

In St. Alphonsus' time there were many churchmen and moralists who were more concerned for uniformity of order and discipline than for the dignity of conscience. St. Alphonsus was warned by friends that his emphasis on respect for the sincere but erring conscience could cause trouble even for the congregation he had founded. He responded that even in such a threatening situation he would prefer to see his congregation suppressed than the conscience of people oppressed.[38]

An erroneous judgment of conscience can be culpable in varying degrees and for various reasons. There can be a lesser or greater negligence in searching for what is truth and goodness, or there can be the blinding influence of past sins insufficiently repented, or the misguided power of passions not sufficiently controlled.

St. Thomas Aquinas held that, in the case of a culpably erroneous dictate of conscience, the person sins whether he follows its dictate, or acts contrary to it; but the sin is more immediate and evident if he acts contrary to his erroneous conscience, even if, in so doing, he does what is objectively right. By acting against the dictate of conscience he wounds and jeopardizes even more his inner wholeness and his union with what he sees as the objective good and truth.

Although an erroneous verdict of conscience can be rectified, still, as long as it persists, it is actually binding.[39] And yet, according to Thomas Aquinas, it would not be correct to say that the person with a culpably erroneous conscience has only two choices and, therefore, unavoidably commits sin. There exists a third choice, which is to correct the verdict of conscience by purging the sources of error in their very depth,[40] by a deeper conversion. And if one delays conversion or refuses to be converted at all, this attitude contaminates all one's decisions of conscience.

St. Thomas teaches also that if anyone professes faith in Christ and/or the Church, although he is firmly convinced that it is wrong to do so, he is sinning against his conscience.[41] However, St. Thomas could not conceive that a Catholic who had once come to faith would ever, without personal guilt, reach the conviction of conscience that he has to leave the Church.[42] Today we have to consider many more psychological and sociological influences in approaching this and other complex problems of the erroneous conscience.[43]

To any such difficult problems we can apply the general criterion that a particular decision has the unconditioned dignity of a judgment of conscience if the person is sincerely seeking the truth and is ready to revise the decision as soon as he realizes that new pertinent questions call for his consideration. The sign of a truly conscientious decision is the inner peace and a growing sensitivity to all the new opportunities to do what love and justice demand.

5. *The perplexed conscience*

The disturbed or perplexed conscience is a particular type of erroneous conscience arising from a transitory but violent disturbance of the person's capacity to form a serene judgment. Faced with the necessity of having to make a decision, the person can see no apparent choice free from sin. If the decision can be delayed, then one must postpone the solution in order to deliberate on it more quietly. But if it cannot be delayed, the conscientious person will choose what he thinks is "the lesser sin" and thus manifest his correct attitude. In fact, there is no question of sin in this matter, for sin is not merely a matter of intellectual judgment but is also an evil act of free will, which is evidently lacking here.

A moral theology that has multiplied the absolutes that can conflict with each other in concrete situations has produced many cases of "perplexed conscience". A moral education that helps to discern both the urgency and the priority of values will greatly alleviate such pain for conscientious people. It is not enough to tell people that, on the subjective level, they will not be guilty if they make certain choices; we must also insist that there is always an objectively right way to resolve these cases.

III. DEVELOPMENTAL PSYCHOLOGY AND THE STAGES OF CONSCIENCE

Developmental psychology's great contribution towards a better understanding of conscience and of moral education is welcomed by a moral thology concerned with creative freedom and fidelity and a dynamic understanding of the person. Especially helpful are the studies of Erik Erikson, Erich Fromm and Lawrence Kohlberg.

Erikson distinguishes three phases in the development of moral awareness and conscience. "I will speak of moral learning as an aspect of childhood, of ideological experimentation as a part of adolescence, and of ethical consolidation as an adult task".[44] He describes the dangers and chances of each stage. In the first stage, the danger is that education lords over the child .by prohibitions reinforced by frowning faces and moral threats — if, indeed, moral learning is not actually beaten into the child by physical punishment before the child can possibly understand the meaning of it all. But where guidance is given with love and respect, the child can already learn to internalize moral prohibitions.[45]

Adolescence is a time when the critical mind awakens. "The adolescent learns to perceive ideas and to assent to ideals, to take, in short, an ideological position for which the younger child is cognitively not prepared".[46] The adolescent and the young adult are seeking for a worldview coherent enough to attract a total commitment.

In all stages, Erikson sees an affirmative chance for the

superego: it can and must be integrated into higher levels of moral awareness if it is to foster genuine socialization through discerning self-commitment. However, both he and Erich Fromm warn also about the negative possibility, a wrong direction taken during the first stages, if the superego serves mainly the goals of the caretaker. In these cases the prescriptions of authoritarian conscience — their commands and taboos — are not determined by experience of values; they simply echo the pronouncements of external authority.[47]

The child needs more guidance than the adolescent. However, guidance can be given in such a way that the first stage anticipates the second. External sanctions give way to internal perception; prohibition and fear give way to joy and preferences in self-respect; habits of obedience give way to genuine self-guidance and creative responses.[48]

If we understand the contribution made by Erikson for a better understanding of the fundamental option, then we are helped to appreciate also Lawrence Kohlberg's contribution towards a deeper understanding of the moral development of conscience. It seems to me most fortunate that Kohlberg has found such a ready audience among ethicians and educators.[49]

He distinguishes six stages at three levels of development:

I.   The pre-conventional level
     Stage 1: Obedience and punishment orientation
     Stage 2: Instrumental relativistic orientation
II. The conventional level
     Stage 3: Interpersonal concordance of "good boy/ nice girl" orientation
     Stage 4: "Law and order" orientation
III. Post-conventional, autonomous or principled level
     Stage 5: Social contract orientation (with utilitarian overtones)
     Stage 6: Universal-principle orientation.[50]

Kohlberg repeatedly insists on the dynamic aspect indicated by the fact that each stage contains some horizon and some tendency towards the next stage. During the first stage, children experience the good chiefly by the physical consequences which they perceive as reaction. During the second stage there arises a clearer perception of values like fairness and reciprocity, but perception is still on a rather pragmatic level. During the third stage, "good behaviour is that which pleases or helps others and is approved by them. There is much conformity to stereotyped images of what is majority or 'natural' behaviour. One earns approval by being 'nice' ".[51]

During stage four, the growing person especially perceives the values of authority, maintenance of order and reliability. There is already a beginning discernment between good and poor exercise of authority. On this level, danger arises if those in authority are not able to share the knowledge of salvation and prefer to operate on the level of knowledge of control-dominion. Thus, they oppose the inner dynamic of this stage towards the next.

Kohlberg assesses stage five as more or less that of the official morality of the United States' government and constitution. "There is a clear awareness of the relativism of personal values and opinions and a corresponding emphasis on procedural rules for reaching consensus . . . an emphasis on the legal point of view but also with an emphasis upon the possibility of changing law in terms of rational considerations".[52] However, there is gradually developing a sense of the moral good beyond law. In stage six, the universal ethical vision takes over. Right is defined by the decision of conscience in accordance with self-chosen ethical principles.

While all education, if conceived as truly moral education, tends clearly to the sixth stage, the dynamic is best utilized if special attention is given to the gradual transition to the next possible stage. With Dewey and Piaget, Kohlberg is convinced that children can learn early to accept authority when they are helped to understand its goodness and to see the reasons behind the rules. On this point he firmly dissociates himself from Emile Durkheim and his followers who, in their understanding of common life, remain substantially on the level of mere order and discipline.

The growing person is able, and therefore has a right, to be helped to understand ever better that there are ethical principles clearly distinguishable from arbitrary conventional rules and beliefs. It is important to listen to children and their way of arguing. "We all, even and especially children, are moral philosophers. By this I mean the child has a morality of his own".[53] If we respectfully listen to and talk to children, we can discover "that they have lots of standards which do not come in any obvious way from parents, peers or teachers".[54]

From this cross-cultural research, Kohlberg has found that the stages of moral development are common to all cultures. Each child goes, step by step, through the various stages but with varying speed according to the help or hindrance he finds in the world around him. Kohlberg and Piaget emphasize the cognitive development but also affectivity. "All mental events have both cognitive and affective aspects. It is also evident that the presence of strong emotion in no way reduces the cognitive component of moral judgment".[55]

The development of moral thought moves forward in one direction, but it can be blocked at an earlier stage so that it never reaches the fifth or sixth stage. The person who reaches moral maturity recognizes universal values. This does not mean that all values are universal; but the basic one of justice, common to all people, should be expressed towards all. The golden rule is basic and common: "Do unto others as we would have them do to us. Love your fellowmen as you want them to love you". For Kohlberg, this is the most universal principle.[56]

In stimulating moral development through stages five and six, the aim of moral education is to give the individual the capacity to engage in moral judgment and discourse rather than to impose on him a specific morality.[57] The heart of the matter is discernment, based on the knowledge of man and on a recognized hierarchy of values. The great psychologists have abundantly proven how dangerous it is to consider moral life as static. An education based upon such a static concept leads to lack of integration and presents the danger of regression.

IV. A DISTINCTIVELY CHRISTIAN CONSCIENCE

The recent discussions on a distinctively Christian ethics were frequently sterile and frustrating because they centred all around the concept of normative ethics, and in a rather narrow and all too static vision. The following pages suggest a shift of focus.

Christians should be distinguished by their true humanity and co-humanity, for at the centre of faith is the dogma of the incarnation of the Word of God. God reveals himself in full humanity and co-humanity in Jesus Christ, true God and true man. Therefore, if we take seriously our identity as Christians, we develop a distinctively Christian conscience whereby we think, above all, of our solidarity with all of humankind. We believe that Christ is the Redeemer and Lord of all, and that his Spirit works in all, through all and for all.

The great privilege that, through faith, we know Christ and have our life in him does not allow us any superiority complex or exclusiveness. Rather, it gives us a mission to be and to become ever more light to the world and servants to the world. We cannot help others to reach out for the fullness of explicit faith unless we know our own name and live according to the One who calls us by that name.

1. *In Christ — under the law of faith*

The conscience and conscientiousness of a Christian are marked by his encounter with Christ, by his joy at being a new creation in Christ, and by his knowledge, through Christ, of the Father and of his fellowmen. "This is the eternal life, to know you who alone are truly God, and whom you have sent, Jesus Christ" (Jn 17:3).

It is important to understand what the word "know" means. It is a gift of the Holy Spirit who reaches into the innermost depths of our soul. A salvific knowledge of Christ includes confirmation of our fundamental option that gives us wholeness of conscience and a knowledge by connaturality.

A truly Christian conscience is marked by that creative liberty and fidelity that arises from faith in Christ. Faith is the joyous, grateful and humble reception of him whom the Father has sent, and who is our Life, our Way, our Truth. It is total surrender to him who draws us to the Father, a new, liberating experience of friendship with Christ that gives us also a new and intimate relationship with God the Father, in the Holy Spirit, and with our fellowmen, as well as a new self-understanding.

The foundation and the firmness of this Christian conscience lie in faith. The Apostle of the Gentiles contradicts emphatically those who feel that his preaching about the "law of faith" undermines the law or morality. "Does this mean that we are using faith to undermine morality? By no means! We are placing morality itself on a firmer footing" (Rom 3:31). It seems to me that we can replace Paul's word "law" or "morality" by "conscience" without changing his meaning. "To St Paul, faith is the whole attitude of the Christian, assimilating his judgments of moral worth too. The Christian is not divided within himself between a natural economy and a supernatural one; there is only one judgment of conscience and it is determined by his faith".[58]

The Revised Standard Version translates Romans 14:23 as, "Whatever does not proceed from faith is sin". The New English Bible translates it simply, "What does not arise from conscience is sin". Both these translations are right, for St. Paul sees the human conscience and the conviction of conscience illumined and confirmed by faith. Especially in his Pastoral Epistles, "faith" and "conscience" have almost the same meaning. "The aim and object of this command is the love which springs from a clean heart, from a good conscience, and from faith that is genuine" (1 Tim 1:5). For Paul, faith and good conscience are inseparable. "So fight gallantly, armed with faith and a good conscience" (1 Tim 1:19). Christian leadership can be exercised only by persons "who combine a clear conscience with a firm hold on the deep truths of our faith" (1 Tim 3:9). Those who desert faith and spread falsehood are men "whose own conscience is branded with the devil's sign" (1 Tim 4:2; cf. Titus 1:15-16).

A mature Christian conscience will not think of faith as a catalogue of things and formulations. What shapes all the moral dispositions, gives wholeness to the conscience and firmness to the Christian's fundamental option is the profound *attitude* of faith and its responsiveness. Faith, as a profound relationshhip with Christ, awakens in us a deep longing to know Christ and all that he has taught us and expects from us. This faith is marked by gratitude and joy that give direction and strength to all our life (cf. Neh 8:10). Faith can be defined as an all-embracing Christ-consciousness.[59]

A mere inculcation of various doctrines, without a synthesis in Christ and without a sharing of the joy of faith, does nothing to help the formation of a distinctively Christian conscience. Indeed, an over-emphasis on control of doctrines and a militant theology about doctrines can become an obstacle to an integrated faith. Only a joyous sharing of faith and a building up of a profound disposition of faith can guarantee the synthesis between orthodoxy and orthopraxis that unites all believers in Christ.

2. *"No longer under the law but under grace"* (Rom 6:14)

Whoever gives first place to law and moral obligation while assigning only a second place to the grace of Christ perverts the right order and undermines the authenticity of a Christian conscience. Life in Christ means to be drawn to him and to the Father by his Spirit, and into a life that is praise and thanksgiving. Grace and faith take the first place.

Faith itself is a gratuitous gift that can only be received and welcomed in gratitude. It gives us a vista that makes us see everything in the light of the love of God and his graciousness. Grace *(charis)* means, above all, the attractive love of God the Father. He who has given us his life-giving Word and bestows on us the life-giving Spirit turns his face to us, blesses us. It is in this way that he makes us sharers of the covenant and engraves his law — his loving will — in our hearts.

Moral teaching becomes Good News if it is presented as an integrated part of faith-experience (of course, without making everything an unchangeable "dogma") and received in gratitude for God's infinite self-giving love. This is the central message of St. Paul's moral teaching. In view of our sharing in Christ's death and resurrection, we understand that "we are no longer under a regime of law but under grace" (Rom 6:14). "The law of the Spirit who gives us life in Christ Jesus has set me free from the law of sin-solidarity and from death" (Rom 8:2). The Christian conscience is marked by faith in the Holy Spirit and by an all-pervading gratitude that keeps us on the level of the Spirit and frees us from the web of incarnate selfishness.

We repeat the same truth when we insist that a Christian's profound dispositions and outlook are thoroughly formed by the celebration of the Eucharist, which evokes thanksgiving in view of all that God has done for us and promises us. One cannot live under grace without a grateful memory. Openness to the Spirit guides the Christian conscience in the evaluation of every situation. We see at the same time all the gifts God has bestowed on us and the needs of our fellowmen to which we can respond by using rightly all that we have received from God. Only in this readiness to meet the responsibilities of our co-humanity can we praise God and pray, "What can I render to the Lord for whatever he has given me?"

The legalist stands before an abstract law and will ever be tempted to get around it without a full commitment to the Lord, or else to impose it ruthlessly on others, with no knowledge of salvation. He fixes his attention on the minimal requirements of the universal laws. But, whether he becomes more a laxist or a rigorist, he will always be a captive of legalistic thinking. Only if the believer turns his attention to the love of God and to all the many signs and gifts of God's love, can he be set free for his neighbour and become faithful in Christ. When this boundless love of God becomes his main orientation, he no longer looks for the minimum response but aspires, rather, to "let your goodness have no limits, just as the goodness of the heavenly Father knows no bounds (Mt 5:48).

To live under grace means a shift from the prohibitive laws to the orientations of the goal-commandments, the affirmatives presented in the whole gospel, in the words of Christ and the Letters of St. Paul. It is a dynamic morality that never allows the Christian to settle down, content with himself. His gratitude becomes the new noödynamics that gives clear directions to his psychodynamics.

The Lord has expressed this morality of gratitude in his parables about the talents and in practically all the parables about the kingdom of God. A conscience formed by faith and grace knows that all the gifts come from the one God and Father, and that not to use them responsibly and to the full is to show ingratitude to God and injustice to the human community, for every gift is given for building up the kingdom of God. The person who has received two talents and uses them well receives the same praise as the one who has received five and used them profitably. And if the person who has received one talent would have used it, he, too, would have matched the fidelity of the others.

A sacramental spirituality is a great help in reaching maturity of conscience under grace. All Christian education should be, somehow, a post-baptismal formation of conscience. We should see what we have received in baptism, and how we now can bear fruit as members of the body of Christ. The birthright of baptism is sharing in the body of Christ and the blood of the covenant. Christ gives himself so totally to us that his love and his praise of the Father can be alive in us and through us.

In a sacramental understanding of marriage, the spouses receive each other in a spirit of gratitude, and continue to praise God by mutual self-bestowal. Thus, by their very love, they teach their children how to understand the law of grace. And by their gracious, generous and spontaneous expression of appreciation, they help the children to discover their own inner resources and to develop responsible and creative consciences.

The key words of the moral message of the New Testament underline equally the gratuitousness of God's love and gifts and their social dimensions. God draws us together in the fellowship of the Holy Spirit by his very gifts. First we have to see that God's loving us is an undeserved gift that can be received abundantly only to the extent of our gratitude. And since it is the gift of the one Father, who wants us all to be sharers of his own love, it is a gift and appeal to join him in his encompassing love for all people.

Shalom — peace and reconciliation — will draw us into God's reconciling action and make us messengers and channels of peace. If we celebrate them as his gifts, if we render thanks always and everywhere in grateful awareness that his gifts are bestowed on us so that we may share them with our fellowmen, then we will not lose these gifts.

And so it is with the biblical message of justice *(dikaiosyne)*.

We are justified by God's own justice. It is in justice to his name as almighty and all-merciful Father that he calls us sinners into the kingdom of justice and peace. God shows his justice by special care for the sinners and those who are weak and abused. If we live under the law of grace, we will act towards our fellowmen as God acts with us.

In the light of these great gifts, we discover then that all that we are and all that we have are signs of God's love. All our life is then taken up by the dynamics of the goal-commandments: "Love each other as I have loved you" (Jn 15:12) or, as expressed in the beatitudes and in the solemn words that follow the beatitudes, the repeated, " . . . but I tell you . . ." (Mt 5:17-48). If we live according to a kind of normative ethics that is mainly limitative, prohibitive or static, we have not yet truly entered into the new covenant.

We have not yet fully overcome the split between a static moral theology and a lofty ascetical and mystical theology. Moral theology for the use of confessors and penitents was almost unavoidably guided by the knowledge of dominion and control. Since such a theology, written mostly for controllers, could threaten the freedom of believers in the realm of things solicited by grace, it seemed best to leave out or bypass spirituality or ascetical mystical theology.

The dichotomy between moral theology as static normative ethics and a totally different spiritual theology led frequently also to an ethics for two classes: one for those who wanted to become "perfect" (the religious) and the other for those who only lived under the commandments, understood as static norms. Thus, not only the unity of the people of God could fall apart, but there was danger that consciences, too, could separate into two different departments, one for moral norms and the other for "superfluous works".

The beatitudes, all the goal-commandments and the "harvest of the Spirit" were considered as a mere ideal or as *parenesis* and, therefore, not as a part of normative Christian ethics. Surely, we must carefully distinguish what is an abiding orientation and normative ideal from what is time-bound moral or religious exhortation in a particular situation. But it would be most harmful for the specifically Christian self-understanding if all the goal-commandments of the Bible were reduced to mere ideals or even only to *parenesis*.[60]

To love God with all our hearts and to love each other as Christ loved us is not just an ideal but a *normative* ideal that requests that all our desires, deeds and endeavours be energized in this direction. Christ has revealed the true countenance of love to us, and there can be no rest or self-satisfaction for the Christian, since this lofty ideal draws us constantly closer to Christ and reveals itself as both ever more demanding and ever more rewarding.

It is detrimental to the very fundamental norms of Christian ethics, but especially to the formation of a distinctively Christian consciousness, if the law of growth and the criteria for a deeper understanding of Christian love are relegated to another discipline or, in moral theology, only considered as *parenesis*. But it should be equally clear that a distinctively Christian formation of conscience does not belong to those who specialize in "knowledge of control". For it is at the very heart of knowledge of salvation.

3. Filled with hope

Already in the chapter on fundamental option special attention has been given to the eschatological virtues. But not only the development and rootedness of a genuinely Christian fundamental option but also each act of conscience and the whole formation of conscience should be seen in that same light of the eschatological virtues that allows and calls for creative fidelity and liberty. Ours is a pilgrim ethics. Hope brings this home to our consciousness and inscribes it in our conscience.

In view of false forms of secularization we give special attention to a distinctively Christian hope. It arises from faith in the resurrection from the dead and God's promise to grant us a new heaven and a new earth, if we faithfully work to incarnate love, justice and peace in all of life. The sharp conscience of Christians for social justice, their non-violent and most active involvement, and a Church that is watchful for the "signs of the time" should be a real symbol of our hope of the world to come.

A distinctively Christian hope that gives a new and unifying
noödynamic to the psychodynamics of our conscience will never
ignore the cross of our Lord Jesus Christ and his calling us to
follow him on the way of the cross. As the strength of our
fundamental option grows, we accept in the depths of our
conscience the still remaining need to put to death our selfish
self and to take up every day our burden and a part of the
burden of our fellowmen. The Eucharist that nourishes the
expectation of the coming of our Lord will give us joy, strength
and orientation for our mission in this time on this earth.[61]

4. Vigilance and prudence

Vigilance results from the creative tension between the
"already" and the "not yet", perceived and responded to in
thanksgiving and hope. The vigilant conscience is symbolized
by the virgins who are always ready for the coming of the
Lord; for his call reaches us in the here and now, in the kairos.
Each Christian and the whole Christian community are meant
to share in the charism of John, "the man waiting for the
coming of the Lord" (Jn 21:22-23), recognizing him under
whatever disguise he is coming. Through vigilance a distinctively
Christian conscience is seized by the wealth and the tensions of
the history of salvation.

The formation of conscience depends a good deal on how
the virtue of prudence is understood. It should be seen thoroughly
in the light of the eschatological virtues, especially of vigilance.
Vigilant prudence gives the conscience the delicate tact for the
situation and deciphers even in the most confused and confusing events the present opportunities and needs despite all
the darkness that arises from past sins and from the allurements
of a sinful world. Thus, the conscience is sensitive for the Lord's
calling and trustful of his grace. That gives true creativity and
fidelity. The task of vigilant prudence is twofold: to appraise
correctly the objective realities, and to discern and command the
actions which are appropriate as a response to God's gifts and
human needs. Joseph Pieper says that prudence has "two faces,
one turned to the objectively real, the other to the good to be
made real".[62]

To the degree that a decision of conscience is the certain

voice of a sincere conscience, it is neither more nor less than the verdict of prudence. As to the content, the dictates of conscience correspond exactly to the prudential judgment. However, the existential inner awareness of the calling, and the urgency to do the good, come from the whole moral condition and wholeness of conscience.

In St. Thomas Aquinas' teaching, we note the strong insistence on vigilance for the moment of grace. He holds that this is a distinctive function of prudence or, more specifically, a distinctive virtue which is assigned to the virtue of prudence. He calls it *"gnome"*, which is a sensitivity to the wealth of the present situation, which always offers something more than the ordinary.[63]

Thomas Aquinas relates the distinctively Christian character of prudence to the gifts of the Holy Spirit. It is at least partially understood as a fruit of wisdom that gives the person a taste for heavenly things and joy in the service of the Spirit. The special gift of the Holy Spirit which brings prudence to perfection is counsel. Through this gift the Holy Spirit directs deliberation — the first act of prudence — with such perfection that subsequent acts are assured of a solid basis.[64]

Under the inspiration of the gift of counsel, the conscience rejoices in the divine dispositions and directives and thus becomes more sensitive to all the possibilities of the here and now.[65] If the conscience is solidly guided by the Spirit and trusting in the Lord, serenity and courage will guarantee the spiritual atmosphere that provides the proper judgment and joyous fulfilment.

5. Discernment: the virtue of critique

Thomas Aquinas treats matters of discernment (*discretio*) under the virtue of prudence. There are special reasons why we give special attention to discernment today: biblical and patristic renewal, the emphasis on the promptings of the Holy Spirit, greater attention to the creative power of the conscience under the influence of the Holy Spirit, a renewed interest in spiritual experience and, lastly, the new situation of the pluralistic and sometimes confused society that makes the virtue of critique imperative.

More than ever, we have to ask the question, "Whom shall we follow?" The emphasis on reciprocity of consciences makes discernment regarding ourselves and our partners an important aspect of a mature conscience. Besieged by so many ideologies, we have to heed Jesus' warning, "Beware of false prophets... you will recognize them by the fruits they bear. Can grapes be picked from briars or figs from thistles? In the same way, a good tree always yields good fruit and a poor tree bad fruit" (Mt 7:15-17).

Paul mentions a special charism in the Church, "the ability to distinguish true spirits from false" (1 Cor 12:10). But all Christians are admonished to exercise discernment. "But do not trust any and every spirit, my friends; test the spirits, whether they are from God" (1 Jn 4:1). The criterion, "every spirit which acknowledges that Jesus Christ has come in the flesh is from God" (1 Jn 4:2), is pronounced by John against the Gnostics. They denied the incarnation in true humanity and, therefore, they also disregarded commitment to the bodily world. We might draw the conclusion that all who are not willing to co-operate for the embodiment of freedom, fidelity, goodness and non-violence in the world around them are not true prophets.

Whoever is inspired by the Holy Spirit does not contradict the doctrine of Christ transmitted by the apostles (1 Jn 2:24; 4:6). For Paul, the condition of discernment is conversion of heart and mind, which is the work of the Holy Spirit. "Adapt yourselves no longer to the pattern of this present world but let your minds be remade and your whole nature thus transformed. Then you will be able to discern the will of God and to know what is good, acceptable and perfect" (Rom 12:2).

These words of Paul can easily be related to what we have said about fundamental option and the transforming power of fundamental dispositions. We can easily be deceived by the falsehood in the world unless we live fully in the light of Christ. "Let no one deceive you with shallow arguments... Live like people who are at home in daylight, for where the light is, there all goodness springs up, all justice and truth. Try to find out what would please the Lord" (Eph 5:6-10).

Discernment depends upon one's wholeness and the openness of one's conscience to the Spirit. "This is my prayer, that your love may grow ever richer and richer in knowledge and insight of every kind and may thus bring you the gift of true discernment" (Phil 1: 9-10). Profound faith experience and the fulfilment of Christ's law of love are the conditions for recognizing what things are most worthwhile.

St. Ignatius of Loyola follows the pattern of the Scriptures and of the great spiritual tradition when, in his *Spiritual Exercises*, he offers objective criteria for discrimination and points especially to the spiritual level on which a person must live who desires the gift of discernment.

It is noteworthy that in the whole treatise on discernment Ignatius never uses the word "prudence". He is not so much interested in offering a systematic treatise on virtues as in docility to the Holy Spirit. He feels that it is not enough for a person to seek and to welcome help from other spiritual people; even more important is to be on guard against "the kind of behaviour that belongs to the selfish nature: fornication, impurity . . . contentiousness, envy . . . and the like" (Gal 5:19-21), and always to strive for the kind of desires, deeds and qualities that bring "the harvest of the Spirit: love, joy, peace, patience" and so forth (Gal 5:22).

Like Paul and John, Ignatius is positive, focusing on the presence of the Spirit. Everything should be done to keep oneself open to the Spirit and to reach the level where the presence of the Spirit can be experienced. "Then the peace of God, which is beyond our utmost understanding, will keep guard over your hearts" (Phil 4:7). He presupposes that the person can prepare himself to have this kind of experience and then, in moments of discernment and decision, can remember this spiritual experience and judge the present situation in its light. Here, there is neither an alienated objectivism nor a dangerous subjectivism. It is care for both the purity of heart (of conscience) and for spiritual criteria.

Although Ignatius thinks about spiritual persons who help others, he is not primarily concerned with a confessor. His main purpose is to help the person himself to make the discernment. In this same spirit, I would never allow myself to make a decision, for instance, for a priest who wants to leave the priesthood and marry. However, I would offer not only criteria but would insist that he should make the decision only after having made a great effort to live on the level of the Spirit. This might need weeks or months of intensive prayer and vigilance over one's motives.

The uniqueness and creativity of conscience is not just for one's own sake; it is for co-humanity in and for the reciprocity of consciences. Hence, discernment concerns the common good in Church and society, and the good of each of our fellowmen. Church and world need a critical conscience. (The word "critique" comes from the Greek *krinein*, which approximates our "discernment".) In a pluralistic society and world, Christians should be an active leaven of the virtue of critique. There are three options. Either we choose critique in the sight of God or we fall into one of the two extreme deviations of idle conformism or vicious critique. We must also be ready to accept criticism from others and to acknowledge our own shortcomings and faults. We have to listen to the prophets even if they shake us and unmask our errors. Towards community and society, critique must be exercised as a ministry in continuing service for the common good. However, one should have given a hundred signs of solidarity and cooperation before proffering one effective and credible protest.

The virtue of critique presupposes gentle persuasion, self-control and commitment to non-violent speech and action. Generalizing accusations and lamentations do more harm than good; they become part of the confusion. Our critique must be detailed, clear, and always against a background of appreciation expressed for all the good. It becomes virtue only if we believe in the inner core, the divine spark, and the resources of those whom we criticize. As expression of enmity, it is vicious. The virtue of critique is a part of the ongoing dialogue and reconciliation in the world. On this road we must be ready to accept an open-ended compromise, but with the understanding that we continue our shared ministry of discernment and peaceful striving for a healthier community and society.[66]

Summing up, we can say that we have a distinctively Christian conscience if we are deeply rooted in Christ, aware of his presence and his gifts, ready to join him in his love for all his people. Everything will be tested as to whether it can be offered to Christ as fitting response to his love, his gifts, and to the needs of our fellowmen.

V. SIN AND SANITY

Once we have realized that conscience is the inner core, the deepest wellspring of integration and wholeness, it becomes evident that many forms of mental and physical unhealthiness are caused by a corrupted conscience. Whoever has quenched the light that comes from within, and has allowed his will and intelligence to disintegrate through indulgence of the selfish self, has a corrupted conscience. Gradually he has lost freedom for truth and goodness. "To the pure all things are pure, but nothing is pure to the tainted minds of disbelievers, corrupted alike in reason and conscience. They profess to acknowledge God but deny him by their actions. Their detestable obstinacy disqualifies them for any good work" (Titus 1:15-16).

I do not intend now to cover all the dimensions of the interrelation of sin, health and sanity, but it is important to see how health and sanity are related to the healthy or unhealthy conscience.

Since the longing for inner wholeness and the yearning for truth and goodness are the most important dimensions of our human existence, there cannot be full human health and wholeness if conscience is corrupted. As we saw earlier, it is an evil if we make an erroneous assessment about an important decision. But it is a much greater evil for us and for the world around us if our inner integrity is destroyed or handicapped.

Not each ailment or psychic defect has to do with sin. There can be suffering as a truly human condition and a way to greater maturity. We should never judge suffering people in a moralistic way. But by its very nature each sin is an enemy of sanity. It would be a grave error and, for Christians, a sin to consider health and sanity only in a perspective of the functioning of our various organs. A biochemical understanding of health, therapy and sickness is not only simplistic but is dangerous reductionism. The wellspring of human health rises from an inner wholeness and openness; and sin contradicts and diminishes the yearning for these qualities.

I am not speaking here, of course, of the hundreds of "mortal sins" invented by legalists and ritualists, but of sin as acting against one's conscience, and especially the gradual destruction of the integrity of conscience itself. Sin is alienation from one's better self, loss of knowledge of the unique name by which we are called, a plunging into darkness, and a split in the depth of our existence. If our conscience is tainted, we cannot build up healthy relationships with others but, rather, will contaminate the world around us with all the symptoms of alienation, falsehood and abuse.

The relatedness of sin with unhealthiness has been noted down through the ages. And today, what the Bible says about the inner and outer destruction caused by sin is confirmed, illustrated and presented in scientific terms by great psychologists and therapists like Erikson, Fromm, Frankl and many others.[67] Only gradually do we understand scientifically how grave is the noögenic neurosis caused by a negative response to the inner longing of the conscience for wholeness and openness. And how can a person consider himself healthy on a human level, if he has missed finding his true identity and integrity?

Each sin negatively affects man's wholeness and creative liberty. It contradicts the very meaning and purpose of our conscience and our freedom. By losing our own inner freedom and integrity, we are doomed to become slaves of the powers from which Christ has freed us if we believe in him. Sin contradicts our faith and, therefore, our liberation in Christ. Especially habitual sin and lack of repentance deepen the wound in our inmost self, while conscience still cries out for wholeness and health. "The experience of a so-called 'bad conscience' may be viewed as a profound rift in the depth of man's being, leading to a sense of disunity in oneself".[68]

Different types of corruption of conscience have different consequences regarding wholeness, integration and integrity.

1. *Escape into moral theory and compensation scrupulosity*

Habitual sin not only diminishes the noödynamics towards ultimate meaning and towards the "other"; it can also weaken more and more the psychodynamic that strives for personal integration. Sinful man, shackled by selfishness and sloth, can gradually accept the split between moral knowledge and his will. Such a person can become a moralist in a legalistic and ritualistic sense. He can fight for minutiae and can deliver talks on moral theory without being moved or touched in his heart to act on the Word. He will, however, become more and more blind to the great gift and law of love of God and neighbour. He will know many laws with which to deceive himself and others about his lack of knowledge of the supreme law in which the heart of the healthy person rejoices. He will deceive himself by being zealous and even scrupulous about a few small things while at the same time disregarding love, mercy and justice. His moral discourse can take on more and more the character of moral insanity. There is a personality split: a "self" who talks about morals and another who acts and lives without the human longing for wholeness and integrity. In spite of his orthodox moral discourse — but orthodoxy only on small details, without any vision of the wholeness that is distinctively human and Christian — this person falls back on lower levels of conventional and utilitarian morality.

2. *The dark energies of the strong character*

A person with a very strong psycho-dynamic towards inner wholeness can feel deeply the remorse of conscience as a call to conversion. But if, because of pride and arrogance, he nevertheless habitually resists the call, then a mechanism of the stubborn sinfulness activates another kind of inner integration. The strong will, selfish and arrogant, imposes its dictate on the intellect, and the intellect then finds a thousand reasons to approve what the will desires. Finally, the intellect sees only what pride and arrogance dictate, and the result can be a person in the image of a Hitler or a Stalin, who is indeed "integrated" — all of one piece — but whose enormous energies will reach out only for their own dark goals. To find an inner integration he has completely lost integrity and openness. Hence, he will be unable to have healthy relationships with persons or to live in a genuine reciprocity of conscience.

3. Sin as loss of joy, peace and strength

Whether sin destroys integration or integrity, wholeness or openness, it will always deprive the person of a capacity to rejoice and to repose in the good. It diminishes one's capacity to appreciate, to be grateful, to share in other people's joys and to bring joy to them. Where there is no inner harmony or openness to the good and the truth, one cannot have peace and, therefore, cannot radiate peace. Rather, such a person will everywhere communicate his inner disunity and his lack of unity with the good. He may imitate joy by a show of gaiety, but his laughter will be hollow. He may try to project a sense of humour, but it will be sarcasm and irony that hurts relationships. And since he is not at peace with himself, he will always be tempted to war *against* someone or something but is unable to be *for* a common ideal.

4. Loss of dignity

Article 16 of the Constitution on the Church in the Modern World, quoted above, asserts that through habitual sin conscience itself gradually loses its dignity. It is tainted and becomes more and more perverted. The person becomes unable to respect the conscience and dignity of others and thereby reveals the loss of his own dignity.

5. Sinful loss of liberty

A partial loss of liberty can be caused by the sins and errors of others. Some repressions that block the normal functioning of conscience and liberty can be due to oppressive authority. But nothing can so much damage one's own liberty, especially one's creative liberty for the good, as habitual sin. The loss can be greater or less according to the gravity and number of the sins, and the duration of unrepentance. It is particularly great if there is a sinful fundamental option which, because of the long time of unrepentance, has inscribed itself in erring dispositions and attitudes.

6. *A catalogue of sins against liberty and sanity:*

Not to outgrow the lower levels of conscience; not to learn and unlearn; not to overcome a static view of life, norms, rules and conscience; to learn many things but not what is good and what is true;

To refuse to be committed to work for the freedom and dignity of all and, in consequence, not to increase one's own freedom but, rather, to endanger it;

To foster passivity in education; to look more for submission and uniformity than for growth in moral responsibility; to stifle initiative and creative liberty;

To avoid risk and to prefer flight and non-involvement rather than commitment to common ideals and arduous vocation; to favour a merely intellectualistic or voluntaristic education;

To support centralism and authoritarian forms of government that stifle subsidiarity and collegiality, and favour uncritical obedience;

To allow others to manipulate one's conscience; not to protest the manipulation of other people's conscience by a system of reward and punishment instead of offering genuine motivation and appeal to the sincere conscience; to tolerate manipulation of public opinion;

To refuse to listen to the prophets and to acquire discernment;

To split religion into a separated dogmatic (abstract doctrines not concerned with man's wholeness and salvation) and morals proposed without a convincing value system; orthodoxy separated from orthopraxis;

To yield to pressure groups instead of taking up the cause of the weak and oppressed; to justify violent oppression or to speak and act about liberation only or mainly in terms of violent reaction;

To propose an ethics of prohibitions and controls to the detriment of an ethics of creative liberty and fidelity.

VI. REPENTANCE AND REBIRTH OF THE INTEGRITY OF CONSCIENCE

Our discourse on conversion and reconciliation would be somewhat abstract if it did not relate to the rebirth of consciousness, wholeness and integrity.

Max Scheler's treatise on repentance is presented in the great perspective of rebirth.[69] Conscience that is tainted and corrupted by sin can be restored because it is never totally destroyed except in the case of "sin against the Holy Spirit", where all wholeness and integrity are thoroughly destroyed. God calls to repentance and thus to a new life by touching, through his grace, the depth of our conscience where the wound still cries for healing. And if the sinner turns to God with all his heart, God's powerful action grants him wholeness and integrity again. If the sinner repents, the blood of the covenant "will cleanse his conscience from the deadness of his former ways and fit him for the service of the living God" (Heb 9:14).

This promise of God, offered by his grace, should be the most urgent calling to the sinner to desire his own inner wholeness, integrity and openness. Even if we have not definitely turned away from God but realize that our conscience has been obscured and weakened, we hear the insistent call of grace: "So let us make our approach in sincerity of heart and full assurance of faith, our guilty hearts sprinkled clean, our bodies washed with pure water" (Heb 10:22).

If the sins, although grave, were "only" venial, there remains still a precious alliance between one's inborn desire for wholeness and one's fundamental commitment, freely affirmed, towards the good. Our remorse of conscience can then much more easily become a salvific contrition, though always only through God's healing forgiveness and purifying grace.

But if it is a case of mortal sin, then the fundamental option was made for evil and the chaos is so great that repentance is indeed a great miracle of God's grace, a rebirth in the full sense. Yet, man is so much God's good creation that even after a mortal sin there is still in him a remnant of God's image and likeness, a natural longing for wholeness on which grace can build. Rebirth, however, is not possible without profound sorrow, without a contrition in which the whole soul is shaken by the acknowledged insight about the terrible injustice committed against God and good. All good resolutions are weak and inefficient if they are not born of a profound contrition.

"Contrition is the most revolutionary force in the moral world".[70] It is a new encounter with God and good, and a new espousal between the will, longing for true love, and the intellect searching for truth and goodness. But this is not possible without the pangs of a new birth. "The Christian knows that every resolution which is not born in the pain of sorrow for sins remains stale and sterile, because it did not arise from the ultimate depth and, above all, did not come from God, was not conceived in God. Only sorrow softens the hardness of our nature so that a permanent 'new orientation of will' towards God, founded on that which is ultimate, can be impressed on us".[71]

The honour of God requests that each time we have sinned even venially we repent and ask forgiveness and healing as soon as possible.

There is no greater danger for our wholeness than to postpone repentance and conversion. Unrepented venial sins prepare the downfall of the good fundamental option. And we should realize how difficult it is to return to God and find inner wholeness and integrity again after a fundamental option against God.

VII. RECIPROCITY OF CONSCIENCES

1. *The meaning of reciprocity of consciences*

The root words, *con* and *scientia* (to know together) already indicate a mutuality of consciences. We have to see the reciprocal action. The healthy conscience allows wholesome relationships with neighbour and the community. Equally and perhaps more fundamentally, wholesome relationships in mutual love and respect, and a healthy community and society, greatly promote the development and health of the individual conscience.

Surely, conscience also means self-reflection, self-awareness, to be at peace with oneself, to experience one's growing wholeness or the threat against it. But genuine self-awareness and self-reflection are existentially not possible without the experience of encounter with the other.

This is the theme of a profound book by Maurice Nédoncelle on the reciprocity of awareness, consciousness and conscience.[72] The person comes to his or her identity and integrity only in the reciprocity of awareness and conscience. One knows about one's own unique self only through the experience of relationship between Thou and I, which leads to the experience of the We. It is a matter of genuine love and respect when the other is accepted in his selfhood, his uniqueness. "Any kind of love that has another purpose or reason than the openness of I and Thou for a reciprocal communion is an illusion about love".[73]

Genuine reciprocity of knowledge, awareness and conscience enters into the other's perspectives or, better said, two distinct perspectives enter into a collegial conscientiousness.[74] This meeting of people in each one's singularity and identity, in mutual respect for each other's conscience, is a process of reciprocal liberation.[75] Where this bond of fidelity to the other's true self is established, each person can be freed from his mask.[76]

The two who have mutually accepted their diversity and their equal dignity in the profound sharing of conscientiousness, and with radical respect for their conscience, are no longer slaves of the superego; they are no longer just playing roles to please each other. They have come to genuine creative liberty and fidelity, free from that boring repetition which characterizes the mask of the superego.[77] When persons can enter into that ultimate solidarity without giving up their own identity, but rather in profound reverence and cooperation in the Spirit, then they are best prepared to discover the horizon of the divine.[78]

Through mutuality of consciences, a true ego-strength and self-respect arises that allows an ever greater respect and freedom for one another's conscience. Without this synthesis between the reverence that allows the other to be who he is and the solidarity by which the persons are a source of identity, integrity and authenticity for each other, there can be neither true freedom nor creative fidelity. The reciprocity of consciences is disturbed not only by lack of love and respect for others; it is a most painful experience for our own conscience to realize that we are, ourselves, unable to love. Thus bridges that sustain our own worth are destroyed.[79]

Kenneth Clarke makes some insightful remarks about empathy and humour in the context of reciprocity of consciences and the goal of absolute respect for the conscience of the other in self respect. "Humour puts the ego in perspective; it demands that if man accepts himself — respects himself and his fellowman — he must do so with a totality of acceptance. Humour unmasks pretence ... Empathy, like humour, has the capacity to identify with the joy, the anguish, the aspirations, the defeats and the transitory successes of the human beings ..., it demonstrates the interdependence, the oneness of mankind".[80]

2. Reciprocity of consciences in Paul's Letters

An individualistic concept of conscience it totally alien to Holy Scripture. Paul shows us how sensitive is the conscience of those who are freed by the law of the Spirit. They understand the deep desire of all people and even of all creation to have a share in the liberty of the sons and daughters of God. Those who live on the level of the Spirit are no longer under the power of the superego; they are not looking just for approval by others but are responding to their deepest desire to come to fullness of life and a full experience of saving solidarity. This is particularly a theme of the Epistle to the Romans, chapter 8.

Paul's call to be renewed in heart and mind in order to "be able to discern the will of God and to know what is good, acceptable and perfect" (Rom 12:2) is followed by a vision of building up the Body of Christ through all the gifts that God has bestowed on people. "Care as much about each other as about yourselves" (Rom 12:16). This concern extends equally, and even particularly, to those who are hostile to us. "If your enemy is hungry, feed him; if he is thirsty, give him a drink; by doing this you will heap live coals on his head. Do not let evil conquer you, but use good to defeat evil" (Rom 12:20). The Church becomes a visible sign of Christ's presence on earth — as it were, the Body of Christ — insofar as the disciples use all their talents and charisms in complementarity (Rom 12; 1 Cor 12:14; Eph 4).

In Romans 14 and 1 Corinthians 10, Paul discusses a very specific example of reciprocity of consciences: the loving attention which those who have progressed in faith give to the weaker consciences of their fellow Christians. Paul himself is convinced that there is no distinction between ritually clean and unclean food, yet he reminds the Christians to respect the conscientiousness of others. "For instance, one person will have faith enough to eat all kind of food, while a weaker one eats only vegetables. The person who eats must not hold in contempt the other who does not, and he who does not eat must not pass judgment on the one who does; for God has accepted him" (Rom 14:2-3).

This mutuality of conscience is rooted in our faith relationships with Christ. If we live for the Lord, we also live for each other in concern and respect for one another's conscience. "For no one of us lives and no one dies for himself alone. If we live, we live for the Lord; and if we die, we die for the Lord" (Rom 14:7-8). "Let no obstacle or stumbling block be placed in a brother's way. I am absolutely convinced, as a Christian, that nothing is impure in itself; only if a man considers a particular thing impure, then to him it is impure. If your brother is outraged by what you eat, then your conduct is no longer guided by love. Do not, by your eating, bring disaster to a person for whom Christ died" (Rom 14:13-15).

While Paul appreciates his own freedom from taboos and traditions that are no longer meaningful, he warns that it is something quite different to have contempt for fellow Christians who are still wavering or still have strong convictions about laws and traditions that, by one's own values, would no longer be binding. "Happy is the man who can make his decision with a clear conscience! But a man who has doubts is guilty if he eats, because his action does not arise from his conviction, and anything that does not arise from conviction (conscience) is sin. Those of us who have a robust conscience must accept as our own burden the tender scruples of weaker men, and not consider ourselves. Each of us must consider his neighbour and think what is for his good and will build up the common life" (Rom 14:22—15:2).

Again, in the First Letter to the Corinthians, chapter 10, Paul shows how he understands the reciprocity of consciences. The Council of the Apostles in Jerusalem had decided that Christians should "abstain from things polluted by contact with idols" (Acts 15:20). Paul does not conclude that it is intrinsically and absolutely evil to eat meat that was sacrificed to the idols and then sold on the market. He approaches the problem in a perspective of the reciprocity of consciences. The liberals, who were insisting on their own insight that the food is always the gift of the good God, ignored the injunction of the Council of the Apostles. They bragged of the freedom of their consciences, saying, "We are free to do anything". But Paul asks them, "But does everything help the building of the community? Each of you must regard not his own interests but the other person's" (1 Cor 10:23-24).

If nobody's conscience is hurt, he agrees that they can eat the meat with thanksgiving to God. "You may eat anything sold in the market without raising questions of conscience; for the earth is the Lord's and everything in it. If an unbeliever invites you to a meal and you care to go, eat whatever is put before you, without raising questions of conscience" (1 Cor 10:25-27). But the situation is quite different if the fact that the meat is sacrificed becomes a part of the context of eating. Even if an illumined conscience sees it only as a gift of the one God, the person must consider the conscience of the other. "But if somebody says to you, 'This food has been offered in sacrifice', then, out of consideration for him, and for conscience's sake, do not eat it: not your conscience, I mean, but the other person's. 'What?' you say, 'Is my freedom to be called into question by another man's conscience? If I partake with thankfulness, why am I blamed for eating food over which I have said grace?' Well, whether you eat or drink, or whatever you are doing, do all for the honour of God: give no offence to Jews or Greeks or to the church of God" (1 Cor 10:28-32).

According to Paul, it is evident that we cannot honour God from the depth of our conscience unless we are thankful but also respectful about the impact of our action on the wavering conscience of our fellowmen. Those who were not yet completely freed emotionally from their ancient cult might well have thought that those stronger characters took a double insurance, one with

Christ and one with the pagan gods. For Paul, it is the conduct, and not the material thing itself, that is always to be judged in the reciprocity of conscience, in the collegial solidarity for wholeness and salvation.

3. Religious freedom in a Humanist and Christian perspective

One of the most important dimensions of the reciprocity of consciences is the full recognition of liberty of conscience and, even more specifically, of religious liberty. Everything we have said so far about conscience would be disowned if we were to refuse a full acknowledgement of freedom in religious matters as a specific case of freedom of conscience. The history of the problem is highly relevant for the whole development of moral and religious consciousness. A full understanding of it sheds its light on the diversity of historical circumstances but also on our own earlier question, "How free was theology?"

a) The history of freedom of conscience and of religious freedom

The striving of the churches and of secular society towards full recognition of religious freedom is among the most significant signs of our times. The *Universal Declaration of Human Rights*, adopted by the General Assembly of the United Nations on December 10, 1948, says in Article 18: "Everyone has the right to freedom of thought, conscience and religion or belief, and freedom, either alone or in community with others and in public or private, to manifest his religion or belief in teaching, practice, worship and observance".

Article 30 underlines this declaration: "Nothing in this declaration may be interpreted as implying for any state, group or person any right to engage in any activity or to perform any act aimed at the destruction of any of the rights and freedoms set forth herein".

The encyclical of Pope John XXIII, *Peace on Earth*, and the declaration of Vatican II on religious freedom are clear and profound responses to these signs of the times. It is a major breakthrough in the life of the Church. And in all honesty, it must be recognized also as a real development and conversion.

To do justice to the Church about her different approach that would be considered today as unfaithful to the Gospel, we

have to see the historical context. For a long time the Church
fulfilled her role as teacher in a totally Catholic culture in which
even such liberal-minded men as Abelard — who strongly asserted that there is possibility of invincible error in religious
matters — denied emphatically that a person can err in matters
of faith in Christ and in the Church without a guilty conscience.[81]
A strong theological trend also tended even to hold that the
conscience of a Christian is always, or almost always, guilty if
it dissents from the doctrines of the Church, even if it is not
a matter of doctrine revealed by Jesus Christ.[82]

In the Constantinian era, when the state wanted support by
the Church, and considered uniformity in faith and morals as
one of its absolute foundations, and where the Church was
strongly supported by this very state, it was almost normal that
there would be more emphasis on the objective truth and on
conformity with the Church's teaching than on the personal
conscience. It was an age when most people lived on the conventional level of conscience. There was a general tendency to
judge severely as guilty those who publicly dissented from any
of the teachings of the Church — Galileo, for example, for his
opinion that the earth is not the centre of the universe. There
was more emphasis on the essence of things or the objectivity
of doctrinal formulations than on the existential truthfulness of
the person in the community.[83] Religion was somehow viewed
as the common bond to a system of truths and an absolute
allegiance to religious authority representing God on earth.

Although she continued always to teach that the act of faith
is, by its very nature, a free act, the Church also manifested her
uncertainty by frequent opposition to freedom of religion: by
the very institution of the Inquisition, by the burning of heretics,
and by a number of documents opposing the modern idea of
religious liberty without the necessary distinctions.

The declaration of the Second Vatican Council on religious
freedom recognizes the Church's past failures in this matter. "In
the life of the people of God as it has made its pilgrim way
through the vicissitudes of history, there have appeared at times
ways of acting which were less in accord with the spirit of the
Gospel and even opposed to it".[84] A widespread theory about
religious freedom regarded as normal the "thesis" that whenever

Catholics are in the majority they can request the state to restrict the freedom of other religions; and the "hypothesis" was accepted that where Catholics are in the minority they would approve and claim for themselves equal freedom for all. This surely did not work for the credibility of the Church in the modern world.

The development of the doctrine of religious freedom is a classical example of how the official doctrine of the Church can be prepared by constructive dissent by theologians to the official position of the Church. Already in the last century, Montalembert, Bishop Dupanloup, Lord Acton and many others, and in our century especially Jean Jacques Maritain and John Courtney Murray, were teaching practically what Vatican II affirmed as the official position. An outstanding Protestant ecumenical author was probably accurate when he wrote, before the Council: "It would be an understatement to say that for each book or article in favour of the traditional doctrine, ten have been published defending religious freedom".[85] "This long-suffering cause of dissent within the Church was vindicated in the declaration".[86]

The history of this problem can show us how the Church can and must grow in an understanding of both the natural law and the Gospel. I agree with Panikkar and others who insist that the Vatican Council's declaration of religious liberty means a profound spiritual mutation and a transition into a new phase of history.[87] The Church now fully accepts the focus on the person and the reciprocity of consciences as a basis of community life and evangelization.

b) The autonomy of the secular society and the state

Old Israel and most of the pagan societies did not distinguish temporal society from the religious community. Constantine the Great brought into his alliance with the Church the Roman tradition in which the emperor considered himself as *Pontifex Maximus*, supreme pontiff. In reaction, the Roman pontiffs (the popes) affirmed themselves not only as supreme pontiffs of the Church but also as supreme authority over all the states.

The strongest such affirmation was made solemnly by Boniface VIII in his famous Bull, *Unam Sanctam*. It taught that temporal power was in the hands of kings only "at the nod and suffrance of the priest".[88] And one year after the solemn publication of the Bull, Boniface instructed Albert of Halsburg that "no earthly power has anything except what it receives from the ecclesiastical power" and that "all powers are from Us, as the Vicar of Jesus Christ".[89]

The official change of this doctrine was made possible through the courageous dissent of St. Robert Cardinal Bellarmine. His thesis was that the Church has power over the temporal sphere only indirectly, insofar as she proclaims to all men, including the temporal authority, the doctrine and commandments of God. The official change that made possible the teaching of Vatican II on religious liberty was initiated chiefly by Leo XIII and Pius XII. Leo XIII thoroughly rejected the medieval concept of relations between Church and state. "The Almighty has given charge of the human race to two powers, the ecclesiastical and the civil, the one being set over divine and the other over human things. Each in its kind is supreme, each has fixed limits within which it is contained".[90] And Pius XII called the teaching of Boniface VIII in this matter "a medieval conception . . . conditioned by the times", and expressed his firm hope that these errors will not be repeated again.[91]

The official teaching of the Church has gradually clarified the fact that the purpose of the state is not to protect certain Church doctrines but to protect the equal dignity and freedom of all citizens, including and especially their freedom of conscience. The declaration of Vatican II makes this particularly clear. "For the rest, the usages of society are to be usages of freedom in their full range. These require that the freedom of the human person be respected as far as possible, and curtailed only when and insofar as necessary.[92] The conciliar teaching is a firm promise that Church authorities will not interfere in the functions of the state, and that when she speaks out about legislation concerning moral questions she will do so not by imposition but by arguing in view of the common good.[93]

c) Full recognition of the dignity of the human person

Church and state are equally interested in respecting and protecting freedom of conscience and of religion, since otherwise they would not fully recognize personhood, the fundamental dignity and right of all persons, and thus would betray an essential part of their task. A state cannot flourish and does not truly promote human culture unless it realizes how all life in community and society depends on personhood: on the freedom of and respect for people's conscience. It is a duty of the Church to recognize and to underline this mission of the state as such, but also on behalf of the religious message. "It is on this dignity of the moral agent that religious freedom is grounded, the freedom to act in conformity with the religious conviction to which one loyally adheres. In order to acknowledge and protect effectively the dignity of moral subjects in their members, temporal societies — states or international society — must, therefore, sanction religious freedom in their legislation".[94]

The state cannot prevent people from erring. However, it can protect and promote people's right and readiness to search freely for truth and thus become capable of genuine cooperation. Nobody can dispense the human person from his or her personal responsibility to act in conformity with the judgment of conscience. The more the freedom of conscience is respected and protected, the greater is the hope that people will truly live according to their conscience. Only for the sake of the freedom, dignity and the rights of all can the state legitimately restrict people's freedom.

The Vatican Council's declaration on religious freedom recognizes that respect for conscience and protection of its freedom promotes genuine co-existence, collaboration and co-participation. "Let them form human persons who will be lovers of true freedom, persons, in other words, who will come to decisions on their own judgment and, in the light of truth, govern their activities with a sense of responsibility, and strive after what is true and right, willing always to join others in cooperative efforts".[95]

In our pluralistic society and world we understand better what Thomas Aquinas taught: that "human laws cannot hinder everything that the natural law forbids".[96] It would not only contradict the declaration of Vatican II but also be unwise if a Catholic majority, or a Catholic minority with great political power, would try to impose on others what they consider to be requirements of the natural law. Not only have we found out that we sometimes have erred in natural law teaching and must seek truth with all people of good will, but we also realize now that efforts to impose our teaching on others do not serve the good purpose, since laws on moral matters are ineffective If they do not re-echo in people's consciences.

It is not difficult to illustrate this truth. When, after World War I, the poor people in Germany had lost almost all their property through inflation and other causes, the government proposed a law to redistribute a part of the property of great landowners who were mostly of the high nobility. The Catholic hierarchy gave an order to Catholics to vote against this law in the name of the "natural right of property". That bill was only against the selfish interests of a small rich minority, and the hierarchy's advice was based on a rather individualistic and static understanding of the doctrine on the right of property. By trying to impose that doctrine on the state, the Church lost credibility in her moral and religious teaching.[97]

The 1948 declaration of the United Nations, in Article 29, Section 2, also sets forth its purpose to grant as much freedom as possible, and to do so in view of the common good. "In the exercise of his rights and freedoms, everyone shall be subject only to such limitations as are determined by law solely for the purpose of securing due recognition and respect for the rights and freedoms of others and of meeting the just requirements of morality, public order and the general welfare in a democratic society". The last words may be open to some misinterpretation if "democratic society" is not understood as expression of the consensus of the people. There can be arbitrary decisions about what morality, public order and the general welfare might be.

Respect for conscience and religious liberty is a great service to the good of society and to peace on earth. Most political conflicts could easily be resolved peacefully if respect for these basic and most important rights reigned in all societies.

d) For the sake of genuine faith and evangelization

It is not enough for Christians to give only grudging tolerance to dissent. More than anyone else they should appreciate freedom of conscience and of religion for the very sake of faith and evangelization, and of course also for the sake of the responsibility of persons created in the image and likeness of God. "To tolerate dissent is today merely prudent; to respect the conscience and the person of another is noble. The cornerstone of religious freedom is *religious*, not political".[98]

The Vatican Council's declaration on religious freedom makes clear the point that it is not a matter of political prudence or adjustment but a response to revelation as the Church can understand it here and now. "Religious freedom in society is entirely consonant with the act of the freedom of Christian faith".[99] The Council was aware that the act of faith and all expressions of religion can only gain when there is a climate of respect for conscience and religion. There can be no statistical census of the kingdom of God. Only those who search with a sincere heart for truth, and act on it, belong to the kingdom of truth and justice.

If applied in the whole life of the Church, the declaration on religious freedom is probably the most decisive step on the road to Christian unity.[100] The Church manifests her fidelity to the design of God, who does not destroy the wheat in order to remove the cockle (cf. Mt 13:13; 30:42).

Christ emphatically refused to be a political messiah because he wanted to draw all people freely to himself and to the Father. "God calls men to serve him in spirit and truth. Hence, they are bound in conscience but they stand under no compulsion".[101] If God has risked creating us in freedom and for freedom, the Church has to do the same in fidelity to God. Only thus can she herself be enriched by creative fidelity and liberty.

Firm adherence and profound dedication to religious freedom foster the best conditions for witnessing to the truth and gaining credibility. The Gospel can touch only the free will, and to touch it we must provide the external conditions necessary for that freedom and never allow any kind of manipulation in matters of faith. St. Paul teaches us that love is the plenitude of the law; but he also teaches us that Christ has freed us for the very freedom of love. Therefore, we must do everything possible so that faith and love can unfold our creative energies.[102]

Nobody is saved by mere ritual or by insincere adherence to dogmas. We are saved by a faith that implies a firm self-commitment to good and to God, and a sincere search for truth in order to act on it. Religious freedom has nothing to do with indifference in matters of morality or truth. Rather, it is an essential condition for the Christian's commitment to give witness and to win everyone for Christ, and to serve the salvation of all humankind.

With Karl Barth, today's theology speaks of *analogia fidei* as way of salvation. This analogy of faith is given where a person is searching for what is true and good, and acts in his own freedom according to his conscience. All pressure in matters of religion, and any form of manipulation of conscience, causes temptations that could lead people away from the way of salvation.

The Spanish theologian, Julian Marías, is surely not alone in his conviction that the paralysis of theology since the seventeenth century has been largely due to the oppressive spirit of the Inquisition that expected the Catholic theologian to commit no error in the search for truth. As a consequence, errors in theology could not be creatively corrected.

Religion is not something that can be applied as a juridical code; it is rather like a language, and if one knows the grammar, the vocabulary and the genius of the language, he can make creative use of it. "It is similar with religion. It has a structure, a content. The religious act should be creative. Therefore freedom is the condition for the very possibility of religious life".[103] Especially the evangelization of all nations and cultures depends on this vitality and creativity of our faith and of all of the life of the Church.

e) Freedom for the people's conscience first

The Church must affirm the freedom of conscience *itself*, and not just for herself or with stress only on freedom to choose membership in the Catholic Church. Christ has come to set all people free for truth. He addresses his message to people's conscience. He does not want to have submissive slaves but friends. "I call you servants no longer, for the servant does not know what his Master is about. I call you friends, for I have shared with you whatever I have received from the Father" (Jn 15:15).

The choice of the Catholic faith is possible only when conscience is fully respected; hence the Church's prime mission is not to claim freedom for herself but, rather, to be a sacrament of liberty and liberation. She is a servant of the people. "Religious freedom, in sum, makes not only a better Church and a firmer obedience among Christians; its constitutional recognition and protection also makes a better government. Thus, again, in the end, God's will for the realm of the redemption and his purpose for the created order blend in a final harmony".[104]

The Vatican II declaration on religious freedom, art. 9, underlines that "Christians are bound to respect it (the doctrine of freedom) all the more conscientiously". They thus give witness that they are truly concerned for the cause of Christ, for the liberty of people to search for truth and to act on it as they best understand it. It is always deplorable if people's consciences are not allowed freedom to search and to act according to their sincere judgment. But the evil is much greater if consciences are stifled in favour of the true religion, for in such a case the very truth and love of that religion is concealed.[105]

In order to preach faithfully and effectively the Gospel of our Lord Jesus Christ, the Church will present the message in the context of "religion as liberty", and will promote the religiosity of freedom for the sake of salvation of humankind.[106] It does not serve the Church if abstract truth is inculcated; she is sacrament of salvation and truth only to the extent that she promotes genuine growth of freedom in the search for and dedication to the truth which comes to us in the person of Christ and should come to all nations in the persons of his disciples.

The proclamation of the Good News and the call to conversion should make people fully conscious that they are called in freedom and for true freedom. Morality, as witnessed and proposed by the Church, should follow the prophetic tradition so that people can grasp, as gift of the Lord, the new historical situation *(kairos)*, with its opportunity to realize something new, to grow in liberty, in goodness and truthfulness.[107]

The Council's declaration on religious freedom is not at all an option for the individualism that has branded most of the liberalism of the last century. It is an option for covenant morality, a common commitment to freedom in responsibility. "Religious freedom . . . ought to have this further purpose and aim, that men may come to act with greater responsibility in fulfilling their duties in community life" (art. 8). To my mind, the declaration is a profound option for a greater faith in the Holy Spirit and, dependent on it, a moderate optimism in people's fundamental goodness that allows us to appeal to their conscience and help them to discover their inner resources in genuine freedom.

The declaration stresses also the Church's freedom to proclaim the Good News and to teach Gospel morality. She has a mission and, therefore, a right and duty to assist people in discovering truth and the exigencies of the law written in their hearts. However, there should be no doubt that the freedom of the Church as a prophetic voice in the world will be the harvest of her own faithfulness to the freedom for which Christ has freed all people. For the freedom she claims is not so much for her own sake as for her ministry which sustains the consciences of her members and of all people of good will.

There is more hope that the Church's prophetic voice will be heard even by non-Christians if her members and office-holders present themselves not as a power or pressure group but as moral agents uniting with all who search with sincere conscience for what is good and truthful. "Certain elementary principles of a moral and religious character exist which constitute the fundamental inheritance of all people and on which there is agreement as inevitable foundation for common life, in order to attain the construction of a true social and world-wide order of justice and peace".[108]

The Christian duty to promote justice, honesty and peace in social, economic and political life falls first on those citizens of the secular world who enjoy a Christian vision, along with competence in their respective fields. If Church authorities speak out on matters concerning the secular city, they cannot, according to the understanding of religious freedom set forth in the Vatican II declaration, impose their authority but can argue and try to convince the consciences of citizens and of the authorities in the secular city. They aim above all at educating the citizens' consciences and at respect for conscience itself.[109] This is an important part of the social mission of the Church.

f) The prophetic ministry of dissent in the Church

Humanly speaking, we can say that the official Church would never have come to full recognition of the intrinsic value of religious freedom without the prophetic ministry of dissent within the Church on this matter. The official teaching of the Church needs those who dedicate themselves to the humane sciences — the study of anthropology, sociology, psychology and so forth — together with the study of the Scriptures. The Church needs, above all, absolute sincerity and honesty in her own ranks, so that those who enjoy special competence will be free to speak out against any trends towards ossification of doctrines and against all temptations of ideologies within the Church's life and teaching.

The declaration on religious liberty did not address the matter of right to dissent within the Church, but the Council did so in other documents. The Dogmatic Constitution on the Church (art. 32 and 37) stresses the right and duty of lay people to speak out freely on matters concerning not only the secular world but also the Church, if they enjoy a particular competence.

The same emphasis is found in the Decree on Lay Apostolate (art. 3); and the Constitution on the Church in the Modern World (art. 62) is even more articulate. After having spoken on freedom as the basic condition for progress of culture, the latter text speaks of the necessity of freedom for theologians within the Church. "It is to be hoped that many lay people will receive an appropriate formation in the sacred sciences, and that some will develop and deepen their studies by their own labours. In order that such persons may fulfil their proper function, let it be recognized that all the faithful, clerical and lay, possess a lawful freedom of inquiry and of thought, and the freedom to express their minds humbly and courageously about those matters in which they enjoy competence".

Obedience in the Church makes sense only through the reciprocity of consciences and the common dedication to truth which is possible only if there is freedom of inquiry and freedom to speak out even in dissent from official documents, as has happened frequently in the past, but sometimes only too late and after many losses.[110]

Dissent will have a constructive effect on the whole Church only if it comes from men and women who are thoroughly dedicated to the Gospel of Christ and to the service of the Church. It needed the prophetic dissent of Friedrich Spee against torture and burning of so-called witches to bring the official teaching of the Church more in concordance with evangelical leniency and respect for the dignity and conscience of people.[111] And it needed the prophetic and competent voices of men like Heribert Doms and others to overcome the Augustinian trend in the Church that considered the conjugal act fundamentally as shameful and to be excusable only by the explicit and direct intention to "use" the intercourse for procreation.[112] The chapter on marriage in the Pastoral Constitution on the Church in the Modern World could come into being only through a greater freedom of thought and speech in the Church. It is unthinkable that the Church can be an effective prophetic voice in the world unless the Church authorities allow prophetic voices within the Church to be heard.

g) Freedom of religious education and education for freedom

Those who are suspicious that the Vatican II declaration on religious freedom might mean indifference regarding truth should note, for instance, the emphatic reaffirmation of the freedom of religious education and specifically the freedom for Catholic education in Catholic schools.[113]

I do not see it as a clear and right solution about freedom of conscience and of religion if religious schools are only tolerated by the state, and parents who want their children to go to religious schools have to pay the full tax for state schools without receiving any subsidy for the education of their children in the equally accredited schools of their choice. Surely, on this matter, the United States has still some things to learn about freedom of religion from Western Europe and from Canada. A state monopoly of schools will always tend towards a conventional morality of obedience, whereas a diversity of schools can better serve the education of a creative conscience and constructive dissent, made with discernment.

VIII. CHURCH AUTHORITY AND THE RECIPROCITY OF CONSCIENCES

A sincere conscience is, for everyone, the supreme authority under God. It is by respecting this authority that we can adore God in spirit and truth. However, we have seen that our conscience comes to its fullness only in reciprocity with other consciences. We receive light and strength through the authority of conscientious persons, the saints, the prophets, who are at the same time competent in important areas of life.

Our conscience does not receive so much light and impulse from abstract laws as from the exemplary person who lives truthfully under the authority of his conscience and respects wholly the conscience of others. We live the communion of saints by sharing our reflections and our moral and religious experiences, by encouraging each other to ever greater depth of conscience. The greatest gifts to the Church and to each of us are the saints who have brought themselves totally under the authority of the loving God through a pure heart, a sincere conscience.

The creativity of God's people depends on the prophetic people who are always vigilant for the coming of the Lord and can communicate to our conscience their experience: "It is the Lord who calls you". The office-holders will enjoy greater authority in the Church if they are grateful for the "authority" of the prophets and the many humble saints who live fully the reciprocity of consciences under God and in full co-responsibility with and for all of God's people.

Christ has sent apostles as witnesses, people who have lived with him, have come to know him and have allowed themselves to be guided by the Holy Spirit. The Church flourishes when popes and bishops are truly charismatic, zealous shepherds and proclaimers of the Good News. Their authority for the conscience of all open-minded people grows if they are outstanding observers and listeners, able to learn from the example of the saints and from the voices of the prophets and of men and women competent to speak by their learning and by their spirit of prayer

In our difficult times of transitions and worldwide meetings of various cultures, the cooperation of the papal and episcopal magisterium with theologians is of paramount importance for a better understanding of the signs of the times. Headed by the pope, bishops and theologians stand together in the service of the Word of God. All are guardians and promoters of the faith in mutual complementarity. They can be leaders of the people only if they are the most outstanding listeners, listening to the word of God, listening to each other, listening to the faithful, especially to those who embody the moral and religious authority of life, competence and experience, while listening always to the Spirit who prompts their hearts to search, in absolute sincerity, for truth.[114]

Only where and when this reciprocity of consciences comes to its full bearing will magisterial interventions and the ongoing research of theologians strengthen the teaching authority of the Church.[115] The hierarchical authority and the theologians are, together, leaders and learners in a pilgrim Church. Nobody possesses a monopoly of truth, and nobody can hope to be inspired by the Spirit unless he honours the Holy Spirit who works in all and for all.

Nobody should be distressed or surprised when neither the pope nor the theologians have always ready responses to all new problems, but have to go through painstaking effort to discern the abiding truth, to decipher the signs of the times, and to free themselves and their fellow Christians from ossified formulations and partial ideologies.[116]

There must be the authority of those who teach and make decisions, and there must be a spirit of loyalty and obedience towards them. But in order to understand the specific quality of authority and obedience in the Church we must think, above all, of the truth embodied in Jesus Christ and in his communion of saints, the apostolic faith passed on, confessed, celebrated and preached. It is the common faith of all Christians, that can be shared and better understood in the reciprocity of consciences. The more consciences express purity of heart, and the more authority of the upright conscience is recognized, the more all will come to a deeper understanding and a greater moral authority.[117]

James Gustafson, a competent and benevolent observer of Catholic renewal, gives a very interesting and challenging assessment of the present picture. There is a struggling for a better understanding of law and teaching authority "in favour of a Christian ethics of responsive and creative action for human well-being". There is a liberation from scupulosity and from all too many doctrines about absolutes that can be imposed and are fit for control, in favour of a morality that is mainly concerned "to be freely self-giving in the service of others in the world. The Church becomes more the enabler of freedom than the proscriber of conduct and judge of mistakes". There is more emphasis on action and interaction, and everything is directed towards persons who can be conceived "as responders and initiators".[118]

The magisterium of the Church, in all its forms and on all levels, is authentic and faithful to Christ when the overriding concern is not for submission but for honesty, sincerity and responsibility. The Church is present where the superego morality is unmasked and where mere acceptability yields to co-responsibility in reciprocity of consciences. All the saints, the prophets, those who enjoy particular competence, and the hierarchical authorities have to join energies to withstand all kind of manipulation of consciences, and to educate persons who are open to the Spirit and have the courage to shoulder together their responsibilities. Thus the earth will be filled with the knowledge of the Lord.

IX. A NEW LOOK AT PROBABILISM

1. *Blending old and new things*

From the sixteenth to the eighteenth century, Catholic moral theology was shaken and sometimes preoccupied with the problem of "the moral systems". Fundamentally, it concerned the tension between law, traditions, Church authorities and confessors on one side and, on the other, the individual conscience.

In both the extreme traditionalists and the boldest theologians of that time, we see the same concerns and polarizations that beset our Church and the consciences of people today in this time of profound changes. But I think we must have and can have more hope and courage than the old probabilists when we examine these problems with a sharper awareness of the primacy of conscience and, at the same time, in a perspective of a covenant morality in which the reciprocity of consciences is fundamental. Things can change radically when these questions are examined in the light of a covenant morality rather than a one-sided defence morality.

A better understanding of past tensions and disputes between traditionalists and innovators can help us greatly in approaching our own problems when the dignity of conscience is in conflict with external laws, traditions and doctrines.[119] Provided we keep in mind the different social context, the past and present momentum of history, and yet the similarity of mentalities and approaches to basic problems of the Christian conscience, an informed appreciation of past tensions, sufferings and pastoral solutions can indicate for us the less and the more promising openings to be explored.

As in the past disputes about tutiorism and probabilism there was a clash not only of two eras but also of two opposed mentalities, so today we live again, but more intensively, the contemporarity of two eras, and suffer deeply under the clash of two different mentalities.

2. *The social context of probabilism*

We cannot learn from traditional moral theology unless we are fully aware of the different contexts in which it served the Church and the consciences of the faithful. The disputes around probabilism happened in an extremely authoritarian and oppressive society and within a centralistic Church whose structures of government and decision-making were greatly influenced by the surrounding society. This is no cause for wonder if we realize that many popes and bishops gave more time to administration in the temporal sphere than to the spiritual care of their flock.

It was a society and a Church too much preoccupied with control and law. Conventional morality in the service of stability was over-developed, to the detriment of discernment. Moralists who realized the situation had to be extremely cautious not only in view of ecclesiastical censorship but even more because of most severe censorship by civil authorities. Furthermore, moralists were writing chiefly for confessors and penitents, and many confessors understood their role mainly in view of law and discipline, as delegates of the institutional church. The role of confessor as judge was, for many, too pre-eminent. Others, however, like St. Alphonsus, understood quite well that the confessor's real purpose is to be an image and likeness of God's compassionate love and to serve the growth of the person in holiness.

The probabilists were to some extent aware of the great historical change, but even they had not the historical consciousness that characterizes today's generation. As for the traditionalists (the tutiorists, legalistic rigorists and probabiliorists), surely they were in no way aware of the profound economic, cultural and social changes.

One concrete problem may exemplify the situation: the taking of interest for loan of capital in the new capitalistic economy. Past laws and doctrinal documents of the Church had severely forbidden the charging of interest for any reason, since the loan was given to the poor to help them in special needs, and no Christian should profit from such a situation. Traditionalists were looking only to the formulations of past documents, while the probabilists were aware of the distress of many penitents and sensitive confessors. Interest had a totally new function in the economic society where savings could help create new jobs and where those who received the capital were not the poor but the economically strong groups.

Moralists tried to find solutions that would not oppress people's consciences, yet would allow a constructive participation in the new situation.[120] They could not easily contest the Church's teaching or challenge its validity for a new era;

therefore, to help people in the conflict of conscience, they had to treat matters within the prevailing legal system.

The conflict was not only between clinging to traditions, order and discipline and, on the other hand, allowing a sincere and creative decision of conscience; it was deepened by the contrast between theological pessimism and optimism. Rigorists, and especially the Jansenists, were convinced of people's profound corruption and, therefore, decided for a severe system of legal controls and sanctions. On the other side were theologians who believed with St. Paul in the superabundant redemption. "Where sin is abundant, God's grace is superabundant".

St. Alphonsus, who was one of the chief proponents of a moderate probabilism, was fully aware of this contrast. The direction of all his activity as moral theologian and pastor was, "With the Lord is plentiful redemption" (Ps 130). From that followed a greater confidence in the sincerity of people's conscience and, of course, a greater emphasis on proclaiming the Gospel instead of focusing on social and ecclesiastical controls.

It cannot be denied that many tutiorists, rigorists and probabiliorists were trapped in a completely legal system and legal approach. They did not see conscience in its own dignity and right, and did not believe in the creative conscience of those who have received the Gospel truth by witness and with joy. "Can one more humiliate conscience than to treat it just as a slave of the law?" [121] On the other hand, some of the probabilists, frequently labelled as laxists, were also at least partially caught in the system of conventional morality, at least regarding the methods by which they wanted to free the overburdened conscience.

3. *The authentic concern of solid probabilism and especially St. Alphonsus*

Great Christians, totally dedicated to the Church and to the dignity of consciences, were frequently considered less faithful to the Church because their explanation of formulations of doctrine and laws was less rigoristic and less adequate for complete control.

Their intentions could not be understood by those who

were only concerned for the upholding of traditions, of order and discipline in a sometimes self-defensive Church. The mentality of the besieged diminished the chance of the great probabilists to be properly understood. Their main concerns were the following:

(1) They wanted the conscience of people and the public consciousness of the Church to be open for the signs of the times, to respond to new needs and opportunities in a creative way. They wanted each Christian to be allowed to respond to his concrete situation by a creative conscience, in genuine responsibility. They realized that responses and laws given in a former situation were frequently no longer appropriate. They also were aware that too many laws, and an all too strict interpretation of them, could stifle the creativity and joy of Christians.

(2) They wanted to break out of a system of uniformed formulations and a system of schools which did not allow the individual theologian to search creatively for truth. Especially St. Alphonsus, a most loyal son of the Catholic Church, expressed his protest against a school-thinking and against any kind of uniformism that would not allow a search for truth in freedom. He even ridiculed people who were just reproposing the arguments and formulations of their school: "Look how the Scotist school has battled for centuries against the Thomists. In all this time we do not hear of even a single Friar Minor who agrees with the school doctrine of the Order of Preachers, and the reverse is just as true: no Dominican admits that anything in Scotism is valid. And yet, if one of these men had become a Dominican instead of a Franciscan, would he not battle arms and legs against Scotus? And similarly, if a man had entered the Franciscan Order instead of the Dominican, would he not act as if he were a declared opponent of Thomistic teaching? What does rule here, passion or reason? Certainly not reason".[122]

He stated clearly that not only people in their personal decisions have to follow conscience but, even more, a theologian in his teaching has to follow his own conscience, which is not possible unless he dares to use his own reason and his own experience. "I venerate the Jesuits and the other Orders, too, but in what concerns moral theology I follow my own conscience".[123] It was a more mature way of loving the Church by absolute sincerity and honesty of thought and expression than to honour an institution just by conformism.

St. Alphonsus had been taught by a rigoristic probabiliorist of the Dominican Order; but when, as a young priest, he gave his main attention and care to the marginal people, he just could not make use of that way of thinking and turned to the great Jesuit probabilists. After the suppression of the Society of Jesus, he continued in the same pattern; but in order to avoid too strong opposition from the mighty traditionalist wing, from then on he called his always moderate probabilism "equiprobabilism". The very word indicated that he would ponder equally both sides, the opinion in favour of law and tradition and that in favour of a creative exercise of freedom and fidelity beyond law.

(3) Writing a moral theology chiefly for confessors and churchmen, he stressed above all the dignity of the individual conscience that must never be manipulated. Even if the confessor or person in authority is convinced that his conviction is the right one and the penitent or another "subject to the Church" is erring, St. Alphonsus holds that the main concern cannot be "objective truth", as the man of authority understands it, but the sincerity of people's conscience. One should never try to impose what the other person cannot sincerely internalize, except the case of preventing grave injustice towards a third person. In the light of today's psychology we would say that one should not cause a split between the conscience that arises authentically from the inner depth of the person and, on the other side, the superego that is pressed to conform with external order. It would be an insult to the Church to present the conspiracy between the superego and a manipulator as ecclesiastical conscience. The Church can build itself up only in a genuine reciprocity of consciences.

Probabilists were truly concerned that people should overcome the merely conventional stage of morality and live their own life by acting according to their own sincere conscience.

Therefore, they warned that people must not be overburdened with laws, especially with laws whose value for the person and for genuine communities are doubtful or cannot be realized in one's own conscience. Their concern was not just liberation from too great a burden but equally, or even more, a liberation for a creative judgment of conscience that takes into account both the scale and the urgency of values.

4. *Rules of prudence for taking moral risks*

Authoritarian parents and legalists do not allow other people to take the risk of making mistakes, a risk that is unavoidable if one lives according to one's own conviction and courageously searches for truth and goodness beyond the conventional level of conscience.

Some people do not want to be allowed to live according to their own conscience; they want to be guided by others, to be told what to do. They do not want to take the risk inherent in living one's own life in creative liberty and fidelity. There is a widespread security complex among immature people, and this complex is constantly endorsed by authoritarian people who do not so much search for truth as for conformism and, through conformism, power over others. Long before the heated disputes between traditionalists and probabilists started, a great moral theologian and bishop, St. Antonine of Florence, O.P., (1389-1459) warned against this security complex. "It is a sign of a disciplined person to be, in every instance, content with the degree of certainty fitting mortals".[124]

St. Alphonsus and all great probabilists did not aim at legal security but at a covenant morality by which everyone lives according to his own conscience and in full co-responsibility. The first concern must be that people are helped, not hindered, by Church authorities to be sincere in their decisions of conscience, and that they learn to see creatively not just the legal boundary but the enormous realm of the good beyond the boundary. In other words, moral theology should show people that there are many levels of good and many ways to do the good, which is much more urgent and valuable than to follow dubious laws or the letter of a law which may be even against the needs of people.

If we understand the Church as a spearhead of humanity fostering genuineness of conscience, then we understand better the main concerns of the best probabilists.

(a) The great tradition of the Church and of probabilism gave prime attention to the inner reasons that convince the conscience of the goodness of an opinion or a conviction rather than to external authorities. This does not include an arrogant conscience, because genuine sensitivity is always exercised in the reciprocity of consciences and is an expression of covenant morality. But there is a covenant of people only if everyone searches for well-grounded personal convictions. St. Alphonsus writes: "All agree that the authority of the learned teachers has not great weight where the intrinsic reasons appear certain and convincing".[125] Of course, he surely does not ignore what is taught by others, especially by learned men in good standing with the Church; but "authors are not to be counted but weighed".[126]

(b) Some modern liberals accuse probabilists of having spent their energies uselessly in discussing traditions, laws and official teachings. My view is that they have to be praised for having always taken very seriously the authoritative expressions of the Church in her teaching and in her laws. However, genuine probabilists were not inclined to absolutize one law above others or one doctrinal formulation above others. Rather, they tried to understand the historical context of moral teaching and laws, and thereby came to the conclusion that sometimes these formulations were not at all applicable in a new historical situation where the person feels obliged to give preference to higher and more urgent values.

(c) Ongoing learning in dialogue: While traditionalists try to quote proof-texts out of context, good probabilist tradition has realized that even such great doctors of the Church as St. Augustine and St. Thomas Aquinas — indeed, especially these great doctors — have revised some of their earlier opinions and, if they had lived longer, would have continued in that ongoing revision.[127] Why, then, in our times, should we not think that Church authorities are also a part of this ongoing learning process in a reciprocity of consciences that brings together the various competences? We would be altogether unfaithful if we just quoted earlier expressions of teaching and did not personally try to understand better the truth in the historical context, so that we might come to the best possible solution here and now, in view of our present knowledge.

No one should be quoted as authority on a certain topic about which he later has corrected his stand. In 1959, Léon Suenens, in a book which at that time was courageous and forward-looking, described, with no further distinction, the cooperation of the wife in interrupted intercourse as "a kind of moral dissimulation and way of spiritual mediocrity",[128] despite the fact that St. Alphonsus and other probabilists had considered it as sometimes the "best possible". But Cardinal Suenens has later come to a thorough revision of the whole problem of responsible parenthood and the various ways it can be carried out.

(d) Classical probabilism does not at all condone an arbitrary decision of conscience. Arbitrariness contradicts conscience in its dignity. The purpose of probabilism is to allow a careful evaluation of the present opportunities, of the needs of fellowmen and community in view of God's gifts, and always in the light of our vocation to holiness. Such an evaluation and sincere judgment of conscience cannot be hoped for if there is a system that constantly produces legalistic scrupulosity or looks more for conformism than for a deepening knowledge of God and of man. Such a system can only increase individual and group egotism. Ecclesiastical conformism, under the pressure of people's own superego and under external reinforcements, contradicts both the Church as community of salvation and liberation and the very nature of conscience.

Whoever believes in "the life-giving law of the Spirit in Christ Jesus" (Rom 8:2) will not have recourse to an over-harsh imposition of changeable traditions or timebound doctrinal formulations. "It is an injustice to weaken the observance of the divine law; it is nevertheless no lesser evil to make a yoke imposed by God more difficult for others than is just. Exaggerated legal severity that wishes to oblige men to the most difficult prescriptions obstructs the way of salvation".[129]

Have we the courage to study, for instance, the problem of enforced celibacy under the grave sanction of lifelong exclusion from the sacraments for divorced people who have struggled sometimes heroically to save their marriage? While we must be faithful to the Lord's severe condemnation of ruthless divorce in order to marry another person, should there not be a greater fidelity towards the goal-commandment, "Be compassionate as your heavenly Father" (Lk 6:36)?

Moral teaching must proclaim with Mary, Queen of the Prophets, "Holy is his name; his mercy sure from generation to generation towards those who fear him" (Lk 2:49-50). All our moral teaching must confront the fundamental question, "What image of God are we conveying?" And how do we present the self-understanding of the Church?

(e) Classical probabilism is still of great actuality. There are many important issues that can be divisive for the Church if we do not meet in that dialogue and mutual respect which can manifest creative fidelity towards tradition and creative responsibility for the here and now and for the future of humankind and the Church.

I think that the declaration of Vatican II on the freedom of conscience and religious freedom, along with many other texts, gives us a light on how to live diversity in the Christian expression of co-humanity. We should rejoice that we are united in one faith, in the love of our Lord Jesus Christ, and then accept disagreement on some specific questions in a constant dialogue and reciprocity of consciences.

The Constitution on the Church in the Modern World gives us a very realistic guidance: "Let the lay people not imagine that their pastors are always such experts that, to every problem which arises, however complicated, they can readily give them a concrete solution, or even that such is their mission . . . Often enough the Christian view of things will itself suggest some specific solution in certain circumstances. Yet it happens rather frequently, and legitimately so, that with equal sincerity some of the faithful will disagree with others on a given matter. Even against the intentions of their proponents, however, solutions proposed on one side or another may be easily confused by many people with the Gospel message . . . they should always try to enlighten one another through honest discussion, preserving mutual charity and caring above all for the common good".[130]

X. THE TROUBLED AND SCRUPULOUS CONSCIENCE

A moral education that focuses on responsibility and on creative liberty and fidelity will prevent or heal many forms of scrupulosity. One that stresses one-sidedly the complete confession, and directs the person's attention chiefly to the sin-borderlines, can be and often has been a cause of overscrupulosity. "It can be historically established when the phenomenon of scrupulosity actually first appeared. It developed in relatively modern times from the juridical attitudes and thought patterns of the Latin moralists. St. Thomas and the Eastern Churches are not even aware of the concept".[131]

However, the word "scrupulosity" can have various connotations. It can include normal, or almost normal, crises or a number of pathologies that manifest themselves in the whole life of the person, and not only in moral and religious matters.

There can be, as Cardinal Gerson, the great theologian of the Council of Constance, remarked, scrupulosity as a wholesome temporary shock when the person ceases to live on a rather superficial level. But, normally, scrupulosity is part of a neurotic fixation, be it an anxiety neurosis or a manifestation of compulsive neurosis. Anxiety neurosis can be greatly aggravated by teaching a religion of fear, especially if the person has had, in childhood or later, an anguishing experience of authoritarian rule.

If compulsive neurosis takes troublesome forms, there is usually need for professional help. But a better understanding of religion and morality can always be of great help too. Healers are those who, in a consistent way, and not only by words but by their whole life, communicate the message of a loving, forgiving and healing God.

What we have said earlier about sin and sanity leads to a better understanding of one specific form of scrupulosity, namely, a compulsive neurotic scrupulosity of compensation. In the last analysis this arises from protracted neglect in the most fundamental areas of religious and moral life.

One who disobeys his conscience in the matter of healthy relationships and the all-embracing gift and law of love tends to take refuge in a cramped and restricted effort to comply with the pettiest details of laws in order to conceal from himself and others his apathy and laxity in the important areas of morality. There can be no healing unless the person understands better the wholeness of ethical life and strives for integration of prayer and life.

Liberation from a scrupulosity of compensation needs a profound conversion. This does not, however, allow a mere shock therapy. There can be no liberation for love and adoration without the experience of healing forgiveness and generous love and understanding. There is always a mixture between sin, consequences of sin and a profound suffering arising from various sources.

Tersteegen, a great Protestant guide in the paths of spirituality, helped people to free themselves from various forms of anxiety and scrupulosity by explaining that looking too much at one's own self makes one ill, and that psychic and spiritual health can be restored if one turns one's heart and will to God in loving attention to the needs of others. Walter Nigg remarks that, in his approach, Tersteegen "was surely on a safer path than those directors of souls who have their penitents occupied with themselves at all times".[132]

There is no objection against the anamneses by which psycho-therapists help their patients to face the past with full con-sciousness. However, the dynamics of therapy requests that they then be freed to look at God and his gifts and at the needs of their neighbour, freed to find creative ways to develop their own potentialities.

Persons who, because of compulsive scrupulosity, try again and again to make a general and utterly complete confession, can sometimes be helped by the penance that, in the future, they may never again confess any past sins committed before the date of this confession. Of course, it must be kindly explained that the penance does not mean in any way to relax God's law but, rather, to set all energies free for joyous service of the Lord. And it must also be explained to these people why they have good reason to hope that they have not committed mortal sins and that, from now on, even in doubt they should decide in their own favour as long as they truly seek God's will.

St. Alphonsus offers a loving instruction to the scrupulous person in the following prayer: "Oh my God, anxious souls deal with you as with a tyrant who demands nothing of his subjects but anxiety and restraint. Therefore, they stand in dread of every careless word they utter and every thought that passes through their minds. They think that the Lord God is stirred to wrath and is ready to cast them into hell. No, no, no. God deprives us of grace only if we scorn him and turn our backs to him, with our eyes open and our wills fully yielding to evil".[133]

While it is important to remind the scrupulous person that God wills his healing, and that, therefore, he should do everything to rid himself from his anxiety or compulsion, he must also learn to accept the slow process of healing and to give meaning to the suffering involved in his situation.

NOTES

[1] *Gaudium et spes* 16.
[2] R. Schnackenburg, *Moral Teaching of the New Testament*, New York, 1965, 69f.
[3] Cf. C.A. Pierce, *Conscience in the New Testament*, London, 1955, 113.
[4] D. Stanley S.J., *Boasting in the Lord*, New York, 1973, 131.
[5] Cf. J. Stelzenberger, *Syneides im Neuen Testament*, Paderborn, 1961; Id., *Die Beziehungen der frühchristlichen Sittenlehre zur Ethik der Stoa*, München, 1973.
[6] Cf. J.L. McKenzie, "Conscience in the New Testament", in his *Dictionary of the Bible*, Milwaukee, 1965, 147; C.H. Dodd, *The Epistle of Paul to the Romans*, London, 1959, 61f.
[7] Ph. Delhaye, *Christian Conscience*, New York, 1968, 36.
[8] R.H. Preston, "Conscience", in J. Macquarrie, *Dictionary of Christian Ethics*, Philadelphia, 1967, 67; cf. Ph. Delhaye, l.c., 42; P. Spicq, "La conscience dans le Nouveau Testament", in *Revue Biblique* 47 (1938), 63-67; E.D. D'Arcy, *Conscience and the Right to Freedom*, New York, 1961, 4-12.
[9] H. Thielicke, *Theological Ethics*, vol. I, Philadelphia, 1966, 298; cf. D. Capone C.Ss.R., "Antropologia, coscienza e personalità", in *Studia Moralia* IV (1966), 73-113.
[10] Cf. H. Schär, "Protestant Problem with Conscience", in E. Nelson (ed.), *Conscience: Theological Perspectives*, New York, 1973, 86; M.B. Crowe, "The Term Synderesis and the Scholastics", in *Irish Th. Q.* 23 (1956),. 151-164; 228-245; see Jerome, *Commentarium in Ezechielem*, lib. I c. 1 PL 25, 22.

11 S.Th., I II ,q 79, a 13.
12 R. Hofmann, *Die Gewissenslehre des Walter von Bruegge und die Gewissenslehre in der Hochscholastik*, Münster, 1941, 107-108.
13 For a more detailed treatment, see my book *Manipulation*, New York and Slough, 1975, 109-133.
14 A.S. Neill, *Summerhill: A Radical Approach to Childrearing*, New York, 1960.
15 E. Durkheim (1858-1917) is considered as the founder of the French school of sociology; he had a worldwide influence. He wrote, among many other books, *Elementary Forms of Religious Life*, Glencoe/Ill., 1947, *Education and Sociology*, Glencoe/Ill., 1956.
16 L. Kohlberg, "Stages of Moral Development", in *Moral Education. Interdisciplinary Approaches*, edited by C.M. Beck and others, New York and Paramus, N.J., 1971, 61.
17 See the chapter on milieu and freedom in my book *Marriage in the Modern World*, Westminster Md., 1966, 53-66.
18 G. Gurvitch, *Déterminismes sociaux et liberté humaine*, Paris, 1955, 12. See also G. Gurvitch, *The Social Framework of Knowledge*, Oxford, 1971.
19 S. Freud, *An outline of Psychoanalysis*, London, 1949, 3-4.
20 E. Erikson, *Life History*, 261.
21 E. Fromm, *Man for Himself*, Greenwich, 1969, 149ff.
22 J. Glaser S.J., "Conscience and Superego: A Key Distinction", *Theol. Studies* 32 (1971), 36.
23 G. Baum, *Man Becoming*, New York, 1971, 223f.
24 l.c., 143.
25 E. Fromm, l.c., 162.
26 P. Lehmann, *Ethics in a Christian Context*, New York, 1963, 253f. We find the same emphasis on a holistic vision in C.J. Van Der Poel, *The Search for Human Values*, New York,1971, 106ff; J. Fuchs, *Theologia moralis generalis*, Rome, 1971, 154ff; Ph. Delhaye, l.c., 51-58.
27 E. Mount, *Conscience and Responsibility*, Richmond, Va., 1969, 33.
28 J. Mullrooney, "Covenant and Conscience", *The Way* 2 (1971), 283-290.
29 Cf. S. Breton, *Conscience et intentionalité*, Paris, 1956; D. Capone, La verità nella coscienza morale, *Studia Moralia* VIII (1970), 7-36; R. May, *Man's Quest for Himself*, 174-222: "The Creative Conscience".
30 S.Th., I II, q 45 a 2.
31 K. Rahner, *The Dynamic Element in the Church*, New York, 1964, 13-41.
32 See especially A. Maslow, *The Farther Reaches of the Human Nature*, New York, 1973, 299-340.
33 B.J. Lonergan S.J., *Method in Theology*, New York, 1977, 115.
34 J. Glaser S.J., "Connatural Knowledge and the Spontaneous Judgement of the Faithful", *Theol. Studies* 29 (1968), 748; cf. J. Fuchs, *Theologia moralis generalis*, 154.
35 *Gaudium et spes*, 16.
36 J.H. Newman, *Apologia Pro Vita Sua*, New York, 1950, Part VI, 212.
37 St. Alphonsus de Liguori on "invincible ignorance", *Theologia moralis*, lib. I, tr. 2, ch. IV, dubium 1; pastoral conclusions, see *Praxis confessarii*, n. 8. It is for St. Alphonsus not so easy to accuse another of error of conscience, since not only man-made laws but even formulations of natural law allow *epikeia*; that means that a concrete judgment not conforming with a natural law formulation in conflict situation might well be a truthful judgment; see *Theologia moralis* I, 4, n. 170.
38 See Archive of the Generalate of the Redemptorists, Rome, Letters of St. Alphonsus, ch. III, nos. 342, 347, 402, 421 and Letters of Pierpaolo Blasucci XXXII, vol. II, 1. See my book *This Time of Salvation*, New York, 1966, 53-72: "Is the Moral Theology of St. Alphonsus Relevant?".
39 *De Veritate*, q 17 a 4; cf. a 5.
40 S.Th., I II, q 19, a 6 ad 3.
41 S.Th., I II, q 19, a 5; cf. *De Veritate*, q 17, a 4, and Th. Deman OP, "The Dignity of Conscience", in *Blackfriars* 34 (1953), 115-119.

42 This opinion is clearly proposed by K. Adam, *One and Holy*, New York, 1951, and by M. Laros, "Autorität und Gewissen", *Hochland* 36 (1938/39), 265-280; however, the argumentations based on Thomas Aquinas, *De Veritate* q 17, are not conclusive.

43 Cf. X.G. Colavecchio, *Erroneous Conscience and Obligations: a study of the Teaching from the Summa Halesiana, Saint Bonaventure, Saint Albert the Great, and Saint Thomas Aquinas*, Washington, 1961; F. Kaiser, *The Concept of Conscience According to John Henry Newman*, Washington 1958.

44 E. Erikson, *Life History*, 206.

45 l.c., 261.

46 *Insight and Responsibility*, 225.

47 E. Fromm, *Man for Himself*, Greenwich, 1969, 149. Cf. R. May, l.c., 187ff.

48 Cf. G. Allport, *Becoming*, New Haven, 1955, 71-72.

49 Cf. L. Kohlberg, *Collected Papers on Moral Development and Moral Education*, Cambridge/Mass., 1973; L. Kohlberg and E. Turiel (eds.), *Moralization Research: the Cognitive Developmental Approach*, New York, 1971; L. Kohlberg, "Stages of Moral Development: a Basis for Moral Education", in *Moral Education: Interdisciplinary Approaches*, edited by C.M. Beck and others, New York, 1971; Id., "Education for Justice: a Modern Statement of the Platonic View", in *Moral Education, Five Lectures* (J. Gustafson, R.S. Peters, L. Kohlberg, B. Bettelheim, K. Kenston), Cambridge/Mass., 1970, 56-83; R. Duska and M. Whelan, *Moral Development: A Guide to Piaget and Kohlberg*, New York, 1975; J. Piaget, *The Moral Judgement of the Child*, New York, 1962 (first published 1932); C.E. Nelson (ed.), *Conscience: Theological and Psychological Perspectives*, New York, 1973.

50 L. Kohlberg, "Stages of Moral Development", 86f.

51 l.c., 87.

52 l.c., 88.

53 l.c., 34.

54 l.c., 35.

55 l.c., 44.

56 l.c., 65.

57 l.c., 54. The religious educator should be aware of the limited scope of L. Kohlberg's theories. He does not refer to a distinctively Christian formation of conscience (cf. the following section of this chapter). We should also take a critical look at his Kantian philosophical approach and the one-sided emphasis on the cognitive dimension of the conscience. Cf. W.E. Conn, "Postconventional Morality: An Exposition and Critique of Lawrence Kohlberg's Analysis of Moral Development in the Adolescent and Adult", in *Lumen Vitae* 30 (1975), 213-230; P. Philibert, "Lawrence Kohlberg's Use of Virtue in His Theory of Moral Development", in *International Philosophical Quarterly* 15 (1975), 455-479; P. Philibert, "Some Cautions on Kohlberg", in *The Living Light* 12 (1975), 527-534.

58 R. Schnackenburg, *Moral Teaching of the New Testament*, 294.

59 Cf. J. Leclercq, *Christ and the Modern Conscience*, New York, 1962; J. Coventry S.J., "Christian Conscience", in *Heythrop Journal* 7 (1966), 145-160; X.G. Colavecchio, "Conscience: A Personalist Perspective", in *Continuum* 5 (1967), 203-210; T.E. O'Connell, "A Theology of Conscience", in *Chicago Studies* 15 (1976), 149-166.

60 This is to a great extent the thought pattern of B. Schüller; see his article "Zur Diskussion über das Proprium der Christlichen Ethik", in *Theologie und Philosophie* 51 (1976), 321-343. In his overview of the latest discussion on this subject R. McCormick synthesizes this tendency — seemingly approving it — in the following way: "Where morality is concerned, Schüller argues, Scripture is largely parenesis. That is why so many rich and excellent studies in biblical ethics never come to grips with the problem of normative ethics", "Notes on moral theology" (regarding the specificity of Christian Ethics), in *Theological Studies* 38, (1976), 64-71, quote from p. 67.

⁶ Cf. my book *Hope is the Remedy*, New York and Slough, 1972.

⁶² J. Pieper, *Prudence*, New York, 1969, 27.

⁶³ S.Th., II II, q 51, a 4; q 57, a 6 ad 3; cf. R. Doherty, *The Judgement of Conscience and Prudence*, River Forest/Ill., 1961.

⁶⁴ II II, q 52.

⁶⁵ I II, q 68, a 1

⁶⁶ Cf. P. Freire, *Education for Critical Consciousness*, New York, 1973; G. Goulet, *La Conscience critique*, Paris, 1971.

⁶⁷ Cf. E. Fromm, *Anatomy of Human Destructiveness*, New York, 1973, M, *Esscape from Freedom*, New York, 1941.

⁶⁸ G.M. Regan, *New Trends in Moral Theology*, New York, 1971, 167.

⁶⁹ Cf. Max Scheler, "Reue und Wiedergeburt", *Vom Ewigen im Menschen*, Berlin, 1933 (3rd ed.), 5-58.

⁷⁰ l.c., 41.

⁷¹ D.v. Hildebrand, *Transformation in Christ*, New York, 1948, 31.

⁷² M. Nédoncelle, *La réciprocité des consciences; essai sur la nature de la personne*, Paris, 1942. Id., *De la fidelité*, Paris, 1953; *Love and the Person*, New York, 1966. The French word "conscience' has a much broader meaning than the English "conscience"; it is awareness, self-awareness, consciousness but not without relationship to the moral conscience and consciousness.

⁷³ *Réciprocité des consciences*, 11f.

⁷⁴ l.c., 18.

⁷⁵ l.c., 23ff.

⁷⁶ l.c., 51. The French word "masque" and the English "mask" remind of the Greek word "persona" which meant the mask one used in the play. The word "mask" in Nédoncelle's writing comes close to the meaning of the superego, that drives people to play the social game without attention to their authenticity and conscience.

⁷⁷ l.c., 64ff.

⁷⁸ l.c., 86-90.

⁷⁹ Nédoncelle, *Réciprocité*, 182f.

⁸⁰ K.B. Clark, *Pathos and Power*, New York, 1974, XIV.

⁸¹ Petrus Abelardus, *Ethica seu liber scito teipsum*, PL 178, 656.

⁸² Cf. L. Janssens, *Freedom of Conscience and Religious Freedom*, Staten Island, 1965, 21-53.

⁸³ R. Panikkar, "Hermenéutique de la liberté de la religion; religion comme liberté", in E. Castelli (ed.), *L'herméneutique de la liberté de la religion*, Paris-Rome, 1968, 58-61.

⁸⁴ *Declaration on Religious Freedom of Vatican II*, 12.

⁸⁵ A.F. Carillo de Albornoz, *Roman Catholicism and Religious Liberty*, Geneva, World Council of Churches, 1959, 8f. Cf. also his book *Le concile et la liberté religieuse*, Paris, 1967.

⁸⁶ R.J. Regan S.J., *Conflict and Consensus. Religious Freedom and the Second Vatican Council*, New York and London, 1967, 185. John Courtney Murray deserves our special gratitude; cf. his book *The Problem of Religious Freedom*, Westminster/Md., 1965; D.E. Pelotte, *Theologian in Conflict (John Courtney Murray). Roman Catholicism and the American Experience*, New York, 1976.

⁸⁷ Panikkar, l.c., 75.

⁸⁸ Denzinger-Sch., *Enchiridion symbolorum, definitionum et declarationum de rebus fidei et morum*, 33rd ed., Freiburg, 1965, p. 280. Bulla *Unam Sanctam*. 18 Nov. 1302, (Denz. 1948), p. 280.

⁸⁹ *Monumenta Germaniae historica, Leges*, sect. IV, tom. IV, part I, 139.

⁹⁰ Leo XIII, *Immortale Dei* - DS 3168, 3685)

⁹¹ Pius XII, Address to the 10th International Congress of Historical Studies, AAS 47 (1955), 678.

⁹² *Declaration on Religious Freedom of Vatican II*, 7.

⁹³ Cf. J.C. Murray S.J., *Church and State in US*, New York, n.d.; Th. T. Love, *John Courtney Murray: Contemporary Church-State Theory*, Garden City/N.J., 1965.

300   CONSCIENCE

[94] Cf. L. Janssens, l.c. 132.

[95] Declaration, 8.

[96] S.Th., I II, q 96, a 2 ad 3.

[97] L. Janssens, l.c., 114.

[98] F.H. Littel, "A Response", in W.M. Abbott (ed.), The Documents of Vatican II, Notes and Comments by Catholic, Protestant and Orthodox Authorities, p. 697f; cf. E. McDonagh, Freedom or Tolerance?, Albany/N.Y., 1967.

[99] Declaration, 9.

[100] Cf. A. Bea, Unity of Freedom, New York, 1964; II. Küng, Freedom Today, New York, 1965; J.C. Murray (ed.), Religious Liberty: An End and a Beginning, New York, 1966; H. Thielicke, The Freedom of the Christian Man, New York, 1963; W.C. Bier (ed.), Conscience: Its Freedom and Limitations, New York, 1971.

[101] Declaration, 11.

[102] Cf. Panikkar, l.c., 75-84.

[103] J. Marías, "Les niveaux de la liberté religieuse", in E. Castelli (ed.), l.c., 402-403.

[104] F.H. Littel, l.c., 700.

[105] A.F. Carillo de Albornoz, Le concile et la liberté religieuse, Paris, 1967, 185.

[106] Cf. Panikkar, l.c., 57; J.M. Diez Alegría S.J., La libertad religiosa, Barcelona, 1965.

[107] R. Schäffler, "La liberté comme principe herméneutique de l'intreprétation des textes religieux", in E. Castelli (ed.), l.c., 253-283, p. 277.

[108] Cardinal Roncalli (John XXIII), Discourse of June 18, 1951 (UNESCO), in Osservatore Romano of June 29, 1951.

[109] R.J. Regan S.J., Conflict and Consensus, 179ff.

[110] Cf. K. Rahner, Free Speech in the Church, New York, 1959; K. Rahner and others, Obedience in the Church, Washington, 1968; D. Callahan, Honesty in the Church, New York, 1965; Th.A. Shannon, Render Unto God: A Theology of Selective Obedience, New York, 1974; B. Häring, A Theology of Protest, New York, 1970; J.L. Segundo S.J., The Liberation Theology, New York, 1976 (the original Spanish title expresses the purpose clearer: Liberación de la teología, Buenos Aires, 1975); cf. ch. II of this book: How Free was and is Moral Theology?

[111] Cf. G.R. Dimler, Friedrich Spee's Trutznachtigal, Bern, 1973.

[112] Cf. H. Doms, The Meaning of Marriage, New York, 1939.

[113] Declaration on Christian Education, esp. 7-10.

[114] Archbishop Robert Coffi, "Lehramt und Theologie - Die Situation heute", in Orientierung 40 (1976), 63-66.

[115] Cf. R. McCormick, "Notes on Moral Theology", in Theol. Studies 38 (1977), 84-114, esp. p. 90; cf. also International Theol. Commission, "Theses de magisterii ecclesiastici et theologiae relationibus ad invicem", in Documentation cath. 73 (1976), 658-665; M. Flick S.J., "Due funzioni della teologia secondo il recente documento della commissione teologica internazionale", in Civiltà Cattolica 127 (1976), 472-483; Bishop A.L. Descamps, "Théologie et Magistère", in Ephem. Theol. Lov. 52 (1976), 82-133; A Dulles S.J., "What is Magisterium?", in Origins 6 (1976), 81-87.

[116] Cf. B.C. Butler, "Letter to a Distressed Catholic", in Tablet 230 (1976), 735f and 757f.

[117] Cf. Y. Congar O.P., "Pour une histoire sémantique du terme 'magisterium'", in Revue des sciences Phil. et Theol. 60 (1976), 85-98; Id., "Bref historique des formes du 'magistère' et de ses relations aec les docteurs", ibid., 99-112; A.B. Calkins, "John Henry Newman on Conscience and the Magisterium", in The Downside Review 87 (1969), 358-369; Associazione dei moralisti italiani, Magistero e coscienza, Bologna, 1971, with an article of mine under the same heading, 319-345.

[118] J.M. Gustafson, "Education for Moral Responsibility", in J. Gustafson and others, Moral Education, Cambridge/Mass., 1970, 12-13.

[119] For a more detailed treatment of this whole problem see my books *The Law of Christ*, voi. I, Westminster/Md., 1961, 169-189, and *This Time of Salvation*, New York, 1966, 53-72.

[120] Cf. J.T. Noonan, *The Scholastic Analysis of Usury*, Cambridge/Mass., 1957.

[121] Th. Deman O.P., "Probabilisme", in *Dict. Théol. Cath.* XII (1936), 418. I do not think that Deman has truly understood the purpose and spirituality of genuine probabilism while he rightly condemned all the legalistic background of the disputes.

[122] St. Alphonsus, Dissertatio from the year 1773, n. 49.

[123] "Risposta apologetica circa l'uso dell'opinione egualmente probabile", 1764, in *Quattro apologie italiane della teologia morale del beato Alfonso Maria de Liguori*, Torino, 1829, 36.

[124] St. Antonine of Florence, *Summa moralis*, P. I, tit. III, cap. 10.

[125] St. Alphonsus, *Theologia moralis*, lib. I, tr. I, n. 79.

[126] l.c.

[127] Ch. E. Curran, *Ongoing Revision of Moral Theology*, Notre Dame, 1975.

[128] L. Suenens, *Amour et maitrise de soi*, Bruges, 1959, 81.

[129] St. Alphonsus, l.c., lib. I, tr. I, n. 82.

[130] *Gaudium et spes*, 43.

[131] J. Regnier, *Le sens du péché*, Paris, 1954, 33.

[132] W. Nigg, *Great Saints*, Hinsdale/Ill., 1948, 219.

[133] St. Alphonsus, *The Way of Salvation and of Perfection, Complete Ascetical Works*, 2, edited by E. Grimm, Brooklyn, 1926, 482f.

Chapter Seven

Traditions, laws, norms and context

People can become slaves of traditions, rules and particular situations. It would be an error, however, to consider traditions, laws, norms and total context chiefly or only as a threat. They can promote fidelity, creativity and freedom itself, if each generation discovers in them the liberty, creativity and fidelity embodied by past generations and is willing to embody, ever anew, these qualities in the traditions, laws, moral norms and total context of its own time.

I. LIBERTY AND TRADITION

1. *Christ and tradition*

The eternal Word of the Father is incarnate in our humanity; he lives in it. He took on our humanity in view of all, and at the same time he became incarnate in a concrete social, cultural and religious context.

Both in his own humanity and in his growth in wisdom, Christ was deeply rooted in the Hebrew tradition. The way he acted and the words he spoke manifest the fruitfulness of the great tradition of Israel and especially of the prophets. Jesus' coming is prepared by a long history that reaches him humanly through the community and its tradition. Some of these traditions were written in the holy books, but they were also embodied in the people of Israel, especially in the humble *anawim*, the class to which Mary and Joseph belonged.

Christ also took upon himself the burden of history, of the solidarity of sin embodied in all of humankind, and in the particular sin-solidarity of his people which made him suffer so directly. This second aspect can be properly understood only in view of the first: Christ's rootedness in tradition and his gratitude for the living tradition of Israel.

Oriented to the prophetic history that reaches him directly in Mary, the Queen of the Prophets, and in John the Baptist, Christ is the very embodiment of discernment. He focuses on all good traditions in order to bring them fully to life, but he takes a strong stand against traditionalism, especially that of the priestly class and the influential people of Israel. He bitterly denounces the Pharisees for clinging to useless traditions and imposing them on people in a way that is unfaithful to the living God.

The Pharisees were captives of traditions that had become ossified and they accused Christ and his disciples of not observing all their traditions. "The Pharisees and the lawyers asked him, 'Why do your disciples not conform to the ancient tradition, but eat their food with defiled hands?' He answered, 'Isaiah was right when he prophesied about you hypocrites in these words: This people pays me lip-service, but their heart is far from me; their worship of me is in vain, for they teach as doctrines man-made laws . . . You neglect the commandment of God in order to maintain your traditions'" (Mk 7:4-9).

In the Pharisees' approach, the very lack of fidelity to the living God and his first law of love, mercy and justice distorts all of tradition. Jesus' plain prophetic language angered the Pharisees and the lawyers. "Then the disciples came to him and said, 'Do you know that the Pharisees have taken great offence at what you have been saying?' His answer was: 'Any plant that is not of my heavenly Father's planting will be rooted up. Leave them alone; they are blind guides, and if one blind man guides another, they will both fall into the ditch'" (Mt 15:12-14).

Christ desacralized and demythologized all those traditions that allowed Judah and its priestly class to be arrogant and self-righteous, and to set themselves apart from the crowd and from other tribes and nations. He, the Son of the almighty God and Father of all, tore down those absolutizing trends that separated the Jews from the Samaritans and from the Gentiles. He broke the traditions that did not allow a Jew to speak with Samaritans and especially with a Samaritan woman (Jn 4:4-30). He affirmed that Salvation comes from the Jews; but with the very coming of the Saviour, disputes about sacred places between Judah and Samaria had become meaningless, because God wants "adorers in spirit and truth". No longer, then, may man-made barriers separate humankind into different classes and tribes opposed to each other (cf. Jn 4:21-36).

2. Theological reflection on tradition and mores

a) Meaning and value of the mores

Tradition reaches us in doctrines relevant for moral life, in written laws and norms and in unwritten mores. The mores, which throughout history have played a greater role than written laws and tradition, contain a number of models of behaviour and socialization. According to Toennies, they have sign-values of the particular practice insofar as it is accepted as binding norm.[1] They can be called the grammar of human conduct, and their observance is expected as much as that of the grammar and syntax of language. The mores have a much greater binding force than written law and ethical norms if the norms are not themselves rooted in the mores; and moral norms become effective for the long run only if they inscribe themselves in the mores. However, if the mores are accepted uncritically as binding forces then they will become ossified, degenerate, and will greatly hinder people's ability to outgrow the merely conventional level of morals.

b) From mores to morality

William Frankena writes, "Moral philosophy arises when men like Socrates pass beyond the stage in which we are directed by traditional rules".[2] It is not just a matter of internalizing rules and traditions but of discerning the very rules, traditions and mores, and of affirming a kind of autonomy of the moral agent. Long before Socrates, and even before Confucius, this discernment and transformation of mores into morality happened again and again through people with a profound faith. It is the great merit of the ethical prophetism of Israel that it is willing to challenge the mores and traditions in order to uproot what is useless or harmful and to bring all the good tradition to fresh life.

A better understanding of the historical context shows us the much-discussed story of Abraham, and his intent to sacrifice Isaac, in a new light, as a radical challenge and change in the tribal mores. By faith, Abraham accepted the calling to an exodus from his culture, as Noah had made an exodus from the mores of the people around him. In the culture in which Abraham had lived, the sacrifice of the first-born was at the very core of the mores. People thought they knew the conditions under which the gods would require the sacrifice of the first-born to placate them. Abraham was conditioned by this belief rooted in the mores. But the faith-exodus allowed him a new confrontation with God's "angel", who liberated him from his erroneous conscience. Or we might say that Abraham began to live on the level of a faith-conscience of true morality.[3]

This explanation is quite different from the one given by Kierkegaard who, like so many others, was wrestling with the problem of how God could tell a father to kill his first-born son. "In Abraham's life there is no higher expression for the ethical than this, that the father shall love his son".[4] How, then, could Abraham intend to kill his son who had done no wrong? Kierkegaard answers, "He acts by virtue of the absurd . . . Abraham is therefore no instance of a tragic hero but something quite different, either a murderer or a believer". For Kierkegaard, he is a model of the believer who, for the sake of faith, ignores and offends the ethical value. "So despite the universal moral imperative about killing, and for the sake of God, Abraham overstepped the ethical altogether. He showed that the religious individual is higher than the ethical universe".[5]

The tragic hero sacrifices, with great pain, one ethical value for the sake of a higher expression of the ethical, but Kierkegaard's believer sacrifices the ethical altogether, and he thinks that this is a characteristic sign of the higher stage, the religious one. Instead, I am convinced that, precisely through his faith, Abraham reached a higher stage of morality by being freed from slavery to the mores which, in good conscience, he had followed up to then. From that moment on, for Abraham and his descendants, sacrificing one's first-born was an abominable crime, an offence to the true God.

So often in history, imperfect and even distorted mores have received the sanction of an imperfect religion or, rather, of imperfect religious people; and, in the name of a tradition and its sanctions, harmful mores have been observed and embodied where people should have been critical. It suffices to remember torture and witch-burning in many parts of Christendom, crusades and "holy" wars, where peaceful solutions would have been possible. Energies that could have served justice and mercy were swallowed up in trivia surrounding legalism and ritualism. For centuries, reasons have been given for the terrible mores of war, while we should long ago have freed ourselves from its evil. "Warned by the calamities which the human race has made possible, let us now make use of the interlude granted us from above and in which we rejoice. In greater awareness of our own responsibility, let us find means for resolving our disputes in a manner worthy of man. Divine Providence urgently demands of us that we free ourselves from the age-old slavery of war. But if we refuse to make this effort, we do not know where the evil road we have ventured upon will lead us".[6]

The inner strength of faith, a lively faith-community and rational reflection will discern the mores, strengthen what is good, purify what is acceptable and radically eliminate what contradicts the total vocation of mankind. Scientific ethics and Christian ethics are worth nothing if they do not join the best efforts to transform mores into morality.

c) Tradition and traditions

We have seen Christ's challenge to the Pharisees and lawyers who had betrayed divine Tradition in favour of man-made traditions. It is one of the great tasks for religion, and especially for religious ethics, to distinguish painstakingly between Tradition and traditions. The Tradition that is activated by

God's creative and redemptive action and revelation is a torrent of life; it is the history of cooperation between God and humankind. Those who have a living faith, a developed conscience and who want to live freely, creatively and faithfully can enter into this stream of life.

There are also good human traditions and mores that become a part of this stream at certain historical moments if, there and then, they are the best expression of fidelity to one's own conscience and to the best available knowledge of God and man. But traditions can become frozen, ossified, in many ways. Traditions that from the very beginning were wrong or at least imperfect responses to God's gifts and human needs may be held onto long after better knowledge has become available and prophetic voices have called for change. Other traditions which, in a concrete historical moment, were well adapted to people's knowledge and needs can be actually harmful if they are not discarded when new knowledge or new needs arise.

The incapacity or unwillingness to discern between Tradition and traditions is frequently called "fundamentalism". A typical example is the teaching of the Jehovah's Witnesses that blood transfusion is against biblical teaching. But the Old Testament texts did not at all face this life-saving means, and it is unintelligent and irreverent to hold God responsible for the loss of lives when this kind of "tradition" is observed.

Another typical example is the misinterpretation of Genesis, Chapter 38. The story is that Jacob's sons, especially Onan, refused to fulfil the law of the levirate. Onan did not want his brother's wife to have children. "Onan knew that the offspring would be his; so when he went in to his brother's wife he spilled the semen on the ground, lest he should give offspring to his brother" (Gen 38:9). It would surely be an unhistorical effort to prove, by this and other texts, that married men in our present culture should take the widow of their brother as second wife in order to awaken offspring for the dead brother. However, it should not be excluded that the text might be a challenge to the Church when she prohibits the fulfilment of the levirate duty to African tribes who are, as much as were the sons of Abraham, convinced that this is their duty. Their whole cultural tradition does not allow these people a sudden change without harming the good of persons. But one other thing seems sure: that this text of Genesis 38 cannot at all be used in discussion of today's problems of responsible parenthood and of overpopulation in some parts of the world.

The question can also be raised here about whether a long rooted tradition that has excluded women from the ministerial priesthood and from all sharing in the decision-making process in the Church is a sufficient argument when this tradition coincides with both a male-centred culture and with some very poor justifications for the practice.

The Church has always found it difficult to free herself from past traditions. It needed a prophet like the Apostle of the Gentiles to free the infant Church from the temptation to absolutize Jewish traditions and impose them on all peoples as condition for membership in the Church. It was hard for prophets to free the Church from a long-standing tradition of practising and teaching torture. And it needed even a longer time for the Church to see that the earlier, well-justified teaching about usury was not suitable for an age with totally different economic conditions.

Solutions which the Church gave in the first centuries do not automatically resolve our problems when we are faced with a wholly new historical context. Yet, the Church is and must be deeply rooted in the past history and tradition. This means "that in present reflection, the community does not have to begin *de novo*, as if God's will for present and future had no consistency with God's will for the past. Moral discernment is in continuity with the past, not discontinuity. It learns from, and is thus informed and directed, without being determined, by the past".[7]

Gratitude for the past experience and reflection should go hand in hand with celebration of openness for the present opportunity and responsibility for the future. We are never allowed to sacrifice the present and the future to the past. "Now" is always the time of salvation.

Wherever parts of Christianity became captives of a frozen tradition and a system of unchanging doctrinal formulations, the most dynamic people were tempted against faith in such a

Christianity. If God-talk is bound up with ossified mores, then it can happen that faith in God and all traditional values are falling at the same time.[8]

Misinterpretations that followed the model of Kierkegaard's explanation of Abraham's case made Christianity blind to new signs of the times. Friedrich Nietzsche, despite his exaggerated generalities, represents many others in his reaction. "From the very beginning the Christian faith is a sacrifice, sacrifice of all freedom, all pride, all self-assurance of the mind, at the same time it is servitude, self-mockery and self-mutilation".[9] It is in this bitter reaction of a wounded heart that Nietzsche sets up the morality of the superman against the "flock" morality which he sees as an uncritical following of traditions in blind obedience. "Become mediocre, is now the sole morality that makes sense, that finds ears".[10] To those who, in the name of God, had been clinging to traditions inimical to man and the earth, Nietzsche responds, "I beseech you, my brothers, remain faithful to the earth . . . Once the sin against God was the greatest sin; but God died, and those sinners died with him. To sin against the earth is now the most dreadful thing".[11]

It is one of the most urgent tasks of Christianity to discern profoundly between Tradition and traditions. If we want to prevent the rebellious spirit expressed by Nietzsche, then we have to confront first the traditionalists who disown the living God, the God who indeed was but who also comes and will come.

c) A difficult task

Many of our contemporaries are not contemporaries of each other. There are those who, plagued by security complexes, live thoroughly in the past; and there are those who impatiently want to anticipate the future without rootedness in the past and without patient work for organic change. On the one side we have the traditionalists who need to be challenged by Jesus, Paul and the Church of Vatican II; and on the other side we have those who are unrooted, overcritical of all traditions, mores and laws.

We can and must speak against traditionalists, as Paul did; but we must never forget that our discourse will be listened to also, and possibly misunderstood, by those who need to be challenged wherever they follow the modes and the fads of the day and are yielding, in this particular day, to the permissive society. For many in this generation it is no longer tradition that is followed but the loudest voice and the latest modes. They are not rooted in history but look to modernity in an uncritical, uninformed way. And since the mores and the tradition have yielded to passing modes and present legislation, there are all too many people who discern wisely neither the past traditions nor the present modes; they simply accept as good whatever is not forbidden by present law.

Mature Christians are not only critical towards past traditions and mores but extremely critical towards the present modes and fads. They also do their best to embody their informed and critical response to the signs of the times in new mores, new customs and new ways of thinking, in a vital tradition of community and society. They tend not only to be carriers of tradition but also, in some manner, creators of the culture. It is the mission of the faith-community to help people to live according to their conscience in the reciprocity of consciences. Then they will be sensitive to the accumulated wealth of historical tradition and, in its light, will be able to discern the signs of the times. Thus, they will live their own unique life and become active partners in a living tradition.[13]

II. THE APOSTLE OF THE GENTILES FACED WITH JEWISH LAW AND TRADITION

Many good Jewish people and also converts from Judaism to the Catholic Church were never helped to discern time-bound laws and traditions from the abiding will and design of God. Especially those who did not give particular attention to the prophetic history of Israel knew thousands of laws and traditional practices without truly knowing the one all-embracing law of God's love that gives meaning to everything and helps us to discern the signs of the times.

Paul, the Apostle to the Gentiles, had been himself a slave of tradition and law, and had therefore persecuted Christ in his disciples. He had considered them as enemies of the sacred tradition and law. But, when converted and sent to the heathen, he realized that the Jews' desire to make proselytes for their law and tradition could be the greatest obstacle to evangelization. His attitude towards the Mosaic law and the Jewish traditions is essentially defined by his position as missionary to the Gentiles.[14]

He understood Christ as the one who had torn down all the obstacles to faith in the one God and Father for the unity of all mankind in one Church. To use the Gospel in favour of one tradition and one culture or nation was, therefore, in his eyes, a serious sin against the universal mission of the Christian Church. "God has no favourites" (Rom 2:11). Overemphasis on traditions and laws would be not only a practical obstacle to evangelization but also a grave injustice to Christ, the Saviour and Lord of all. Tradition is for Christ and not Christ for tradition.

Therefore, while Paul is sensitive to the feelings of the Jews, and observes their traditions wherever he can, he is equally sensitive to the Gentiles to whom he is sent. Christ has freed him from the idolatry of tradition and law. "I am a free man and own no master; but I have made myself every man's servant, to win over as many as possible. To Jews I became like a Jew, to win Jews; as they are subject to the law of Moses, I put myself under that law to win them; although I am not myself subject to it. To win Gentiles, who are outside the Mosaic law, I made myself like one of them; I am not lawless, neither am I under the law, but in the law of Christ" (1 Cor 9:19-21).

Many of Paul's expressions are polemical and can be rightly understood only as challenge to a legalism and traditionalism that obscured the primacy of Christ and salvation through faith in Christ. This is also somewhat true of many expressions of Martin Luther. It is misleading to focus one-sidedly on their polemical expressions which were necessary against a dangerous traditionalism. To use the same words and emphases today in a discourse with our present permissive society distorts the meaning they had in the original social context. Paul and Luther protested vigorously in a context in which their attacks against a slavish terror of law and against idolatry of man-made traditions could not be easily interpreted as invitations to licence. Had Paul been dealing with religious situations in which permissiveness and the absence of rootedness in tradition were present, rather than oppression by law and tradition, his responses would surely have been quite different.[15]

However, Christianity in the Western world finds itself to some extent in a situation analogous to Paul's. The future of humanity will have its focal points in the Third World, in Asia, Africa and Latin America. The Christian Churches of the West are all, to a great extent, enslaved in their traditions. There seems to be no hope that they will come to unity in one Church, and equally no hope that they can bring the living Gospel to the cultures of the Third World without a painstaking discernment between the deposit of faith and man-made formulations, and especially between the new life in Christ Jesus and the many moral laws and traditions based on the mores of the Western world.

The best that Westerners can do is to bring the Gospel in its original simplicity and beauty, as found in Holy Scripture, and allow the indigenous Christian communities the freedom to embody it in their own culture. We could thereby give them a good example of how we discern our mores, the new trends, the spirit of the era, in order to adopt whatever is good and beautiful, purify what is potentially good and eliminate what contradicts the history of salvation.[16]

III. NATURAL LAW IN THE LAW OF CHRIST

1. *Knowledge of salvation or knowledge of control*

What we call "natural law", as part of the Church's teaching, must be explored, above all, in the light of Holy Scripture. There, it is presented as a part of the Good News of salvation.

The disciples, who had come to know Jesus as the only Saviour and the Saviour of all, had to ask themselves how those whom the Gospel had not yet reached might come to salvation in Jesus Christ. A first and beautiful response is given in Matthew 25. There will be those at the right hand of Jesus when he comes to judge the living and the dead. He will call them blessed, for they have received him in the poor, the downtrodden, the prisoners; they have fulfilled the great law of love. Many of those whom the Lord calls into his eternal kingdom had not known him explicitly when they fulfilled that law. So it is clear that God gives his grace, merited by Jesus Christ, and the essential knowledge of his law also to those outside the pale of the Judaic law and even outside the institutional church.

The Apostle of the Gentiles responds to the same question in his Letter to the Romans. It is a part of his powerful message that God, the Father Almighty, is the God of all, and Jesus is the Saviour of all people. "For God has no favourites: those who have sinned outside the pale of the law of Moses will perish outside its pale, and all who have sinned under the law will be judged by the law. It is not by hearing the law but by doing it that men will be justified before God. When the Gentiles, who do not know the law, carry out its precepts by the light of nature, then, although they have no written law, they are their own law, for they display the effect of the law inscribed on their hearts. Their conscience is called as witness and their own thoughts argue the case on either side, against them or even for them" (Rom 2:11-15).

What appears in these two biblical passages as a kind of law in which all people share "by the light of nature" is in line with the great promises of the prophets, that God will write his law into people's inmost being, that he will engrave it in their hearts. It is quite clear that in this perspective we are not faced with a law that is imposed from without. It is not a teaching of the Church, although it agrees with the heart of the Church's teachings. It is not a law that can be seen in a perspective of dominion and/or control.

Quite the opposite is true about the "natural law" theory of the Romans. In the Roman empire the inquiry about the customs and mores of the different tribes and nations submitted to Roman rule was an instrument of dominion and control. In the service of the colonial power, Roman officers carefully compared the mores and laws of the various people who were submitted to the *Pax Romana*. In the tradition of Greek philosophers, they tried to discover what was common

to all these cultures. It was a great step beyond the early
Greek natural law philosophy, where all the interest was focused
on the Greek-speaking people or, more narrowly, on the Greek
male inhabitants of all the cities and kingdoms of Greek origin.
It was, however, the "natural law" for the ruling class. The
Romans had their civil law as a special statute for the privileged class, and were looking for what was common to the
submitted peoples for the purpose of legislation, the *jus gentium*.
This was issued as law for second-class people, tough enough
not to leave any hope for independence, yet broad enough to
unite all in a colonial empire.

This, of course, is simply not the natural law but a theory
about it and a use of it that is born under the sign of original
sin. It is disruptive of the unity of the children of the one
God and Father; it disowns the equal dignity and freedom of
all persons. So, while the Romans did a creditable job of
research about the mores and customs, they did not truly
discover the main purpose of that law which is written in all
people's hearts and tells them to love each other as equals and
as free persons.

Natural law is not something to be imposed for any purpose
of dominion or control. Whoever wants to honour the law
which God has written into the human heart will first try to
read it in his own heart and then explore it further in shared
experience and reflection with others, so that together all
may come to a better knowledge of the human person as a
moral being called to live in justice and peace.

2. *Man's nature and natural law*

No systematic thinking about morality can avoid the basic
question: What is man's nature? And from that question follow
others: What is man meant to be? What are his relationships
with others, with himself and with the world around him meant
to be?

If a physiologist or a sociologist asks about man's nature
within the narrow goals of his discipline, he can forget about
the ethical question. But that means that he never asks about
the whole nature of the human being. As soon as the ethical

question arises, we have to see the human person in his or her wholeness and his or her essential relationships. Always it is a question of meaning and purpose. "Discussions on ethics always include the delineation of some view of man. Indeed the understanding of the nature of man is one of the keystones in every ethical system" [17]

a) A merely "natural" approach to human nature

Few expressions are used with such diverse meanings and intentions as "natural law" or "natural right".[18] Things become even more confused if natural law is taken as the result of merely "natural law thinking". This "natural law thinking" sometimes meant the understanding of what belongs to man's humanness in all thinkable orders of creation. It was an effort to come to the indispensable essentials by philosophical extrapolation; and very frequently this extrapolation eliminated some aspects which we find very fundamental such as, for instance, the historicity and the dynamism of human nature.

Another form of extrapolation did not try to construct a static concept of human nature but simply to find out what human nature would be without the gifts of faith and revelation, without our being called to discipleship in Christ and to adoption as children of God. The purpose of that extrapolation was to emphasize the gratuitousness of the present historical order, which is one of salvation and revelation. Yet another form of extrapolation asks what human nature would be if there had been no Fall, no sin. Here, one had to imagine a pure state without the fallenness and with or without adoption as children of God. All these extrapolations could only lead to unreal constructions of what never does exist and what might be thinkable only in the abstract.

However, there is one extrapolation which has an important purpose. As people who simply do not and cannot renounce the full consciousness of our identity as Christian believers, we try to find out on what insights about human nature we can base our dialogue with unbelievers. We view the human being in the real historical order, as we see it; that is, in the order of revelation and salvation in Jesus Christ. On this level we are willing to conduct the dialogue, taking as point of departure what is shared experience and shared reflection in a common history of value insights and awareness of betrayal of ethical values. The purpose can be cooperation to build a better world in which we accept diversity and pluralism but emphasize what can unite us. In such an approach we do not extrapolate sin and fallenness, since experience of faults and perversions is common to all the partners in the dialogue.

The original purpose of theories about natural law in the first Christian centuries was evangelization.[19] The servants of the Gospel did not want to destroy or discard what people already knew about God and about good. Rather it was their conviction that Christ, the Saviour, had already reached out to those who did not belong to the Jewish tradition, and that they had a law written in their hearts. But while Paul (Rom 2:15f.) believed that this law in the hearts of holy Gentiles was a part of the saving action of Christ and the Holy Spirit, others later considered it as a merely natural thing which, as such, could not enter into the realm of salvation.

b) Nature as givenness and nature as norm

The enormous and complicated problem for ethics is how we can make the transition from nature as givenness to nature as ethical norm. The various extrapolations that lead, for instance, to the concept of a "pure nature", where the reality of history and human experience is disregarded in favour of the idea of what human beings could be and must be in all thinkable orders, surely does not appeal to today's thinking. It could serve neither for evangelization nor for building a more humane, just and brotherly world. If we want to conduct a dialogue on human nature with today's people of various cultural, religious and ideological backgrounds, then we have to ask ourselves first: what do we know about man in his fundamental experiences? Do we find something that all have in common, on which to build further reflections and collaboration?

If we speak as today's people, then we cannot take as point of departure the experience of just one culture. Rather, we will try to bring home all the experiences of the present humanity and of past cultures insofar as we can still reach out to them. We cannot discard the behavioural sciences: ethnology, anthropology, sociology and the various branches of psychology. If our concern is specifically the ethics, then we will give particular attention to the sociology of morals in a comparative approach.

The human life sciences study, for instance, biology. The knowledge can serve health care, genetics, efforts for good nutrition, and so on; but we cannot jump from biological trends or biological givenness to ethical norms. We can only conclude that, in our total assessment of human life, we cannot ignore what biology has to tell us. For biologists, sociologists, ethnologists or psychologists, there can be a great temptation to build their worldview and their ethical code on their own science without taking into proportionate account all the dimensions and perspectives of the human being. For the ethician or moralist, it is even more imperative to avoid the danger of any such reductionism.

c) The absolute need for a wholistic understanding

Nothing is more deadly for Christian ethics and for all ethics than to jump from one particular aspect of human nature to ethical imperatives. Our first task, before we ask the question of normative ethics, is to try to understand man's total vocation, the human person in all his or her relationships and in the concrete historical order. In this context, it is well to remind ourselves about the theories on conscience: any theory that does not come to grips with man's innermost longing for wholeness in his own faculties, and wholeness and integrity in his relationships with God, his fellowmen and the world around him is of little help for the understanding of natural law.

We should also remember that Christianity could live through many centuries without speculations on a mere nature conceived outside the context of salvation and friendship with God. We should, therefore, realize that a person turning away from salvation is not in a natural but in a most unnatural situation. We can, however, distinguish what we understand through shared experience and shared reflection without revelation from the full understanding of historical humanity in the light of revelation and with all the accumulated knowledge that is at hand.

d) From self-understanding to ethical norms

The original meaning of natural law emphasizes the great difference between laws that are imposed and laws which man finds in himself. The word "natural" comes from *nasci*, and means inborn. St. Thomas Aquinas synthesizes the best of our tradition when he says that neither the new law promulgated by Jesus Christ nor the natural law is a law imposed from without. Both are inborn laws that man discovers as his own, appeals to a good life that come from within.[20]

The discovery is made by the person *as* person, and that means in interaction, in sharing, in the mutuality of consciences. The humanist clinical psychology frequently comes very close to this understanding. Erich Fromm, for instance, says that if man "faces the truth without panic, he will recognize that there is no meaning to life except the meaning man gives to life by the unfolding of his powers, by living productively".[21] The emphasis is on the *unfolding* of what man discovers as his best endowment for becoming more humane and for helping others to make the same discovery.

For an extreme existentialist like Jean Paul Sartre, the approach is quite different. He does not believe that man can discover a law that is written into his heart but, rather, that man has to realize "that he is the being by whom value exists. It is then that his freedom will become conscious of itself and will reveal itself in anguish as the unique source of value and the nothingness by which the world exists".[22] I agree with Sartre that, on earth, only the human person can bring ethical values into existence. But he finds ethically relevant realities. And there is more than just the naked existence of an arbitrary freedom. Sartre's life companion, Simone de Beauvoir, makes at least one important step towards our understanding of natural law. "To will oneself free is also to will others free . . . The precept will be to treat the other as a freedom so that his end may be freedom".[23]

The existentialism that emphasizes one-sidedly the freedom to be and the freedom to let others be is an extreme reaction to those kinds of natural law theories that gravely neglected man's inner call to be free and to become ever more so. Typical of that neglect of inner freedom is the utilitarian approach of

Jeremy Bentham and John Stuart Mill to natural law. Bentham writes, "Nature has placed mankind under the governance of two sovereign masters, pain and pleasure. It is for them alone to point out what we ought to do, as well as what we shall do".[24] This jump from "ought to do" to "shall do" leaves no place whatever for genuine freedom under the "two sovereign masters". And it is only a naive optimism that allows Bentham to hope that these twin masters will achieve the greatest happiness for all those whose interest is in question.

Any form of natural law theory that does not honour the freedom and dignity of the human person, any theory that submits the person, as such, to mere drives or other "sovereign masters" is worth nothing or, rather, is inimical to ethics.

3. *Natural law and the historicity of humanity*

The present uneasiness about natural law will not be overcome unless moral theology is ready "to move from a classicist methodology to a historically conscious methodology".[25] Historicity, as an abiding and essential dimension of the human being, must be given great attention. But before approaching this basic matter, we should be reminded that natural law theories, too, are historically dated and need, at least partially, a contextual explication. Not only the lowly people are conditioned by their traditions and their environment; also those who engage in theories about the nature of man and the ethical demands that flow from it work with the tools of their time, and are conditioned by their educational background and the social and cultural milieu in which they move.

We can see, for instance, how the Greek philosophers began to compare the thinking and the mores of the various Greek colonies that were in contact with each other; but while speaking about human nature, they had in mind only the free Greek-speaking male. They did not even question the presupposition that females had not the same nature and that the slave and the non-Greek-speaking people were simply barbarians. A new encounter of their culture with the major cultures of Asia Minor, Mesopotamia and Egypt, in the wake of Alexander the Great, brought a broadened approach with some fresh insights. So, should we not realize today, in our thinking about natural law, that we are faced with a new encounter of all present cultures? The historical and behavioural sciences provide us with new knowledge. It would be the most unnatural and self-defeating attitude, then, to quote only what Holy Mother Church said about natural law in previous centuries.

a) Consciousness of historicity

It is distinctive of the human being that he has history, is history and makes history. Animals do not have the kind of memory and consciousness that allow history. The human individual and the human community and society have a memory. We can consciously view the present moment in the perspective of the past from which it arises and in conscious responsibility for the future that we are shaping here and now.

Through growth in historical consciousness, mankind and the human person are growing in humanness. Our present era has a newly informed consciousness of our rootedness not only in the immediate past but also in the billions of years in which life on earth developed and the millions of years in which the human race made its ways through history. We are aware of the development and decay of cultures. Besides, we see the conscience of the human person in a perspective of developmental psychology. The person is fully alive and human by learning, unlearning and discerning the direction of his development and growth. Where this process stops, there we are faced with obvious signs of senility.

We also know better today how the desire to search for new dimensions of life is conditioned by the historical context. Greek philosophy was strongly marked by the idea that history simply repeats itself; there was little or no awareness that man can create a new future. Under the impact of Hinduism, the caste system was sacralized and fixed and traditions — even traditional work-tools — could not be changed without fear of sinning against the Dherma.

We are more aware now that the Judaeo-Christian vision of religion as history of God with man, marked by the Exodus and new breakthroughs, has influenced the modern world; and the modern world, in turn, has made us more aware that our faith is not a philosophical system or a system of unchangeable formulations of doctrines but a history of life with God. In our present era of profound transformation of cultures, we are more aware than our predecessors of the centrality of the Exodus in the Old and New Testaments. We, therefore, see more clearly the importance of the Pauline breakthrough in the apostolic time when a part of Christianity was tempted to lock itself into a static vision of mores, tradition and law.

b) Historicity as all-pervading dimension

In man, there are essential and abiding components and faculties. We can say that it belongs to his very nature that he is rational, endowed with free will, with affectivity, emotions and passions; that he has an inborn sense of beauty, of play, of joy and a sense of humour; that he is an embodied spirit and, last but not least, he is a social being. However, we should not forget for one moment that all these dimensions are lived and thought about under diverse historical conditions.

(1) Man is a rational being. He is self-conscious and can consciously reflect about himself, his relationships and all his desires and doings. However, if we compare the various cultures, we see that rationality, too, manifests itself differently according to the historical context. The rationality of Jesus, characterized by the constant use of parables and proverbs, is quite different from that of Greek philosophers. Jesus and the apostles have not given us definitions, as Scholastic thinking likes to do. The rationality of the old Chinese culture as expressed in Taoism and Confucianism, the rationality of Hinduism and the cultures impregnated with the contemplative way of Hinayana Buddhism, the mythological intuitions of Africans, and the more empirical approach of today's scientists, all fall under the same general concept of "rationality"; yet, there is a whole world of difference between them. Similarly, the rationality of the new generations, influenced by the audio-visual mass media, does not fit into a certain philosophy and ethics of rationality of earlier times.

(2) Free will belongs to the essential nature of man; but mankind has not yet explored all the dimensions of and obstacles to the freedom of the will, depending on the quality of the environment and the recognition or denial of the freedom and

dignity of all people. In today's anthropology, psychology, sociology, and especially in today's ethics, there can easily be seen dimensions that were lacking in earlier ethical systems.

(3) Not all cultures have given the same attention and evaluation to affectivity, emotions and passions. Consider the difference between the Stoic Greek thinking about *apatheia*, which disowned the value of compassion and all other passions, and treated love mainly as one of the suspect passions and, on the other side, the emphasis on compassion and love in the biblical teaching and in Hinayana Buddhism.

(4) A human being can hardly be envisioned without some thought of a sense of humour, the many expressions of joy, a child's smile; yet, how different are the various cultures in their expressions and evaluations of humour and gladness! There are cultures that foster play, dance, the varied expressions of relaxed humour, while other cultures are as stolid as oxen. The quality and strength of humour is a main criterion for the validity of a culture. Yet, what kind of humour would one make the standard for all cultures? Diversity of expression is "natural" for historical man.

(5) Consider, too, how different are the views on the body and the treatment people give to the body. While biblical tradition gives to the body the highest praise by the ethical challenge to glorify God in the body, and the expectation that the resurrected body will share in God's glory, certain trends in Parsism and in Hellenistic philosophy considered the body as an unworthy prison of the immaterial and immortal soul. All this had enormous influence on the understanding, for instance, of sexuality, of asceticism, of care for the body, and so on. Theology did not always remain faithful to the biblical vision of the body.

(6) Greek and Roman philosophy already defined human nature in view of sociability. Man is a social animal. Only modern historical study, the sociology of sexuality, of marriage and family, of the mores and morality, and the sociology of religion, have made us fully aware of the profound interdependence of all these aspects in a totality of economic, social, cultural and political situations, relationships and processes. Any theory of

natural law ethics that did not try to take all this fully into account would be, for the active and well-informed modern man, a pitiable fossil.

St. Paul, St. Matthew and the Church Fathers of the first centuries developed thought patterns about natural law in view of the appreciation of what is good, right and truthful in the various cultures where the Gospel was preached. It prevented them from imposing time-bound mores, traditions and laws on cultures different from their own. Today, there is a special need to return to this kind of approach. Otherwise we can be tempted to impose everywhere a ready-made system of natural law ethics that is expressive of only a limited part of humanity. We have to be keenly aware of the danger of an ethical colonialism that would greatly harm the Gospel and be unfaithful to the right understanding of what the Christian faith is all about. In this respect, moral theology has an enormous task in the service of the Church and her mission to preach the Gospel to all nations, as well as in her service to the whole of mankind by promoting mutual respect, genuine dialogue and cooperation.[26]

4. What is abiding in natural law?

Neither Christian ethics nor any humanist ethics depends on a natural law theory that proposes to establish, by way of a rational procedure, an ethics for all people. However, accepting historicity and the possibility of various approaches to natural law does not entail an unlimited relativism. We always insist that man has to discover what is good and evil; he cannot determine it arbitrarily. There are abiding truths. And we can even hope that, throughout history, humankind will come to acknowledge ever more clearly those abiding human rights and moral values. We can mention the abolition of slavery, the declaration of the United Nations on human rights, the right to conscientious objection to military service.

There is one abiding design for humankind, and it requires fidelity to knowledge of the past, openness to the present opportunities for better knowledge and evangelization and growth in responsibility for the future. This growth can be constantly jeopardized, however, by the sins of individuals and by the cultural decay that is so often just the expression of the many sins of many people and especially of those in positions of influence. A broadening of the dialogue and a sharing of human experience and reflection should lead to greater enrichment of our moral knowledge as well as to greater discernment between what is abiding and what is time-bound.

Our understanding of human nature is *relational*. That does not mean that we disown selfhood and individuality. It means, rather, that the individual person understands himself in interaction and solidarity with other people and communities. However, the concrete shape of morality cannot be understood without this total context.

In this relational vision, there remains one firm pillar already emphasized in the Stoic ethics and confirmed by Christianity: "The human person is a sacred reality for the human person".[27] Earlier we came to a deeper understanding of conscience in the reciprocity of consciences: the individual cannot be a moral being without honouring humanity in all other people. The golden rule is applied to all. We affirm that slavery should not recur anymore, that it does contradict the golden rule. The individual person cannot reach an existential knowledge of his own freedom, dignity and basic rights without being committed to the same dignity, freedom and rights of others.

A better understanding of the relational character of human nature bridges the very important and abiding insight that no group, no nation, no part of the Church may impose any time-bound norms on others. This is a warning for all times against a superiority complex that leads to ethical colonialism, to dangerous tensions and even to wars. The United Nations' affirmation on basic human rights to be acknowledged and protected by all civilized states is an important milestone in the understanding and promotion of the unalterable requirements of human nature.

5. *Natural law and revelation*

a) What God has disclosed to the eyes of reason

Martin Luther and many other Christians have rightly opposed a natural law theory which presented practically a closed system of an autonomous human reason. Luther follows Old Testament language calling human reason a "whore" whenever man makes himself the centre of everything and thus practically turns away from God. Therefore, we have to distinguish between two totally different mentalities and attitudes in their approach to a rational foundation of normative ethics.

One mentality is closed-minded, unresponsive, anthropocentric in the bad sense. This can be described as a rationalistic approach that constructs a system of thought where there is no place left for new insights, no appreciation for the values and experiences of other cultures and subcultures. The causes and shades of this closed-mindedness are multiple: the kind of upbringing, a security complex or a superiority complex of the individual worsened by that of the social group, a previous failure to resolve the identity crisis and/or other crises of development, as shown in the presentation of the various phases in Erikson's theory (see the chapter on Fundamental Option). One principal cause is the prevalence of "knowledge of dominion" over and above "knowledge of salvation". The rivalries of Christian Churches, a defensive posture in relation to others was a permanent obstacle to the readiness to learn and to unlearn.

On the other hand, we find an approach to natural law marked by the capacity to listen and to learn in dialogue with others, with a vivid sense of the continuity of life. This attitude fits easily into the great dimensions of the history of salvation and revelation. Humbly sharing experience and reflection makes people attentive to the signs of the times. The open-minded person is a listener and, thus, he is attuned to natural and supernatural revelation. All of God's creation is a word, a message, a gift and a calling for man's response. In this vision, natural law cannot be conceived as a closed system. It can easily be seen as an integrated part within the one unfolding revelation that comes to its fullness in Christ. Through the things God has made and through the events that happen under his providence he discloses his attributes to the eyes of reason (cf. Rom 1:19-20).

Only in a radical openness to the truth of the other, in the readiness to learn together, does man gradually discover the significance and finality of his being. In this openness and reciprocity of consciences man is on the wavelength of the order of revelation and salvation. This readiness to share in the common quest for truth is already a sign of redemption.

b) Uniqueness and fullness of revelation in Christ

Speaking, as Christians, of natural law, we must be extremely careful about our own identity. No thought, no word and no theory must disown our faith that God has revealed himself fully in Jesus Christ. All things are made in him, who is the Eternal Word of the Father, and in view of him, the Word Incarnate (Col 1:16). Everything God has created is created in that Word who, in the fullness of time, has taken on our human nature. And there is something specific in the history of Israel by which God has prepared humanity for this fullness of revelation that comes in Jesus Christ alone.

The honour we owe Jesus Christ requires that we also appreciate everything that is right, good and beautiful in cultures outside of Israel and outside of the Christian Church. For, whatever is true and good has its centre in Jesus Christ. He is the focal point, and we are to discern everything in his light. Therefore, the honour we owe Jesus Christ demands our absolute attention to everything that people outside of Israel and outside of the Church have discovered about truth and goodness and what they have realized. For the Spirit of God works in all and through all for all, always in view of Christ. That means that we consider the natural law from within the law of Christ.

However, we distinguish what is open to the eyes of reason from what can be understood only through the special revelation that comes to us through Jesus Christ and which was prepared for by the prophets.

What holy and humble people outside the history of Israel and outside the Christian Church understand about God, truth and goodness, and what they frequently consider as a revelation coming from God, truly enters into the perspective of revelation because, under the influence of the Holy Spirit, they have discovered what God has revealed, by his work and his Word, to the eyes of reason and to the hearts of all who seek him sincerely.

Although dependent on the revelation that came in Jesus Christ, we may never renounce the use of our reason. Rather, as redeemed people, we will use it in openness and integrity. This obliges us to be particularly careful in our arguments and assertions made in the name of the natural law, just as we have to be extremely careful about what we teach as revealed in Jesus Christ.

c) Restoration of human nature in Jesus Christ

The words "human nature" can have various meanings. We have to realize that, throughout history, theology and the documents of the magisterium followed various trends and traditions. The extrapolation of a "pure nature" is a rather late philosophy. For the Church Fathers it was in the true humanity of Christ that the original and true human nature was revealed; and this faith determined everything they said about natural law and righteousness. This vision, which prevailed until the Middle Ages, considered natural law as the expression and order of the integral human nature as it is restored in Jesus Christ and as it can be understood in the light of revelation and under the grace of God. Since then, other approaches have come to the foreground. Following the thought-patterns of the philosophy of antiquity, Christian thinkers developed an autonomous realm of ethical insight distinct from, or even separated from, Christian morality.[28]

Christ has restored the original nature which is a graced nature. He did not come to confirm an autonomous system of natural law teaching but, rather, to restore, confirm and bring to fullness the original design of God. It is dangerous, or at least ambiguous, therefore, to present Jesus Christ simply as a legislator. He is, rather, the fullness of the covenant and the fullness of the law in the perspective of the gospel of John: "While the law was given through Moses, grace and truth came through Jesus Christ" (Jn 1:17). Christ's restoration is not the result of a dictate; it is an ongoing event that comes to completion through faith and grace. To realize this is so important that it has to be illustrated by a few examples.

Christ came to tear down the barriers between Jews, Samaritans and Gentiles. He has revealed that, before God, there is no difference between those born in freedom and those born in slavery and no difference between male and female. But only those who have a living faith and who live totally under the influence of the grace of Jesus are able to draw the conclusions and to do the hard and patient work necessary to tear down the barriers of prejudice, such as the superiority complex of a Latin culture or of the Western world and the many prejudices prevailing even in parts of the Church against the full role of women in the family, in society, in public life and in the Church.

It was through lack of faith and of docility to the grace of the Holy Spirit that Christian thinkers justified the institution of slavery. Moreover, by doing so, they did not properly use their reason but followed an estranged form of reasoning tainted by their membership in a privileged class. It could have happened that people not belonging to the Church understood better than some Church people the issue of freedom and dignity of all people, and committed themselves to it. This does not mean, of course, that reason can be stronger than faith but that those who live on the level of analogy-of-faith, and are totally open to the Spirit, can bring forth a harvest of the Spirit over and against those who follow a heterodox-orthodoxy which subscribes to a code of dogmas without being truly open to Christ and his grace.

Another example. Christ has restored and confirmed the original design of indissoluble fidelity in marriage. To the Pharisees who insisted that Moses allowed divorce, Jesus responded, "It was not like that when all began" (Mt 19:8). One would deeply misunderstand the order of salvation by thinking that it suffices that Jesus promulgated this in a kind of code and, therefore, the Catholic Church has to see to it that all states enforce this promulgated law. Something quite different happened. Jesus revealed the design of his Father by his whole life and death, by being the living Gospel. Restoration of God's original plan is possible only through faith and grace. Graced people outside Christianity may grasp this gift of God while people who live more on the level of law than of grace may distort or thoroughly misunderstand the words of Christ. The Church is committed to this restoration of the original plan, not by teaching and reinforcing an autonomous law of nature but by preaching a living faith and entreating people to let themselves be guided by the Spirit. In other words, the indissolubility of marriage may not be made a mere legal system.

d) Dialogue on natural law between Christians and others

Dialogue and participation among Christians and other believers is surely not fostered by a natural-law thinking that creates practically a closed and autonomous realm of a pure nature. Taoists, Confucianists, Hindus, Mohammedans and the most ancient inhabitants of the Americas and Africa believe in a God who has revealed himself to their ancestors and in many other ways. Much of what we call "natural law" was conceived by them as a part of God's revelation. Therefore, we would do well to follow an approach similar to that of the Apostle of the Gentiles in his epistle to the Romans, chapter 1 and 2. We would then distinguish carefully what our particular faith tells us from what are good arguments proposed, however, in a perspective of God's revealing himself through his work-as-word and especially what he has revealed to humankind through the humble ones and holy, inspired persons. Keeping in mind this dimension does not diminish our good use of reason and our careful pondering of arguments. It allows a more congenial sharing of experience and reflections.

There is also a place for natural law arguments in the dialogue with unbelievers. In that dialogue we should remember the following points. First, we should never think that all those who reject organized religion have automatically the mindset of unbelievers. Some reject organized religion because they do not find enough life and truthfulness in some aspects of the institution. They may be longing for greater dedication to truth. Second, we would do well to search for the hidden unbeliever in our own thinking and conduct. Third, we need not disown our identity while searching for common ground with those who call themselves unbelievers.

We can and should acknowledge all the good and sincere concerns of those on the other side. Thus we honour God and may help them to discover more than they were able to perceive until now. After all, Christians should prophetically "bear witness to the aboriginal law of man's creation. The count against the great anti-Christian systems is not just that they reject *our* ethic, the ethic we happen to prefer . . . It is that they repudiate the law of man's creation".[30] In this prophetic denunciation we can rightly give special attention to the common sense of people and to the best in the common human tradition.

But why should we not also refer to Jesus Christ, whose humanity frequently appeals to people who are not attracted to organized religion? Jesus Christ is present in today's world through his Church, though unfortunately somehow concealed by the divisions among the Christian Churches. He is present to the world in the saints, in the Christian prophets and the humble people. He is also listened to by Mohammedans, by many Jews belonging to Judaism and by many great leaders like Mahatma Gandhi who, through their profound understanding of Christ, have greatly influenced the consciousness of the modern world.

e) The ongoing revelation

In Jesus Christ, in his incarnation, life, death and resurrection, the revelation of God has come to its summit and can never be surpassed. Christ is the final word of the Father to humanity. Yet, it would be erroneous to consider the revelation given two thousand years ago in Jesus Christ as a kind of dead heritage. Rather, it is the active leaven that gradually permeates the whole of history. The Christ-event goes on. All the good that happens between the first and the final coming of Jesus Christ is history in the Word, an effective presence of the Saviour and Lord of the world. The Holy Spirit introduces the disciples of Christ gradually to a fuller understanding of the Christ-event and what it means for the whole of human life.

Before Jesus left this world he said to his disciples, "There is still much that I could say to you, but the burden would be too great for you now. However, when he comes who is the Spirit of truth, he will guide you into all the truth; for he will not speak on his own authority but will tell only what he heard; and he will make known to you the things that are coming" (Jn 16:12-14).

The Holy Spirit will never teach us anything opposed to Christ's doctrine but will lead the Church and humanity gradually to a deeper understanding of it. And here we should not think that this deeper understanding is based only on Scripture. For, besides Scripture, but never opposed to it, there is the living tradition. This is not only a tradition from mouth to mouth throughout the centuries; it is a torrent of life in which God remains always the source and power, the One who was, who is and who will be. Historical events and especially the life of the Church are, therefore, to be understood as the ongoing active presence of God. And wherever there is an active presence, a work of God, there is also a message, an ongoing revelation.

The Spirit introduces us not only to an understanding of the Bible but, also and equally, in the light of Jesus Christ, to an understanding of "things that are coming". For the community of believers, the whole history between the first coming of Jesus in the flesh and his final coming in the *parousia* is the opening of the sealed book of history (cf. Rev ch. 4-7). History, therefore, and particularly the important "signs of the times" may never be neglected in our search for a better understanding of the revealed truth and equally of the will of God.[31]

The renewal of the Church, as willed by Vatican II, is strongly marked by this openness to the signs of the times, an openness that brings with it a great freedom for dialogue. That freedom includes the capacity to learn and to unlearn while guaranteeing a genuine continuity of life in Christ Jesus. This distinguishes an authentic Christian understanding of tradition, history and what we call "natural law" from that of the traditionalists whose ears need to be attuned to Christ's clear statement: "My Father has never yet ceased his work, and I am working too" (Jn 5:17).

f) The role and competence of the magisterium in matters of natural law

How frequently the Roman pontiffs throughout the last century have emphasized their role and competence in matters of natural law cannot be overlooked.[32] Many papal documents about justice, chastity, liberalism and other moral questions are mainly based on natural law considerations. The teaching office in the Church would not be fully faithful to Jesus Christ if it failed to give great attention to the ongoing revelation which we see especially as the "signs of the times". The magisterium cannot at all disregard the broad realm of morality that is accessible to the eyes of reason and is, in fact, understood by the conscience of the common people and of those who have a prophetic role in the world.

I see the primary role of the magisterium in the preaching of the Gospel in a way that will help people to find the synthesis of faith and life. The successors of the apostles ought always to promote the broadest dialogue in a sharing of experiences and reflections, in order to bring everything home into the light of Christ. The teaching Church relies by necessity on the living Church; and a very definite part of that living Church is represented in the growing insights into moral problems, and the sensitivity to the present opportunities and dangers.

Church leaders, together with those who are endowed with a special prophetic charism, have to promote discernment constantly, not only by offering solid criteria but also by educating a discerning membership. It is, then, also their right, and sometimes their duty, to speak a prophetic word, to open new horizons and to challenge whatever contradicts the spirit of Christ and jeopardizes the common good of humanity. But a prophetic challenge is effective only to the extent that it shows a high level of discernment and of readiness to listen and to learn.

When theologians rely almost exclusively on a time-bound natural law philosophy, it is unavoidable that some documents of the magisterium will follow the same trend. We all realize that we need a thorough-going hermeneutic for a right interpretation and application of scriptural texts to the moral problems of today's world. The awareness of these difficulties may lead some to base their thinking almost exclusively on natural law. But natural law thinking needs an equally profound hermeneutic. In each era we have to bring home the best insights about what human nature and human history mean in the present life context and what they mean in the light of Jesus Christ.

What is most needed today, and what should be particularly promoted by those who have authority in the Church, is a distinctively Christian vision of the natural law — one that is seen within the law of Christ. This Christian vision is needed also in view of the Church's dialogue with the modern world, where the first necessity is our own Christian identity.

6. *Understanding the law of Christ in the Bible*

The law of Christ is one and undivided; of course, we rightly distinguish between those parts and aspects that are accessible to the "eyes of reason" of all men of good will and those that come to us only through special revelation. As a result we are faced with the question: how does the Bible transmit to us moral guidelines and norms? [33] However, our gratitude for the unique revelation in Christ and in view of Christ and the special light we receive from the Bible should not distract our interest in a synthesis. The modern distinctions between "natural" and "supernatural" are, in this form, not to be found in the Bible. But the Bible tells us a lot about the proprium of a "life in Christ".

a) Exegesis and hermeneutic

Moral theology refers to exegesis to discover what the biblical texts really say and how they can be rightly understood by giving full attention to the literary form as well as to the cultural and historical context. Biblical theology helps us to see the main perspectives of that morality that is rooted in faith. It alerts us also to the gradual growth of moral sensitivity and moral insights. Therefore, it is not correct to quote discrete biblical texts as proof texts, unless proper care is taken to discern the dynamics of historical development of ethical knowledge and the very diversity within the books of the Bible, for instance, the tension between the prophetic and the priestly tradition. While the Old Testament conveys a wealth of wisdom and gives us most valuable insights into a morality marked by the covenant between God and his people and into God's patient pedagogy, when it comes down to a more concrete moral guidance everything has to be tested again in the full light of the New Testament. By comparing the various writings not only of the Old but also of the New Testament, exegesis helps us to see a healthy pluralism of approaches within the oneness of faith. Therefore, moral theologians will not try to prove the abiding and universal value of norms found in one inspired author without awareness of the complementarity of the others.

While exegesis is principally concerned with discovering what really happened and was said in those times *(in illo tempore)*, theological hermeneutics seeks to answer the question: What does the Bible teach us in order to understand God's will here and now, in our time? Hermeneutics requires knowledge both of that time and our time, sharp awareness of the biblical horizon for understanding, including the time-bound worldview of the inspired writers, and of our own culturally conditioned way of approaching the problems.

b) Abiding teaching in the Bible

The way one seeks moral teaching in the Bible makes an enormous difference. Some ask whether there are abiding norms in the Bible while thinking mainly or only of limitative norms. Or we can take a much broader approach by seeking in various directions an abiding orientation for our moral life deriving from revelation as found in the Bible. In this work, we have already stressed the importance of the context of understanding offered by the whole of Scripture. All our moral discourse should be illumined by that vision and the main perspectives that are found in the whole of the scriptures or at least in an important part of them; for instance, the prophetic tradition. We also remind ourselves here of what was repeatedly said about the biblical emphasis on the goal-commandments, the normative direction for on-going conversion and growth. Furthermore, we find in the Bible strict norms that present a very lofty ideal, for instance, the words of the Lord against divorce. There are also general norms in the sense of universal criteria for discernment both from the angle of the normative ideal and from that of the absolute minimum. On the one hand, for instance, are the "fruits of the Spirit", on the other the sins that exclude from the kingdom of God (cf. Gal 5:19-23).

c) Transcendental orientations

The motivations and, to some extent, the very content of the lofty biblical orientations, requiring corresponding dispositions and offering criteria for discernment, are based more on what God has already done in creation and redemption (*unumnusu*) than on our expectations and hopes, although we do not wish to minimize the eschatological horizon insofar as it describes God's promises for the things to come and the road we have to walk. The uniqueness of God's marvellous deeds climaxing in the incarnation of the Word of God, the Paschal Mystery, the effusion of the Holy Spirit, is more than an additional motivation for keeping norms which are naturally known; it opens up new dimensions and orientations that also lead to more concrete norms, setting us on the road and obliging us to a clear direction that has always to be kept in mind.

d) Abiding and transient emphasis on certain dispositions

The Bible speaks very frequently of virtues and dispositions that can be expected from those who know the Lord's goodness and his marvellous deeds. But there is no doubt that special emphasis can, at least partially, derive also from the cultural environment and from special needs. The sacred authors bring the ethos of their culture into the light of revelation, into the horizon of the covenant morality, excluding what is not fitting, strengthening what is simply good and purifying other parts of the traditional ethos. We learn from biblical scholars, for instance, how Paul, the Apostle of the Gentiles, meets differently the Jewish and the Hellenistic mentality; the way he approves or disapproves the virtues taught by the Stoics, bringing them home into a new horizon. But the eschatological virtues, frequently referred to in this work, are originally biblical, emphasized at all times and normative for Christian ethics.

e) Concrete material norms: abiding or time-bound

The inspired authors did not intend to write something like today's scientific moral theology. Their teaching is kerygmatic and pastoral. It is, however, theology in the true sense, a ministry of salvation. They have little interest in treating separately the more transcendental guidelines and, then, the more concrete material "norms". For instance, in Romans 12:1-15:13, Philippians 2:1-18 and 1 Thessalonians 4:1-12 we find a number of rather concrete general norms and particular imperatives integrated into the broad horizon given by the mysteries of salvation and by transcendental orientations.

The first impression, and the rightful presumption, is that the general material norms derived from the main perspectives of faith are meant to be abiding and binding teaching for all times. This does not, however, exclude that throughout the ages, the very same truth can find different formulations and form part of various systematizations.

Not infrequently the very context and the formulation of the inspired authors indicate that it is a matter of guidance in a unique historical context or even a response to a very special local problem. The latter is evidently the case in Paul's argumentation about the women's veil in Corinth (1 Cor 11:33-36, 1 Tim 2:12). However, this does not at all mean that these passages are irrelevant for the moral teaching of today; on the contrary, they are very helpful as "models" of how to deal with particular traditions and how to incarnate the Gospel morality in other cultural contexts.

Paul's advice on slavery is not at all a divine approval of that practice. On the contrary, his vision is a gigantic step forward towards totally renewed human relationships that, one day, would bring about new institutions and abolish old ones, like slavery. The same holds true of Paul's words about obedience to state authorities (Rom 13:1-7). It would be a misunderstanding to think that Paul means blind or unconditional obedience. He has his strong reservations about earthly authorities and knows about the frequent abuse (cf. 1 Cor 2:8; 6:1-7). But his expectation of a rather near *parousia* and the smallness of the Christian communities surely did not favour the development of guidelines, so necessary today, about how Christians should fulfil their social and political responsibilities also by bringing about a profound change in structures. Finally, moral theology will never confine itself to the interpretation of an isolated text; it will rather always look to the total biblical teaching, for instance, on our relationships to the earthly

authorities and the total experience of Christianity and other
religious people throughout the thousands of years.

Norms can be found which are consistently inculcated in
the Bible and in a considerable part of Church tradition, about
which we can come to the awareness that they are not binding
for all times when profound changes in the societal life happen.
A well known example was the severe prohibition of taking
interest from capital loaned to others. A new socio-economic
situation enforced a change regarding the concrete material
norm. Unfortunately, the transition was not at all elegant.
But, again, it should be stressed that the biblical teaching on
this and on other points brings to light an abiding "rule":
never to take advantage of our neighbour's distress. An enforced
change of the concrete norm can even lead to better understanding of the biblical orientation and to a more demanding
challenge.

f) Approximations in the fulfilment of the Lord's words

The Lord's own words forbidding divorce and remarriage
seem to be absolute. We can see how seriously they were taken
by the primitive Christian communities. Yet, Paul (cf. 1 Cor
7:12-16), and probably also Matthew, while inculcating the
Lord's command, allows approximations, that is, the best
possible fulfilment and not an always literal application. However, Paul, in his very wording, shows that he does not give the
same weight to his own practical solution as to the Lord's
own word. "To the married I give this ruling, which is not my
own word but the Lord's . . . To the rest I say, as my own
word, not as the Lord's . . ." (1 Cor 7:10-12).

Summing up we can say: Moral theology is neither biblicistic
nor a mere philosophical endeavour. It is either under the
authority of the word of God or it is not theology at all. But
the way it is guided by the Bible needs to be discovered by
painstaking effort of research and reflection. The Bible offers
much more than a moral code, something quite different from
a list of ready-made norms, but, nevertheless, does offer binding norms. However, the more concrete some biblical norms are
the more carefully must the question of concrete historical
circumstances be raised; and the universality of norms binding

for all time is not to be asserted on the basis of one or two texts. We need to pay attention always to the whole Bible and to Tradition. Finally, theological hermeneutics, using all the resources of philosophy and of the anthropological sciences, should always take place within the faith-community.

IV. NORMATIVE ETHICS

Let it be said again, a Christian moral theology is more than normative ethics; it is the theology of life in Christ Jesus, an effort to come to a full understanding of what discipleship means for Christians and for the world. Normative ethics, however, is an indispensable part of Christian ethics.

How much space and emphasis are given to concrete norms depends on the various types of understanding of Christian life. In a moral theology for confessors who understand themselves as judges and guides, or even controllers, the normative part prevails absolutely. In a certain type of Protestant ethics one-sidedly concerned with acts and the question "what ought I to do?" the result is similar.

An outspoken morality will give the main attention to the formation of the Christian personality, the discerning person. Here, the chief concern is to make good the tree, with the hope that the fruit will then also be good. There is a profound difference in whether rules are presented as "Thou shalt"/"You ought" or as the full and attractive picture of the truly Christian person endowed with eschatological virtues. Whoever knows what these virtues mean knows also what is expected of him, even though he does not yet know the details.

What has been said about norms, rules and laws in this chapter should not take away our attention from what was said earlier about the fundamental option and the formation of a distinctively Christian conscience. The understanding of the reciprocity of consciences leads us to what could be called "relational virtues". Once they are understood, they give guidance but, again, the emphasis is on the gift-character of these virtues and the effort to acquire them is understood not so much as "thou shalt" but, rather, "you can", inviting a willing response to the call.

Only if we have come to realize what morality is all about, and what a distinctively Christian morality is, can we address ourselves to the question of norms in a Christian context. Here, we have to distinguish between the various levels of the moral discourse about norms.[34] The first and lowest level is the expressive, evocative use of norms: the guidance of others through norms. The second and truly moral level is the discerning use of moral norms and rules, their intelligent and free application. The third is the ethical level where we ask the critical questions about whether certain principles, norms or rules are appropriate in a new historical context. Especially in a time of profound cultural changes, the third, the ethical level, is of particular relevance.

1. *Creative fidelity and liberty as normative*

The greatest gift that divine liberty offers us is God's own love and the human capacity to reciprocate love. Love is not, first of all, a norm; it is a gift, a self-bestowal. But love faithfully received makes us free to love each other and to love God.

Once we have understood from what and for what Christ has freed us, we can easily see that this very freedom is an all-embracing norm with many detailed aspects. As Christians, we cannot speak of freedom without thinking equally of creative fidelity in which we use our freedom. Norms are different when they form an essential part of a covenant morality from when they are expressed within a defence morality.

Christian morality is the acting out of a covenant, and therefore is a morality of creative fidelity. And this, for human beings who are justified and yet still sinners, requires clear norms in the sense of role expectations and of the reliability so necessary for mutual trust, healthy self-trust and genuine love. God has freely committed himself to his world. He has made a special covenant of fidelity with his people, and this becomes a basic norm for an ethics of fidelity. Moreover, all norms have to be faithful to that freedom for which Christ has set us free.

Norms are necessary for a peaceful life in community and society. They should serve to educate us to become ever more discerning persons and are indispensable for our own examination of conscience. "The good may be wrought without the use of norms but it cannot be taught or even thought without some kind of cognitively meaningful ethical statements. And what is more, the good cannot be meaningfully wrought without some meaningful ethical norm to determine what the good thing to do is".[35]

Even proponents of "the new morality", like J.A.T. Robinson, insist on the necessity of some norms and rules. A Christian "cannot but rely, in deep humility, upon guiding rules, upon the cumulative experience of one's own and other people's obedience. It is this bank of experience which gives us our working rules of 'right' and 'wrong', and without them we could not but flounder".[36]

It is for the sake of peace and equally for the sake of the freedom and respect of all that we need acknowledged norms. However, this does not mean that we accept traditional rules blindly. On the contrary, we have constantly to use our critical mind and common endeavour to work out the best possible rules in view of present opportunities and needs. "A moral code there must be in any society. Christians must be to the fore in every age, helping to construct it, to criticize it, and keep it in repair".[37]

History teaches us that rules and norms can live on, independent of their original purpose, just as authorities can forget that their purpose is service to the common good. There is unavoidably a tension between a fixed set of norms and freedom for creative and timely action in fidelity. Therefore, the fundamental question of normative ethics is: How do we evaluate, here and now, the adequacy of norms and rules?

2. Deontological and teleological criteria for norms

As Christians, we live under the law of faith and grace. We receive them in joy and gratitude as supreme gifts of God and as our supreme law. God's freedom has manifested itself in his love for us through Jesus Christ and in the outpouring of the Holy Spirit and, thus, all our energies are set free for that supreme norm which Jesus formulated at the Last Supper: "This, then, is my commandment I share with you: love one another as I have loved you" (Jn 15:12). And since Christ reveals for us the freedom of the Father to love us, this commandment coincides with another: "Let your goodness have no limits, just as the goodness of the heavenly Father knows no bounds" (Mt 5:48).

If this supreme gift of love is the all-embracing law, it follows that we have to do everything in our power to know this love. And that means to know Jesus Christ and to know the Father.

Love is not just a sentiment. If we have faith in Jesus Christ, we cannot be agnostics about true love. God has revealed his countenance, the countenance of true love in Jesus Christ. We can know it only if we abide in the love of Christ and let his words dwell in us, for Christian love is sharing in Christ's own love as he shares in the Father's love for all people. However, it is not enough to abide in Christ's love. We must also search, consciously and explicitly, to discover and understand the essential qualities and demands of this love. We call this kind of reflection "deontology", well aware that others have another somehow legalistic vision of deontology, limiting it to a "normative ethics" of the borderlines.

We can agree with Bishop Robinson that "The various commandments are comprehended under the one command of love and based on it. Apart from this there are no unbreakable rules".[38] Against the extreme situation ethics of Joseph Fletcher, Paul Ramsey rightly emphasizes that it does not follow from the above vision that a most general formulation of love is the only absolute rule. On the contrary, we have to conclude that "In and from love there *are*, or there may be, unbreakable rules, and the question relentlessly pressed is what these rules are".[39] But they are not to be found "apart from love".

Anyone who would try to justify, on the basis of the freedom of *agape*, his own inability to bind himself one way and not another for love's sake, would thoroughly misunderstand the meaning of this freedom. There is an order of love that goes beyond the immediate response of one person's depth to another's depth. They both stand before that love that has a countenance and has bound itself in a covenant. Paul Ramsey opposes Fletcher's structureless "act-agapeism". His own concept is one of "rule-agapeism". This means that we are asking not only which act is the most loving but are asking also profoundly, "Which rules of action are most love-embodying?"[40]

In order to work out or to discern these more specific rules, it is not enough to have a general knowledge of love as Jesus Christ has revealed it; we also need a knowledge of our own human nature and of our historical context and experience as it pertains to the foreseeable consequences of our actions. A utilitarian pragmatism looks only at the foreseeable results of actions. Behind this tendency there is a kind of agnosticism, a despair about the possibility that we can know the true countenance of love. For Christians, this is tantamount to denying our faith in Jesus Christ, through whom we do know what true love is.

An ethics of responsibility also gives careful thought to the foreseeable consequences of our actions. In other words, we do not neglect teleological consideration. But these foreseeable consequences must be evaluated in view of the true countenance of love as revealed in Jesus Christ and in view of the inborn powers that allow us and urge us to become truly an image and likeness of God. Our attention to these inborn tendencies or laws (*telos*) and to the foreseeable results is a teleological approach that is quite different from a one-sided utilitarian pragmatism. And, as Christians, we should give our greatest attention to forming a harmonious synthesis of deontological and teleological reflections. We cannot accept an "either/or" approach: either deontological rules or attention only to results.[41] We need and we have deontological criteria that allow us to evaluate the foreseeable consequences.

3. "The impossible ethical ideal"

From the countenance of love as revealed in Christ, described in Holy Scripture and represented again and again, although imperfectly, by the saints, the disciples of Christ, there follow two kinds of rules: (1) The prohibitive rules which indicate those attitudes that absolutely contradict the gift and norm of love, and (2) the goal-directed norms as expressed, for instance, in the beatitudes and in the solemn words of Jesus, "but-I-tell-you" (Mt 5:17-48).

The first kind of norms are clearly and concisely prescriptive. "In the prescriptive use of the principles, the centre of gravity is on the reliability of traditional moral propositions and their reasonable application in a relatively open contemporary situation".[42] The second kind are illuminative. But this does not mean that they are merely optional. They are truly to be considered as norms for Christian attitudes and actions, in that Christians ought always to be guided and dynamized by them. In the illuminative view of principles, the centre of gravity is on the newness of the life in Christ Jesus, the openness for ongoing conversion and growth, the absolute readiness to go far beyond the realm of prescriptive rules.

A distinctively Christian ethics gives the greatest attention to the normative ideal expressed in the New Testament and already indicated by the covenant law: to love God with all our heart and all our energies. But, as soon as we work out a normative ethics for the economic-social-political realm, that perfect and normative ideal seems to be, as Reinhold Niebuhr expresses it, an "impossible ethical ideal". We are not able to build on it a code of public morality. Therefore, we need approximations. "The law of love is involved in all approximations of justice, but as an ultimate perspective by which their limitations are discovered".[43] Nevertheless, the "impossible ideal" disallows a static, self-complacent view of the approximate rules.

The approximations must never be arbitrary. They should be a response to the present opportunities, to the signs of the times, and always open for more ideal means and goals. We have to be attentive to both the prescriptive rules and the highest normative ideals if we are to determine goals which represent God's purpose for our time. As John Bennett suggests, we have to work out, with all people of good will, "middle axioms" that can somehow build bridges between the transcendence of Christian ethics and the technical competence of the autonomous sectors of the temporal spheres.[44]

Gene Outka speaks in the same sense about "intermediate norms".[45] Above all, it is a matter of "relational norms" that regulate the relationships between persons and of persons and communities. As example we could mention the declaration of the United Nations on basic human rights or the "fundamental ground rules of the society" in the Bill of Rights of the Constitution of the United States. These ground rules are different from merely positive laws that pertain to their clarification, protection and implementation.

As believers in one God, Father of all people, we know infallibly that no person may exploit another, no group may manipulate or exploit another. While we must strive untiringly towards this ideal, we can reach it only gradually. Therefore, we need, as Mahatma Gandhi frequently emphasized, a readiness for open-ended compromises. Here I would not think only of concrete political arrangements but also of normative rules that are helpful as criteria in the difficult situations where we have to work out patiently these open-ended compromises. A *casuistry* that works out a certain typology based on unbreakable prescriptive laws and also in view of the dynamics of the "impossible ideal" should not be lightly discarded.

4. Over and above rules

The necessary emphasis on rules and norms should never let us forget the "life-giving law of the Spirit in Christ Jesus" (Rom 8:2). We have constantly to remind ourselves that "Christian morality, then, does not mean only fidelity to the catalogue of the commandments, but the uncataloguable, dynamic liveliness of the good, spirit-inspired man who detects opportunities for good with fine sense and, above all, who does not deal so much with the 'Thou shalt' of the commandments but under the impulse of the 'Thou mayest' of love".[46]

On the one hand we need the ongoing battle against the selfishness that is incarnate in us and in the collectivity; and in that battle we have to look carefully to rules and norms. But on the other hand we also rejoice in the gifts of the Spirit and praise him for the harvest that he brings forth in our life: "But the harvest of the Spirit is love, joy, peace, patience, kindness, goodness, fidelity, gentleness and self-control. There is no law dealing with such things as these" (Gal 5:22-23).

When we allow the Spirit to guide us, we are less tempted to break the prohibitive laws that mark the boundaries of the order of love. Rather, we joyfully approach the will of God as a manifestation of his saving justice. We shall never discard the use of proper criteria since we are justified and yet sinners at the same time. But, if we allow the Holy Spirit to guide us, then sin no longer has power over us. "Therefore, I implore you by God's mercy to offer your very selves to him: a living sacrifice, dedicated and fit for his acceptance, the worship offered by mind and heart. Adapt yourselves no longer to the pattern of this present world, but let your minds be remade and your whole nature thus transformed. Then you will be able to discern the will of God and to know what is good, acceptable and perfect" (Rom 12:1-2).

On one hand, this classical text of Paul warns against the morality of the superego that so easily yields to the pressure of the selfish environment; on the other hand, it expresses the optimism of faith and hope. If we are ready to accept Christ's sacrifice as the pattern of our life, and if we test all that we do by whether we can offer it, with him, to the Father in thanksgiving for all he has given us, then we will be guided by the Spirit and able to discern the will of God. The real Christian does not just stand before rules and criteria; he has his centre of life in the Eucharist and makes his decisions on whether his response can be brought home into the celebration of God's goodness and mercy as revealed in the Paschal Mystery.

5. *Tension between norm and liberty in the Church of today*

In a time of profound cultural upheaval, and in a Church that tries to overcome the besieged mentality of the past centuries by opening itself to ecumenism and dialogue with the whole of humanity, it is not surprising that two models for the understanding of norms are clashing. This clash reflects the profound tension between the self-understanding of the Church as a perfect society, an institution where the hierarchy simply calls itself "the church" and claims total control over the conduct and consciences of the "subjects of the church" and, on the other hand, a new and yet older model in which the Church understands herself as a community of love and a fellowship in the Holy Spirit.[47]

We live in the painful transition from an era of the Constantinian "church of the empire" where people became by birth subjects of the church, to an era of faith by free decision and commitment to the community of faith as active, co-responsible members. Besides, the Church has to undergo an enormous exodus from an era dominated by a Western mentality and structure to an era in which the Third World will be decisive for the Church and the future of humanity.[10]

There was always a tension between those people who looked mainly for security and stability and those who were spearheading historical developments. This tension is presently sharpened by the new constellation in Church and world. Our presentation of moral theology tries to work for reconciliation without, however, renouncing its clear decision in favour of a theology of co-humanity, co-responsibility, creative liberty and fidelity, reciprocity of consciences.

The mere discussion of individual norms, and their absoluteness or lack of it, will lead nowhere unless we are more aware of the clash between the two mentalities and even two purposes of moral teachings. There is still the concept of moral theology as guide for confessors who understand their role mainly as judges and controllers of consciences; and there is also a moral theology whose purpose is to present the whole of Christian life in the Church and the secular society as co-responsibility. So, it is no wonder that the clash becomes particularly evident when we come to the fundamental questions and conclusions concerning normative ethics and the role of norms in the life of Christians.[49]

The one school, supported by a part of the hierarchy, overstresses the authority of Roman documents even when they are historically dated or when it can be shown that they fall short in the historical dimension of morality. Although the magisterium has seldom, if ever, proposed moral norms with the specific claim of infallibility, time and again one school of morals has posed these norms as if they were practically infallible, "at least until such time has elapsed or such a volume of dissent arisen that this position is simply no longer tenable".[50] This attitude greatly damages the credibility of the magisterium of the Church, and particularly her moral teaching, in the eyes of critical persons who might be the most decisive people for the future.

In the light of the Second Vatican Council, today's moral theology can offer some clear perspectives:

(1) The whole moral teaching and particularly the proposition and critical refinement of norms and rules are not so much for the service of the Church as institution as for the service of the Church as a community of love and as servant to the kingdom of God. An absolute condition for proclaiming the kingdom of God is profound respect for the sincere conscience of people and an ongoing effort to enlighten and strengthen their consciences.[51]

(2) Moral theology exercises a role of mediation between the magisterium and all believers. Its purpose cannot be just to explain the rules laid down in earlier Church documents; it also has to assist the magisterium by bringing home the experiences and reflections of the lowly people as well as of those who enjoy particular competence. Moral theology has constantly to revise critically the former efforts and, also, to offer to those in authority the results of its concerted studies.[52]

(3) Since the Church understands herself more consciously as a servant of all humanity, she feels obliged to engage in a dialogue that requires also the willingness to learn from the world. The Pastoral Constitution on the Church in the Modern World, article 44, speaks of the help which the Church strives to give to human activity throughout the world. But in the following article she speaks also of "the help which the Church receives from the modern world". It is, therefore, not sufficient to consult only the faithful in matters of morality;[53] it is also imperative that the Church be willing to listen to those outside her fold, especially when they are highly qualified and manifest a prophetic spirit and special sensitivity to the signs of the times. Openness to the views of others and patient dialogue are signs of the authority of the Church's freedom.[54]

(4) All who critically discern and propose ethical norms must be fully conscious that they stand under the authority of the Word of God. It must be recognized, however, that the interpretation of the Word of God requires a great effort for good hermeneutics and the best possible knowledge of the historical context of the individual writings of the Bible.[55]

(5) The Church needs office-holders of human and religious competence, endowed with a prophetic spirit and willing and able to listen to prophetic voices. Their authority will be strengthened if they keep themselves within the limits of the competence of both their office and their knowledge.[56] Not all questions must be authoritatively resolved, but there is sometimes a need for the authority to urge the faithful to solidary action in a certain direction.

6. The uses of law and norms in ecumenical dialogue

a) The vision of the Orthodox Churches

Catholic-Protestant dialogue should never overlook as partners the Orthodox Churches which frequently can make a contribution towards a higher synthesis. This is particularly the case in the matter of 'uses' of law and norm in the respective theologies.

In the tradition that was common to East and West at least until Leo the Great, there was never any talk of law as such, or of law as an isolated realm. There was always the great sacramental vision: God has made his love visible in Jesus Christ who is the great sacrament of his love, the covenant, and thus the law. And he continues to be present in the visible Church, a community of love and fellowship in the Holy Spirit, a sacrament endowed with sacraments to manifest his grace and gracious presence, his love, and thus also his saving will. The centre of Christian life is the Eucharist which turns our eyes and our hearts to Jesus and, at the same time, to the Holy Spirit. "The Spirit alone gives life; the flesh is of no avail; the words which I have spoken to you are both spirit and life" (Jn 6:63).

The Protestant Churches have been, time and again, tempted to see everything in the word alone and in the preaching of the word. Certain Catholic trends have been tempted to put law and merit first. But the genuine common tradition, still alive in the Orthodox Churches, is the Word Incarnate, the visible image of God, the sacramentality of all of creation and history, and the sacramentality of human persons who, in

Jesus Christ and in the fellowship of the Holy Spirit, have truly become a living sign of the loving God and of the new creation in the Holy Spirit. Law and norm must never be separated from this total sacramental experience in the Word Incarnate, in the Paschal Mystery, in the risen Lord.[57]

b) From reciprocal protest to common search

Luther's position on the uses of law touches abiding Christian concerns, but it can be understood only in the light of the situation in which his protest took place. Against a widespread legalistic control, Luther, like Paul, appealed to the liberating power of the Gospel. He held that Christians are meant, above all, to be hearers of the Word of God and to receive it as Good News and not mainly as law. Against Scholasticism, and especially against the naturalism and rationalism of renaissance philosophy, Luther emphasized salvation through faith alone, firmly rejecting an autonomous reason. He could not accept a system of natural law teaching outside the realm of faith. Against the overemphasis on merits and good works, Luther emphasized that we are saved by grace alone.

The Lutheran Church lived to a great extent in a reciprocity of protest with the Catholic Church, where we also see a counter-Reformation and counter-protest trend. The legalist manuals of moral theology again and again gave occasion to Protestants to reaffirm their ancient protests. Joseph Fletcher might well be considered as one of the last protestors, sharpening the one-sidedness so that, in the end, there remains nothing but "love alone" in an unprincipled ethics.

Good Protestant theology, transcending the phase of protest, has made us aware that we are, above all, responding beings, answerers.[58] On this ground, biblically renewed thinking in Catholic moral theology meets with the main representatives of the Protestant tradition. Both parts of Christianity are aware, however, that God does not speak only through the Bible. Our common awareness of God's presence in history and our cooperation in secular ecumenism broaden the horizon also about the use of law.

c) Luther's theological use of the law

In Luther's theology the main use of the revealed law of the Sermon on the Mount, as well as of the Decalogue, is the call to conversion. He calls this the "theological use of the law", the second after the "civil, political use of the law", but always the main purpose of law. It is a call to repentance. The sharpening of God's command in the New Testament is given in order to fully unmask our sinfulness and to lead us to Christ, not insofar as he is legislator but because he is the Saviour and Redeemer.

Luther correctly emphasizes that Christ does not save us as legislator but as the One who brings us the Good News and who gives himself for our salvation. He rightly sees the foundation of Christian life in the liberating action of Christ. But, as Protestant theologians of today acknowledge, his presentation of the function of the law is sometimes biased, due to his own experience and his opposition to a system that presents the Bible mainly as a law.

As frequently happens, the protest takes up a mistaken approach of the other side. In his *Small Catechism* Luther presents first the Decalogue. "But Luther's greatest mistake in this connection is that he left out the opening words of the proclamation of the Ten Commandments: 'I am the Lord your God who brought you out of the land of Egypt, out of the state of slavery' ".[59] Whenever he speaks of the law in its theological use, he presents the sequence as law and Gospel, giving first place to law insofar as it drives man to despair about himself and thus unmasks his radical sinfulness and drives him to Christ.

Karl Barth, who follows the Calvinist tradition which has always given more emphasis to the "pedagogical use of law", stresses, in his ground-breaking book *Gospel and Law* (1934), the basic perspectives of Old and New Testament law: "The tables of the law were kept in the ark of the covenant of grace". The strongest critique comes, however, from within the Lutheran Church through Dietrich Bonhoeffer. His chief emphasis is that "the law cannot be preached without the Gospel".[60] Bonhoeffer feels strongly that it is not meaningful for modern man to be told about law mainly or only in terms of unmasking his miserable situation. He considers it even ignoble and unchristian to take as one's starting point only what is wrong with man instead of presenting first what is in reality God's good work and helping man to discover the good in himself.

Moreover, Bonhoeffer rejects as unacceptable Luther's use of Galatians, where Paul speaks of the role of law in the Old Testament. "Before this faith came, we were closed prisoners in the custody of law, pending the revelation of faith. Thus the law was a kind of tutor in charge of us until Christ should come, when we would be justified through faith; and now that faith has come, the tutor's charge is at an end" (Gal 23:24). The Old Testament law which "was a kind of tutor" was not just a law to unmask sinfulness but was, first of all, the law of the covenant that prepared for the final covenant in Christ.

There is, however, an abiding value in what Luther really wanted to say about the theological use of law. I understand it in this way: We must never speak of sin and law without making our chief concern the Good News that we can and must be converted. And what is especially important is that this conversion is not just a conversion from sinfulness to law, but one from a sinful relationship with people and the law to friendship and trust in Jesus Christ. We can say with St. Augustine, "The law is given in order that grace may be sought after; grace is given in order that the law may be fulfilled".[61] But we shall never forget that for St. Augustine "the law" means, above all, life in Christ Jesus under the "law of the Spirit".

While preaching the Good News to those who do not yet believe in Jesus Christ, the Saviour, the Truth, the Way and the Life, we should never forget that many people are prepared for faith by an attitude — openness, sincere search for truth and goodness, dedication to the good they have discovered — which Karl Barth calls "the analogy of faith". We have to build on what the Spirit of Christ has already prepared. The same is true for the evangelization of non-Christian cultures and religions. We should not first see evil, as if God had given them nothing but their share in original sin.

On the other hand, we cannot deny that many modern people know the burden of guilt and, as Victor Frankl has shown, experience the emptiness and absurdity of human life until they have found ultimate value and purpose. "And this may, as it were, be an introduction into the right listening to the Christian message of salvation. But not until man is confronted with divine *agape*, as revealed in Christ, will he come to real knowledge of sin and of the utter vanity of life left to its own resources".[62] So, the basic theological sequence or order is always Gospel first and then law, and not law and Gospel, even in view of conversion. We preach on the great evil of sin, pointing to Christ crucified: "So much was needed to rescue us". The Christian will come to a keener sense of sin and of the need for conversion especially through the celebration of the Paschal Mystery.

In his polemic against legalism, Luther emphasized so one-sidedly that the role of law is to unmask the sinner that he denied that Christ is also the legislator. He was surely right if Christ were seen first of all as a legislator who comes to change the world by law. In genuine Catholic tradition, there is no such thing as law in itself but only that law that flows from life in Christ Jesus. Christ is legislator through faith and grace. However, it cannot be denied that legalism, within the Christian and especially the Catholic tradition, sometimes spoke of Christ as lawgiver outside the context of the new life.

Luther's friend Melanchton, in a more balanced approach, stressed as a third use of law the *usus didacticus*, the guidance received from God's revealed law. For Calvin, this is even the primary use of law, just as in the Catholic tradition. But the best tradition in all Christian Churches holds the truth that an imperative of the law, seen as guidance for a Christian conscience, must never be severed from its foundation, "the law of faith" (Rom 3:31).

The main guidance given by the Sermon on the Mount and the whole gospel is not so much an "ought" as a gracious invitation to live on the level of the Spirit, to live the new life. There is a basic consensus in Christian ethics that the law of Christ guides us more by the indicative of the new life than by the imperative. But, since we are limited beings, not always able to draw the conclusions from the indicative, and especially since we are still sinners, we need also the explicit guidance of the imperative.

In a realistic evaluation of our life in pilgrimage, there can be no doubt that the indicative of the Gospel does not make the imperatives of the Gospel superfluous. Calvin rightly stresses the point that for the Christian, insofar as he is lazy, there is a need for law in the sense of a "whip".[63] But, when we emphasize with Scripture, that where sin is abundant, grace is super-abundant, we can say with Paul Lehmann, "This is why the definitive question with which Christian ethics has to do has been formulated, not as 'what ought I' but rather as 'what am I, as a believer in Jesus Christ and as a member of his Church, to do?' "[64] Furthermore, while it makes sense, in a protest against a disintegrating legalism, to reject Christ's role as primarily a legislator, it makes even more sense to honour this role when opposing a "tendency towards moral defeatism and anti-nominalism in the Reformation".[65]

When Luther seemed to deny the didactic or pedagogical use of the law, his concern was to exclude man's boasting about "works", "merits" and laws. Protestant, and especially Lutheran scholars stress, however, the point that this boasting is more radically excluded by the "law of faith" (Rom 3:27), by the experience of and faith in the Holy Spirit (cf. Jn 16:8-9). "And yet the law is hereby not overthrown, it is confirmed" (cf. Rom 3:31). But first and foremost, it shows what God's gracious will really is and for what purpose it was revealed.[66]

I think that if we follow the theological line of thought of Thomas Aquinas, we can reach a truly ecumenical consensus about the didactic use of the law in the total context of the New Testament. "The New Testament consists in the pouring forth of the Holy Spirit who teaches us from within . . . therefore, it is said in the Scriptures: 'I will put my laws into their mind' (Heb 8:10). The plural form 'laws' is used because there are many commands and counsels. He also prepares the heart for good deeds. Therefore, it is said: 'Upon their hearts I will write them' which means that upon knowledge I shall inscribe love. 'The charity of God is poured forth in our hearts by the Holy Spirit' (Rom 5:5)".[67]

After having emphasized thus the primacy of grace and Gospel, Thomas speaks explicitly on what Melanchton called the third and Calvin called the first use of the law. The written law has only "a secondary place in the new law . . . for what is most characteristic in the law of the new covenant, and what gives it its entire efficacy, is the grace of the Holy Spirit which is given through faith in Christ. And so the new law is fundamentally (principaliter) the grace of the Holy Spirit himself". Beyond this, the word and letter of the law "pertain to the preparation for the grace of the Holy Spirit and to the right use of this grace".[68] Mere agreement with these words is not sufficient, however; what is needed is that all our moral teaching and Church practice manifest this basic insight.

d) "The political use of the law"

For Luther, civil obedience or the political use of the law is the very first and most direct use of law. Especially in his fight against licence and disorder, caused by enthusiastic followers and rebelling farmers, Luther calls strongly for civil obedience to Christian princes. Lutherans had a good tradition of civil obedience. They also generally approved the principle that the Christian ruler may decide the denomination to which his citizens had to belong, a principle that humiliates all Christians today.

As Catholic moral theology, after the horrifying experience of the slavish obedience of Christians in the time of Hitler, attacked a one-sided education for obedience, so Protestant ethics, led by Dietrich Bonhoeffer, sharply attacked the Lutherans' traditional concept that the first use of the law is for civil obedience. Not only the passivity and the too uncritical acceptance of civil law and the power of the rulers but also the separation of the two realms in Luther's theology came under fire.

Christians should not be the patrons of a static civil order or of any particular established system, nor should they separate the two realms, the realm of faith and the realm of civil order. Christian preaching calls man to responsible obedience or, when necessary, to civil disobedience, because it calls man to faith. Faith in Jesus Christ, the Lord and Redeemer of all creation, gives us a specific dimension and motivation for our activity in the temporal realm. We recognize its autonomy in respect to Church authoritieis, and we realize that there is much ethical insight and good reason outside the Christian community for the ordering of society. But we also realize that there is a fundamental difference "between those who know of divine *agape* and those who do not".[69]

This difference concerns mainly our basic convictions and motives, but the focus on faith and the "law of faith" is, again and again, helpful to us in our approach, for instance, to reconciliation in contrast to the approach of dialectic materialism. Soe concludes, "If this exposition is correct, it means that the old doctrine of the 'first' or 'civil' or 'political' use of the law is absorbed into the 'third' use".[70] This means that we turn our attention first, in all things, to Christ, in order to come to know God's will.

e) Luther's doctrine of the two realms

Luther was rightly opposed to the doctrine of Boniface VIII and Innocent III and their followers who wanted to submit the whole temporal sphere to the rule of the popes. He rightly stresses the relative autonomy of the secular realm, expressed by his "first use of the law". Lutheran doctrine has surely made its contribution to the recognition of "the rightful independence of earthly affairs".[71] It fell short, however, in regard to the prophetic role of Christians and the necessary search for integration of faith and life.

Outstanding theologians of the Protestant Churches think that Luther failed to express fully the biblical doctrine of the kingdom of God because of his polemical approach. "The realm at the left hand of God" was not fully brought home into the Gospel vision.[72] We find similar difficulties concerning integration in today's Catholic moral theology, especially among those who assert the autonomy of the world ethos or the autonomy of the secular sphere with relation to Church authorities.[73]

7. Norm and context

a) Norm and casuistic reflection

Traditional Catholic theology knows quite well the importance of the context or the situation referred to as "circumstances". In the first place, there was always mention of the decision-maker himself: his uniqueness, his background and his place. We are surprised, however, to find him mentioned only under the heading "circumstances". The point I want to make, along with James Gustafson, is that "no serious Christian moralist who champions the place of principles avoids the issues involved in their appropriation and application within unique situations. The defenders of principles seek to move from the general principles to the particular in a disciplined way".[74]

The main focus of a personalist Christian ethics is, however, on the human person and the reciprocity of consciences. We give greater attention to the individuality of persons and the uniqueness of historical occasions, although this does not at all rule out the need for serious study of the ethical traditions, norms and rules. "Yet, it does free one from the paralysing effects of excessive scrupulosity, from the emasculated idealism that retreats to the eternal verities and universal values and principles in order to avoid the possibility of being culture-bound or mistaken in a particular judgment".[75]

Whatever the shift of focus may be, we cannot dispense ourselves from the work that casuistry tries to do. Besides the main purpose of forming discerning persons, we also must seek criteria for making choices in complicated situations. Casuistry sets forth the morally relevant aspects which frequently recur in various situations. Without ever forgetting the uniqueness of the person and his conscience, special attention has been and will always be given to cases where values and duties conflict.[76] The scale of value must always be fully recognized, even if the particular urgency of another duty prevents a person from cultivating the highest value here and now. It is never to be disowned nor its place in the scale of values denied. On the contrary, before a decision is made, it is taken seriously into consideration. Moreover, the value response abides beyond the particular decision.[77]

As a basic rule of preference, personalism stresses that persons must never be sacrificed for things, that the conscience of persons ought never to be manipulated, and that healthy personal relations and community structures are more important than merely biological or other "laws" pertaining to the sub-human world.

b) New consciousness and conscience-raising regarding the context

The total context in which the person lives was first emphasized by ideologies inclined towards determinism. Today, however, it is chiefly the theology of liberation that awakens our consciousness and sharpens our conscience in this regard. If we face the interdependencies we can greatly change the way and mode of interaction. Those who unite with others to create a healthier community, society, world — a healthier context — can free themselves from many stereotyped slogans, ideologies and manipulations.

As Christians, we should look at the Church as a possible "divine milieu" that enables us to become free and discerning persons, helping one another on the road to fuller truth and to the best possible decisions on this road. Paul Lehmann [78] brings this truth into focus, although he takes the beneficial influence of the Church all too easily for granted, and unconsciously yields to a certain secular messianism of the "social gospel" type of Christianity. If we are conscious of the enormous impact of the total context, and believe in the mission Christ has given to his Church, we will give great attention to our mission to build up a divine milieu, not only for our own benefit but so that we may truly become, in Christ, the light of the world and salt of the earth.

c) "Love alone" — Situation ethics

The matrix of modern situation ethics without law is the age-old legalistic situation ethics so strongly condemned by Jesus. "How well you set aside the commandment of God in order to maintain your tradition" (Lk 7:9).

The commandment of God is love, justice, mercy. Yet, how

frequently legalists have ignored the good of persons and of healthy personal relations in favour of man-made laws and legal situations! The legalistic situation ethics is frequently vague in its absolutized definitions. Indeed, it absolutizes rules without testing whether they truly apply in all situations and in all possible understandings of the law of God.

Modern situation ethics, that sets aside everything in favour of an equally vague understanding of love, is at the other end of the spectrum. The most extreme representative is surely Joseph Fletcher, who calls himself a "utilitarian consequentialist". A less extreme and more profound representative is J.A.T. Robinson. He holds that "Love alone, because it, as it were, has a built-in moral compass enabling it to 'home' intuitively upon the deepest need of the other, can allow itself to be directed completely by the situation . . . It is able to embrace an ethic of radical responsiveness, meeting every situation on its own merits, with no prescriptive laws".[80]

Robinson does not totally exclude guidelines and criteria. He also acknowledges that there are certain actions like cruelty and rape that "are always wrong; that is, it is so inconceivable that they could ever be an expression of love".[81]

But in practice, an ethics that operates with love and situation alone is unrealistic and impractical. Very seldom do persons reach such high connaturality with the good by pure and strong love that they can approach all situations without attention to norms, traditions and rules. Fletcher and, to a lesser extent, Robinson allow themselves a "massive nominalism".[82] A mere "act-agapeism" is particularly unrealistic and misleading if one is, like Fletcher, basically agnostic about the very nature of love itself. Moreover, Christ is strikingly absent in Fletcher's work; even though it is only in him that the true countenance of love is fully revealed.

While all serious moral theologians agree that love is the supreme principle and God's all-embracing gift and law, it has to be recognized that it is not easy to determine how, on the cognitive level, love reveals its rules and norms. Fundamentally two approaches are possible. The first sees love as unfolding itself in rules. These rules have to be constantly tested in the light of love and transformed and determined by it. The second approach demands a knowledge of man and competence in the various fields of ethical relevance and, then, tries to see all this in an "ultimate perspective of love". Here, love does not yield ready-made rules but rejects or confirms and gives final coherence to all the rules.

I think Frankena is quite right in his observation about the cognitive and practical level when he says that love is the basis of rules "not by it own nature alone, but by its nature together with effects about the world in which it is seeking to fulfil itself or to reach its object".[83] Take, for instance, conscientious objection against all forms of military service, asserted on the basis of unselfish love. Even if we know what love means for us Christians, love alone cannot tell us that this is our duty, unless we have enough knowledge of peoples' tendencies and reactions, and can reasonably assess what might be the consequences if many people of one country or even all were to accept and follow this principle of conscientious objection. Will it be an encouragement for ruthless aggressors or will it, with high probability, lead to a general change of mind and help to free humanity from war?

There was, and still is, a tendency within a part of Catholic moral theology to give love only the role of sanctioning laws which are drawn up from other sources. Gene Outka criticizes Gilleman who, like many other moralists, affirms the absolute and exceptionless evil of contraception, even if it may be the only means available to save a marriage or the mental health of a spouse. He also teaches the exceptionless duty to tell the truth even if the life of a friend is at stake.[84] One may doubt whether, in these cases, love is still the supreme principle and norm. Otherwise, one would have to prove that the very nature of love guarantees the absoluteness of similar rules.

d) For an authentic contextual ethics

We saw earlier that the problem of pluralism and probabilism became such a burning issue because many of the established norms and laws were no longer appropriate in a time of profound change. The situation is sharpened today. One cause of an extreme situation ethics is surely individualism; but another reason for a widespread unease is the rapid change of our own culture and, even more, our encounter with quite different cultures. We suddenly realize that many of our moral rules and norms were a product of a concrete culture that will not recur in the same form. "Modern Western man, trained through four centuries of emphasis on rationality, uniformity and mechanics, has consistently endeavoured, with unfortunate success, to repress the aspects of himself which do not fit these uniform and mechanical standards".[85]

Especially for the evangelization of the new generations and of the Third World, as well as for the cooperation of all nations and cultures, we have to acquire a totally new critical consciousness of the context in which our thought-patterns, our language and even a great part of our moral rules were worked out. For instance, it does not make sense for Western missionaries to teach the Greek cardinal virtues in nations influenced by Confucius.[86] This would seem only an unnecessary import and colonial attitude.

The International Theological Commission appointed by Pope Paul VI has published an important document entitled *Faith and Theological Pluralism*. This document touches also on the moral problem. "Pluralism in the moral field appears, above all, to be in the application of general principles to concrete situations. This becomes yet more extensive when contacts are established with cultures which at the beginning were ignored, or on account of rapid changes in society. All the same, a fundamental unity is manifested through the common esteem of human dignity, which implies imperatives for the conduct of lives. The conscience of every man expresses a certain number of fundamental exigencies recognized in our age in public declarations on the essential rights of man. The unity of Christian morals is founded on constant principles contained in the Scriptures, presented to each generation by the magisterium. Let us remember the principal lines of thought: the teachings and examples of the Son of God who revealed the heart of the Father, his death and resurrection, the life according to the Spirit in the bosom of his Church, in faith, in hope and in charity to renew us according to the image of God. The necessary unity of faith and communion does not impede a diversity of vocations and personal preferences in the manner of approaching the mystery of Christ and of living it".[87] Note that the text of the Commission mentions only the most general principles and guidelines.

Traditional Catholic philosophy distinguished the primary and secondary principles of natural law and agreed that the latter allowed variance. "Thus Christian ethics is both absolute and relative. It is absolute in that its ultimate norm of obligation (principle) is context-invariant. It is relative in that its contingent norms of obligation (rules) are context-variant".[88]

In the process of evangelization it is not just a matter of extending some of our rules or transforming some of them. Rather, there exists the necessity to meet the ethos, to understand its dynamics and, based on the context-variant norm, to discern and to perfect whatever is acceptable and, if necessary, to eliminate whatever contradicts the basic Christian vision of life.

8. *Absolutes in moral theology*

The creative freedom for which Christ has set us free is able and ready to commit itself to a covenant morality; and this includes those norms and rules that guarantee reliability. On the other hand, the demand for absolute obedience and the multiplication of absolute norms is a necessary weapon in the arsenal of authoritarians. Therefore, we must be on guard. Absolutes [90] can be accepted only to the extent that they can be shown not to overlap or to lead to hurtful conflicts.

Frequently, a better understanding of the very meaning of norms can resolve the conflict, as can be seen, for instance, in the conflict between absolute truth-telling and life-saving. Kant, in accordance with a long tradition, tried to redefine lying in such a way that the life-saving expression or the refusal to communicate does not contradict our commitment to truthfulness. When German nuns, who were responsible for a large number of mentally and physically handicapped children, were asked by Hitler's obedient slaves how many children they had of this and that category of deficiency, they responded simply that they had none of them. Did they lie? They did not, because in the context there was no communication about children and children's sickness; the real question asked was, "How many children do you have to deliver for our gas ovens?" And the only truthful and, at the same time, life-saving response was, "None".

The denial of any absolutes in moral theology resulted sometimes from a false understanding of the Bible. We saw earlier that this was the case with Kierkegaard. "Love of God may cause the knight of faith to give his love to his neighbour the opposite expression to that which, ethically speaking, is required by duty". "Faith is capable of transforming a murder into a holy act well pleasing to God".[91] In our time, Karl Barth and Joseph Sittler — to mention only the most representative men — presented a similar vision. Their theological purpose is to stress God's sovereignty and absolute freedom that request from man total obedience, whatever he commands. It is on this ground that they exclude absolute norms. "Service to this will is presented to the believer not as a general programme in advance, but as an everchanging and fluctuant obligation to the neighbour in the midst of history's life".[92] The point of departure is, time and again, the sacrifice of Isaac (Gen 22). They understand the text as God manifesting his sovereign right to request even the killing of the firstborn as a sacrifice. Can we accept this image of God? They would respond: it is the image God himself has revealed in Scripture. Walther Eichrodt offers the historical elements for a quite different exegetical understanding of the text: God freed Israel gradually from taboos and religious concepts contradicting God's holiness. Israel's forefathers had inherited certain convictions that God sometimes can be placated only by the sacrifice of the firstborn. The better knowledge of the cultural context from which Abraham came and the greater attention to the literary forms suggest the following understanding of the Genesis story: Abraham found himself in conditions in which the devout men of his environment would have felt the obligation to offer the firstborn. He, too, felt in conscience this obligation as concerning him here and now. The willingness to act according to his conscience counts before God. But on this occasion, through revelation, there is a unique breakthrough of faith. From now on Abraham and his descendants know by faith that God never requests the killing of the firstborn; on the contrary, they consider it as an abominable perversion of religion.[93]

For those who grow up under a moral teaching permeated with the spirit of absolutism, and are now shocked by the heart-searching question of theologians about absolutes, it will be a surprise to discover how careful and broadminded was Thomas Aquinas' approach. For Thomas, the absolutes in ethics coincide practically with the precepts of the Decalogue "insofar as the precepts of the first table contain the very ordination towards God, and the precepts of the second table contain the order of justice among men; namely that nobody should be wronged and everyone should receive what is right".[94] He was not afraid to insist that this formulation left open a number of questions. "Thus the precepts of the Decalogue are immutable as to the very justice which they contain; but as to the determination in view of the application to individual acts (for instance whether this or that is murder, theft, adultery, or not) there is place for change".[95]

Others will be more surprised to learn that such a moderate moralist and Doctor of the Church as St. Alphonsus acknowledged that even precepts of the natural law are not necessarily absolute and, in their time-bound formulation, allow exceptions. In the same sense as St. Thomas Aquinas, he speaks of the *epikeia* which does not look just for loopholes but rather for a wholistic understanding of God's will and can truly be called the virtue of freedom.[96] St. Alphonsus writes, "*Epikeia* means the exception of a case because of the situation from which can be judged, with certainty or at least with sufficient probability, that the legislator did not intend to include it under the law. This *epikeia* has its place not only in human laws but also in natural laws where, because of the circumstances, the action could be freed from malice".[97]

In view of this tradition, nobody should be shocked or scandalized if most of today's Catholic moral theologians ask the question: "Can all secondary prohibitive norms claim an exceptionless, absolute validity?"[98]

One should not think, however, that today's approach leaves us nothing but the categorical imperative of Immanuel Kant:

"So act that the maxim of your will could always hold, at the same time, as principle establishing universal law".[99] Kant himself was concerned with showing that this most universal principle leads to well-defined norms far beyond all considerations of one's happiness.[100] Everyone, except extremists like Fletcher, acknowledges that there are some particular prohibitive norms that must be considered as absolutes: for instance, the prohibition against blasphemy, rape, sexual promiscuity, cruel punishment of children, torture.

Pope Pius XII, when teaching emphatically that the use of torture is always and absolutely against the natural law, was quite aware that Pope Innocent IV (1252), in his well-known Bull on torture and the burning of witches, had made this very conduct once compulsory, while centuries earlier, Pope Nicholas I had condemned it.[101] The same is to be said about slavery and against any form of heinous manipulation of persons and their consciences. Paul Ramsey rightly warns extremists who say that "there is nothing man should never do" that this is the "most uncivilizing, unacceptable principle".[102]

9. Conflict and compromise

Situation ethics of the extreme left resolves conflicts easily because, outside of its faceless love and utilitarian pragmatism, it does not know of any principle that can make absolute claims. This kind of love is, in a strange way, free because it does not even know its own countenance!

The approach of Nicholas Hartmann is quite different. He strongly emphasizes that a person is frequently faced with a conflict between various values and even spheres of values. "There is nothing else left to the human person than to accept the conflict of the values and to decide by his own initiative. Whatever may be the decision, it is at the same time a positive response to some values and an offence against others. By necessity the person makes himself guilty regarding one side".[103] For Hartmann, this is unavoidably so because there does not exist one cosmos with a visible hierarchy of values, but only diverse and conflicting spheres of values. Indeed, he thinks that this constitutes the condition for man's dignity, for through it man can become the creator of his own world of values.[104] This is a basic condition for Hartmann's postulatory atheism.

Totally opposed is the "solution" of a certain mysticism of sin. In view of the frequent experience of conflicts, this kind of thinking consoles people by posing that sin is unavoidable, and whoever suffers under it is already forgiven. There is no rebellion in this approach; however, it does undermine the very concept of sin and reconciliation, for sin is never something unavoidable.

Legalists, with their armour of hundreds of absolutes, assert that, objectively, there can be no conflict caused by any of these absolutes. They argue that only people's ignorance in matters of moral theology causes the "perplexed conscience". All conflicts between their many absolutes are condoned and resolved on the subjective level. The same moralists, however, do not condone those who question the absoluteness of some of their norms that cause constantly disturbing conflicts.

With the mainstream of Christian tradition, I firmly believe in a cosmos and a hierarchy of values. However, people are sometimes faced with a chaotic teaching that presents many norms, rules and laws, causing anguish and scrupulosity, and frequently debilitating people's moral energies and their trust in God. The right solution is a more careful elaboration of norms and clear distinctions between the most universal principles, general and specialized laws and rules. Max Scheler offers a ground-breaking vision of an ethics of values with criteria for determining the scale of values and the urgencies of value responses.[105] Norms concerning lesser values can be absolutely binding regarding the relationship they cover, *as long as* that relationship does not overlap with another more binding relationship. The morally most relevant norm ought to prevail in cases of conflict.[106]

To elaborate carefully an ethics of conflict and compromise is one of the most urgent tasks of moral theology.[107] It demands a more careful formulation of norms, clear criteria or specified norms for cases in which a very general norm allows or necessitates a specified application. The law of growth and ongoing conversion in the life of individuals and society must be more proportionately taken into account.

An example here might be the compromise St. Paul accepted in the matter of slavery. We might say that, throughout the centuries, Christians accepted all too easily a similar compromise even when the institution of slavery was already out of tune and Christianity could have ended the shame of it. In a genuine ethics of conflict, the emphasis is not so much on the role of the controller as on the formation of a discerning person who is always on the road to greater maturity.

The various and opposing approaches can easily be seen in today's discussions about abortion. Extreme situation ethics boastingly asserts that abortion can be as much an expression of loving concern as any other solution. The mysticism of sin makes no distinction, puts not even a semi-colon between contraception, sterilization and abortion, making them all and always equally mortal sins.

Most moralists would insist that the commitment of Christians to the value of life is among the very highest and, therefore, it is not enough to propose just a general rule that declares abortion a crime and then to ask the legislator to enforce this norm with the strongest sanctions. The emphasis is, rather, on the general commitment to life and, therefore, to heart-searching reflection about how the main causes of abortion can be removed, even by accepting the "lesser evil" or "the best possible solution", regarding civil and penal law. In conflict situations concerning the highest values of the life of the mother and the life of the fetus, we truly share the agonizing conflict and opt for life saving action.

Gene Outka points out the several alternatives that are possible in the extreme conflict in which it is clear that the life of the fetus cannot be saved while that of the mother could be saved by an intervention. (a) One may simply say that the rule prohibiting murder applies without further qualification, and that it would be preferable for both mother and fetus to die than for one individual to survive by means of an act which, by prior determination, has been prohibited. (b) One may deny that the formulated rule applies. The fetus might be held, for example, not to be a 'person'. (c) One may formulate the rule in a different way, so that it does not apply. Or the fetus may still be regarded as a person in the relevant respects, but one qualifies one's definition of murder so that, perhaps, its meaning does not include directly and intentionally taking the innocent life (of the fetus) if this innocent life will die in any case and another innocent life (the mother's) will be saved. (d) One may say that the prohibition is always relevant and generally counts against abortion but in some cases, where it does not apply, it may come into direct conflict with another rule (e.g., in certain situations of agonizing moral choice one ought to save one innocent life rather than to lose two) and it is not necessarily decisive for one's final evaluation. Thus one establishes a priority among formulated relational norms and/or moral rules.[108]

Whatever may be the preference, one must take into account a change of mentalities. While in earlier ages there was little possibility to save either life and mankind accepted most of the conditionings passively, today many people, and especially the medical profession, consider the passive attitude "to let die", when a life-saving intervention would be possible, a transgression of their basic rule to do everything to save life.

V. COVENANT MORALITY AND MAN-MADE LAW

A detailed treatment of the many-faceted relationships of the followers of Christ towards the authority and law of the Church and of the various parts of secular society (the state and international organizations) belongs to special moral theology. General principles of moral theology belong, however, to the basic horizon of covenant morality. Yet there can be a conflict between covenant morality and defence morality; or a synthesis between the two can at least be difficult, especially in the realm of man-made law.

1. *Can morality be legislated?*

One could quote a great number of Church documents that required civil authority to sanction the doctrines of the Church in matters of public and even private morality. This trend was not exclusively a phenomenon of the Catholic Church. Calvin went even further than most of the papal documents. All this has become untenable and should be dealt with in the light of the declaration of the Second Vatican Council on religious liberty. The same is true of the relation between canon law and civil law.[109]

In order to make their specific contribution, Christians who are at the same time citizens of the Church and of the secular society have to question themselves thoroughly about the role of law and the state authority. We have already touched this problem in the discussion about the civil use of law in Protestant ethics. Here we address ourselves to a limited and yet important question in today's relations between Church and state. Has the state a competence to legislate in moral matters and to enforce moral norms as such?

The state and international organizations have an invested interest in common moral values and ideals. Therefore, they do well to fulfil a part of their obligation towards the common good by giving full liberty to organized religious groups and to all those free associations committed to uphold and foster insight into and commitment to those common values and ideals.

The state has no competence to legislate matters of religious doctrine or moral norms as such. It has, however, a duty to define and defend the basic rights and the shared freedom without which the common good of the secular city cannot be sustained. It is not, for instance, the duty of the state to lay down the moral norms regarding abortion. It is not the state's concern to reinforce the norms taught by the Church. However, the right to life and the respect for the life of all human beings belong to the pillars that support society and the organized state. The state has to do its very best to foster respect for all human life and to protect the weakest, among whom is the human fetus. What "the very best possible" means in this regard depends also on the extent to which there are still common convictions about the dignity of the fetus in the mother's womb. And here, not only the official Church but, above all, the citizens as such have a particular obligation. They should do their best to enlighten public conscience.

Insofar as it is necessary for the common good, for peace and order, for progress in economic and cultural life, the state can and must legislate. Throughout the ages, state authorities have appealed to the conscience of the citizens. This appeal was not always genuine; frequently it degenerated into manipulation in favour of unjust laws and privileges for a minority. It is in the state's best interest that the legislator should explain the justice of the laws, and thus — and only thus — appeal to the conscience of the people. It can also be in the best interest of the common good and, therefore, of the state when citizens challenge the legislator by conscientious objection in all those matters which they consider unjust and damaging to the common good.[111]

The state has the right to enforce its just laws against those who transgress them. It can enforce them even with force against those who act violently. However, it cannot enforce *unjust* laws, even against those who oppose them violently. Rather, it has to correct them.[112]

2. *Co-responsibility and obedience of the citizens*

Citizens are not only obliged to obey laws; they are called by conscience to unite their efforts to obtain good laws and to promote common convictions that make good laws operative. Christians are called to exercise a prophetic role in the secular society by unmasking injustice and the abuse of authority. They can do so effectively and truthfully, however, only if they are outstanding in the fulfilment of their civic duties. They will give support to authority wherever they can do so for the common good. And in all things, they will act with a sincere and concerned conscience. "You wish to have no fear of the authorities? Then continue to do right and you will have approval, for they are God's agents working for your good . . . That is why you are obliged to submit. It is an obligation imposed not merely by fear of retribution but by conscience. That is why you pay taxes. The authorities are in God's service and to these duties they devote their energies" (Rom 13:3-6).

All just laws bind in conscience by their very justice and according to the relevance they have for the common good. Therefore, strictly speaking, there are no mere penal laws. The theory about mere penal laws was somehow necessary in a time of absolutism when, because of the heavy censorship by the state and the Church, moralists could not speak publicly about unjust laws. They helped citizens by calling "penal laws" those laws which people could not generally recognize as necessary laws.

There is, however, a broader meaning in the concept of "penal laws". Citizens sometimes have a good reason not to observe some directives or laws when their observance here and now is not necessary for the common good. However, when caught by the authorities, they have no right to resist violently when they are punished. They should try to defend themselves peacefully, or try to avoid these inconveniences as far as possible.

An impossible law cannot oblige anyone; and the state must take into account the moral possibilities of people. A law is unjust if the burden is out of proportion to the contribution its observance could make to the common good. State authority is obliged to recognize the proper use of *epikeia*. It has no right whatsoever to reinforce a literal observance of laws if citizens act responsibly.

Unjust laws, because of their lack of justice, cannot bind the conscience of the citizens. Citizens, however, need discernment and must ask themselves what kind of action, here and now, would be best for the common good and for their own good.

Usurpers cannot make any claim upon people's conscience until they have legitimate approval by the people and act for the common good. But sometimes it is out of concern for the common good, for peace and security, that citizens obey just laws even when issued by usurpers. Citizens have, however, a right and sometimes a strict duty to oppose privileges granted by law to certain groups when these privileges do not entail a service to the common good.

3. Covenant morality and Church law

The purpose of the Church is not to legislate morality but to educate the believers in faith, so that they can discover the law written in their heart and understand ever better the law proclaimed by Jesus Christ. It is not the mission of the Church to impose moral norms from above, but to promote openness, sharing of reflection and experience which can help people to discover the moral norms. However, the Church has a right and a duty to propose and to explain the norms which are their heritage by divine tradition and by a living tradition that helps people again and again to decipher the signs of the times and to respond to them creatively.[113]

Positive Church law — Canon Law — is for the service of the Gospel and the Church as a community of love, a fellowship in the Holy Spirit and a sacrament of the covenant with Christ.

Church law must make clear that it is submitted to "the life-giving law of the Spirit in Christ Jesus" (Rom 8:2). There must be no unnecessary law in the Church, and the process of revision of all man-made laws must be continuous. Nothing in the Church should conceal her being the spearhead of humanity on this earthly pilgrimage. Canon law ought to reflect the best self-understanding of the Church. "In the explanation of canon law, the mystery of the Church should be kept in mind as it is set forth in the Dogmatic Constitution on the Church promulgated by this holy synod".[114]

Pope Paul VI applied this text in depth, underlining that it is necessary "to derive the canonical law from the essence itself of the Church of God, which is the new and original law, the law of the Gospel, the law of love, by the grace of the Holy Spirit given by faith in Christ. Thus if this is the interior principle which guides the Church in her work, it should always be manifest in her visible, exterior and social discipline. It is, however, easier to insist on this vision than to foresee all the consequences".[115]

Because the Church is, first of all, a *koinonia* (fellowship, communion) in the Holy Spirit, she transcends, in her legislation, the laws of earthly societies. The concern of those who formulate and explain ecclesial discipline, and the action of those who carry it out, should be inspired by the word of the Lord: "The Sabbath was made for man, not man for the Sabbath" (Mk 2:27).

The legislation of the Church should always be a manifestation of her vigilance for the *signs of the times* and, therefore, should exclude any ossification. The pilgrim Church has to examine the signs of the times constantly in order to grasp new opportunities and face new difficulties. "The human race has passed from a more static concept of reality to a more dynamic, evolutionary one".[116]

The discipline of the Church is at the service of the genuine dynamism of growth and expectation. It is the discipline of a living community on the march to the final fulfilment. Enough freedom ought to be given to the local Churches to take responsible initiatives in view of their concrete situation. This diversity is a sign of our faith in the Holy Spirit, and helps to create a climate of mutual confidence and co-responsibility.

The life of the Church should be marked by a sober use of positive laws. In this way she testifies that she puts her confidence in the power of the Holy Spirit and gives more importance to witnessing to the Gospel than to her own law and discipline. However, as long as the earthly pilgrimage lasts, pastoral directives and the necessary disciplinary norms which sustain unity and cooperation should never be lacking.

A study of the penal law as expressed in the Code of Canon Law (issued in 1917) alerts us to the danger that "knowledge of dominion" was marked by an overemphasis on control, by excessive concern for the protection of property and privileges of the institutional Church. A revision presupposes, therefore, a renewed spirit that gives first place to salvation knowledge and trust in the power of the Gospel and the corporate witness to it.

In the course of her history, the Church has articulated and incarnated her original mission in the socio-cultural context to which she was sent to announce the Gospel. She needs creative fidelity and a keen sense of discernment, as well as patience and courage, to readjust her ministries to the present opportunities and needs. Her very fidelity to her Founder and Lord obliges her to make all the changes in her traditions and legislation that are necessary for the evangelization of all people and all cultures. Moreover, she should test everything in the light of the Lord's testament "that all may be one".

NOTES

1 Cf. F. Toennis, *Sitte*, Frankfurt, 1909, 12f.
2 W.K. Frankena, *Ethics*, Englewood Cliffs/N.J., 1963, 3f; cf. Frankena, *Perspectives on Morality*, Notre Dame, 1977.
3 Cf. W. Eichrodt, *Theologie des Alten Testaments*, 6th ed., Göttingen, 1959, I, 88-90, 105-100.
4 S. Kierkegaard, *Fear and Trembling*, New York, 1954, 70.
5 l.c., 29-30.
6 *Gaudium et spes*, 81.
7 J.M. Gustafson, "Moral Discernment in the Christian Life", in G. Outka and P. Ramsey (eds.), *Norm and Context*, New York, 1968, 34f.
8 N.L. Geisler, *Ethics: Alternatives and Issues*, Grand Rapids, 1971, 33.
9 F. Nietzsche, *Beyond Good and Evil*, Chicago, 1966, n. 46, p. 53.
10 l.c., n. 262, p. 211
11 F. Nietzsche, *Thus Spoke Zarathustra*, New York, 1966, Prologue, p. 125.
12 R. May, *Man's Quest For Himself*, 206, cf. 209.
13 Cf. D.Th. Jenkins, *Tradition, Freedom and the Spirit*, Philadelphia, 1951; J.R. Geiselman, *Die überlieferung als Norm des Glaubens*, Freiburg, 1959; Id., *The Meaning of Tradition*, New York, 1966; J. Beth & H. Fries (eds.), *Kirche und überlieferung*, Freiburg, 1960; J. Pieper, *Tradition als Herausforderung*, München, 1963; K. Rahner, *Offenbarung und überlieferung*, Freiburg, 1965 (*Revelation and Tradition*, New York, 1966); Y. Congar, *Tradition and Traditions; An Historical and Theological Essay*, New York, 1967; G. Biemer, *Newman and Tradition*, London, 1967; J.R. Mackey, *Tradition and Change in the Church*, Dayton/Ohio, 1968; B. Häring, "Tradition and Adaptation in Light of the Mystery of Incarnation", in *This Time of Salvation*, New York, 1966, 93-108.
14 Cf. F. Böckle, *Law and Conscience*, New York, 1966, 36; K. Wagenast, *Das Verständnis der Tradition bei Paulus und in den Deuteropaulinen*, Neukirchen, 1962.
15 Cf. L. Long Jr., "Soteriological Implications of Norm and Context", in *Norm and Context*, 293f.
16 Cf. my Book *Evangelization Today*, Slough and Notre Dame/Ind., 1974, 45-77; 141-163; W. Bühlmann, *The Coming of the Third Church*, Slough, 1976; Maryknoll/N.Y., 1977.
17 J.M. Gustafson, *Christian Ethics and the Community*, Philadelphia, 1971, 91.
18 Cf. Ph. Delhaye, *Permanence du Droit Naturel*, Paris, 1961. The author mentions twenty different concepts of natural law.
19 Cf. E. Osborn, *Ethical Patterns in Early Christian Thought*, 183-191.
20 S.Th., I II, q 106 a 1 ad 2.
1 E. Fromm, *Man for Himself*, New York, 1947, 45.
2 J.P. Sartre, *Being and Nothingness*, New York, 1956, 627.
3 S. de Beauvoir, *The Ethics of Ambiguity*, New York, 1948, 72-73.
4 J. Bentham, *Introduction to the Principles of Morals and Legislators*, (1789), ch. I, I.
5 E. Osborn, l.c., 187; cf. F. Flückiger, *Geschichte des Naturrechts*, Zürich, 1964.
6 Cf. F. Henrich (ed.), *Naturgesetz und christliche Ethik*, München, 1970; A. Knoll, *Katolische Kirche and Naturrecht — Zur Frage der Freiheit*, Wien, 1962; J. Fuchs, *Natural Law*, Dublin, 1965; F. Böckle (ed.), *Das Naturrecht im Disput*, Düsseldorf, 1966; K.H. Peschke, *Naturrecht in der Kontroverse. Kritik evangelischer Theologie an der katholischen Lehre vom Naturrecht und natürlicher Sittlichkeit*, Salzburg, 1967; A.P. D'Entrèves, *Natural Law*, 2nd ed., London, 1970; B. Häring, *Morality is for Persons*, New York, 1971; F. Brasnahan, S.J., "Rahner's Critical Natural Law in Relation to Contemporary Ethical Methodology", in *Journal of Religion* 56 (1976), 36-60; S.

27 Privitera, "La fondazione della norma morale...", in *Rivista di teologia morale* 9 (1977), 125-135.

27 Seneca, *Epistulae morales* 95, 33: "Homo sacra res homini".

28 F. Flückiger, *Geschichte des Naturrechts*, Zürich, 1964, 359 and 435.

29 Cf. E. Osborn, l.c., 183.

30 C.H. Dodd, *Gospel and Law*, New York, 1951, 82.

31 Cf. B. Häring, *Evangelization Today*, 6-24; 79-182.

32 A. Valsecchi/L. Rossi, *La norma morale*, Bologna, 1971, 79f, quoting many texts in which Roman Pontiffs assert their competence in matters of natural law.

33 Cf. W. Schrage, *Die konkreten Einzelgebote in der paulinischen Paränese*, Gütersloh, 1961; D.H. Kelsey, "Appeal to Scripture in Theology", in *Journal of Religion* 48 (1968), 1-21; Th. Beemer, "The Interpretation of Moral Theology" in *Concilium* 5 (1969), 62-72; E. Hamel, "L'Ecriture âme de théologie morale", in *Gregorianum* 54 (1973), 417-445; Id., "La théologie morale entre l'Ecriture et la raison", in *Gregorianum* 56 (1975), 275-319; F. Lage, "Puntos para una introducion al problema de la fundamentacion biblica de la moral", in *Pentecostes* 12 (1974), 293-331; J.G. Ziegler, "Zwischen Vernunft und Offenbarung" — Zur Quellen — und Methodenfrage", in *Theol. Revue* 70 (1974), 265-277; J.T. Sanders, *Ethics in the New Testament: Change and Development*, Philadelphia and London, 1975; W. Kerber, "Grenzen der biblischen Moral", in K. Demmer/B. Schüller, *Christlich Glauben und Handeln*, Düsseldorf, 1977, 112-123; Y. Congar, "Réflexion et propos sur l'originalité d'une éthique chrétienne", in *Studia Moralia* 15 (1977), 31-40; H. Schürmann, "Haben die Paulinischen Wertungen und Weisungen Modellcharakter?", in *Gregorianum* 56 (1975), 237-271 (with abundant bibliography). My exposition follows for the most part the studies of Schürmann and Hamel.

34 Cf. H.D. Aiken, "Levels of Moral Discourse", in *Reason and Conduct*, New York, 1962; J.M. Gustafson, *Christian Ethics and Community*, 192ff.

35 N.L. Geisler, l.c., 27.

36 J.T. Robinson, *Honest to God*, London, 1953, 118.

37 J.T. Robinson, *Christian Morals Today*, Philadelphia, 1964, 12.

38 l.c., 16.

39 P. Ramsey, *Deeds and Rules in Christian Ethics*, New York, 1967, 35.

40 l.c., 3.

41 Cf. N.L. Geisler, l.c., 20.

42 J.M. Gustafson, *Christian Ethics and the Community*, 117.

43 Reinhold Niebuhr, *An Interpretation of Christian Ethics*, New York, 1935, 140.

44 J. Bennett, *Christian Ethics and Social Policy*, New York, 1946, 76.

45 G. Outka, "Character, Conduct, and the Love Commandment", in *Norm and Context*, 44ff.

46 J. Fuchs, *Human Values and Christian Morality*, Dublin, 1970, 63.

47 Cf. B. Häring, *The Sacraments in a Secular Age*, Slough, 1976, 36-89; *The Sacraments and your Everyday Life*, Liguori, 1976.

48 Cf. W. Bühlmann, *The Coming of the Third Church*, Slough, 1976.

49 A good survey on the critical efforts of Italian moralists during the past ten years by S. Pivitera, "La fondazione della norma morale...", in *Rivista di teologia morale* 9 (1977), 125-133.

50 J.P. Mackey (ed.), *Morals, Law and Authority*, Dayton/Ohio, 1969, XI.

51 This was forcefully asserted by R. Lombardi, *Chiesa e regno di Dio*, Bologna, 1976, 51-62; 89-99.

52 Cf. Ch.E. Curran, *Ongoing Revision. Studies in Moral Theology*, Notre Dame, 1975; B. Häring, "Reflexionen zur Erklärung der Glaubenskongregation über einige Fragen der Sexualethik", in *Theol.-praktische Quartalschr.* 124 (1976), 115-126.

53 Cf. Cardinal Newman, *On Consulting the Faithful in Matters of Doctrine* (ed. J. Coulson), New York, 1961, 104-106.

54 J.Ch. Hampe edited a three-volumes commentary on the Second Vatican Council, written by authors of the various Churches, under the title *Autorität der Freiheit*, München, 1967; cf. my article "Das Recht auf Verschiedenheit im Bemühen um geschichtsgerechtes Handeln", l.c., III, 113-119.

55 Cf. J.M. Gustafson, "The Place of Scripture in Christian Ethics: A Methodological Study", in *Interpretation* 24 (1970), 430-455; E. Hamel, S.J., "L'usage de l'Ecriture en théologie morale", in *Gregorianum* 47 (1966), 53-85.

56 Cf. B. Häring, "Norms and Freedom in Contemporary Catholic Thought", in *Thought* (Fordham) 52 (1977), 5-17. Id., "Norm und Freiheit", in R. Hammer/ B. Schüller, *Christlich glauben und handeln*, Düsseldorf, 1977, 171-194.

57 I have treated these questions in my book *Prospettive e problemi ecumenici di teologia morale*, Roma, 1973; and *Sacraments in a Secular Age*, Slough, 1976.

58 Cf. J.M. Gustafson, *Christian Ethics and the Community*, 110f.

59 N.H. Soe, "The Three 'uses' of the Law", in *Norm and Context*, 308.

60 D. Bonhoeffer, *Ethik*, München, 1949, 237-249.

61 Augustine, *De Spiritu et littera*, cap. 19 PL 44, 221; cf. G. Söhngen, *Gesetz und Freiheit*, Freiburg-München, 1957.

62 N.H. Soe, l.c., 308.

63 Calvin, *Institutio Christianae religionis* (1559), II, 7, 12.

64 P. Lehmann, *Ethics in a Christian Context*, New York-London, 1963, 159.

65 Reinhold Niebuhr, *Nature and Destiny of Man*, London, 1943, II, 147.

66 N.H. Soe, l.c., 309; R. Bring, *Gesetz und Evangelium und der dritte Gebrauch des Gesetzes in lutherischer Theologie*, Helsinki, 1943; W. Geppert, "Zur gegenwärtigen Diskussion über das Problem des tertius usus legis", in *Evangelische Kirchenzeitung* 9 (1955), 387-393; W. Joest, *Gesetz und Freiheit. Der tertius usus legis bei Luther und die neutestamentliche Parainese*, Göttingen, 1951.

67 *Commentary on Hebr.* VIII, Lectio II, last lines.

68 S.Th., I II, q 106 a 1.

69 N.H. Soe, l.c., 320.

70 l.c., 320.

71 *Gaudium et spes*, 36.

72 Cf. N.H. Soe, l.c., 322; W.A. Visser't Hooft, *La royauté de Jésus Christ*, Geneva, 1948; F. Lau, *Luthers Lehre von den beiden Reichen*, Berlin, 1953.

73 A. Auer, *Autonome Moral und christlicher Glaube*, Düsseldorf; R. Mehl, *Catholic Ethics and Protestant Ethics*, Philadelphia, 1971.

74 J.M. Gustafson, l.c., 112.

75 J.M. Gustafson, "Moral Discernment in the Christian Life", in *Norm and Context*, 26.

76 Cf. R.M. Hare, *Freedom and Reason*, New York, 1965, 48f.

77 Cf. G. Outka, *Norm and Context*, 56; a very good information about this whole problem is given by N.L. Geisler, *Ethics: Alternatives and Issues*, Grand Rapids/Mich., 1971, 47-136. He stresses particularly the following point: "Why should a man be punished for doing his best. He should be rewarded for doing the so-called 'lesser evil', for it is really the greater of (two) goods", l.c., 112.

78 P. Lehmann, *Ethics in a Christian Context*, New York, 1963. J.M. Gustafson approaches the same problem with remarkable balance and in an ecumenical openness; cf. his book *Christian Ethics and the Community*, Philadelphia, 1971; *The Church as Moral Decision-maker*, Philadelphia, 1970.

79 J. Fletcher, *Situation Ethics*, Philadelphia, 1966. Among the many critical responses see: J.C. Bennett (ed.), *Storm over Ethics*, Philadelphia, 1967; G. Outka and P. Ramsey (eds.), *Norm and Context*, New York, 1968; B. Häring, *The Christian Existentialist*, New York, 1968.

80 J.A.T. Robinson, *Honest to God*, 115.

81 Robinson, *Christian Morals Today*, Philadelphia, 1964, 16.

82 R.A. McCormick, "Human Significance and Christian Significance", in *Norm and Context*, 246.

[83] W.K. Frankena, "Love and Principle in Christian Ethics"; A. Platinga (ed.), *Faith and Philosophy*, Grand Rapids/Mich., 1964, 213.

[84] G. Outka, *Norm and Context*, 52; see G. Gilleman, *The Primacy of Charity*, Westminster/Md., 1961, 174.

[85] R. May, *Man's Search for Himself*, 33.

[86] Cf. M. Hinrichs, *Die Bedetung der Missionstheologie, aufgewiesen am Vergleich zwischen den abendländischen und chinesischen Kardinaltugenden*, Münster, 1954; J. Müller, "Missionarische Anpassung als theologisches Prinzip", in *Zeitschrift für Missionwissenschaft und Religionswissenschaft*, 1973, 1-24; K. Rahner, "Theological Pluralism and Unity in the Profession of Faith", in *Concilium*, 1969, N. 5.

[87] *Settimana del clero*, June 1973, 4.

[88] F.S. Carney, "Deciding in the Situation", in *Norm and Context*, 11.

[89] B. Häring, *Evangelization Today*, esp. the chapters "The evangelization of Morals", 45-78, and "Evangelization in the age of Exodus", 141-163.

[90] The literature on absolutes in moral theology is abundant; only a few publications can be mentioned: J. Gründel, *Wandelbares und Unwandelbares in der Moraltheologie*, Düsseldorf, 1967; Ch.E. Curran (ed.), *Absolutes in Moral Theology*, Washington D.C., 1968; D. Maguire, *Moral Absolutes and the Magisterium*, Cleveland, 1970; J. Fuchs, "Absoluteness of Moral Terms", in *Gregorianum* 52 (1971), 415-457; F. Scholz, *Wege, Umwege und Auswege der Moraltheologie. Ein Plädoyer für begründete Ausnahmen*, München, 1976; J. Sauer (ed.), *Normen im Konflikt*, Freiburg, 1977.

[91] S. Kierkegaard, *Fear and Trenmbiing*, New York, 1954, 80 and 64.

[92] J. Sittler, *The Structure of Christian Ethics*, Baton Rouge/Louis., 1958, 73.

[93] Cf. W. Eichrodt, *Theologie des Alten Testaments*, 6th ed., Göttingen, 1959, I, 88-90; 185-188.

[94] S.Th. I, II, q 100, a 8.

[95] l.c., ad 3.

[96] L. Reily, *The History, Nature and Use of Epikeia in Moral Theology*, Washington D.C., 1948; A. Adam, *Die Tugend der Freiheit*, 2nd ed., Nürenberg, 1952, 142-162; E. Hamel, *Loi naturelle et loi du Christ*, Bruges/Paris, 1964, 70-106; Id., "Epicheia", in *Dizionario enc. di teol. morale*, 4th ed., Roma, 1976, 357-365 (with abundant bibliography); A.M. Dolorosa, *La tradizione dell'Epikeia nel medioevo latino*, Milano, 1976.

[97] *Theologia moralis*, lib. I, n. 201. Of course, it is clear to us that not natural law as such — the law written into the heart and mind of man and to be discovered in shared reflexion and experience — allows epikeia; it does disallow a clinging to imperfect formulations of the natural law or to one principle and norm when this conflicts against higher principles, values and duties. St. Alphonsus draws some conclusions which still might be considered actual. While with other moralists he teaches that interrupted intercourse is against natural law, he also asserts: "It is lawful to interrupt intercourse, provided there is a proportionate reason" (l.c., lib. VI, n. 947). Note that he does nor request, as others did, a most serious reason (gravissima causa), but only a "proportionate reason" (justa causa).

[98] F. Schulz, *Wege, Umwege un Auswege der Moraltheologie. Ein Plädoyer für begründete Ausnahmen*, München, 1976 (with good bibliography); cf. B. Schüller, "Problematik allgemein verbindiicher Normen", in *Theologie u. Phil.* 46 (1970), 1-23; C.E. Curran, "Absolute Norms in Moral Theology", in *Norm and Context*, 139-173.

[99] *Critique of Practical Reason* (1788), English tr. by Lewis, New York, 1956, 30.

[100] l.c., 36.

[101] Pius XII, Discourse of Nov. 3, 1953, in *Herderkorr.* 8 (1953/4), 79.

[102] P. Ramsey, *Norm and Context*, 135.

[103] N. Hartmann, *Ethik*, Berlin, 1935, 683.

[104] l.c., 263, 266, 269.

[105] M. Scheler, *Der Formalismus in der Ethik und die materiale Wertethik*

Neuer Versuch der Grundlegung eines ethischen Personalismus, Bern, 5th ed., 1966.
[106] Geisler, l.c., 130f.
[107] H. Boelaars, "Towards a Theology of the Imperfect Response", in *The Clergy Review* 55 (1970), 445-450; N. Crotty, "Conscience and Conflict", in *Theological Studies* 32 (1971), 208-232; E. Quarello, "Per il superamento dei conflitti di coscienza", in *Salesianum* 33 (1971), 127-154; K. Demmer, "Entscheidung und Kompromiss", in *Gregorianum* 55 (1972), 323-351; Ch.E. Curran confronts this problem in almost all his books; see *Catholic Theology in Dialogue*, Notre Dame/Ind., 1972, 216-219; *Ongoing Revision*, Notre Dame/Ind., 1975,186-189; M. Attard, *Compromise in Morality*, Rome, 1976. See also the literature on "Absolutes in moral theology" which mainly concerns the problem of multiplying "absolutes" and thus causing unnecessary conflicts and requiring a kind of compromise.
[108] G. Outka, *Norm and Context*, 58f.
[109] B. Lonergan, S.J., "The Transition from a Classicist Worldview to a Historical-mindedness", in J.E. Biechler (ed.), *Law for Liberty: The Role of Canon Law in the Church Today*, Baltimore, 1967.
[110] B. Schüller, *Herrschaft Christi und das weltliche Recht. Christologische Rechtsbegründung neuerer Protestantischer Theologie*, Roma, 1963.
[111] Cf. J. Finn (ed.), *A conflict of Loyalties: The Case for Selective Conscientious Objection*, New York, 1969; Th.A. Shannon, *Render Unto God: A Theology of Selective Obedience*, New York, 1974.
[112] D.C. Rayne, *Conscience, Obligation, and the Law: The Moral Binding Power of the Civil Law*, Chicago, 1966; E. Hamel, S.J., "La scelta morale tra coscienza e legge", in *Rassegna di teologia* 17 (1976), 121-136.
[113] B. Häring, *Evangelization Today*, 68-80: "Evangelization of Canon Law"; B. Schüller, *Gesetz und Freiheit*, Düsseldorf, 1966; J. Hainz, *Ekklesia-Strukturen: Paulinische Gemeindetheologie und Gemeindeordnung*, Regensburg, 1972; E. Hamel, S.J., "La legge nuova per una comunità nuova", in *Civiltà Cattolica*, 1973, III, 351-360.
[114] *Optatam totius*, 16.
[115] Paul VI to the participants at the International Congress of Canonists, *Osservatore Romano*, June 20, 1970, AAS 62 (1970), 109.
[116] *Gaudium et spes*, 5.

Chapter Eight

Sin and conversion

Conversion is the ongoing activation of creative freedom and fidelity in Christ. In a comprehensive text of moral theology its role is of great significance; and in a dynamic moral theology, it is, by necessity, all-pervasive.

While John Baptist Hirscher and John Michael Sailer have given particular attention and an essential place to conversion in their moral theology, the more juridical manuals have treated conversion only as a coming back to the Catholic Church. All their attention is given to sin. My own feeling is that this text can do without a specific chapter on sin: not because we speak everywhere of sin, but because all the chapters, and especially this one, speak of conversion. Sin has no place in its own right. We treat it only as the power from which God has freed us and which threatens us only to the extent that we are lacking in our freedom for Christ and our faithfulness to him.

I. HOW TO SPEAK OF SIN

1. Sinful talk of sin

We can sin by talking of sin, if our purpose is to excuse ourselves while accusing others. Some would explain sin by blaming the devil, while doing nothing to overcome the bedevilment of the world. Some would hang all sin around the neck

of Adam or Eve, or of both, in order to forget that each of us,
when we sin, acts as Adam did, and increases the sinfulness of
the world. We can excuse ourselves, disowning our freedom and
denying our task to increase the volume of freedom in the world
around us. If we excuse ourselves because of a lack of freedom,
we are ungrateful and we sin against Christ who has set us
free and shows us how to grow together in freedom and fidelity.

We can speak of sin in a way that increases guilt complexes
in others and in ourselves. This kind of talk brings sadness
whenever it is alienated from its true context of redemption
and healing forgiveness. If we are reconciled people, truly
Christian people, we speak of sin by praising God's mercy,
acting as ambassadors of reconciliation, and healing the wounds
of those who are afflicted by their sins or the sins of others.

Our talk of sin is most sinful if we talk as if the sin of
Adam and Eve were greater than the grace of Jesus Christ. It is
my conviction that we are sinning against our heavenly Father,
who truly wants the salvation of all, if, in our talk, we condemn
to everlasting alienation the innocent children who, without
fault, have not received baptism. Our talk of original sin is
always sinful and alienating if we speak of it outside the context
of redemption or in a way that belittles the power of the
Redeemer.

It is sinful if we speak more of sins against laws and precepts than of the sin of refusing God honour, gratitude and
love. We are sinning against the right order if we speak more
of sins against sacred things — sacred stones, sacred vestments,
sacred places, sacred times, sacred rituals — than of sins
against the human person and the human community. Our talk
is sinful, too, when we emphasize the sins against biological
functions more than those against healthy human relationships
and reasonable responsibility.

What are we doing when we speak of mortal sins of children
who have not at all the capacity yet to sin mortally? And what
kind of God are we portraying if we teach that, in all matters
of the sixth commandment, the presumption is that even the
slightest transgression such as an intemperate kiss means mortal
sin deserving everlasting punishment? Our talk of sin is sinful
whenever we have not made all the effort necessary to come to

a better knowledge of God and man. And it is sinful whenever we are lacking in our resolution to be converted and to share with others the Good News of conversion.

Very frequently in the past, in the old and new covenants as well as in all religions, the kings' priests spoke sinfully of sin by being most concerned with their own privileges, with the status quo in favour of the powerful and wealthy, inventing hundreds of mortal sins about rituals while forgetting the sins against justice and peace. The kings' priests sinned when they talked too sharply against the sins of the poor, the downtrodden, the outcast, while they kept silent about the sins of the kings, the priests, the powerful.

To know how to speak of sin, we have to look to the prophets. They proclaim the possibility, the need, and the urgency of the conversion of all: the conversion of each person and the renewal of the community. They speak of the sins of those who disregard their responsibility for the world around them. They shake the consciences of the powerful and wealthy. By manifesting the mercy of God, they unmask the sins of the merciless. By proclaiming the God of love, they accuse the sins of lovelessness. By revealing the holiness and justice of God, they make known our obligation in justice to forgive, to heal and to be on the side of the victims. By presenting the message of wholeness, the synthesis between love of God and love of fellowman, the synthesis and tension between justice and mercy, they call us to a conversion not just to laws but to God and fellowmen. By proclaiming the messianic peace, they leave no excuse for those who remain uninvolved and uncommitted although they are called to receive the gift of peace and to promote peace at all levels.

Priests of the new and everlasting covenant cannot be excused if they speak as priests of the mighty of this earth. They are called by *the* Prophet Jesus Christ to share in his prophetic mission, to suffer with him in order to rejoice in him, to be raised to life. The prophets have a joyous message, even if they speak of sin, because they believe and they share their faith in conversion and reconciliation.

When speaking of sin, the kings' priests and moralists support group interests, taboos, traditions and laws that set

kingdoms against kingdoms and churches against churches.
The prophets, who know the name of the one God and Father,
tear down the man-made barriers so that all may be one,
honouring the one God and Father and the one Lord Jesus
Christ in the one Spirit.

The kings' moralists know the catalogue of sins once and
for all, while the prophets interpret the signs of the times
and call all to vigilance and readiness.

2. *The Gospel of conversion and the evil of sin*

In Holy Scripture, the discourse on sin forms an integrated
part of the Gospel of conversion, which is gladdening news to
those who want to respond to the call to holiness, and threat
to those who obstinately refuse to respond to God's call.

The Bible speaks of sin and conversion in a very concrete
form. It speaks in the *kairos*, the concrete 'now', in keen awareness of the partners in the dialogue. We can surely learn from the
Bible abiding norms on how to speak of sin. It always speaks in
view of God whose name is holy and whose mercy lasts from
generation unto generation. It tells of the unfolding of God's
history with humankind; it opens the horizons of history and
calls for the next step to be taken. The Bible does not have
just one word for sin; rather, in various images, parables and
words taken from everyday life, it expresses the experiences of
sin and conversion and, thus, teaches us how to take the next
step in the right direction.

Earlier, we spoke of the controversy concerning "law and
Gospel" or "Gospel and law". Although there is a great diversity
of discourse on conversion and sin in the Old and New Testaments, there emerges from it the clear truth that it is not law
that unmasks sin; it is the revelation of God's saving justice
and mercy, and the Father's final revelation in Jesus Christ that
tears away the mask of sin and reveals it.

"The negative reality of the sin cannot be the last word
of a Christian theology, any more than it is the last word in
Scripture".[1] Sin can be neither the first nor the last word.
The first word is always God's creation, his original design, and
all the good which, through his grace, was and is present in the
world. Even when preaching conversion to unbelievers, we start

with the good; and when preaching conversion to Christians this especially applies. When speaking to Christians, we should never start with law and sin but always with the Good News of God's superabundant grace. When preaching to believers, we should build on the reality of faith, which remains always a gift. Indeed, all our discussion on sin makes sense only if we communicate the Good News. "Conversion is possible; Christ has set us free".[2]

There is a considerable difference between the preaching of the prophets of the Old Testament on sin and conversion, and that of Jesus, the Prophet and Saviour. When the fullness of salvation is present, there must necessarily be a greater emphasis on salvation, liberation and conversion than before the event of redemption.

We should also notice the different emphases in Christ's preaching, which correspond to the capacities of his hearers. At the beginning, in Galilee, when he preaches to the poor, the simple people, there is not the same need to unmask hypocrisy and hardness of heart as there is when he preaches to the higher clergy and those Pharisees and lawyers who manifest stubborn opposition and closed-mindedness when faced with the Good News.

a) God's saving justice and man's injustice (*adikia*)

God the Father has revealed in Jesus Christ his saving justice, through the unsolicited and wholly undeserved manifestation of his saving love. He does justice to his own name, "Father", when he acts mercifully. We are justified by his grace, his graciousness. If we refuse to accept this gift gratefully and thus lose it, then we are unjust not only to our own legitimate interest and salvation but, above all, to God's saving justice.

He who manifests his mercy and his saving justice lays down at the same time the rule that we should act with others as he acts with us. "Let your goodness have no limits, just as the goodness of the heavenly Father knows no bounds" (Mt 5:48). Hatred, enmity, harshness and lack of mercy against our fellowmen are a crying injustice against our own name as children of God, and an assault on God's saving justice. The refusal to respond to the just claims of our fellowmen, and especially to the cries of the needy and to those who have offended us, is, above all, a violation of God's holiness who asks from his children that they act as he did (1 Jn 5:17).

Because God lays claim to sovereignty over us by his revelation in Jesus Christ of the dominion of love and by the mission of the Spirit of love, the refusal of filial love and mutual justice and love manifests the most outrageous injustice against God himself. The most violent injustice is the rejection of Jesus Christ (Jn 15:22f). Since God reveals his love through his saving justice and mercy, all refusal of love of God and of neighbour falls under the actual (biblical) concept of injustice.

The injustice is particularly great if one hardens one's heart, especially since we live in the messianic age in which the prophecies are fulfilled that God will give us a new heart. Sin, then, does not only deny our heart its proper role but also, by ingratitude, shows the greatest injustice towards the Holy Spirit. One can easily understand this if one has received Christ's message as synthesized in Mark 1:14: "The time of favour has come, the kingdom of God is at hand. Be renewed in your heart and put your faith in the Gospel". To live as if Jesus had not come and the Spirit had not been sent is plain injustice to God, to oneself, to our fellowmen and to all creation.

Sin as injustice flows from impiety (*asebeia*), which means refusal to honour God as God and to render thanks (Rom 1:18f). The injustice of sin is to prefer the "polluted world" of arrogance, selfishness, deception and self-deception, to the infinite love of Christ (2 Pt 2:20). If a believer turns away from God in a fundamental option, then the injustice of the sin is as great as "trodding underfoot the Son of God" and "profaning the blood of the covenant" (Heb 10:26-31).

One who prefers to live on the level of selfishness ("flesh"; *sarx*) when one could live on the level of the Spirit is living the injustice of sin. It is both alienation and an unjust refusal of gratitude to put one's trust in one's own strength and in what is controllable by man, instead of seeking the things of the higher realm and manifesting trust in God and gratitude through prayer and thanksgiving.[3] To those who know the gift of the Eucharist as ongoing thanksgiving in Christ the grave injustice of ingratitude is particularly evident.

Holy Scripture, especially the preaching of the prophets and the New Testament, makes it clear that all sin against oneself and one's fellowmen is also an injustice against God, Father of all. Religion and morality are inseparable. Whoever refuses to love his neighbour and to work for God's kingdom of justice and peace on earth, refuses by this very fact to love God. Faced with the marvellous works of God's self-revelation, man can give a wholehearted and fitting response. This response includes, by necessity, involvement as partner in the ongoing creation and redemption and in the final battle between God and the inimical powers. Non-action, non-involvement is an injustice to the Creator and Redeemer as well as to God's people.[4]

b) Turning away from God's life-giving law (*anomia*)

With Paul the Apostle, the redeemed person sings the song of praise, "In Christ Jesus the life-giving law of the Spirit has set you free from the law of sin and death" (Rom 8:2). When we are offered life in Christ, friendship with God, fullness of life and liberty guided by the Spirit, then we can realize what sin really is and what liberty is. The sin of both lawlessness and senseless cult of laws is evident to those who know life in Christ Jesus as their innermost law (1 Cor 9:21).[5]

Betrayal and refusal of the law of the Spirit is something quite different from transgression of those laws, traditions and norms that are not known as being part of the law which God writes into our hearts by his Spirit. Whether one yields to permissiveness or to over-scrupulosity under man-made laws and abusive authorities, the evil and misery lie in one's refusal of the law of the covenant[6] which is a law of friendship and salvation.

Sin as individual or group egotism can become, as it were, a second nature, the law of the sinner; and that is self-punishment for abandoning the life-giving law. Scripture shows us history as the drama between the law of liberty in Christ and the dominion of sin that in many ways establishes its inimical ways over men (cf. Rom 3:9; Eph 2:1-5). The liberating law of Christ is given to bring man to God, to true life. The law of sin binds man to himself, to selfish thinking, to slavery under the godless world and under death (cf. Rom 7). It does this by turning laws, human traditions, taboos and other powers into ends in themselves. The sinner can know many laws and obey many traditions and norms, but he does not know anymore the saving law of unselfish love.

In sin, man's true self is lost to his selfish self which binds him to all the inimical powers. He is lost to his selfish self even when he observes laws and traditions. But through the prophetic teaching, and even more through the life-giving law of the Spirit written in man's heart, God liberates man for himself, so that in adoration, in faith, hope and love, man comes to true membership in the people of God and thus finds his real self.

The "law of sin" tends to harden man's heart more and more, to the point where he becomes hostile to God. "The outlook of the selfish self is enmity with God" (Rom 8:7). "This thought of hostility became a constitutive element of the Pauline concept of sin".[7]

God's life-giving law is a law of growth, of ongoing conversion. One begins to turn away from this law when one refuses to grow, to learn and unlearn, to be more fully converted.

c) Turning away from the saving covenant to sin solidarity (*hamartia*)

From the very beginning, humankind has never been simply condemned to sin. The history of salvation is marked by God's promises and by his covenant (cf. Gen 3:15; 9:8-17; 17:1-7; Ex 34:10-27). The people are assured of his fidelity, and they experience liberation and salvation insofar as they live faithfully in the covenant, trusting in God and being united among themselves under his saving rule.

Sin is not only transgression of individual laws. In the full sense it is *breaking the covenant*. This is drastically symbolized by Moses breaking the Tablets containing the laws of the covenant. "And I looked, and behold, you had sinned against the Lord your God; you had made yourselves a molten calf; you had turned aside quickly from the way which the Lord has commanded you. So I took hold of the two Tablets and cast them out of my two hands, and broke them before your eyes" (Deut 9:16-17).

Sin is understood as "missing the point" *(hata)*. It is not only missing precious opportunities to do good and to escape evil; it is missing the point of the covenant. In the Old Testament, the concept of sin depends greatly on the covenant reality. No other aspect is stressed more than the social dimension of sin. Those who abandon the saving covenant fall into sin solidarity. They do not only lose their share in the covenant but also tend to involve others in the same misery. It was not until the time of the Babylonian exile, when each family of the scattered people had to take up its own responsibility, that the prophets brought the individual aspect of sin more into focus — however, without diminishing the social dimension.[3]

As disciples of Christ, we know that we are redeemed and sealed by the blood of the covenant. Christ himself is the covenant and, thus, the law. Sin, therefore, is an assault against Christ, the Saving Covenant. This truth is expressed by Paul in his symbol of the Body of Christ. "Christ is like a single body with its many limbs and organs which, many as they are, together make up one body. For indeed we are all brought into one body by baptism in the one Spirit" (1 Cor 12:12-13). "If one organ suffers, they all suffer together. If one flourishes, they all rejoice together" (1 Cor 12:26). It is the very "law of Christ" to bear the burden of one another, to be concerned for the salvation of all (Gal 6:2). Each sin diminishes the effective presence of salvation and increases the powers of evil. And since it affects the salvation of our fellowmen, it is an offence against Christ who died for all.

The Bible sometimes presents sin as if it were a personified power that subjects the sinner and exercises its deteriorating influence even on the environment (cf Gen 3:17). The created world suffers under the sin-solidarity of man, and with man, is groaning to share in the liberty of the children of God (Rom 8:19-21). The created world and all humanity protest against our sin.

The individualist who is concerned only with his own well-being and salvation cannot escape the dark powers of sin-solidarity until he makes the conscious choice for saving solidarity, expressed in day-by-day co-responsibility. The whole community must be concerned for its health and bring this home to the consciousness of each individual. "Have you never heard the saying, 'A little leaven leavens all the dough?' The old leaven of corruption is working among you. Purge it out, and then you will be bread of a new baking" (1 Cor 5:6-7).

The New Testament frequently uses the expression *hamartia* for sin in the singular. If sin is used in the plural, it means the individual transgressions, the acts of sin. If in the singular, it means the state of sin, the hardened heart, including the dimension of sin-solidarity.

Individual sins are not only multiplied numerically; they also create a hardened heart. They diminish the freedom for good and increase the poison of evil. The more the sinner is subject to the power of sin, the more he comes under the power of collective sinfulness. Personal sins, by a dialectic that can be analyzed, are translated into social alienation; alienation of person from person, alienation of communities and societies. They lead to an alienated understanding of man; and they poison the whole environment which, in turn, diminishes the freedom for good and tempts individuals to join in collective falsehood, injustice and perversion.[9]

Everything we have said here about sin is fully verified in mortal sin, that fundamental option for evil which, by necessity, is an implicit option for sin-solidarity, an option to fight with the evil powers against saving justice and solidarity in Christ.[10] Venial sin weakens one's wholeness and endangers healthy relationships. If the venial sin is grave, the person is somehow divided. While in the deepest depth he is still on the side of Christ, he contradicts himself and increases the inimical powers.

d) Turning away from the truth to the bondage of falsehood

As we saw earlier, Christ, who is the Truth, has set us free from the bondage of falsehood to live in his light and to become a light for the world. Christ, the Light, shines in the world, but there are people who prefer the darkness (Jn 1:5f). They shie away from him who is the Light, since they are not ready to repent for their dark sins. While the sinner takes part in the barren deeds of darkness and allows himself to be deceived by shallow arguments (cf. Eph 5:6-10), true believers walk in the daylight where all goodness springs up, all justice and truth. The Bible presents sin in its individual and social dimension as darkness *(skotos)*, plunging into errors, self-deception and lying *(pseudos)*, which makes people sons of Satan, the father of lies (cf. Jn 8:44f). Sinners have "bartered away the truth of God for the lie" (Rom 1:25).

How grave is the option of idols, self-deception, a lying life under the bondage of Satan the liar, becomes evident through the fact that in Jesus Christ the Father has revealed his truth, his wisdom and his love. Jesus says of those in Israel who have made the fundamental option against him and the Father, "If I had not come and spoken to them, they would not be guilty of sin; but now they have no excuse for their sin: he who hates me hates my Father" (Jn 15:22-23).

The sinful world and the individual sinner have no excuse when they are sinning despite God's having sent us the Spirit of truth. "When he comes, he will confute the world, and show where wrong and right judgment lie. He will convict them of wrong by their refusal to believe in me" (Jn 16:8-9).

Those who are guided by the Spirit of truth, and give full witness to truthfulness in their allegiance to Christ, are unmasking idols and ideologies, and call sinners to the truth. "On the one hand the sinner is responsible for the sins he committed. Through his own fault he wanders in the darkness. On the other hand, once he has fallen, he continues to sin by a kind of necessity because he cannot do otherwise than to continue to stray in this darkness and slavery to the devil . . . But he can break the chains of this fatal enslavement through faith in the divine revelation in Jesus".[11] The call to conversion comes normally through the faith community, through those who walk in the light.

3. *Temptation*

Our God-given freedom, as such, does not incline to evil; it is given for the good. However, the possibility of sin is inherent in man's imperfection. Temptation is something quite different from the mere possibility of sin. Free will can be tempted by one's own concupiscence, the evil inclinations that are the harvest of past individual and collective sins, by the evil invested in the world around us, and by the devil.

The devil is "the tempter" (1 Thess 3:5; Mt 4:3). On the one hand, we should not ignore the cosmic powers of sin that transcend our environment; on the other hand, we ought never to speak of the devil in order to discharge our own responsibilities.

Evil spirits have no power over those who put their trust in God and join hands with all men of good will for creating a divine milieu that invites goodness, justice and peace.

We should know what it means to pray, "and do not bring us to the test, but save us from the evil one" (Mt 6:13). God does help us to overcome temptations. By converting our hearts and soliciting our co-responsibility, he preserves us from many temptations. "No one under trial or temptation should say, 'I am being tempted by God'; for God is untouched by evil, and does not himself tempt anyone. Temptation arises when a man is enticed and lured away by his own lust; then lust conceives and gives birth to sin" (Jas 1:13-15). The evil one has no power over man unless man's individual and collective selfishness and arrogance empower him to be the tempter. In temptation, the sinner's own concupiscence (selfishness) meets with a sinful world around him whose tempting power is the result of all the sins of individuals and groups.

Whoever puts his trust in the Lord, gives and finds support in the community of believers, and is docile towards the Spirit of God, will be given discernment to judge rightly about the deceitful spirit of the world, whereas a person who is unspiritual and refuses what belongs to the Spirit of God is easily tempted by the deceitful world. The selfish self (*sarx*) invites temptations coming from the sinful world.

The power of the godless world and of what remains of the "old man" in ourselves is broken by the solidarity of salvation. Believers fulfil the law of Christ by fraternal encouragement and correction, knowing quite well that they too can be tempted (Gal 6:1-2). We have become well aware that fraternal correction alone does not suffice; we have to create healthy communities and work together for justice, truthfulness, fidelity and authentic liberty.

Therefore, while we pray that God may free us from temptations, we directly pray that, with God's grace, we may come to purity of heart, intentions and motives, and at the same time remove from ourselves and from others the many temptations that come from a deceitful and unjust world. We should be aware that we offend God by praying that he may not lead us into temptation while we seek culpably the tempting situation or, by our sloth in prayer and vigilance, turn normal situations into a danger for salvation.

We do not pray that God will spare us any kind of test; we ask him only to preserve us from the dangerous tests. From God comes a test of our sincere faith, the providential tribulation in the form of an external visitation, together with abundant inner grace, at least to pray. This providential trial is in the apostle's mind when he says, "My brothers, whenever you have to face trials (*peirasmoi*) of many kinds, count yourselves extremely happy in the knowledge that such testing breeds fortitude" (Jas 1:2; cf. 1 Pt 4:12).

While allowing trials to come upon us, God wants to purge our character and live the pure gold of faith and a life according to faith (Sir 27:6). It was thus that he tried Abraham, Job, Tobias. "I was sent to put you to the test. At the same time, however, God commissioned me to heal you" (Tobit 12:14). "The Lord, your God, is testing you to learn whether you really love him with all your heart and with all your soul" (Deut 13:4).

To the allurements of a sinful world, the Christian response is not flight but, rather, a purposeful commitment to change the world and thus to respond to its yearning to have a share in the liberty of the children of God. For this life-effort, the followers of Christ will prepare themselves by prayerfulness, by rootedness in the community of salvation, by meditation on the wisdom of the cross, and the Christian's mission to be light for the world. They will pray for the gifts of wisdom and discernment. They will also assess, individually and together, their own strength before deciding the type of personal and communal involvement, and will always give proper attention to the foreseeable consequences of their acts, so that they may help others and not become for them an occasion of temptation.[12]

4. *Punishment for sin*

Today's moral theology places less emphasis on the ideas of reward and punishment than the manuals of the last three centuries did. The reasons are various. In the first place, we have to be aware of the crisis of faith induced in many people who are appalled by the idea of an avenging deity.[13] A second reason is the shocking awareness, aroused by men like Pavlov and Skinner, that manipulation works through the twin masters of reward and punishment alone. God does not live in a contractual relationship with man; he offers a covenant of love and fidelity. Believers come to their proper stature if their motivations transcend those of external reward and punishment.

Yet we cannot ignore the fact that the good itself brings forth, as precious harvest, the self-actualization of the person. It leads to the road of beatitude if it is not done just for the sake of obtaining reward or avoiding punishment. Similarly, we realize that sin, too, brings forth its own fruit in all kinds of evil. The apostle Paul follows the Old Testament line of thought when he explains perversion and alienation in the world as the natural outcome of sin, understood as refusal to honour God as God, and to render thanks to him (Rom 1:18-32).

God is not vindictive. In his saving justice he calls man to repentance in such a way that the suffering that comes from sin becomes part of the calling. "Or do you think lightly of his wealth of kindness, of tolerance and of patience, without recognizing that God's kindness is meant to lead you to a change of heart? In the rigid obstinacy of your heart you are laying up for yourself a store of retribution" (Rom 2:4-5).

Man is indeed cruel to himself by sinning. If he does not repent, he gradually destroys his own liberty for the good. He ruins his own inner wholeness, loses his integrity, opts for slavery. "Everyone who commits sin is a slave" (Jn 8:34).

We should not think lightly of venial sin. Continual neglect of God's grace leads to repeated venial sins that become ever more grave. They gradually destroy the sensitivity of conscience and the inner dynamics for wholeness and integrity.

Eventually they can bring the terrible temptation to mortal sin.

Sin inscribes itself in the cerebral cortex, in one's memory and tendencies. It makes a devastating investment of evil in one's life and environment. Humankind has punished and still punishes itself by its sins. The Incarnate Word of God himself has suffered to the utmost under mankind's sinfulness. However, he has also shown us how to transform suffering into saving solidarity.[14]

The Lord has clearly revealed to us that our fundamental option entails the choice either for everlasting life and friendship with God or for irrevocable alienation.

II. SIN AND SINS

Holy Scripture distinguishes between sin as power, alienation and perversion of man's heart, and the various acts and expressions of sin which are here called sins. Throughout the ages, various concerns led to catalogues of sins, to special attention to the specific and numeric diversity of sins, to the distinction between sins of omission and sins of commission, as well as to the need to envision the gradation of the gravity of sins.

1. Catalogues of sins

Concern for cataloguing sins or vices arose out of concrete situations, and for pedagogical or societal reasons. For example, we find in Deuteronomy 27:15-26 curses connected with twelve crimes which at that time were a special threat to the people of the covenant. The Mosaic law, as it was taught at the time of Jesus, contained some six hundred and thirteen precepts which were thought to provide a complete moral code and, of course, a catalogue of sins.[15]

St. Paul has short catalogues of sinful attitudes and deeds which are directly opposed to the coming of the kingdom of God. In I Corinthians 6:9-10 he mentions the vices currently prevailing among the pagans. His warning is probably directed to an antinomian misinterpretation of his message on Christian freedom. Similarly, Galatians 5:18-21 is a short and sharp description of those attitudes which contradict the freedom for which Christ has set us free.

Throughout antiquity, there existed a short common catalogue of sins which were so gravely scandalous that the sinner had to be submitted to a special discipline (Canonical Penance). Each local Church had a short list of scandalous sins which, in the particular environment, created an especially condemnatory reaction from the Church. The penitential books of the Irish Church enlarged greatly the number of sins on the list. It was, however, mainly a catalogue of penances.

Catalogues of sins should not be stereotyped repetitions of earlier warnings. They should be a challenging reaction against the principal sins and disorders in a certain culture or environment.

2. *Specific diversity of sins*

By its law that the faithful must confess all mortal sins committed after baptism according to their specific and numeric diversity, the Council of Trent gave new impetus to treatises on the specific diversity of sins.[16] An all too strict interpretation of this law led to over-scrupulosity and to artificial criteria for distinguishing the various species of sins.

The specific type of sin may be determined by the kind of duty, value or virtue contradicted by it. For instance, carelessness about revealed truth or neglect or even denial of those truths of faith calling for a change in one's life: all these are sins against the virtue of faith. The virtue of religion demands that we adore God and him alone. Adoring false gods — idolatry — is radical contradiction. The same virtue demands that God be honoured in a manner worthy of his supreme dignity and goodness. Carelessness in worship and especially all forms of superstition contradict this aspect of the virtue of religion.

To transgress a just law of the Church or of the state violates the virtue of obedience, and above all the rights, values or duties protected by this just law. If a positive command or precept is concerned only with obedience as such, and no other virtue or value is demanded by the command, its transgression is neither a sin of disobedience nor a sin against another virtue. If, however, one endangers the life and integrity of others, for instance by transgressing traffic and speed laws, one is sinning not only against obedience but also against regard for life, and that means against the virtues of justice and love as well.

Manuals written for confessors have surely exaggerated the specific diversity of sins. Their main purpose was to obtain a "materially complete confession". Our principal concern should rather be the sharpening of peoples' conscience about the values, duties, rights or virtues that are at stake. Scrupulosity must be carefully counteracted.

3. The numeric distinction of sins

In today's society, a crime is rightly considered particularly grave if one repeats it. From the moral point of view, we realize that sins committed repeatedly, because of a lack of repentance, might be a sign of a fundamental option against God and good, or at least a great danger gradually undermining the good fundamental option. The danger of opting against the love of God "above all things" is most evident if a Christian says to himself after a serious sin, "I have to confess it anyway, why not repeat it!"

Attention to the fundamental option makes it impossible to indulge in a somewhat mathematical approach, counting mainly the number of acts instead of asking, above all, how seriously one is struggling against a habit and how soon after a sinful act one repents before God. It is evident that a long lasting disposition for a sinful disorder creates a greater sin-bondage than a number of evil acts while the person is still struggling against temptation. Much more important than the number of sinful acts is — even in view of a good confession — the more basic question whether there is an over-all growth or an ever more visible decay.

4. Sins of omission and commission

It may be that sins of commission of evil do not constitute as grave a peril for the kingdom of God and the growth of the human person as the more numerous sins of neglect of the good that could and should be done. God's kingdom is not only a matter of well-defined obligations. For the Christian, the acceptance of the kingdom of heaven is the fundamental option to live on the level of grace. That means gratefully using all our energies and present opportunities to do good, to meet the needs of people. Whoever gives conscientious attention only to the sins of commission will never conquer the powers of evil.

Among the great sins of omission are the neglect to search for what is good, truthful and beautiful, the neglect to reflect and to meditate, sloth and non-involvement, which is a main cause of the power of the perverted world. A catalogue of sins that is merely concerned with prohibitions and borderlines is a sinful way of speaking of sin, because it can distract the person from the road of salvation. One of the great sins is the unwillingness to grow according to the measure of gifts received from God, and in response to the needs of those whom we can help.

5. *Sins of the heart and sins of action*

Biblical ethics emphasizes purity of heart and the relevance of man's emotions, thoughts, desires, intentions and motives. All evil deeds are born of the disorders in the heart of man. Although there are certain sins which are entirely interior, we should not forget that they are the bad tree which brings forth all kinds of bad fruit. The principal interior sins are:

(1) Mental complaisance about one's imagination and thoughts regarding evil things *(delectatio morosa)*. Still more dangerous is the interior complaisance about the evil one has done, or the inward regret for having missed the opportunity to commit sins as, for instance, not having used an opportunity to commit adultery. Such thoughts, complaisance or regrets betray the unconverted heart.

(2) Evil desires about sinful actions that are not within one's power to accomplish. In this instance one does not actually decide to do the evil thing but only because it is not possible. This sin is sometimes called "inefficacious desire for evil".

(3) Evil purpose, the actual resolve to do evil. It is called "efficacious desire", even though some external circumstance may prevent the evil deed.

All these interior sins belong to the same species as the external act to which they refer, but they do not always have the same degree of malice as the external act (cf. Mt 5:28). If a person does not have a keen consciousness about the sinfulness of these interior acts, it is a sign of moral and/or psychological immaturity.

Since there are often also some positive values or aspects in sinful acts, it is lawful to rejoice about what is good as long as one does not interiorly approve the evil. If, for instance, an unmarried mother rejoices in having her child, this does not necessarily mean that she is happy about having committed sin. She can be happy for having shown responsibility after the sin has occurred, and she can praise God for all the good that is in her child and in her motherly love.

III. MORTAL AND VENIAL SINS

1. Are all serious sins mortal sins?

If we compare the history of moral theology in the past several centuries with the preaching of the Apostles and the teaching of the first centuries of Christianity, we are struck by the disproportionate efforts to determine what constitutes mortal and venial sin.

The Bible and the Church Fathers surely warned about the dangers of sin which could turn man away from God. It was, however, only after the sacrament of penance had taken its present form that there appeared a real obsession in the minds of moralists and of many scrupulous people to determine accurately the borderline between mortal and venial sin.

The change of emphasis and perspective must be evaluated in the total context of culture and in the light of the Church's self-understanding at the time. In a Church that strongly asserted her direct or indirect power over all events in the secular world, the question of mortal and venial sin fell too much under the power of "knowledge of control".

Rigoristic trends brought about total confusion by identifying all grave sins as mortal sins, leaving the impression that venial sins could be neither grave nor serious. The situation greatly worsened under the impact of Jansenistic rigorism which spread in a great part of the Roman Catholic Church, meeting similar trends in sectors of the reformed Churches.

This brand of rigorism held that the greatest part of humanity is doomed to eternal condemnation, and this by divine decrees which predestined some for the good but the great majority for the evil. Adhering to the teachings of the most rigoristic theologians of his time, Calvin preached that "every sin is mortal because it is a rebellion against God's will that necessarily provokes his wrath".[17] He taught that if these sins are pardonable by God, it is because of his mercy for the predestined ones and not because of their venial nature. And if God punishes those predestined to eternal damnation, he is just. This is a terrifying image of God. For both Calvinists and Catholics, a rigoristic concept of sin produced innumerable traumas and concealed faith in God who is love for all.

Taking seriously the challenge of some atheists who tell us that if there is a God he is surely infinitely greater than the one we may have manifested to them, we are forced to examine painstakingly our thinking about mortal and venial sin. However, many other reasons besides secularism and atheism force and help us to consider the question in a new light.

We have already addressed ourselves to this problem in the perspective of a better psychological understanding of the fundamental option. The self-understanding of the Church, as expressed by the Second Vatican Council, is a major contribution to the solution of our problem, for the Vatican II Church sees herself more clearly in a perspective of "knowledge of salvation" and as a living Gospel for the world of today. Faced with a critical generation, she asks herself whether she conveys the message of the living and loving God in all her formulations of doctrines and in her practices.

2. *Gradation of sin in the Bible*

There is no doubt that the Bible often points clearly to a gradation of sin,[18] but surely not in the sense of distinction between sins that must be confessed (mortal sins) and sins that may be confessed (venial sins). When the Bible speaks of sin, the main context is always the call to conversion, whether from a total or a partial alienation.

The call to conversion becomes particularly urgent for Israel, since she has received the covenant and the law of the covenant, as well as many other signs of God's goodness and mercy. The sins of Israel are, therefore, more serious than those of the Gentiles who had not received so many signs of God's mercy and so much knowledge of his holiness.

The greatest of all sins is committed by that part of Israel which, despite the full manifestation of God's love in Jesus Christ, refuses the new covenant. It is to that great sin that we can compare the terrifying sin of Christians who, after illumination by faith and a solemn commitment to Christ, turn away from him again. "If we wilfully persist in sin after receiving the knowledge of the truth, no sacrifice for sin remains: only a terrifying expectation of judgment and fierce fire will consume God's enemies. If a man disregards the law of Moses, he is put to death without pity on the evidence of two or three witnesses. Think how much more severe a penalty that man will deserve who has trampled underfoot the Son of God, profaned the blood of the covenant by which he was consecrated, and affronted God's gracious Spirit!" (Heb 10:26-30). This text is especially aimed at those who had a clear and firm fundamental option for Christ and then turned radically away.

However, not only apostasy but also a life which constantly contradicts the faith one confesses is a fundamental option against Christ. Those who have dishonoured the Lord by mere lip-service will hear at the end the terrifying judgment, "I never knew you; depart from me, you workers of iniquity *(anomia)*" (Mt 7:23). The sin of "heterodox orthodoxy" is here called by the same name, *anomia*, as that of the Pharisees. "Outside you look like honest men, but inside you are full of hypocrisy and iniquity *(anomia)*" (Mt 23:28). Whoever, by the fundamental option of his life, rejects the law of the covenant participates in his own way in the absolute opposition of the anti-Christ against God's kingdom (Mt 24:12).

In the writings of John, *anomia* means the decisive rejection of God's loving way by lovelessness and injustice against one's neighbour (1 Jn 3:4). But John insists that the true believer surely does not commit the sin of *anomia*. From the context we can conclude that the sins of believers who, after their fault, continue to seek and to love Christ are of a totally different nature.[19] There are, on the one side, thoroughly alienated sinners who do not "know" God and, on the other side, believers who do not at all commit the sin of iniquity, yet confess humbly before God that they are sinners and in need of forgiveness. "If we claim to be sinless, we are self-deceived and strangers to the truth. If we confess our sins, he is just and may be trusted to forgive our sins and cleanse us from every kind of wrong; but if we say we have committed no sin, we make him out to be a liar, and then his word has no place in us" (1 Jn 1:8-10).

In an optimism that is common in the New Testament, St. John asserts that "We know that no child of God is a sinner; it is the Son of God who keeps him safe, and the evil one cannot touch him" (1 Jn 5:17-18). Yet all believers confess daily and pray that God may forgive their sins of weakness. The sins of Christians can be serious without turning them away from Christ. "If a man sees his brother committing a sin which is not a deadly sin, he should pray to God for him and he will grant him life — that is, when men are not guilty of deadly sins. There is such a thing as deadly sin, and I do not suggest that he should pray about that; but although all wrongdoing is sin, not all sin is deadly sin" (1 Jn 5:16).

Without weakening the Christian optimism that we can abide in the love of Christ, James says, "All of us often go wrong" (Jas 3:2). We need mutual help and mutual healing forgiveness, and all of us should be holy penitents praying daily, "Forgive us our sins as we forgive those who sin against us" (Mt 6:12; Lk 11:4).

At one end of the scale there is the sin against the Holy Spirit, which is unpardonable because it means an absolutely hardened heart, the total refusal of conversion even if faced with all the graciousness of Christ (cf. Mt 12:31ff; Mk 3:28f; Lk 12:10; 1 Jn 5:16ff). At the other end there are the daily weaknesses of which even the saints accuse themselves. In between, there is a noticeable gradation. There are very grave sins, such as the sin of incest, which are, at the same time, particularly scandalous and provoke sharp reactions by the

Church leaders (1 Cor 5:1). Then there are other sins that might not be deadly but need "fraternal correction" (cf. Gal 6:1f; 1 Jn 5:16).

There is not the slightest indication in the Bible that there is a quantitative measurement to define the borderline between mortal and venial sin. The Bible perspective is always the call to conversion: either the radicalness of total conversion from darkness to light or the conversion from serious fault that presents at least a danger of turning away from God, and the ongoing conversion of the saint-penitents, that is, of all Christians. The Bible does not allow all grave or serious sins to be equated with deadly or mortal sins, nor does it allow all venial sins to be considered as not grave or not serious. It is not biblical to reduce the gradation of sins to just two categories, mortal and venial. To think that venial sins cannot be serious or grave is as unreasonable as to consider all wounds and ailments as not serious, as if death alone were serious.

3. Theological reflection

The Church's credibility could be greatly jeopardized if, after the biblical renewal, the new insights brought forth by the best anthropology were not to be taken into account for a better understanding of the distinction between venial and mortal sin.[20] This reconsideration is necessary, first for the right preaching of conversion and then also for the still urgent renewal of the discipline regarding the sacrament of reconciliation. The main vision must always be the effective proclamation of the Good News that conversion is possible and, therefore, necessary.

The call to conversion does not require one to know whether one's serious sin is mortal or not. As already mentioned, the Church of antiquity submitted certain very grave sins, like apostasy, murder, abortion and publicly known adulterous relationships to the canonical long-lasting penance. The main criterion was the gravity of the scandal caused, and therefore the necessity of public reparation. In no way did the early Church intimate that only those sins submitted to the canonical penance were mortal sins. She always proclaimed the biblical catalogues of sins opposed to the acceptance of the kingdom of God (Mt 25:41-46; 1 Cor 6:9-10; Gal 5:19-21; Rom 1:24-32; 13:13; 1 Pt 4:3; 2 Pt 2:12-22; Rev 21:27; 22:15). This was done not for measuring whether or not mortal sin is given but for bringing the message home that every Christian has to fight firmly and unceasingly against these attitudes in his heart and in the world around him, in order to abide in God's love.

When, about the sixth century, the institution of the canonical penance decayed, a new form of penance emerged in the Celtic Churches in Ireland and Scotland, and spread very quickly over the whole of central and western Europe. The old rule that absolution would be given only once in a lifetime was abolished in favour of reconciliation whenever there was serious conversion and the will to do penance.

However, the catalogue of sins that had to be confessed to the priest was greatly amplified, although with no intention to declare that all the sins that had to be confesesed were mortal sins. The catalogue was clear and complete; the gradation of sins appeared in the tariff of penance attached to each sin. Since this practice looked more to sin and satisfaction in view of the objective transgression than to subjective guilt, there was no need to deepen the question about the borderline between mortal sin and venial sin. Everyone could know the catalogue of those grave sins that had to be submitted to the priest in sacramental confession, whether mortal or not.

When, during the eighth and ninth centuries, the Irish-Scottish version of the sacrament of penance was adopted over most of the continent, there was a growing concern for internalization, a trend already quite evident in the theological renaissance at the time of Charlemagne. Later, Abelard emerged as one of the strong voices opposing the mere external, quantitative measurement of sin and penitential work.

As time went on, the call for conversion of the heart was being made more and more in theological works on penance, while the practice of imposing objectively determined penances remained still widespread. The vision of great theologians, like Thomas Aquinas and Bonaventure, and many others who emphasized the fundamental option of the heart, was in strong competition with the approach of canonists and other church-

men who were more concerned for precise external control
than for discernment about profound attitudes in people's
hearts.

The decrees of the Council of Trent on justification and
the sacrament of penance [21] reflect the best theological
endeavours and keep, as the main perspective, conversion by a
deepened faith: the basic or first conversion from total alienation
that corresponds to the "first justification", and then the
ongoing conversion corresponding to the "second justification".
The Council of Trent gave theology all chances for a healthy
development. However, under the impact of legalism, rigorism,
and later of Jansenism, and the influence of the empirical
sciences with quantification as a primary means of objectivation,
the moralists of the seventeenth and eighteenth centuries
yielded all too often to quantitative and merely objective
determination.[22]

Awareness of this rather recent and historically conditioned
development affords greater liberty for changing the latest
tradition. Even among the more conservative moralists of the
past century, a protest against the all too quantitative considerations was not uncommon.

A quantitative approach never came to the mind of the
great medieval theologians. Since they approached the problem
from the viewpoint of God, it would have been a perfect
absurdity for them to assert that God takes his will and his
commandments seriously only up to a certain point.

Arthur Landgraf, who has made a major contribution to the
investigation of the history about venial sin, is convinced that,
after St. Bernard, "perhaps no Scholastic has ever dared to
doubt the principle that everything that is against God's commandments is a grave sin".[23] The Scholastics insisted that the
fully free and deliberate refusal of one commandment in any
quantity means, on principle, a total refusal of God's will.
However, insofar as they did not fully realize all the dimensions
of man's imperfection, their own principle caused them great
difficulty in explaining the possibility of venial sin. Some followed
Scotus by teaching that venial sin is possible only as neglect
of a counsel, while the transgression of a commandment is
always a mortal sin. But none of the great Scholastic theo-

logians of the middle ages drew the conclusion that later characterized the theology of the rigorists and of John Calvin, who taught that "every sin is mortal because it is a rebellion against God's will which necessarily provokes his wrath".[24]

The main intention of the medieval theologians and of Calvin was to inculcate the teaching that God's will has to be accepted integrally, and everyone has to strive, with all the energies of heart and mind, towards total conversion. But as soon as quantitative thinking came into the game, a legalistic rigorism distorted the theological insights.

A Catholic contemporary of Calvin, Johannes Major, taught that theft of one to five ears of grain from a rich man's harvest was no sin; theft of from six to ten ears was a venial sin, and theft beyond eleven ears made it a mortal sin.[25] A number of moralists tried to explain how the smallest quantitative difference could make an absolute qualitative difference between mortal and venial sin. The example of Claudius La Croix[26] was often used; he explained that one more drop of alcoholic beverage could make a man drunk and thus make him guilty of mortal sin. Thus mathematics prevailed over knowledge of man in his greatness and in his weakness.

The point of departure for my own reflection is the same as that of the great Scholastics: God's will must be accepted in its totality. However, we know more today about human imperfection and about developmental psychology. Not every human act and action expresses the person in his totality. Mortal sin is a fundamental option that happens only where a sinful decision arises from the depth of consciousness and freedom or reaches into that depth and thus reveals the person's fully accountable misuse of the liberty. In the fundamental option, a person expresses and determines himself in his basic existence.[27]

This approach in no way negates the importance of the object of the act or the gravity of the matter; but gravity or relevance assumes moral meaning only in proportion to the actual development of a person's knowledge and freedom, and to the extent that the deep self-determination that we call fundamental option can be evoked.

However, there is no possibility whatsoever of giving a

general quantitative and exact determination of where mortal sin begins and venial sin ends, because of the great diversity of psychological endowment and moral and religious giftedness of persons, and the great diversity of environment.

This solution to the crucial problem of the ultimate reason for the possibility of venial sin is a pastoral one. It is an urgent appeal to accept fully the law of grace in which one's own talents and charisms meet the present opportunities and the needs of others. A Christian should never yield to the temptation to make a kind of mathematical calculation about the upper and lower limit of God's will in order to remain "safe" from mortal sin.

This approach must be completed by a moral teaching that sensitizes people to their responsibility, and by a better knowledge of psychology. Although it is characterized by the radicalness of the call to conversion, it should not lead to rigorism, since we always have to take into account the graduality of the human person's growth and the manifold influences that explain why many sinful acts do not arise from the inner depths in which the fundamental decisions of life are made.

A better understanding of the fundamental option in the light of the behavioural sciences will also prevent us from easily talking about mortal sins of pre-adolescents or even of seven or eight-year-old children. Canon 906 of the Code of Canon Law seems to suggest that children, from the moment they come to the age of discernment, can commit mortal sin, since they come under the obligation to confess annually, in the sense of canon 901, which binds in strict obligation only those who are conscious of having committed mortal sin.

But what image of God do we present if speak of "mortal sins" of children deserving eternal damnation from an all-merciful and all-holy God, although not even the most totalitarian type of civil government would intimate that children of seven or ten years of age can commit a crime deserving the death penalty or life-long imprisonment? Do we not risk becoming the "scandalizers" of children whom Christ condemned so forcefully? However, we have also to be reminded that venial sin is not to be identified with "not serious". Developmental psychology also tells us about the great importance of childhood and youth for growth towards maturity of conscience.

4. *Formulations of preconciliar catechisms*

The various catechisms used before the Second Vatican Council have almost identical formulations for determining when a person commits a mortal sin: When he transgresses the law of God in a grave matter, with full knowledge (deliberation) and full freedom of will, his sin is mortal. If he transgresses the law of God in a matter considered relatively unimportant, but also if he transgresses it in a grave matter but without full knowledge and freedom of will, he commits only a venial sin.[28]

Evidently, these formulations insinuate that an accurate line can be drawn quantitatively, separating grave from unimportant or less serious matter. The formula ignores problems of how a small quantitative difference can account for the total qualitative difference between mortal and venial sin. There is no indication of a synthesis of how the two elements make venial sin possible: how the object of the act and the imperfection of the act itself are related to each other. There is no consideration of the psychological or cultural development of the person. Hence the formula can invite either laxism or excessive rigorism. Those who have received five talents from the Lord can then, without scruple, hide four of them in the earth, as long as they have fulfilled the minimum law, while those who have received less than one talent, and are therefore less able to cope with a fixed line of demarcation between mortal and venial sin, can only fall into despair.

The catechisms fail to alert their readers to the danger of misunderstanding. They provide a thousand excuses for those who take the words literally. Where do we find perfect knowledge, perfect deliberation, perfect liberty? The least we can expect from a catechism is a more careful formulation about *proportionate* knowledge, *proportionate* deliberation and freedom: that is, the degree of knowledge and freedom that is commensurate with the penalty of mortal sin, eternal damnation. But this problem is left out because the formulation is made on the level of "knowledge of control". Thus deeper knowledge, the knowledge of salvation, is left out in all the aspects that are not accessible to human control.

5. *Mortal sin — ex toto genere suo*

As soon as a quantitative determination of the borderline between mortal and venial sin is established, there arises the question of whether this type of determination applies to all areas of values, duties and virtues. In other words, are there certain areas which do not allow parvity (smallness) of matter? Many, but not all, moralists of the past centuries taught that there are some areas where the presumption is always that transgressing the law or a virtue even in the smallest degree should be considered as mortal sin. This is what was meant by the expression *"mortal sin — ex toto genere suo"*, that is "deadly in all degrees and dimensions".

At a time when absolutist monarchs and Church authorities were extremely concerned with the control of orthodoxy by formulations, and with total submission of the faithful, many moralists asserted that the smallest doubt in matters concerning orthodox formulations, whether in thought or word or in superstitious practices, had to be a mortal sin. At the same time, they allowed a quantitative measurement of transgression in matters of God's main commandments of mercy, justice, peace, and respect for every person's dignity.

As we have seen, any quantitative measurement of sin is de-personalizing and, in today's milieu, unacceptable. With Marxist collectivism seeking to guarantee uniformity by imposition of the same quantitative measurements on all, and exercising frustrating controls in favour of the party line, religious people are all the more allergic to any mathematical approach in moral and religious questions.

A teaching in which a small quantitative difference in the amount of disorder would explain the absolutely qualitative difference between hell and purgatory gives a distorted image of God and can become a real temptation against faith. Fortunately, contemporary moral theology is making a concerted effort to revise traditional categories which led to the idea that in some fields of morality every fault would be a mortal sin while in other fields mortal sin would begin only at a certain well-defined point of disorder.

Sensible moralists have always realized that their categories regarding gravity of matter can serve only as a rule of thumb. They could be understood as a form of warning, "Danger". But they become senseless if they are used as criteria by a confessor-judge who wants to control the consciences of the faithful in accordance with these determinations of borderline. While a prophetic warning makes sense if it includes all important values, duties and virtues, and especially social justice, peace and healing forgiveness, it cannot move modern man if it is restricted to matters only of orthodoxy and the sixth commandment.

Furthermore, one can speak and warn prophetically only if one has a knowledge of historical humanity, of actual life situations, and is able to read the signs of the times. A moral theology that wants to stimulate conversion and shake the superficial conscience has no place for abstract classification, precise measurements of personal guilt, or for that rigorism that suspects mortal sin everywhere in some fields. In this regard, it is interesting to discover from scholarly studies that the traditional concept of mortal sin *"ex toto genere suo"* has, in the past, often changed its meaning, and does not fall within a commonly established tradition.[29]

6. *Is every sin against the sixth commandment mortal?*

During the last centuries, the faithful were particularly troubled by the specific emphasis given by many moralists and by the Roman Universal Inquisition who taught that all sins in thought, desire and deeds against the sixth commandment are *ex toto genere suo* mortal sins. The reasons and motives behind such an assertion were quite varied.

One of the principal reasons was that chastity was thoroughly related to the sanctity of human life. It was the conviction of Thomas Aquinas and of many moralists of past centuries that man's sperm was "something divine because it is potentially a human person".[30] The result was, for them, that each sin of lechery is similar to murder since "it is an attack on potential human life because of a disorder concerning the act of human procreation".[31] On the pastoral level, the doctrine was 'intended as a pedagogical warning that whenever man, with full advertence and freedom, selfishly seeks sexual or sensual pleasure, he makes himself liable to all the temptations and disorders that might follow, if he keeps such deliberate intentions.

The very careful study by Kleiber gives sufficient evidence that this doctrine took on different meanings and often met with strong opposition from theologians in good ecclesial standing. It is, therefore, impossible to claim a common doctrine or an established tradition. However, in its declaration of January 15, 1976, on matters concerning sexual morality, the Congregation for the Doctrine of Faith not only confirmed this rigoristic tradition but even added a new dimension by teaching that no parvity of matter can be admitted not only objectively but also that everyone has to presume that subjectively, too, a mortal sin is given unless there are particular signs to the contrary.[32]

What is more important in this field is the authority of good reasoning, good argument and pastoral sensitivity. Today's moral theologians concur more and more on the thesis that the sixth commandment is subject to exactly the same norms as other commandments. In biblical perspective, it is not possible to accept the relative smallness (levity) of matter with respect to fraternal love, justice and peace, while asserting in matters of chastity that everything is mortal.

A common effort on how to resolve this problem goes in two different directions coming, however, to almost identical conclusions.

(1) One direction is to take as starting point the medieval doctrine that taught that every perfectly deliberate and free act against any of God's commandments is, on principle, mortal sin, and can become venial solely because of the imperfection of the act. Then we apply this same principle in the same way to all fields of morality including, of course, the sixth commandment. We have to warn that nobody can stubbornly transgress any of God's commandments at any time without danger of mortal sin. But, then, we should be aware that we speak of acts that have fully that character of free and deliberate decision that meets the condition of a fundamental option. For the person

who earnestly seeks God as his ultimate goal there is no presumption of having committed a mortal sin as long as the
profound disposition of good will abides. Individual acts may
be grave or serious, but they are most probably not mortal
in the case of a person who is struggling to overcome a habit
and soon or almost immediately after the sin repents seriously.
In matters of chastity, too, particular attention should be given
to the over-all direction. Is it one of growth or of increasing
carelessness?

Psychology makes it impossible for us to admit the "presumption" that the average Christian commits a mortal sin
even if it is only a matter of *delectatio morosa* (pleasureful
thinking about sexual things) or, a matter of excessive sensual
pleasure when spouses or fiancés exchange kisses and so on.
Against rigorism it must be repeated that the presumption is
rather that mortal sin is not committed as long as persons
are striving for chastity as they, with good will, understand it.

(2) The approach of most of the traditional manuals was to
take as starting point the distinction between grave and
relatively small matter. Although we assert that the possibility
of committing venial sins, while transgressing a commandment
of God, comes simply from the imperfection of the act, we can
accept the distinction between small and grave matter somehow
as a rule of thumb. But then it seems to be wise to accept it
in the sixth commandment as well as in the others. But we
speak on *relatively* small matter, that is, we see everything in
relation to the psychological and spiritual development of the
person and insist on the necessity to grow. Therefore what at
one time might be experienced as relatively small matter will
be taken much more seriously after further conversion and
growth.

On the practical level the results might be similar in spite
of the different points of departure. Whatever may be the failure
to actualize his freedom in decisions about matters that seem
to him less relevant, the conclusion is that if this person, who
generally displays good will, has not acted with malice and
a stubborn bad purpose, although he has partially yielded to
temptation but not to the point of offending God through
relatively serious external acts, he can always abide in the hope

that he has not commited a mortal sin. However, nobody should think that any sin would be considered as not serious. Everyone has to strive constantly to live perfectly on the level of the normative Christian ideals.

It would be a serious misunderstanding to think that this approach minimizes the importance of chastity. On the contrary, our concern is for a fully Christian commitment to all of God's commandments. With reference to sexual education, the rigorism that compels people to think again and again over their past, wondering whether they have committed a mortal sin, heightens the very danger it tries to combat. It can be a source of obsession, constant temptation, and can lead to diminution of freedom.

Moral teaching must always maintain a pedagogical orientation. A constructive approach that leads to serenity and peace of mind is much more conducive to chastity than rigorism excessively inclined to judge as mortal each sin of weakness against chastity. If everything is declared to be mortal sin, many will lose heart or will think, "Why should I not go further if I have already committed a mortal sin?"

IV. CAN MAN-MADE LAWS BE IMPOSED UNDER SANCTION OF MORTAL SIN?

Most of the sins of which the average preconciliar Catholic accused himself in devotional confession were sins against the laws of the Church rather than against fraternal love, justice, peace and healing forgiveness. At this juncture of Church history, in view of the renewed self-understanding of our Church, we cannot avoid another thorny problem: Can the Church impose, under pain of mortal sin, something that is not demanded by the Gospel or by the law that God has written into man's heart? This question needs to be considered in the broader context of whether man-made laws, as such, can oblige conscience, and under what conditions.

1. *Authority at the service of conscience*

The right exercise of human authority, whether by parents, secular society or by the Church, has to do with the Gospel law and natural law. It becomes a moral factor, however, only when directives, orders, laws and precepts, through their very values, can appeal to the moral conscience. The transgression of a human precept or a man-made law can be morally culpable only when the intrinsic malice of the transgression is recognized at least by implication. If children are deeply convinced that their parents are good and what they ask is good then the children will feel obliged in conscience to respond by loving obedience.

The just laws of the state protect the freedom of all, the right of all persons to the development of freedom and all the other basic rights against arbitrariness and abuses of freedom by individuals and groups. However, we are faced with the sad reality that all too often the exercise of human authority does not promote moral health. Indeed, it frequently becomes a deterrent to moral development. This is the case when exercise of authority is a demonstration of power, control for control's sake, or manifestation of a domineering attitude. The situation becomes worse when those who abuse authority and impose unjust laws attempt to manipulate the consciences of their subjects by hypocritical appeals to moral motives, even to the point of bringing into play a threat of sanctions for the life to come.

2. *Risk of alienation of conscience*

Depth psychology has provided evidence that many neuroses, especially in the form of guilt complexes, have their origin in infancy through the child's fear about being punished but most of all through fear of losing his parents' love. Such a guilt complex is one of the main obstacles hindering people from coming to authentic faith and trust in a God who is love.

In an era characterized by atheism and a serious crisis of faith, which is frequently linked to the authority crisis, the Church has to ponder these things very carefully. One of her first tasks is to examine the question of her right to impose her own laws under grave sanctions, including the sanction of mortal sin.

The Constantinian era brought in its wake countless temptations to use religious sanctions and threats of eternal punishment to enforce laws that served neither the Gospel nor the development of the human person. Many of these laws were geared to the temporal power of the Church and her alliance with the mighty. Perhaps the greatest culprits were the moralists of the past few centuries who so often and easily decided upon the sanction of mortal sin for Church laws that had little or no relevance to adoration of God in spirit and truth or to justice and peace.

Under pain of mortal sin, many things came to be imposed: absolute regular attendance at Mass on Sundays and prescribed feast days, abstinence from meat on Fridays and during the Lenten season, Eucharistic fasts from midnight so strict that some moralists dared to say that a person who had taken a drop of water or who had not spit out a snowflake or a tear rolling down the cheek would commit a mortal sin if he broke the law of the Church by receiving communion. Liturgical celebrations themselves were surrounded by hundreds of laws and rubrics, and moralists considered most of them binding under pain of mortal sin. Some moralists also contrived the doctrine that omitting a very small part of the Breviary would entail mortal sin; some insisted that this was the case even if the neglect came only from human weakness with no malice involved.

Karl Rahner expresses well the reaction of modern man when he asks, "Who today would dare to attribute so easily to ecclesiastical precepts, even down to trivia, the character of an obligation under pain of mortal sin?" [33]

A number of moralists even asserted that the Church, through a positive disposition, can impose under pain of mortal sin what, by itself, would bind only under venial sin.[34] The surprising fact is, however, that none of these theologians has ever questioned himself about the kind of image of the Church, and especially of God, such an opinion reflected. We simply ask: By what authority can the Church, sacrament of salvation, make such declarations adding such sanctions as "under pain of mortal sin?"

3. *Towards a solution*

We are far from having solved all problems. A number of hard questions remain open. However, I dare offer some points of departure:

(1) No man-made law can hold power to oblige conscience if it is arbitrary. It can bind only by its service to the common good, to justice and peace, and to the development and responsibility of the human person.

(2) All positive dispositions of the Church must be thoroughly subordinated to her mission to educate consciences and to call to conversion. All her positive laws must be at the service of the "law of grace", the "law of faith". The laws of the Church that go beyond the Gospel and the law of God written in man's heart and mind must be at least a response to the signs of the times and, therefore, cannot bind the conscience beyond the particular historic context which made them necessary or useful.

(3) Positive laws of the Church must never unduly generalize or be imposed on people of vastly different cultures or social conditions unless it is truly something that is necessary for the good of all these people.

(4) In a critical age, the laws of the Church become more effective through convincing arguments that show their necessity or genuine utility rather than through sanction. Not only can obligation under sin, and especially under pain of mortal sin, arise only from the urgency and importance of the law itself and never from the mere will of the legislator, but this urgency and relevance must be made clear not so much by sanction as by insight. Exaggerated sanctions and threats of punishment appeal merely to the superego and pervert its dynamics.

(5) In my opinion, the Church should never impose any man-made law under threat of mortal sin, which means threat of eternal condemnation. The reason is that I cannot think of any positive disposition that is neither part of the Gospel nor of natural law yet could be so important as to be proportionate to the threat of eternal punishment.

There is no doubt that the Church has to be faithful to the teaching of Christ who also sometimes warned people about the danger of eternal damnation; but the actual problem is how we can speak convincingly of this truth to modern people who are aware of the enormous exaggerations of moralists and priests who have multiplied the threats of mortal sin with regard to trivia.

Surely, today's people will ask how a positive law, which cannot be presented as an exigency of the Gospel or of man's own nature, or as a response to the most urgent signs of the times, can ever have such urgency as to justify "capital punishment" in the terrifying sense of eternal rejection in hell. I am not speaking of contempt or rebellion against authority which is instituted by God, for such a revolt would mean rebelling against an essential part of the Gospel; but if an immoderate protest against officials is provoked by intolerable exaggerations, by misuse of authority, then the sin of those who provoke such a rebellion may be much greater than that of those who suffer psychologically from the oppressive tactics.

(6) The sanction *"sub gravi"* added to a disposition of the Church can mean simply that it is an important matter and that those who did not obey might expose themselves to serious danger of offending God gravely. That can traditionally mean a grave venial sin which always entails the risk of being on the slippery road towards mortal sin.

No doubt the Church can alert the faithful to the fact that refusal to observe very important positive dispositions can constitute a great danger to the development of Christian freedom and to the necessary solidarity of salvation. But a late tradition, followed by many manuals, understood *"sub gravi"* as a direct statement that transgression of such a law would be punished by God with eternal damnation. If a warning has to be given, let it be in respect for God, in full knowledge that God does not take orders from man. Furthermore, it must always be evident that the warning arises from the very justice and importance of the law and not from arbitrary exaggerations.

4. Some classical examples

The approach to this problem is best clarified by some examples. I choose three that are important in themselves.

a) Penitential works

Penance, in the broadest sense, is an absolute exigency of the Gospel for anyone who has alienated himself from God; and, equally, the urgency of continuous conversion for all of us must be asserted if we are in state of grace. It also entails the readiness to atone for one's own sins and to rid oneself of all forms of personal and group egotism. Understood in this way, penance is surely obligatory in the most serious sense.

A totally different question is how certain penitential works prescribed by the Church can oblige under pain of mortal sin. In the first part of the Constitution *Poenitemini*, Paul VI emphasizes penance in a way that practically coincides with the conversion demanded by the Gospel.[35] The Pope has the whole tradition of the Church behind him when, in this matter, he teaches that "all the faithful are obliged by God's own law to do penance".[36] In the second part, the Constitution specifies, with great moderation, a few common celebrations of penance and a few penitential works. Great freedom is given to the Bishops' Conferences to specify the penances in such a way that they can become a call for charity, and for penance insofar as it fosters fraternal love and justice. About the celebrations and penitential works it is then said, "the essential observance of them obliges gravely *(sub gravi)*".

The Church has to determine concrete, tangible forms and certain times in order to call Christians regularly to conversion and reflection on the purpose and expression of penance. The words of the Constitution on the grave obligations of substantial observance can be understood as a serious warning that those who are totally unwilling to accept this invitation of the Church to do penance expose themselves to a great danger of neglecting altogether the call of the Gospel to penance, that is, to conversion.

While a meticulous observance of small penitential rituals and works can be an immense evasion, indeed an alienation, the real aim of the Apostolic Constitution is an incarnate preaching in which penitential rituals and works become only symbols, although real symbols, of the call to total conversion. Those who accept this meaning will also give attention to the pedagogical effort of the Church.

b) The priestly prayer and prayers

By God's calling and grace, the Church is a "house of prayer" (cf. Is 56:7). To educate all the faithful, and particularly priests and religious, to a profound life of prayer constitutes one of the most fundamental tasks of the Church. Therefore she has an obligation to guarantee, in a concrete way, the continuity of prayer and the necessary means for all to learn how to pray better, how to remain faithful, and to give each other mutual support. The Church's law relating to the Divine Office is consequently no mere advice with no obligation; it is a law that truly binds conscience.

To learn how to pray, and to help one another in the life of prayer in order to transform all life into adoration of God in spirit and truth, is a matter of life and death for the whole Church — for each of the faithful and, in a very special way, for priests and religious because of their vocation and particular charism for prayer.

Meticulous casuistry about the portion of the Divine Office which would oblige under pain of mortal sin can only obscure the evangelical call to a life of prayer and give rise to either minimalism or over-scrupulosity, both of which are enemies of true prayer. It would be an insult to the Church to claim that the Church wants God to condemn each priest to hell who, instead of reciting the Breviary, alone and with others is seeking a way of prayer and meditation that helps him towards greater spiritual growth and solidarity in Christ. It should always be self-evident that the Church seeks primarily to be helpful on the road to salvation. The law is for a life of prayer, not prayer for the sake of the law.

c) Regular attendance at Mass

The most delicate example relates to the obligation to attend Mass regularly on Sundays and prescribed feast days. Here again, it is above all a problem of pedagogy. One cannot doubt the centrality of the Eucharist for the whole life of the Church. However, the Church would fail greatly if she were to present the Eucharist primarily as a law surrounded by threats of brimstone and fire. The Eucharist is grace, a great gift of God, and, the Church, therefore, rightly prescribes regular attendance at Mass each Sunday and feast day unless a proportionate reason excuses the individual. But since the *absolute* regularity is by no means a divine law, it seems out of proportion to threaten eternal damnation each time someone exceptionally neglects

Mass. This proportion is particularly shocking if the celebration of the Eucharist in the parish is not at all attractive.

I consider it reasonable to speak of grave obligation in the matter of attendance at Sunday Mass but not in the sense of "under pain of mortal sin". Eternal rejection by God seems to be out of proportion to the occasional neglect when it is not a case of obstinate bad will but only a sign of human weakness or even superficiality.

According to Georg Troxler,[37] St. Anthony of Florence (died 1459) was the first to assert that the absolute regularity to attend Mass each Sunday obliges "*sub gravi*". There is reason to think that, like so many others, he understood "*sub gravi*" as a warning about grave danger rather than in the sense of "under pain of mortal sin". One of the leading theologians of the Council of Trent, Melchior Cano, still sharply distinguished "*sub gravi*" from "under pain of mortal sin". For instance, when he explained that a person who has committed a mortal sin and then has received holy communion after an act of sorrow, while postponing confession through negligence, does sin very gravely but does not commit a mortal sin.[38] Troxler also tells us that before the new Code of Canon Law (1917), canon 1248, there was never such a law given for the universal Church, stating that absolutely regular attendance at Mass obliges under pain of mortal sin. I think that even canon 1248 allows a more nuanced interpretation.

V. THE EMBODIED GOSPEL OF CONVERSION

Christ, true Son of God and true Son of Man is the Living Gospel, the Sacrament of conversion, the Liberator from sin, the source of renewed freedom. He is the Prophet who not only unmasks our alienation but leads us to the homeland of truth and reconciliation. He is the Covenant, the embodiment of saving solidarity, the only Way to freedom from the solidarity of sin. Christ has sent the Holy Spirit to renew the hearts of people and the face of the earth, to bring forth a new creation.

1. *Christ, the original Sacrament of conversion*

Christ symbolizes and brings forth the reality of conversion.

He is the One who comes from the Father and returns to the Father. He brings to humankind the salvific experience of God's nearness, and calls all to turn to God and thus to return to the Father with him, in him and through him. The Paschal Mystery is not only the source of salvation; it also symbolizes in the most realistic way the content and the way of conversion: victory over sin and total dedication to the will of the Father.

The oldest programmatic summary of Christ's activity presents him as the herald of the Good News of conversion. "Jesus came into Galilee proclaiming the Good News coming from God: 'The time of favour has come; the kingdom of God is upon you; be converted and believe the Gospel' " (Mk 1:14-15).

Jesus refers to the "time of favour" announced by the prophets, the time in which he would bring forth a new covenant and give his people a new heart and a new spirit. It is the coming of God's kingdom: God guiding us by his own Spirit and by the many signs of his love, and uniting people in the kingdom of justice and peace. All this is God's unsolicited and loving initiative. From the indicative of God's deed arises the urgent invitation, "Be converted by putting your faith in the Gospel" (Mk 1:15). Conversion is made possible, and therefore it is made mandatory. It is not just an intellectual or moral conversion. Its main content is faith as joyous, grateful and humble acceptance of him who is the Truth, the Way and the Life.

Faith is a total life response, dedication to Christ, patterned according to the Paschal Mystery. Faith is love of Jesus who, by his infinite, all-embracing love has conquered sin. It is grateful allegiance to him who leads us to the Father. Conversion in the light of the Paschal Mystery and the whole Gospel of Jesus Christ means, above all, a total turning away from sin, selfishness, arrogance, pride, alienation: a turn to God who has turned his countenance to us.

The Greek expression for conversion is *metanoia*. It includes repentance, deep sorrow for sins. However, the essential meaning is a new relationship with God, a homecoming, a being-at-home with him who is Emmanuel, "God-with-us". The New Testament's words on conversion are in continuity with the Old Testament, where God promises that the people will return to their country when they turn to him. ("Turn", *shub*, is used 1059 times in the Old Testament). [39]

At the very heart of conversion is faith in Jesus and trust in him who is our hope. But it is more than a vague trust that he will save our souls; it is total dedication to him who is the Truth. Therefore it implies a total "yes" to the truth and the way he teaches us. For us, faith is knowing him with a grateful, loving heart, entrusting ourselves to him who is the Way, the One who guides us.

Conversion involves the whole human being in all his fundamental relations. It is total response to God's call, a fundamental decision.[80] We have seen earlier that conscience spells out a profound longing for wholeness and integrity. The fundamental option, if it is a mature option for God and good, is the road to wholeness. A conversion to the Gospel in living faith is much more than conversion to discrete commandments and even much more than acceptance of a complete code of morality. It is a rebirth to new life, to fullness of life in Christ Jesus; it is insertion into the stream of his love for all humankind and union with his love for the Father.

The focal point of a Christian conversion is always Christ. There is a burning desire to know him in all his relationships, to follow him who is the Lord and Saviour of the world. Christian conversion is, therefore, thoroughly different from the withdrawal of members of the Qumran sect who separated themselves from the masses which they labelled as treacherous, hopeless people. Whoever is converted to Christ is inserted into his kingdom, into his boundless love and concern.[41]

Whoever is converted to Christ knows that he is accepted without any merit of his own. Christ died for sinners, and the convert will humbly follow him in his attitude towards sinners. This will always be an act of thanksgiving. The true convert is with and in Jesus Christ, a living sign and part of the kingdom of God, a kingdom of mercy, of justice and peace.

Conversion is the liberation from the sin of non-involvement and sloth. Whoever knows the merciful Samaritan and is converted to him will not follow the example of the priests and levites whose sin is non-involvement in the needs of the wounded, the victim.

Conversion to Christ is, for his disciples, a share in his creative liberty and fidelity, a role as co-actor in his ongoing work of redemption and liberation.

2. Christ the Prophet — Liberation from alienation

The prophets never taught abstract doctrines. They were called always to preach conversion, and for that purpose they unmasked sin in the light of divine goodness and justice. "Hear, O Heaven, and listen, O Earth, for the Lord speaks; sons have I raised and reared, but they have disowned me" (Is 1:2). The prophets speak not so much of the sins of humble people as against the sins of kings and priests. They do not allow any privatizing of the concepts of sin and conversion. They call for the conversion of each individual in the depth of his heart but at the same time also for renewal of the mores and for change of authority structures.[42]

The kings' priests did not like to listen to the prophets. "To Amos, Amasiah said, 'Off with you, visionary, flee to the land of Judah. There earn your bread by prophesying but never again prophesy in Bethel; for it is the king's sanctuary and a royal temple'. Amos answered Amasiah, 'I was no prophet nor have I belonged to a company of prophets; I was a shepherd and dresser of sycamores. The Lord took me from minding the flock and said to me, 'Go, prophesy to my people Israel'." (Amos 7:12-15).

The prophets unmask the very sinfulness of the concept of sin, the evasion into ritualistic over-scrupulosity and all the catalogues of sins which hide the unwillingness to show mercy and to do justice. Above all they proclaim God's sovereignty and his saving action, so that no one can be excused if he does not respond to the call for conversion.

The latest and last of the prophets to prepare for the coming of Christ is John the Baptist. Not only does he, like all the prophets, preach a total change of life, allowing no ritualistic evasion, but he links his call to conversion with the imminent coming of the kingdom of God.

Christ is the Prophet. In him the kingdom of God is visible. With him, the "end of the times", the "favoured moment" has come. All of Jesus' sermons prophetically resound the call to make wise use of the time of favour. He urgently demands conversion and acceptance in faith of the message of salvation. Faced with him, his listeners and the people as a whole have to make a clear decision. "If anyone hears my words and pays no regard to them, I am not his judge; I have not come to judge the world but to save the world. There is a judge for the man who rejects me and does not accept my words; the word that I spoke will be his judge on the last day" (Jn 12:47-48).

Christ scolds the sins of the self-righteous, of the hypocrites, of those who use religion for their self-exaltation. "The righteous persons 'who need no repentance' (Lk 15:7) are, we think, those whose righteousness is false, the Pharisees, since in the Gospel perspective every man is in need of conversion".[43]

Christ the Prophet calls for purity of heart in a way that outlaws all the temptations to privatize religion and conversion. Conversion to the kingdom of God, made visible in Christ and made possible through the outpouring of the Holy Spirit, is a call to absolute truthfulness and to liberation from all forms of alienation.[44] The kingdom of God allows no separation between individual conversion and common effort to free ourselves from all the alienations in the forms of worship, of devotions, of the presentation of doctrines, of canon law and secular law and their heartless application, of perversion of authority, of depletion and abuse of the environment. If we receive Christ as the redeemer of the world, we have to face truthfully all the dimensions of alienation that have to be eliminated. We can do so because there is redemption for the world if we turn to Christ the Prophet.[45]

3. Christ, the One who reconciles

Our conversion is to be seen wholly in the light of God's own initiative. It is acceptance of the reconciliation wrought by God himself through Jesus Christ and by the promptings of the Holy Spirit. This is the "new creation". "When anyone is united to Christ, there is a new creation; the old order has gone, and a new order has already begun. From first to last this has been the work of God. He has reconciled us people to himself through Christ, and he has enlisted us in this service of reconciliation. What I mean is that God was in Christ reconciling the world to himself, no longer holding peoples' misdeeds against them, and that he has entrusted us with the message of reconciliation" (2 Cor 5:17-19).

Since this new creation is God's unsolicited initiative, it can be received by us only in never-ending gratitude. Where there is no gratitude the gift is lost and God's generosity is dishonoured. This joy and gratitude create the energies to live on the level of reconciliation.

The "new creation" which Paul calls reconciliation means, above all, a new kind of relationship. In grateful faith we know that God accepts us and comes to meet us where we are in order to lead us to where he wants us to go: to his kingdom of love and justice. In grateful praise for his reconciling action, we can accept ourselves, discover our inner powers that come from him, and cope with our shades. Being thus accepted and able to accept ourselves, we no longer consider relationships with our fellowmen as a threat but, rather, as a gift of God. Then diversity will no longer mean opposition but complementarity. Those who are truly reconciled will work together for the kingdom of God.[46]

It is important to see reconciliation as the creative initiative of God. This enables us to give a creative response and to accept faithfully our responsibilities for the reconciliation of our world, to be ambassadors of peace on all levels and in all dimensions.

4. "Your Holy Spirit come upon us and cleanse us"

In ancient manuscripts of Luke 11:2, the petition "Thy kingdom come" is replaced or paraphrased by the prayer, "Your Holy Spirit come upon us and cleanse us". Reconciliation and conversion are the work of the Holy Spirit who gives us a "new heart" without which new relationships would not be posssible. The promptings of the Spirit enable us to carry on the ongoing conversion unto the total purification of heart, mind and will.

Christ brings the great messianic prophecies to fulfilment by sending us the Holy Spirit from the Father. "I will sprinkle clean water upon you to cleanse you from all impurities, and from all your idols I will cleanse you. I will give a new heart and place a new spirit within you, taking from your bodies your stony hearts and giving you sensitive hearts. I will put my own spirit within you" (Ez 36:25-27; cf. Jer 31:31-33; Heb 8:7-12; 10:16).

The coming of the Holy Spirit is the sign of the eschatological age and the most urgent calling to radical change, radical purification, and return to God. From beginning to end, everything is the work of the Holy Spirit, but these promptings enable and require our creative and faithful cooperation.

Paul describes the life of the convert as an ongoing battle between the Spirit who justifies us and the selfish self which is always in alliance with the selfish world around us. "If you are guided by the Spirit, you will not fulfil the desires of your selfish nature. That selfish self sets its desires against the Spirit while the Spirit fights against it. They are in conflict with one another, so that what you will to do you cannot do. But if you are led by the Spirit you are no longer under law" (Gal 5:16-18).

Only by trusting in the Holy Spirit and being docile to his promptings can we live the ongoing conversion that conforms us every day more with the crucified and risen Christ. "Those who belong to Christ Jesus have crucified their selfish self (*sarx*) with its passions and desires. If the Spirit is the source of our life, let the Spirit also direct our course" (Gal 5:24-25).[47]

5. Christ, liberator from sin-solidarity

A merely or mainly individualistic approach will never grasp the mystery of redemption and of original sin. Conversion must be individual and at the same time corporate. We are redeemed by a unique person, Jesus Christ. But he also embodies a saving solidarity, a covenant solidarity in which he manifests the saving justice of the one God and Father of all. Hence the doctrine of sin and conversion must be presented in the perspective of the covenant and never in that of a mere defence morality.

Theologically, there is no possibility of presenting a treatise on original sin outside that on redemption and saving solidarity. It is unthinkable for Christians that God, Father of our Lord Jesus Christ, would ever have submitted humankind to solidarity in perdition without offering a stronger power of salvation in solidarity.

If we were to review mainly the sinfulness of our own heart, the memory of our past sins and, at the same time, all the dark powers in the world around us, we would be needlessly discouraged. But all Christian morality, and especially the call and grace of conversion, reaches us in Jesus Christ who is "the covenant and the law".[48] Nobody can know Christ truly as his Saviour unless he knows him as Saviour of the whole world, the Saviour from sin-solidarity.

In the last fifteen years, a great and concerted effort has been made by biblical, dogmatic, moral and pastoral theology to liberate the treatise on original sin from its abstract and sometimes archaic formulations. The result by no means minimizes original sin. On the contrary, it becomes a much greater challenge to total conversion and renewal. There is a new convergence or a consensus in theology regarding original sin in the light of Christ the New Covenant and Saviour of the world.[49]

Theology has to discern painstakingly between the abiding message of the Scriptures and a time-bound world-view. The inspired writers have approached the question of how sin came into the world, which was a good creation of God, and how it can sometimes gain so much power. The various writers approached the question from different angles. It seems that a careful analysis of the Old Testament allows the conclusion that the main intention of the first ten chapters of Genesis is to portray the unity and the solidarity in freedom of humankind, and not so much a historical Adam.

. We are faced with an inherited sin-tradition (Rom 5:12-21) and with a collective power of sin, called by St. John the "sin of the world" (Jn 1:29; cf. 1 Jn 2:16). Doubtless, the biblical message strengthens our conviction that sin began with a free act: there was a first man (Adam) and a first woman (Eve) who failed to do the good they could have done, or did the evil they could have avoided. But we all are Adam and Eve whenever we fail to do the good we ought to do and do the evil we could avoid. As the first sin had its impact on all humankind, so also our sin is never our own private matter. In all that we do, good or evil, there is always operative a collective responsibility for either good or evil.

To explain the solidarity of all humankind in good and evil, it is not absolutely necessary to recur to monogenism. Rather, we look to monotheism, since the one God, the Creator and

Father of all, has called us into being. He calls us by inner necessity to solidarity.

His purpose is salvation for all. If we refuse salvation, we are still under the law of solidarity but it is then a perverted solidarity of perdition.

For the people of Israel, this message was easily understood. The Israelites were deeply convinced of the commonality binding each person to his family and nation, not to mention to his total environment.[50] But we have to look to the whole Old Testament to come to a balanced view of both the solidarity with the race and the unique responsibility of each person.

The second point is particularly stressed by the prophets of the Exile when the individual Israelite was called to exercise personal responsibility in a totally different world with which he could not identify himself. "Without necessarily bearing any personal responsibility for sin, all men find themselves, by virtue of their origin, in a restraint with regard to him who, in Israel's belief, is all merciful".[51]

Original sin must never be presented as a "fate". Neither should we point to the devil or to the first Adam in order to excuse ourselves. Indeed, we have no excuse for our sins. Scripture treats original sin, or rather "the sin of the world", in the perspective of the salvation that frees man from it if he follows Christ, the Covenant, who is Solidarity incarnate.

We should be sharply aware that we are born into a world that, to a lesser or higher degree, is contaminated by lust for power, by individual and collective selfishness, idols and false ideologies. Many biblical texts (cf. 1 Cor 15:33; Eph 4:14; the whole letter to the Romans) face the fact that a child is born into a world where he does not find the desirable stimulus he needs for his moral and religious formation unless there is a presence of redemption in the form of a divine milieu in families, neighbourhood and communities, which manifest corporate witness to justice, peace, truth and so on.

Many theologians today think that original sin is not a unique catastrophe at the birth of our species — although the first sin was a shocking event — but that we are mainly faced with the continually perpetuated perversion of humankind, in which new sins are conditioned more or less by the preceding sins and carry on the existing disorder. "Everyone is victim and many its authors".[52] It is a kind of chain reaction of the earlier and present sins whereby we suffer more under the sins of those who are closer to us than under the sins of those distant ancestors who, thousands or millions of years ago, committed the first sins.

We suffer above all under the most horrifying sin of rejection of Christ not only by the Jewish people but also by people all over the world to whom the grace of faith was offered. And we suffer particularly under the sins of members of households and communities within the Church.

But the final word, when speaking about this mystery, is always praise and thanksgiving for the presence of the greater mystery of saving solidarity. This, however, makes the sin of those who choose solidarity of perdition yet more sinful.

This vision of original sin and redemption presents the most urgent challenge and call to conversion to Christ the Covenant, a conversion to his kingdom of love, justice, peace and truth, conversion of the heart and, at the same time, total commitment to continuous renewal of the Church and society, of family life, of worship and politics.

VI. THE SACRAMENTS OF CONVERSION

Christ is the original and perfect sign of redemption and the effective call to conversion. He not only sends the Holy Spirit into the hearts of his people; he also extends his sacramentality to the Church, giving her the grace to become ever more a community of converted people who walk always on the road of ongoing purification. Further, he endows the Church with sacraments that are signs and sources of our conversion and of our corporate effort for renewal.

1. *The Church as a great Sacrament of conversion*

"By her relationship with Christ, the Church is a kind of sacrament or sign of intimate union with God and of the unity of all mankind. She is also an instrument for the achievement of such union and unity".[53] Union with God and the unity of mankind are possible. They are the goals and sacred duty to be promoted by the Church by being and becoming ever more a holy pilgrim people striving towards conversion and renewal, and by preaching the Gospel of reconciliation.

The Church is holy by divine grace and calling, by the power of the Holy Spirit who guarantees her infallibility in the fundamental truths revealed by Jesus Christ, and by awakening, again and again, saints in the bosom of the Church. She is holy also in the deposit of divine revelation and in the sacraments.

To understand better the Church's mission for conversion and renewal, it is important to see that she herself is in need of ongoing renewal; and for this purpose, we have to ask the question, How can the sinful world or sin-solidarity be a threat and a danger for the Church herself?

Charles Journet advanced a theology of the "Holy Church" that was more or less typical for the past few centuries. "The Church is not without sinners; however, she is without sin".[54] In this explanation, everything in the institutional Church seems to be perfect: the Code of Canon Law, doctrinal documents, the celebration of the sacraments and so on. The purpose of the Church is, then, to call individuals — somehow including also Church officials — to individual conversion.

The vision of Vatican II, prepared by great theologians like Yves Congar, is different. Because of the many sins of her members and office-holders, the Church is somehow forced to realize her innate vocation and her desire for sanctity in a historically limited form which is often far below her calling to perfection. She is situated and fulfils her mission in a world where good and bad are mixed. For evangelization and celebration, she uses a language and cultural symbols that are in many ways contaminated by alienations. She adjusts her own life to social structures, institutions and laws that are impregnated in various ways by the sin of the world.

By the renewing grace of the Spirit, the Church is always and everywhere a privileged sign of Christ's presence and a call to saving solidarity. Nevertheless, sins committed by her members, by office-holders and communities, and especially the sin of unwillingness to confess shortcomings, become invested in the

Church's own structures. Thus the health and integrity of her visible body is diminished and an unhealthy atmosphere is created wherein many temptations arise from a self-righteousness apologetic.[55]

What the First Vatican Council said about the Church's credibility and holiness cannot be ignored. "The Church herself is a great and enduring motive of credibility and irrefutable testimony to her divine mission by her wonderful growth, eminent holiness and inexhaustible stability".[56] But this vision, which is true only on the level of the normative ideal and as far as the lives of the saints are concerned, has to be completed by the more existential vision of the Second Vatican Council.

The very loftiness of the vocation of the Church, if compared with reality, is the strongest call to a radical conversion and renewal on all levels. The Church is not allowed any complacency about her unity. She should rather ask herself whether she truly acts in all ways as the effective sign of unity of all Christians and as pilgrim Church promoting the reconciliation and unity of humankind.

The whole work of Vatican II is a testimony of a self-understanding that is thoroughly related to the call for conversion and renewal. Especially her greater ecumenical sensitivity has led to challenging expressions. "Every renewal of the Church essentially consists in an increase of fidelity to her own calling... Christ summons the Church, as she goes her pilgrim way, to that continual reformation of which she always has need, insofar as she is an institution of men here on earth. Therefore, if the influence of events or of the times has led to deficiencies in conduct, in Church discipline, or even in the formulation of doctrine (which must be carefully distinguished from the deposit of faith itself), these should be appropriately rectified at proper moments. Church renewal, therefore, has notable ecumenical importance. Already this renewal is taking place in various spheres of the Church's life: the biblical and liturgical movements, the preaching of the word of God, catechesis, the apostolate of the laity, new forms of religious life, and the spirituality of married life".[57]

The Church calls truthfully to conversion, reconciliation and unity only insofar as she herself is a holy penitent.[58] Only a penitent and reformed Church responds to the Lord's testament "that all may be one". Not only the members of the Church as individuals but also the office-holders as such must confess their sins and shortcomings. When the Church acts, it is always people who are more or less saintly and more or less sinful who act. Sinfulness influences decisions and actions done in the name of the Church.

The Church is a holy penitent when she prays daily, "Forgive us our sins as we forgive those who sin against us". Whenever she is partially alienated because of the unreadiness of many to listen, to learn, to be reformed, the embodiment of all these sins is an injustice not only against God but also against the whole of humankind for whom she is instituted. A humble Church which, in creative fidelity and liberty, takes all the risks involved in an ongoing renewal is a great sign, a sacrament of conversion for all persons and communities

The self-understanding of the Church of Vatican II, by bringing into focus the sacramental model and the model of the pilgrim Church — the Church as a sacrament of love, community and fellowship in the Holy Spirit — has an enormous bearing on a better understanding of sin and conversion.

One particular grave sin against the Church's mission to be and to become ever more a sacrament of conversion and renewal is, on the one hand, the bitter criticism of Church institutions and the call for renewal made without personal commitment to conversion and, on the other hand, the preaching of individual conversion by churchmen done without sincere personal commitment to Church renewal. This has to be considered also in view of overcoming the crisis of the sacrament of penance.

Persons and communities who live their faith in the universal vocation to holiness, by giving witness of a life of holy penitents striving towards greater purification, are the greatest gift for the Church. By their firm and generous involvement in the renewal of the Church and of the whole environment, they reveal the Church's self-understanding as a saint-penitent, a sacrament of conversion, and contribute towards a better understanding and greater effectiveness of all the sacraments as sacraments of conversion.

2. The sacraments of conversion

The seven sacraments are privileged signs of the basic and ongoing conversion. The community of faith, hope, love and adoration is called to celebrate the sacraments in a way that unceasingly reminds its members about the loftiness of their vocation in Christ, that makes them more fully conscious that a holy life is possible, and encourages and vivifies them on the road.

These seven sacraments, understood as sacraments of the basic and ongoing conversion, teach us that it is not a matter of just a moral conversion, or conversion to individual precepts, but rather a conversion to a life in the fullness of faith, hope, love, justice and peace, of adoration in spirit and truth. However, whether they truly fill us with faith that conversion is possible, and make us aware of the challenge that further purification is needed, depends greatly on how the sacraments are celebrated.

Both the basic conversion that coincides with the good fundamental option and ongoing conversion have a sacramental dimension.[59] They bring home to our consciousness that conversion is always God's initiative and can be truly effective only insofar as we recognize the undeserved gift and respond to it by praise of God's mercy and graciousness.

This includes grateful praise also for the Church which God has made a sacrament and commitment to her ongoing struggle for renewal and her mission to preach conversion to all people. The sacraments of faith proclaim the indicative, that is, the Good News that God turns his countenance to us and calls us to return to him. The celebration of the sacraments becomes an effective imperative through the very joy and strength of the community of faith.

As privileged signs of hope, the sacraments insert us into the history of salvation which is a history of conversion and renewal. They strengthen in us the eschatological virtues of gratitude, hope, vigilance, discernment and serenity, so necessary for the basic and ongoing conversion. Through the sacraments we come to a deep and joyous realization that it is God's own love that calls us to love him. Conversion is not simply fulfilment of certain commandments but is the joyous, grateful reception of God's love and insertion into his love, so that we can love him and can love each other in and with him.

The sacraments of the new covenant teach us what adoration of God in spirit and truth really is, and that there is no conversion in the religious sense without progress in adoration. Conversion means a radical turning towards the glory of God in union with the High Priest Jesus Christ and in saving solidarity with his Church.

While all the sacraments call forth and promote ongoing conversion, the sacraments of baptism and of reconciliation are related to the basic conversion in the fundamental option for Christ and his kingdom. We see their celebration with all the preparation in faith, hope, repentance and intention. Normally, therefore, the celebration itself finds the sinner already in the disposition of a fundamental option for Christ and for the good. Justification is already given, but in view of the sacrament; and the sacramental celebration should then bring the fundamental conversion to a greater maturity and strengthen the intention to bring it to full fruition in all those dispositions that are its harvest.

a) Conversion and baptism

Baptism is the basic sacrament of conversion. Already in the preaching of John the Baptist, the appeal to conversion and the baptism of repentance were one, a prophetic image of the future baptism in the Holy Spirit which actually completes, perfects and seals the conversion of the sinner (cf. Mk 1:4; Lk 3:16; Acts 13:24; 19:4ff). According to the pregnant phrase of Justin the Apologist, baptism is "the bath of conversion which can purify only those who truly are converts".[60]

Baptism in the name of Jesus is an effective symbol of the sinner's return to his Father's house. It expresses the truth that it is God's goodness manifested in Jesus Christ that attracts the sinner to come with trust and gratitude. In baptism, we call upon the name of Jesus who, for our sake, received baptism not only in the waters of the Jordan but in the power of the Holy Spirit and in his blood for the new and everlasting covenant.

Baptism manifests that conversion is a saving encounter with

Jesus Christ and, through him, with the heavenly Father. The sinner meets Christ as Saviour and Master, with that confidence that honours his saving actions and opens the sinner to the power of Christ's passion and resurrection and to the promise of final salvation. In baptism, Christ himself awaits the sinner to welcome him home into the Father's house and to give him a share in the fruits of redemption. It is Christ's attractive presence and power that give efficacy and direction to all the steps that lead the convert to baptism. Preparation for baptism should be such that the welcome by Christ meets with no obstacle raised by the sinner.

Baptism as efficacious sign of conversion clearly symbolizes its goal. Our configuration with Christ in his death and resurrection, which already bears within it the seed and pledge of the ultimate union with Christ in the kingdom of glory, calls also to a life marked by ongoing conversion. If we have died with Christ and are baptised by the power of the Holy Spirit, we can put to death our selfish desires and thus can be drawn fully into the saving solidarity of Christ in his Church. Conversion by baptism means death to sin. "Have you forgotten that when we were baptised into union with Christ Jesus we were baptised into his death? By baptism we were buried with him, and lay dead in order that, as Christ was raised from the dead in the splendour of the Father, we might also set our feet upon the new path of life... You must regard yourselves as dead to sin and alive to Christ, in union with Christ Jesus. So sin must no longer reign in your mortal body" (Rom 6: 1-12).

Many biblical texts make clear that conversion crowned by baptism calls for a continuing battle against all sinful tendencies in us and around us. "I repeat, you died; and now your life lies hidden with Christ in God. When Christ, who is our life, is manifested, then you too will be manifested with him in glory. Then put to death whatever is rooted in the old existence, fornication, uncleanness, passion, evil desire, and that lust which is idolatry... You have discarded the old trend with its deeds and have put on the new nature which is being constantly renewed in the image of its creator and brought to know God" (Col 3: 3-10).

The grace-filled imperative to bring conversion to completion affects all those who are baptised, whether as adults or as children. For those who have fallen into mortal sin after baptism, this fundamental sacrament of conversion is an urgent call to return to the first conversion.

b) Baptism in the Holy Spirit

The sacrament of confirmation, too, should be seen in the dimension of ongoing conversion. It is the sacrament of growth in the Spirit, a growth which is not possible without the constant purification in the battle against selfishness in our own hearts and against the selfish powers around us that reinforce our own bad tendencies. The mature Christian is involved in the battle between the kingdom of Christ and the evil powers embodied in our environment.

The sacrament of confirmation teaches us, "Find your strength in the Lord, in his mighty power... Take salvation for helmet; for sword take that which the Spirit gives you — the words that come from God. Give yourselves wholly to prayer and entreaty; pray on every occasion in the power of the Spirit. To this end keep watch and persevere" (Eph 6:10-18).

Creative fidelity in ongoing conversion and corporate renewal are the work of the Spirit. It is only by entrusting ourselves to the Spirit that we can conquer the powers of falsehood. Confirmation has to be seen in the broader spectrum of Christ baptising his disciples "in the Holy Spirit" so that they can be holy and one in his love in the midst of the struggle against inimical powers.

c) The canonical penance

For most Christians who receive the sacrament of penance today, it is not a matter of re-conversion but a means of ongoing purification. Yet many Church documents and theological reflections speak of the sacrament of reconciliation (penance) as if it were normally a matter of re-conversion after mortal sin. Hence we have to distinguish carefully the different historical developments and the dimensions of the sacrament of reconciliation and healing forgiveness.

Among the origins of the later form of the sacrament of penance is the "canonical penance" of the first Christian centuries. As a call to conversion in those centuries, the Church excluded from the Eucharistic participation those who committed gravely *scandalous* sins. Those who do great harm to the Church by gravely scandalous sins exclude themselves from the community of salvation, since they cannot truthfully participate in the Eucharist through which the Church celebrates her union with Christ.

The Apostle Paul uses very severe expressions in excluding the man who lives with his father's wife, thus transgressing one of the most sacred traditions, the barriers against incest in Greek culture. "A man who has done such a deed should have been rooted out of your company... This man is to be consigned to Satan for the destruction of the body, so that his spirit may be saved on the day of the Lord" (1 Cor 5:1-5).

The community of Corinth had taken similar measures against a man who publicly had reviled the Apostle. Paul urges the Corinthian community to terminate the measure, since the sinner had given signs of repentance. "The penalty on which the general meeting had agreed has met the offence well enough. Something very different is called for now: you must forgive the offender and put heart into him; the man's sorrow must not be made so severe as to overwhelm him. I urge you, therefore, to assure him of your love for him by a formal act" (2 Cor 2:5-11).

Canonical penance, as an institution that took severe measures against those who diminished the credibility of the Church by gravely scandalous sins, was common in the Church of East and West throughout antiquity. The Church knew that she had the power to bind and to loose. Her action intended to bind Satan and to loose the converted sinner from his power. The Church's action was understood as sacramentally manifesting the nature of the Church who is holy and must withstand the scandal within her, but is merciful at the same time, following the healing forgiveness of Christ. This sacrament has often been called "the second plank of safety after the shipwreck of sin".[61] It is a painful remedy which a Christian should not need after he has received his share in the superabundant salvation through baptism and confirmation.

Not all grave sins were submitted to canonical penance. The

original intention was not based on a distinction between venial and mortal sin but was seen as a weapon against gravely scandalous sins. Nevertheless, the Church was always quite aware that everyone who, with proportionate freedom, commits a sin that directly contradicts the lofty vocation in Christ, excludes himself from the union with Christ celebrated in the Eucharist and, therefore, is in need of conversion.

The Fourth Lateran Council (1215) promulgated a law that all Christians who have committed grave sins have to submit them at least once a year, during Eastertime, to the "keys of the Church". From that time on, grave sin was more and more identified with mortal sin, although earlier documents that spoke of "grave sins" thought mainly about criminal or gravely scandalous sins. Actually, throughout the history of the Church, there has been a great diversity in the way of speaking of grave sins.[62]

Today the crisis of the sacrament of penance makes it necessary for us to be more cautious about classifying what is and what is not mortal sin. One of the main causes of this crisis is the exaggeration by moralists of the past few centuries in their scrupulous efforts to determine accurately what is venial and what is mortal sin. Pastorally, it is much easier and more helpful to determine, as the ancient Church did, what causes particular scandal. It may be that in a future the Church will return to the earlier discipline. It must always be kept in mind, however, that a Christian who commits a mortal sin — that is, who makes a fundamental option contradicting his baptismal conversion — is in profound need of penance in the Church. He has not only offended the Lord but has also damaged his Church.

According to the present discipline, if a Christian, although knowing that his sin was grave, has serious doubts about whether or not he has committed a mortal sin, he is not obliged to submit his sins through individual confession to the keys of the Church. He is, however, always obliged to repent and to seek God's healing forgiveness in the Church. He should also be grateful for the sacrament of penance which is not only reconciliation for those who have abandoned God but also a healing event that prevents a worsening of the situation and leads to greater purity of heart and thus to closer union with the Lord.

d) The Bread and Cup of reconciliation

At the centre of the whole ministry and life of the Church is the Eucharist. It is also the central celebration of the forgiveness of sins. "This is the cup of my blood, the blood of the new and everlasting covenant, shed for you and for all people so that sins may be forgiven".

The Eucharist is not only a source of grace and the centre to which the sacrament of penance leads, it is also an event of healing forgiveness.[63] Through baptism, the fundamental sign of our being reconciled, we are integrated into the Eucharistic community. What baptism has begun, the Eucharist continues and brings to completion, if we understand our life as ongoing conversion and purification in order to reach full union with Christ.

The Eucharistic celebration as a whole has the dimension of *confessio laudis* — the confession of our sins, praising God's mercy. The mercy that the Lord has shown on his cross and the victory of his love manifested in the Paschal Mystery are a gracious calling to deeper conversion, to purity of heart and to configuration with the Lord's own mercy and healing forgiveness.

The Eucharistic celebration should be a peak experience of the contrast-harmony of joy and holy fear (awe) in view of the mystery of God's holiness and the attractive power of his graciousness. In a synthesis of holy fear and absolute trust in God's healing love, we find the outstanding sign of continuing conversion.

In the Eucharist, Christ himself continues to proclaim the Good News that he died for us and wants to live in us. If we hear his word gratefully, we shall experience what the Lord himself expressed: "You have already been cleansed by the word I spoke to you. Dwell in me, as I in you" (Jn 15:3). The proclamation of the word of God includes the homily. In medieval times it was frequently followed by a general confession of sins and by general absolution. I am not inclined to see, either in the short penitential rite at the beginning of Mass or in this general absolution, a sacrament in itself, apart from the whole celebration. Rather, it points to the dimension of the whole Eucharist which cleanses us from our sins and brings us to a deeper repentance and a firmer purpose to live what we celebrate.

The Eucharistic celebrations of ancient times were masterpieces of the proclamation of the Good News that conversion is possible and urgent. Even the incensing of the bishop, or the main celebrant, and of all priests and laity at the beginning of Mass was understood as a grateful acknowledgement that we all need this sacrifice of praise for the forgiveness of our sins, and that we cannot celebrate it fruitfully without a deeper repentance and a firmer purpose to overcome all those attitudes in us that contradict the kingdom of God.

Before Holy Communion, all were reminded by the loud call of the deacon, "The Holy One for the holy". This did not, however, raise the question, "Was your sin only venial or was it mortal?" It was, rather, a more existential question: "Are you truly converted to the Lord and willing to continue on the road to purification?" As in the ancient Church of the East and West, so still today in the Orthodox Churches, everyone (except those whose sins are to be submitted to canonical penance because of grave scandal) can receive Communion without previous individual confession if he is sure about the contrition and good purpose. This does not at all diminish the relevance of individual confession and communal celebrations of penance outside the Eucharist, because they all form part of that important preparation that allows us to hear, with serenity and trust, the warning, "the Holy One for the holy".

e) Fraternal correction

Fraternal correction, as taught by the Old and New Testaments, has probably been the most relevant contribution to the development of spontaneous confession before a priest when there was no obligation for canonical penance. If it can be established that the confession of not gravely scandalous sins has to be understood in the perspective of fraternal correction, then a major dispute between the Eastern Churches and the Latin Church can be resolved.

The Eastern tradition fully acknowledges that canonical penance entails a judgment about the gravity of the scandal and of the necessary reparation. Regarding the other sins, the Orthodox Churches give first attention to the healing power of the Church, and de-emphasize the aspect of judgment, thus keeping the sacrament of penance free from overscrupulosity.

Of course, each action for the forgiveness of sins confronts us with the saving justice manifested by Christ on the cross, and the penitent and the priest honour that saving justice by loving discernment and humble gratitude.

In view of all this, it seems that reconnecting fraternal correction to the sacrament of penance, understood as praise of the Lord's mercy and manifestation of saving solidarity, can help us to a better link between life experience and sacramentality.

A classic text on fraternal correction is contained in the Letter to the Galatians, the great Pauline message on Christian liberty and liberation. A deeper understanding of it might give us the key to interpreting other important texts and a great part of history. "If the Spirit is the source of our life, let the Spirit also direct our course. We must not be conceited, challenging one another to rivalry, jealous of one another. If a man should do something wrong, my brothers, on a sudden impulse, you who are endowed with the Spirit must set him right again very gently. Look to yourselves, each one of you; you may be tempted too. Help one another to carry these heavy loads, and in this way you will fulfil the law of Christ" (Gal 5:25–6:2).

Fraternal correction is presented as a work prompted by the Holy Spirit. All attitudes that betray human selfishness (sarx), such as jealousy or grumbling against others, must be firmly excluded. All Christians are obliged to render the important service of fraternal help, but they can do so only if they are "endowed with the Spirit", bearing the harvest of the Spirit (cf. Gal 5:19-25). The emphasis, therefore, is on gentleness and on the realization by the one who offers correction that he, too, can be tempted and might some day be in need of the same kind of help. Fraternal correction is a most significant expression of "the law of Christ". It exemplifies the solidarity of salvation manifested by Christ; and "life in Christ Jesus" makes it a law written in our innermost being.

Not less important is a text in the Letter of James. It equally excludes any kind of judgmental and grumbling attitudes. "Be patient, my brothers, until the Lord comes. You, too, must be patient and stout-hearted, for the coming of the Lord is near. My brothers, do not blame your troubles on one another or you

will fall under judgment, and there stands the judge at the door...
Confess your sins to one another and pray for one another, and
then you will be healed. A good person's prayer is powerful and
effective" (Jas 5:7-9, 15-16).

When we offer each other the help of fraternal correction
and encouragement, we must honour together the prerogative
of God who alone knows the deepest thoughts of the heart and
alone can judge a person. We do not act as judges but, in the
name of Jesus, the Reconciler, the Divine Physician, the Good
Shepherd, we help each other and praise together the saving
judgment of God for those who repent.

We may understand the words of James as not referring just
to spontaneous fraternal correction but possibly also to a kind
of liturgical confession understood as confession of sin to the
praise of God's mercy. But mutual fraternal correction outside
the liturgy is surely to be included.

While Paul speaks to the Galatians emphatically about the
role of the Spirit, James insists on the necessity of prayer. The
meaning is fundamentally the same: we can help each other on
the road to salvation and conversion only when relying on God's
grace.

For an understanding of the abiding value of fraternal correction and of the historical development of the sacrament of
penance, chapter 18 of Mattthew's gospel is most relevant. Here
Jesus warns against scandals that would endanger the salvation
of the weak. The gospel then offers us the picture of the Good
Shepherd who seeks the lost sheep. Christ invites all his followers to act[1] similarly, never letting down a brother or sister
who may be in danger. "If your brother commits a sin, go and
take the matter up with him strictly between yourselves. If he
listens to you, you have won your brother over. If he will not
listen, take one or two others with you, so that all facts may be
established on the evidence of two or three witnesses. If he
refuses to listen to them, report the matter to the congregation;
and if he will not listen even to the congregation, you must
then treat him as you would a pagan or a tax collector" (Mt
18:15-17). The last advice should be understood in the context
of Matthew's gospel. He himself was a tax collector and was

won over by Jesus, who constantly associated with people of this kind in order to save them. So the text means that we must always follow the Good Shepherd, seeking the salvation of all.

A few manuscripts read, "If your brother commits a sin *against you...*". But while we remember that every sin does harm to each member of the Church and of humankind, we should not think of fraternal correction only or mainly in cases where someone has directly done wrong against us. The essential context is the whole solidarity of salvation.

It should not go unnoticed that the effort to rescue the brother or sister who is in sin is not the task for priests only. When the effort of those who live in closest relationship with the sinner have failed, only then should the matter be brought to the congregation and its office holders. Matthew 18:18 tells of the community's action of binding and loosing. It seems that this includes both fraternal correction exercised by members of the community and action by the whole congregation or office holders. The efforts of the faithful, guided by the Spirit, bind the evil one and set the sinner free. The more authoritative intervention of the office holder is to be included whenever necessary. However, since all disciples of Christ share in his active work of salvation, a promise is given to all that their efforts, prompted by the Spirit, will have value in heaven.

We cannot forget that our efforts must be supported by prayer. "If two of you agree on earth about any request you have to make, that request will be granted by my Father. For where two or three have met together in my name, I am there among them" (Mt 18:19-20). When we meet in saving concern for another, we do so only in the name of the Lord. The very action of fraternal correction, offered and accepted in the right manner, is a guarantee of the Lord's healing and liberating presence.

In this context, too, just as in the Lord's Prayer, Christ teaches us that we can be sharers in his healing forgiveness only if we accept this as a basic law for our own attitudes. When Peter asks whether one should forgive as many as seven times, Jesus responds, "I do not say seven times; I say seventy times seven"

(Mt 18:22). That means "without limit", just as the goodness and mercy of the heavenly Father know no bounds.

The religious dimension of fraternal correction is of enormous importance. Agreeing with a tradition that was unbroken until the thirteenth century, we can say that fraternal correction is a kind of sacrament when it is carried out in a spiritual way, in a profound solidarity between the one who offers and the one who receives the correction, with gentleness and humility on both sides, and with everything being brought before God in humble and trustful prayer. "The prayer of the good person is powerful before God". If we pray together for the forgiveness of our sins, we are truly gathered in the name of Jesus and are sure that our prayer is heard by the Father.

What the Bible and other ancient documents say about the saving value of fraternal correction gives us an understanding of how, during the first centuries, believers in the Church came to make a spontaneous confession of their sins to a spiritual person. Those who are moved by the "law of the Spirit" do confess spontaneously to people "endowed by the Spirit" sins which legalists would consider as not serious or perhaps not as sins at all. This is an expression of the common, solidary effort on the road of ongoing conversion.

Since priests were chosen for their ministry in view of the harvest of the Spirit, and the special grace of the Holy Spirit was called upon them in ordination, it was almost natural that people would confess their sins especially to priests. The laity were never authorized to "hear confessions" in the liturgical setting — this is reserved to the priest. However, in the Orthodox Churches, the spontaneous way of opening one's conscience to a spiritual lay person in order to obtain guidance and fervent prayer, is even now appreciated as a sacramental event.

Since fraternal correction, carried out in the common conditions of life, is psychologically a bridge to the confession before a priest, the point has to be stressed that it is not sufficient to confess one's sins to a priest in the sacrament of penance. We have to be willing also to acknowledge our faults humbly before those whom we have wronged and before all to whom we have given a bad example. This should not be too

difficult if we all make the praise of God's mercy a basic purpose
of our lives.

f) Diverse forms of celebrating forgiveness

The Church has always believed that forgiveness of sins
which involve no particular scandal can be obtained in various
ways. What is always indispensable is conversion at both the
individual and social level.

The Gospel that conversion is possible and urgent was particularly stressed during Lent, Advent and on the vigils of the
great feasts. All these efforts enter into the broad spectrum of
the Church's own sacramentality, her being and becoming ever
more a sacrament of reconciliation and healing forgiveness.
Whenever the Church brings us closer to salvation through
profound contrition, trust in the Lord, and renewed good purpose, she acts as an effective and visible sign of God's mercy.

The latest renewal of the sacrament of penance (reconciliation) is not an innovation but a creative return to a great
tradition. Those who understand the broad vision of the sacramentality of the Church, and her total ministry of reconciliation,
will surely not be disturbed by these changes. They respond to
new needs while being faithful to the total tradition. A constant effort is needed to bring the experience of life and the
celebration of the sacraments into closer contact.

An important means of grace and praise of God is the
examination of conscience in Christian families. It can be a
part of the evening prayer, a sharing in the peace and reassur-
ance of forgiveness. Especially after a serious tension or after
a hurt unjustly caused, the members of a family should be
united in the name of the Lord and pray together, assuring
each other of their wholehearted forgiveness. And in such a
reconciling event, thanksgiving should never be forgotten.
Revision of life in religious communities or in groups of lay
people has a similar role for a corporate experience of our
solidarity of salvation.

The Church has re-evaluated the communal celebrations of
penance. Not only are they a good preparation for individual
confession — an aspect that should not be underestimated —
but they are also a privileged sign of grace for the community.

They help us to understand better the social aspect of sin and conversion. While they do not replace individual confession, they are very helpful in promoting conversion and renewal.

Penitential celebrations that are not followed by general absolution or by individual confession and absolution are not yet recognized as sacraments in the specific sense, but we may see this development in the future, at least under certain conditions. Until the eleventh century, absolution was not given in the form of declaration, "I absolve you", but in the form of fervent prayer offered by the minister of the Church that the Lord might grant forgiveness, peace and liberation from sin. The Church was convinced that this prayer, officially offered by the priest and joined in by holy people, was effective.

Between the eighth and the thirteenth centuries, popes, bishops and abbots frequently gave general absolution [64] after a serious preparation, but with the warning that grave sins — normally understood as gravely scandalous sins *(peccata criminalia)* — had to be submitted to the keys of the Church by individual confession. The present discipline requests the individual confession of mortal sins. This is not an arbitrary imposition but an urgent invitation to deepen one's contrition and good purpose, and to open oneself more fully to Christ's healing action.

On Easter Day, Jesus gave his peace and forgiveness to all the Apostles present, Peter included. However, he favoured Peter also by an individual encounter, asking him three times — the same number of times that Peter had denied him — whether he truly loved him. Although Peter was grieved on that occasion, it became a source of great peace and gratitude for him.

We have already noted that those who have reasonable doubts about whether their serious sins are mortal or not, are not bound by Church law to make an individual confession. But it should not be forgotten that a Christian is not just under the written law; he is expected to respond to the offer of grace. Humble personal confession before a priest is not only an important exercise in humility but also a favoured moment of encounter with Christ. If, because of lack of humility, we refuse individual confession, then the otherwise excellent penitential celebrations could easily be exposed to dangers of superficiality, escapism and alienation.

g) The sacrament of healing forgiveness

Along with the ministry of reconciliation, Christ has entrusted to his Church the mission to heal. In his public ministry we find a surprising synthesis between healing and forgiveness of sins.

Jesus rejects the widespread conviction of the Semitic world of his time that caused it to look down on the sick person as if he were a greater sinner than others. Yet to the paralyzed man who seeks a cure, he says, "My son, your sins are forgiven" (Mk 2:5). There are ailments that, in union with Christ's suffering on the cross, are destined for the glory of God; but there are others that are deeply linked with sin. The best of psychotherapy can help us to see more clearly the connection between reconciliation, conversion and healing, especially in cases typical of psychogenic or noögenic disorders.

Great therapists and humanists define genuine human health wholistically, with particular emphasis on the person's ability to relate healthily to his fellowmen, to himself and to the whole of creation. As an embodied spirit, a person is essentially on the way to health if he finds liberating relationships with God and neighbour, with the community and the whole environment. In the sacraments, the Divine Physician helps us to discover or to rediscover our essential We-Thou-I relationships and to live them more fully. It is only when we seriously seek the ultimate goal and meaning of our life, transcending the selfish self and serving those whom we are in a position to serve, that we find our true self.

In the sacrament of reconciliation we come to an ever-deeper experience that God graciously accepts us, meets us where we are, and guides us on the road to wholeness and salvation. He assures us of his friendship whenever we are ready to accept his gracious calling, and this allows us to accept ourselves. We discover the good in ourselves, gain confidence about coping with dark shades, and in this new self-acceptance and confidence, we accept also our fellow travellers on the way to final union with God.

It is, above all, our gratitude and joy for being accepted and loved by God that fosters our continuing conversion to God and fellowmen. If we are grateful that Jesus was willing to bear our burdens and to share with us the fruit of redemption, we learn to accept gratefully our common vocation "to bear the burdens of one another and thus to fulfil the law of Christ". The new liturgy of the sacrament of penance, following the biblical vision, directs the whole celebration to thanksgiving and praise, which should then mark our own life and create a divine milieu of peace, joy, gratitude and reciprocal trust.

The new rite of the sacrament teaches the confessor and the penitent to join in a dialogue of faith, in humble prayer of supplication, and in praise of the Lord's goodness. This dimension becomes even more evident in the communal celebration.

I think that the numerous healings obtained in the prayer meetings of Charismatic Renewal groups can open new avenues to a better understanding of the healing mission of the Church in general, and especially in connection with the sacrament of reconciliation. The fact that many or most of these events of healing can be explained by psychosomatic medicine or by the findings of logotherapy does not at all diminish their significance as faith healing. On the contrary, it shows that through a divine milieu of faith, goodness, serenity, joy and praise of God, the human person can have a new experience of wholeness and health that always points towards salvation.

VII. THE CONVERT'S SHARE IN CONVERSION

Reconciliation and conversion is God's work from beginning to end. Nevertheless, it is inseparably also the convert's response given in renewed freedom. According to the Council of Trent, sorrow, confession and atonement are three essential parts of the sacrament of penance as acts of the penitent.[65] We treat them here in relation to the sacrament, and also as dispositions and acts which are proper to every genuine religious conversion. They have to be seen always under the influence of God's gracious and renewing initiative.

1. *Contrition*

a) Humble self-knowledge: preparation for and fruit of sorrow

Self-examination is part of the event of contrition. Without basic humility and a humble recognition of our condition, we sinners can never come to authentic contrition. On the other hand, only through contrition can we reach that humility which is indispensable for profound self-knowledge.

The deepest root of every sin is pride. It is a part of the mystery of sin that, while sin is degrading, the sinner tends at the same time to increase even more the dreadful evil of pride. On the other hand, he feels the bitter effects of his sin and his sinfulness on his mind and heart. This experience can become an antidote, a call to humility. On the other hand, enslaved by pride, he tends to suppress this sense of humiliation and to allow pride to gain even more control over his mind-set. In this conflict, contrition greatly helps to free the counter-impulse of humility. It removes the natural suppressive force of the pride of our selfish nature. It crushes the barrier of pride that holds back everything from our past that does not appease and justify pride itself.

The courage to face one's own sinfulness, and not only individual faults, is a great step towards inner freedom. So long as the sinner does not recognize that it is not only a matter of individual transgressions but one of sinfulness itself, of cohabitation with the selfish self, he does not come to that profound sorrow that makes him cry out, "Lord, have pity on me, a sinner".

St. Augustine, the great psychologist among the Church Fathers, says trenchantly that the first step towards liberation from the slavery of sin and for freedom in truth is "humility, and the second step is humility again, and the third step is humility; and as often as you may ask, I would give the same answer: humility".[66] Time and again, experience has confirmed Augustine's conviction that precisely the greatest sinners fail to realize the depth of their abasement and, therefore, do not feel the need for penance.[67]

Each delay of repentance and conversion increases the trend towards repressing guilt consciousness and justifying oneself.

Everything depends on the level of humility. Thus, in Luke 18: 9ff, we see the contrast between the self-righteous Pharisee who boasts of his virtues and the Publican who humbly asks for pardon, and of whom the Lord says, "Everyone who exalts himself shall be humbled, and he who humbles himself shall be exalted". The Pharisee should have asked himself whether abuse of religion for vanity and power is not a much greater sin than the mundane sins of the businessman.

If we examine our conscience we should do it in full consciousness of the Lord's presence and in view of what he has suffered for our sins. To face our sinfulness is already the beginning of praise of the Lord's kindness, the courage to have trust in him.

b) Ethical regret and religious sorrow

To a person who has not lost the dynamics towards wholeness, each decision against his conscience causes pain. However, the kinds of sorrow can be quite different. One may experience only a sense of regret over infractions of the standards of hygiene that safeguard psychic health. He may see no more in his fault than a hazard to his own self-perfection. Another may experience a conflict with a legal norm, or fear of the lawgiver, without attention to the inherent value involved. Sorrow reaches a more noble level when the person experiences both the hurt against his own wholeness and integrity and the offence against a value which should claim his support. Even if God is not yet present on the horizon of one's consciousness, if the sorrow expresses a true longing for wholeness and a basic integrity and openness to values, there is already given an analogy of religious sorrow.

Sorrow, in a fully religious sense, presupposes faith in God who lovingly calls us by name. There is a profound relationship between the God-experience and the sense of sin. Contrition is a central act of the virtues of faith, hope, love and adoration. It honours God who is both holy and merciful. In a fully developed religious sorrow, the sinner is shaken in his innermost being at the thought of the malice of his offence against the all-holy God: "Go, Lord, leave me, sinner that I am" (Lk 5:8). But at the same time, the experience of his own sinfulness hurls him into the arms of the infinitely merciful God. "Lord, to whom shall we go? You alone have words of everlasting life" (Jn 6:69). The repentant sinner holds fast to his sorrow and is healed by it precisely because he realizes how unfathomable is the mercy of God who has revealed himself to us as loving Father.

In the light of the Christian faith, sorrow assumes the form of a "sacramental encounter" with Christ. A Christian who is truly on the road of conversion sees his offences in the light of the divine judgment which Christ took upon himself on the cross, in order to impart to us the saving power of his love. A Christian should be aware that, even in the incipient stages of contrition, the mercy of Christ has already touched him, and this is a sign of Christ's intention to show healing forgiveness. This encounter with Christ, growing in intensity and gratitude, foreshadows the privileged encounter with Christ in the sacrament of penance.

Religious repentance activates the vital forces of the virtues of faith and hope which, through God's mercy, somehow remain in the sinner even after the commission of a mortal sin, as long as the sinner, in basic humility, acknowledges that God's commandments are holy and that he himself is thoroughly wrong, since he contradicts in his acts what he acknowledges in faith.

We conclude that the call to conversion is, above all, a call to living faith. Even though the faith of believers who have committed mortal sins is "dead", it is still a firm bond which binds them to the word of God, a point of departure from which every effort towards conversion must proceed. A sinner who has not given up hope in God can look forward to the glad tidings of forgiveness, and this encourages him to return to the Father's house with deep sorrow and humble confession.

c) Repentance: creative freedom and rebirth through grace

"Contrition is the most revolutionary force in the moral world".[68] The first redirection towards the truth of life after sin is not so much through good resolution as through contrition. In profound sorrow, the sinner faces the dark powers behind his back, and thus gains a new orientation.

In contrition, when it affects his whole being, the sinner overcomes his evil past, leaving behind him not only particular sins of the past but also his whole sinful self. He not only deplores some sinful acts but also condemns his selfish self. He not only confesses, "I have sinned", but also, and even more, "I am a sinner". A profound sorrow reaches into the very depth of man's freedom, affecting mind and will and emotions with a pain that cauterizes the wounds of sin.

Sorrow reveals new horizons as it opens up whole new regions of spiritual freedom, according to the measure of its depth and thoroughness. It is true that mortal sin terribly ravages man's moral and religious freedom. However, the sinner does not cast away the whole treasure of liberty for good with a single sinful deed (apart from the sin "against the Holy Spirit" or "the sin unto death"). He does not squander all his freedom through one single act of evil, just as he develops his freedom for good only through a long series of good acts, according to their intensity. What remains of freedom after mortal sin is gathered up in contrition under the influence of divine grace.

Looking at true contrition from the viewpoint of human liberty, we can truly call it a powerful liberation, a revolution that overthrows the entrenched tyranny of sin. Recognizing God's action in it, we see it as a new birth, a new creation through God's grace. At the lofty level of justifying contrition, the noblest dedication of human freedom for good and for God is thoroughly wedded to the attractive power of God's graciousness. In our sorrow, which is a victory of humble and grateful love of God, we receive again the undeserved gift of the freedom of the children of God. The more the sinner gratefully recognizes this gift, the more he will open himself to the new possibilities of creative freedom and fidelity.

Through contrition, we humbly unite ourselves with the holy God who, on Jesus' cross, shows us how strongly he condemns sin. By this "salutary hatred of our ancient manner of life",[69] we adore God's holiness and reach out for his mercy so that we will "not be condemned with this world" (1 Cor 11:31). Thankfully, we accept God's reconciling action and set out on the road of freedom as children of God, praising him with our whole life in abiding gratitude.

This grateful praise of God's mercy distinguishes contrition as the rebirth of true love from attrition that is still dominated by fear of punishment. If, through gratitude, we are open to God's graciousness, fear of punishment will be gradually transformed into "holy fear", that trembling awe felt before the all-merciful and all-holy God. Thus "perfect love banishes fear", for fear brings with it the pains of judgment, and anyone who is driven by fear has not yet attained love in its perfection. "We love because he loved us first" (1 Jn 4:18). This thankful love that rejoices in God enables and presses us to unite with him in his love for all people.

d) Contrition as permanent disposition and frame of mind

Holy Scripture, theological tradition and, not least, the lives of the saints give evidence that contrition must go beyond individual acts in the process of conversion from sin. The true convert will have a permanent disposition of that "blessed sorrow" that configurates us with the suffering and death of Christ. An individual act of sorrow alone, even though based on true love, does not fully tear open the depths of the heart, hardened and knotted by sin, as complete conversion requires. But with deepening sorrow there is also growth in love, and with the progress of love there is development in sorrow.

Since we see Christian life as grounded in the law of divine grace, it becomes evident that the very graciousness of God is exacting in its demands on our humble and grateful love. It must be a love that praises, extolling the mercies of God with humble and contrite heart. It must be an ongoing "thanksgiving (eucharistia) that arises from a contrite heart", to use the words of Mark Eremita who so well expresses this ideal of holiness in Eastern spirituality.[79]

This permanent disposition of compunction cannot be a fitting response to the gladness experienced by the prodigal son at his home-coming unless it is grounded in a grateful love. Thankfulness and praise keep sorrow from degenerating into depression and despair. Yet, without compunction, our thanksgiving would not properly express our existence as people who live by the unsolicited love and compassion of God.

In the measure that our compunction deepens, the wounds of past sins are healed. An antidote is furnished against the reopening of old wounds. Through this disposition, the convert becomes spiritually attentive to the invitation of grace (an indispensable means of progress), with the result that even the slightest disregard of the divine summons to do good causes profound sorrow for our neglect.

In his sorrow, the Psalmist prays, "I have laboured in my groanings; every night I will wash my bed; I will water my couch with my tears" (Ps 6:7). And the words of Isaiah are not less striking. "I will recount to you all my tears in the bitterness of my soul" (Is 38:15). Whoever has this disposition of grateful compunction can understand the life and message of St. Paul. "I am the least of the Apostles, and I am not worthy to be called an Apostle, because I persecuted the Church of God" (1 Cor 15:9).

Sins, our sins, have ravaged the vineyard of the Lord. The spirit of Christian solidarity compels us to grieve deeply about such great spiritual loss to those for whom Christ has died. When confronted by the failings of our fellowmen, a true spirit of compunction makes us ask humbly: How much has my own failure to cooperate fully with all the graces offered me contributed to the power of sin in the environment? How many sins might have been avoided if I, personally, had laboured wholeheartedly for the kingdom of Christ?

2. *Purpose of amendment essential for true contrition*

Just as the firm purpose of amendment has its power from the grief of contrition, so the sincerity and depth of sorrow are revealed in the purpose of amendment. "For there is no authentic sorrow which does not at least implicitly bear the basic design of a 'new heart' from its very inception. Contrition kills only to bestow life. It destroys only to build up".[71] For the purpose of amendment to be firm and strong, contrition must mature and ripen. Reciprocally, the sinner may not be remiss about the firm purpose to sin no more, since otherwise the ardour of contrition will vanish before the resolution to improve is firmly set.

Good resolution must flow from deep contrition and embody the same qualities and potentialities. Accordingly, it must be universal and comprehensive. Conversion to God does not allow mediocrity. Only the person who seriously accepts the call to holiness and is willing to strive patiently towards it has the divine promise and is sure of gracious and patient help.

Creative freedom and fidelity cannot develop without purposefulness in our life. Explicit, particular resolutions must be directed, above all, towards those obstacles which, up to the present, have caused postponement of conversion or hindered one's growth in love for God and for one's neighbour.

One's purpose of amendment must be serious and decisive, reaching to the very root of the evil. It is not enough — to cite one example — for an adulterer to resolve never to commit the sin of adultery again; he must also be determined to banish the evil desire from his mind and heart.

The purpose of amendment must be both generous and prudent. The resolution to strive towards holiness means to look each time for the next possible step. And there are hours of grace when God calls us to go forward, not by little steps, but by leaps and bounds.

Every resolution on the path of conversion must be humble. To the extent that we are converted to the Lord, we put all our trust in him; we therefore transform every resolution into prayer, for God alone, who has given the beginning, can help us to accomplish what he has promised.

3. Confession of sin — praise of God's mercy

One of the essential acts in every authentic conversion to God is the humble confession, "O Lord, I am a sinner and therefore stand in need of your mercy". Since Christian baptism is given "for the forgiveness of sins" (Acts 2:38; Lk 24:47) the voluntary reception itself entails the confession that one is in need of pardon for sins. Yet the Church does not demand a confession of individual sins for baptism, since it is not her mission to draw before her sacramental tribunal sins which were committed while the person was not yet a member of the Church.[72] But if we have sinned after being baptized into the community of faith and saving solidarity, we confess not only before God but also before the Church. Thus we come to realize more deeply what saving solidarity means, and how each sin fails to live fully the covenant morality.

Christ has given to his Church a special mission of healing forgiveness, to free us from the bonds of sin and to lead us into the full freedom of the children of God (cf. Mt 16:19; 18:18; Jn 20:23). The sacrament of penance is the privileged form in which the Church exercises this gracious mission to proclaim, by word and sign, the Lord's liberating action. The Church knows that she has received this power to make known the Lord's saving justice and mercy to those who humbly confess their sins.[73]

Although this book is not a manual of moral theology written mainly in view of confession and penance, the gratitude for this sacrament is a compelling reason to help overcome its crisis. Hence we try to explain here the significance of confession and also the purpose and limits of the law of the Church.

a) Psychological and theological significance of the confession

The human person is an embodied spirit. The interior disposition of contrition is manifested exteriorly by confession, which is not only a visible but also an effective sign that makes contrition more real, more humble and more powerful for total conversion. It has been shown that in almost all religions outside Christianity the need for confession of sins has been felt and practised.[74]

Christ, by his cross, has made visible before all humanity that he bears our burden, our sorrow. By our humble confession we give praise in a sacramental sign pointing to the Paschal Mystery and prepare ourselves to receive the visible sign and word of absolution. If inspired by deep sorrow and directed to the praise of God, our confession is raised to the dignity of "worship in spirit and truth". A contrite self-accusation adores God's saving justice and glorifies his wonderful mercy. This prevents self-regret, useless self-accusation and harmful repression of guilt.

By its very nature, sin tends to hide in darkness and shut out the light, or to mask itself as something good. "Everyone who does evil hates the light, and does not come to the light, that his deeds may not be exposed. But he who tells the truth comes to the light, that his deeds may be manifest" (Jn 3:20-21). Through humble confession, we bring ourselves into the light of

Christ, with all the good we have received but facing the sinful lack of gratitude. With renewed thankfulness, we acknowledge him as the truth of our life and let his light shine upon us. Confession counteracts the darkening power of sin, for it strips the mask of deceit from evil and pours light into the most hidden recesses of our souls. Thus it is a step towards greater fullness of light, of truth and love (cf. 1 Thess 5:5; Rom 13:11-12).

Through humble confession to the praise of the Lord's mercy, we open ourselves to his saving justice, to the divine light, to the transparency of the divine love which penetrates all things.

Each sin is, directly or indirectly, a shameless criticism of God's holy will. Whether he intends this or not, the sinner makes this kind of critique visible. By confession he visibly acknowledges the wrongness of his critique. He expresses his firm purpose to take no more part "in the barren deeds of darkness, but show them up for what they are . . . Everything when once the light has shown it up, is illumined and everything that is illumined is all light" (Eph 5:11-13).

Each sin makes apparent the distance between the loftiness of our being called in Jesus Christ and the inadequacy of our response. Repentance, manifested in humble confession, protects us against the darkening power of sin. Thus confession strengthens the nöodynamics and psychodynamics towards wholeness, greater fullness of truth and truthfulness of life response.

The courage to speak out clearly our faults and our sinful attitudes brings greater clarity to heart and mind, especially if we are fully aware that we — penitent and confessor — are gathered in the name of Jesus to the praise of his healing forgiveness. The confessor who represents the Divine Physician, the Good Shepherd, and who acts as a brother among brethren, can help the penitent to come to a greater Christ-consciousness and to a new courage to see himself in the light of Christ's truth and to follow him who is the Truth, the Way and the Life.

So many people who have turned away from sacramental confession, or have not found a confessor who has helped them to know the Divine Physician more intimately, feel the need to speak out about their past. Gertrude von le Fort writes movingly about the hazards of those who, instead of going to confession, seek absolution from the psychoanalyst, who does not acknowledge sin at all because he does not know what it means to forsake God or to offend the most gracious Father. With deep compassion she looks on the thousands who live a dreadful existence, for their illness is nothing else than scorn for peace with God.[73]

This remark should not, however, hinder confessors from learning from outstanding psychotherapists how to listen compassionately to suffering people, how to help them discern between sin and suffering, and how to assist them patiently to seek the meaning of life. After all, who can better help their brothers and sisters to find full meaning for their lives than those who help us to see all our life in the light of the Divine Master and Physician?

b) Integral confession: law and ideal

It is essential to Christian life to tend constantly towards the heights. The call to holiness is a most challenging normative ideal. This applies to all our attitudes and also to the quality of humility in confessing our sins. It would, however, be a cause of confusion if, regarding concrete duties such as confession of sins to a priest, we did not discern between what law regularly requests and what might be the ideal.

The effort to be integral in confession can conflict with more important values and duties. We accept the warning expressed by many theologians, and especially by John Baptist Hirscher, "not to palliate our faults in sacramental confession, and never to try to get by as easily as possible".[74] But one should, with total inner freedom, discern what kind of completeness is truly good for one's spiritual growth. The sacrament of penance is given to us as a liberating experience and, therefore, must never occasion compulsive confession or any kind of scrupulosity.

It is by grace that the Lord calls each of us by name. He leads us on, step by step in the spirit of penance, into greater depths of sorrow and a more humble self-knowledge, and on to greater courage to face our shortcomings and to a more liberating trust while confessing our sins. Too much concern for completeness of confession can distract us from the concreteness of our purpose and from clearsightedness about our motives that need to be purified. It is sometimes good to limit confession to those few points that most urgently need to be remedied by a firm purpose of amendment.

By positive divine law specified by Church law, we have to submit to the keys of the Church, through individual confession, all mortal sins committed after baptism, according to their number and species, including all circumstances which change the nature of the sins. A positive precept of the Church forbids one to defer confession of mortal sins beyond the next Easter season.[77] Mortal sins have to be confessed insofar as the penitent is conscious of them after a careful examination of conscience.

If a Christian has a reasonable doubt whether or not his sin was mortal, the urgency of salvation compels him to do everything he can to be sure of his state of grace. However, he is not obliged to confess the sin as long as he can sincerely hope that it was not mortal. If there is serious doubt about the mortal nature of a sin, every Christian who earnestly strives to live a fully Christian life may always decide in his own favour. This means that he is not obliged by any compelling law to confess his sin. Scrupulous persons must always decide in their own favour, at least insofar as the domain of their particular anxiety is concerned. Conversely, a penitent who "drinks in sin like water" cannot prudently decide in his own favour in the case of a serious doubt about his sin being mortal or not. A better understanding of the nature of the fundamental option will give basic criteria.

Theologians distinguish between material and formal integrity of confessions. Material integrity is actual integral confession of all mortal sins according to number and species. Formal integrity is the sincere will to make a materially integral confession, whether or not one succeeds in doing so. Confession of sins is materially and formally incomplete if the penitent, through grievous fault, omits confession of a sin which he considers to be mortal. This does not hold, however, for overscrupulous persons who all too easily judge their sins to be mortal.

The reception of the sacrament is valid and fruitful even though the penitent fails to mention a mortal sin through involuntary forgetfulness or even through carelessness, unless he realizes that this very carelessness constitutes a grave neglect.

By personal experience as confessor, and through the study of psychology, I have come to realize that a psychologically excessive sense of shame or a frightening experience in the confessional can make a penitent unable to confess his sins in spite of all his good will. The fact that he lived the life of a truly converted person and suffered greatly under the inability to confess his sins gives enough evidence that he has not committed the sin of sacrilegious reception of the sacrament.

The indication of the number of mortal sins is not a matter of mathematics but a way of pointing to the dimension of sinfulness. It is not the same, for instance, to seduce a number of persons to adultery as to commit the sin with only one person. It might sometimes be much more important to reveal to the confessor how long one has lived in the state of sin without any serious effort of conversion than to try to count the number of sinful thoughts, desires, purposes and acts.

If a materially integral confession in the realm of the sixth commandment is not possible without exciting impure images and dangerous temptations, then the penitent is not only excused from the obligation but the stricter moral duty to avoid unnecessary temptations simply forbids him, under such circumstances, to attempt to confess integrally by trying to evoke in his memory each individual situation.[78] On two occasions Pius XII brought to the attention of psychotherapists the inviolate moral law that forbids all voluntary excitation of temptation to impurity that can be caused by reflective psychoanalytical disclosures. If this is true for purposes of healing by the psychoanalyst, it is also true for the purpose of the purification of our heart and mind in the sacrament of penance.[79] For the same reason, and for the honour in which the sacrament of penance should be kept, a confessor must refrain from asking questions about the sixth commandment if this is not necessary for healing forgiveness and the effective conversion of the penitent. The law of integral confession has always to be viewed in a perspective of salvation and not one of control.

In view of past exaggerations about the "lowest" species of sin, we should be most careful to avoid subtle distinctions alien to the mind of the average penitent. Both for general instruction and for the duty of the confessor regarding the proper species, the following simple rule can be followed: the penitent should mention in confession everything that, in his own moral awareness, constitutes an entirely new kind of mortal sin. He should indicate circumstances which, according to his own conscience, made a sin certainly mortal while under other circumstances it might have been considered a venial sin.

The precept of material integrity binds only in proportion to the other essential elements of conversion. Any question that makes the sacrament of penance a kind of torture must be absolutely avoided, for this sacrament is a grateful celebration of homecoming and a gracious appeal to ongoing conversion.

If a Christian has sincerely tried to make a good confession, he should put aside all worry about the integrity of his confession and, instead, look forward to living fully in accordance with the law of grace. If, however, he remembers with certainty that he has forgotten to confess a sin that in his own conscience was a mortal sin, then he must mention it in the next confession. In the meantime, he should have no doubt about the validity of the absolution.

c) Reasons excusing from material completeness of confession

Apart from the instances already mentioned, every physical or moral impossibility of confessing integrally excuses the penitent. A moral impossibility has to be determined in view of the good of the penitent and the purpose of the sacrament of penance.

For a dying person, it is sufficient to give some perceptible sign of the interior sorrow and the readiness to confess, provided one can do no more than this. One who is critically ill makes a good confession if he does as much as he can without causing danger of worsening his critical condition. Generally speaking, there is no obligation to prepare for confession through written notes, even if the person is forgetful. Such means are extraordinary and often involve the danger of violation of secrecy and of fostering scrupulosity. If these dangers are not present, the penitent may freely decide to use notes, especially if the weakness of his memory is great.

If the penitent cannot find a confessor who understands his language, he is entitled to receive absolution even though his accusation is limited to mere signs or gestures manifesting his sorrow and his will to confess. The same principle applies in the case of deaf mutes who can find no confessor conversant with sign language. The use of an interpreter cannot be recommended for individual confession.

It is up to the episcopal conference and the Ordinary of the diocese to determine the special needs for general absolution. If, for instance, a region has not enough priests to fulfil the urgent duties of the ministry such as evangelization and the visiting of the sick, a bishop should entitle priests to give general absolution after proper preparation.

It seems to me that an incomplete confession can be justified in instances where the penitent has a special relationship with the confessor, when either the sense of shame would prove excessive or if there is justified fear that the relationship might be deeeply disturbed. However, in this or similar circumstances, this reason is valid only if the penitent cannot make his confession to another priest without disproportionate difficulty, or if he would have to defer his confession for a considerable time. In such a case the penitent should be willing to confess his sins with integrity later on when the reasons for his abstention no longer hold.

d) General confession and repetition of confession

Confession must be repeated and mortal sins must be confessed if one's previous confessions have been surely invalid or even sacrilegious. In these instances the penitent is obliged to confess all mortal sins committed since the last valid confession. In the past, preachers have sometimes made exaggerated statements about the frequency of non-valid confessions, perhaps in a laudable desire to arouse in the faithful a greater appreciation for the benefits of general confession. By doing so, however, they have done great harm to many people and have also discredited the sacrament. Even if past confessions have been very imperfect, the presumption is always that they were valid unless the contrary is quite clear.

Except for those who tend towards scrupulosity, a general confession can be a salutary practice when undertaken with full freedom on occasions of special grace, when God grants a livelier and more heartfelt sense of sorrow, for instance, during retreats, parish missions, or at one's entry into a new state of life. The deepening of sorrow for our sins and a humble confession open the profound recesses of the heart to the grace of the sacrament, so that deep wounds not yet fully healed may be exposed to its healing power.

Those who make a general confession for the sake of greater devotion should know that there is no need of an integral confession of all past sins. It is better if the penitent accuses himself of only the more serious and the more typical sins, not only to humble himself before God and men but also to reach out for greater purity of heart.

4. *Creative atonement*

Penances usually imposed in this sacrament were frequently lacking in creativity and, therefore, did not strengthen the penitent's creative liberty and fidelity. Yet it is my conviction that a distinctively Christian moral theology will easily discover the fecundity of penance, satisfaction and atonement for the freedom and fidelity of both person and community. But only if all our understanding of Christian morality is marked by this basic attitude to atonement can there be hope that all the aspects of conversion, and the basic acts of the convert in receiving the sacrament of reconciliation, will manifest liberty and fidelity as signs of the new creation.

a) Fruit befitting repentance

The "blessed sorrow" that unites us with the suffering, death and resurrection of Christ brings forth the firm purpose of amendment, the humble courage to face our sinfulness and to confess our wrongdoings before God and man. It bears fruit in love and justice for the life of the world. John the Baptist's preaching of conversion is synthesized in the words, "Prove your repentance by the fruit it bears" (Mt 3:8; Lk 3:8).

Similarly, Paul describes his ministry as a call to people "to repent and turn to God, and to prove their repentance by deeds" (Acts 26:20). The fruit of repentance and conversion is the new life of the disciples of Christ in the community of faith, a life that bears the harvest of the Spirit: love, peace, kindness, goodness, justice and the like. Because of the ongoing battle against concupiscence in one's own heart and the allurements of sin in the world around us, and for many other reasons, the new life implies also atonement, satisfaction and reparation for past sins.

For various reasons, the Council of Trent formally condemned the assertion that "the best penance is only the new life".[80] Some Reformers seemed to deny that the merits of Christ would give to tribulations and sufferings sent by the Lord himself, to the penance imposed by the priest, or to penitential works like fasting, prayer, almsgiving and other works spontaneously chosen by the penitent, any value of atonement for their past sins. An exaggerated battle against the concept of justice proved by good works seemed to imply that faith, understood as trust in God, would produce the new life "automatically". The Council of Trent was concerned both with justification understood as unsolicited gift and with active freedom as man's response to God's grace. Some innovators held that works of penance, as such, were an insult to the perfect sacrifice of Christ, and that they were in no way worship of God "but human traditions which conceal the doctrine of grace, the true adoration of God and the benefit of the death of Christ".[81]

It should be noted that this false teaching does not represent the common position of Protestantism. Emile Brunner, a highly esteemed Protestant theologian, says on this point: "The modern view that the idea of expiation is sub-moral has unfortunately infected a large number of Christians. Expiation means restoration of the disturbed order by a suffering corresponding to the transgression. But the opinion that, because Christ alone made atonement, no atoning character must be introduced into human atonement is untenable. Human atonement is no more abolished by the divine atonement than human punishment by forgiveness. Besides, without atonement all improvement is an illusion. Only he who feels that just punishment to be necessary, that is who regards it as atonement, has admitted his wrong and can improve".[82]

Indeed, many do not reveal themselves as converted in spite of their tears and good intentions, because they are not willing to carry on the laborious battle against the selfish selves and the collective selfishness and pride of the world. The spirit of atonement is grateful praise for the atonement offered in our name by Jesus Christ. It is the road of fidelity opened by the new creation and chosen in gratitude.

The Council of Trent praises "God's wonderful graciousness that enables us to offer satisfaction to God our Father through Jesus Christ". We do this "not only through spontaneously chosen penances for the condemnation of our sins or through the penance imposed by the priest according to the gravity of our sins, but also — and this is the greatest sign of love — through the divine visitation, if accepted with patience".[83]

The penitential work (satisfaction) should prepare us to appreciate better and to accept more generously whatever suffering we have to undergo (satispassio).[84] The humiliation implied in a humble confession before the priest and before our fellowmen and the pain implied in the various forms of atonement are a natural development of what is implicit in all sorrow that assimilates us with Christ. But it also deepens and purifies the contrition or attrition, the conversion of the heart. For man is an embodied spirit.

Penitential efforts should not be thought of as the soul of repentance, but humble atonement does help to ripen the "fruits befitting repentance" (Mt 3:8). And should these fruits be entirely lacking, one can only conclude that the repentance itself is not genuine enough. Surely the tree comes before the fruits. While Christ speaks of repentance in "sackcloth and ashes" (Mt 11:21), this does not imply that penitential works are the very essence of the metanoia proclaimed as the gladdening tidings of salvation. Nevertheless, atonement is rightly expected to flow from the conversion of the heart ever more spontaneously and generously as repentance itself grows deeper and richer.

The ancient Church, with all her insistence on penitential rigour, was keenly aware that true repentance of heart, with the inner disposition to do penance, is indispensable for the sinner's return to the Father's house in love and gratitude. She considered it sufficient, and consequently pardoned and reconciled the sinner with God in the hour of death, even without previous performance of penance, although not without calling attention to the need to accept suffering and death in a spirit of atonement.[85]

If, on the contrary, the same Church showed herself inexorable in enforcing a strict discipline of prescribed penance, it was mostly for reparation of the damage done by the sin, since the canonical penance was concerned chiefly with the gravely scandalous sins. However, the Church always realized that the performance of meaningful penances brings about a deepening of the penitent's sorrow and prepares his heart to receive sacramental reconciliation with greater efficacy.[86]

b) Grateful homage to God

Penance arising from the sacramental encounter with Christ the Reconciler is grateful acknowledgement of the saving justice and undeserved mercy of God. The sinner, converted and doing penance, recognizes in the sorrow of his heart the wrong he has done to God, whose law is holy and good and spiritual. He puts his faith in God who, because of his own name as Father, acts mercifully. He has sent Jesus Christ to be our peace and to do atonement for us. Although the sinner knows that he is contrite only by God's grace, he fully realizes that works of penance, no matter how great, cannot give him a rightful claim to pardon. His penance is expression of trust in God's mercy as revealed in the cross of his beloved Son, Jesus Christ.

It is through the sacrament of reconciliation that we are assured and we experience that all this was done for us. Through penitential works we then join in the infinite praise Christ has offered to the Father in our name. These works have value as worship in spirit and truth only through our trust in that satisfaction brought by Christ who alone imparts value and dignity to the fruits of penance. Whoever keeps this in mind, while celebrating the sacrament or receiving it, will never consider the sacrament of penance as a "tribunal of wrath and punishment".[87]

Penance becomes truly a part of adoration of God the Father, and praise of his saving justice in and with Christ, but under the condition that we accept God's saving justice as the very rule of our life. Therefore we will embrace those sacrifices which are necessary if we want to bring God's justice to earth by healing forgiveness and by special commitment to the cause of the downtroddden, the oppressed and the poor.

c) Sacramental dimension of penance

The penance imposed by the confessor and readily fulfilled by the penitent receives its full significance as part of the sacrament. All the convert's steps — repentance, self-examination leading to deeper self-knowledge, purpose of amendment, humble confession and works of satisfaction — are given value by the Gladdening News effectively proclaimed by the Church in the name of Jesus Christ. Sacramental satisfaction is a modest but real symbol that points to all our sufferings, our frustrations, the endurance in our battle against the consequences of our sins and those of others, so that everything is understood and accepted as a sharing in Christ's sufferings.

The Council of Trent has beautifully presented this sacramental assimilation to Christ: "In offering satisfaction for our sins, we are assimilated to Christ Jesus who has satisfied for our sins (cf. Rom 5:10; 1 Jn 2:1ff) and from whom comes all our qualification (cf. 2 Cor 3:5). We have also the certain pledge that if we share his suffering now, we shall share his splendour hereafter (cf. Rom 8:17). The satisfaction which we offer for our sins is ours only insofar as it is offered through Jesus Christ. For we cannot do anything by our own strength, but only through him who strengthens us can we do all things (cf. Phil 4:13). Thus if a man has to boast, let him boast in Christ (1 Cor 1:31; 2 Cor 10:17; Gal 6:14). In him we offer atonement, bringing forth fruits worthy of repentance (cf. Lk 3:8), which have all their value from Christ, are offered to the Father by Christ, and are accepted by the Father from Christ".[88]

The penance imposed by the confessor and all our sufferings accepted in the spirit of repentance and atonement have their value in view of Christ who is *the* sacrament of reconciliation, and in view of the sacramentality of the Church. The great sufferings of the Church on behalf of all the sins committed by her members and communities have a great sacramental value if she accepts them as a holy penitent. Thus we learn to bear each other's burden in gratitude for Christ who has taken upon himself all our burden, and in gratitude for all the holy penitents who bear a part of our burden.

It is surely not because of any lack in the suffering offered by Christ as atonement that we find our need to atone. Rather, it is in view of the superabundant redemption wrought by Christ that our repentance becomes a sharing in his redemptive action. The Apostle of the Gentiles speaks convincingly of this mystery. "It is now my happiness to suffer for you. This is my way of helping to complete, in my poor body, the full tale of Christ's affliction still to be endured, for the sake of his body which is the Church" (Col 1:24). It is the overflowing power of Christ's suffering and resurrection that calls and enables us to share in his saving solidarity for our good and the good of all his Church and of all humanity.

In this perspective, the doctrine of the Church on indulgences, now emerging in a better balance, will not become empty ritualism but part of the call to solidarity of salvation. Cardinal Cajetan explains the doctrine of the so-called "treasury of the Church" thus: "All the saints, as living members of the body of Christ, expressing by all their sufferings and good works solidarity with the disposition of Christ, cannot do otherwise than gain merit and offer satisfaction not only for themselves but also for the whole Church".[89] To say "Yes" to the doctrine of indulgences, therefore, means to rid oneself from all self-indulgence and all individualism. It is a "Yes" to saving solidarity in all things, including atonement.

d) The dimension of history of salvation

To better appreciate the sacramental satisfaction and the virtue of atonement, we should remind ourselves of the historical dimension of our faith and our hope. While sin has flooded the earth in the course of human history, redemption has become even more incarnate in history. Christ is the redeemer of the world and the Lord of history. He did not come to show us a way to evade history; he fully entered into it with its joys, its sorrows, and with all its burdens. He opens a future for all humanity by taking up the heavy load of the past and giving a new significance to all the remaining consequences of sin. In atonement, we can express our praise of God and our saving solidarity, and thus take an active part in the hope of humanity.

Each of us has to act historically. In the process of our conversion we face our past and by taking up the present burden we increase creative liberty and fidelity for our own future and that of all mankind. Sacramental satisfaction allows no evasion of a ritualistic kind. It is an expression of covenant morality in its historical and social dynamic, and only thus an indispensable part of the history of liberation and fidelity.

Whoever lives in constant praise and thanksgiving to Christ for having taken upon himself the whole burden of the past ages and for having given the value of atonement to all his life and to his death, will follow him on the path of freedom for the future. If we humbly bow to this law of personal and corporate satisfaction in Christ, new meaning will be imparted to our sinful past or, rather, to its consequences that are still with us, as we strive to live fully the power of atonement given to us in Christ.

e) Creative approach to sacramental satisfaction

We should always realize that penitential works are a call to understand and to fulfil the significance of the spirit of atonement; that sacramental satisfaction, serious as it may be, is looked upon mainly in its symbolic meaning as a call to ever greater co-responsibility in all our life.

In the past centuries, sacramental satisfaction has frequently been emptied by routine. Most of the time, a few "Our Fathers" were given as penance. It is true that faithfulness in prayer and meditation requires a patient effort that can also entail some aspects of penance. But of itself, prayer is the greatest privilege and a constant source of joy. In times when, as confessor, I have no imagination, I would not say,"For your penance, say three Our Fathers", but rather, "In praise of God's mercy, pray and meditate for a while on how all your life can become praise and thanksgiving". On some occasions of very profound conversions following a long time of alienation, I have sometimes suggested as a kind of penance in praise of God's kindness, that you make a daily examination of conscience (for a certain period of time) on how to render thanks to the Lord for the experience of his compassionate love.

We should become more creative in the search for appropriate penances. This is a task not only of the individual confessor but of the whole community, priests and laity. Reparation should be a kind of antidote against our sinful tendencies, a remedy and a reminder. Priest and penitent may sometimes seek together what is most fitting and helpful. Many times I have seen that a concrete "penitential purpose" was especially effective when worked out between confessor and penitent. For instance, adolescents who confessed excessive masturbation, due to a long-lasting habit, were ready to put aside for a good purpose (for the poor, foreign missions, developmental help, etc.) a reasonable part of their pocket-money each time they fell back, and to increase the sacrifice a little bit each time if their failure became more frequent. The results were excellent. Efforts became much more serious. Similar penances can be offered for explosions of impatience and unkindness, for loveless talk about other people, and similar faults.

A German judge for juvenile delinquents helped many youngsters with his creative "penances". Their probation was for instance, to visit, two or three times each week, old and lonely people, to bring them flowers or to offer modest services, and to listen for a while to their talks. It proved an effective means of education in social mindedness.

The rediscovery of the social dimension of all our life, and especially of the sacrament of penance, should also find its proper expression in penitential works. If the whole celebration of the sacrament of conversion is more clearly marked by creative fidelity and spontaneity, it will then also bring home the same qualities not only to the works of atonement but also to all the steps of conversion.

Conversion is God's new creation foreshadowing the new heaven and the new earth. Our part in this great event, our grateful "yes" to God's grace and calling, will participate in God's own creative fidelity. It will lead us ever more to the liberty of the sons and daughters of God to the benefit of all people.

NOTES

1 A.-M. Dubarle, O.P., *The Biblical Doctrine on Original Sin*, New York, 1964, 8f.
2 A. Descamps, "Le péché dans le Nouveau Testament", in Ph. Delhaye (ed.), *Théologie du péché*, Tournai, 1960, 67.
3 Cf. R. Bultmann, *Theology of the New Testament*, New York, 1951, I, 239f.
4 A. Descamps, l.c., 63.
5 Cf. E.M. Maly, *Sin. Biblical Perspectives*, Dayton/Ohio, 1973, 15.
6 W. Eichrodt, *Theology of the Old Testament*, I, 356.
7 Grundmann, *Th.W.z. NT*, I, 312.
8 Cf. Maly, *Sin*, 17; A.-M. Dubarle, l.c., 28f.
9 G. Baum, *Religion and Alienation*, 203.
10 Cf. chapter V on Fundamental Option, where many aspects concerning the subjective side of sin and conversion have been treated.
11 A. Kirchgässner, *Erlösung und Sünde im Neuen Testament*, Freiburg, 1950, 257.
12 J. Leclercq, "Tentation", in Ph. Delhaye (ed.), *Pastorale du péché*, Tournai, 1961, 17-64.
13 Cf. Maly, *Sin*, 47.
14 Cf. P. Eder, *Sühne. Eine Theologische Untersuchung*, Wien, 1962; M. Oraison, *Love, Sin and Suffering*, New York, 1964.
15 Maly, *Sin*, 33.
16 Council of Trent, Denz. Sch. 1630 and 1707.
17 Calvin, *Institutio religionis christianae*, Bk. 2, ch. 8, n. 59.
18 G.C. Berkower, *Sin*, Grand Rapids/Mich., 1971, 285-322; Maly, *Sin*, 33ff.
19 E. de Potterie, "Le péché c'est l'iniquité", in *Nouv. Rev. Théol.* 70 (1956), 785-797.
20 Cf. K. Rahner, "Bussandacht und Einzelbeichte. Anmerkungen zum Römischen Erlass über das Bussakrament", in *Stimmen d.Z.* 190 (1972), 363-372.
21 Denz. Sch. n. 1528, 1544, 1667-1693.
22 See A.M. Meier, *Das peccatum mortale ex toto genere suo. Entstehung und Interpretation des Begriffs*, Regensburg, 1966, K.H. Kleiber, *De parvitate materiae in sexto. Ein Beitrag zur Geschichte der Moraltheologie*, Regensburg, 1971.
23 A. Landgraf, *Das Wesen der lässlichen Sünde in der Scholastik bis Thomas von Aquin*, Bamberg-München, 1923, 190.
24 Cf. above fn. 17
25 J. Major, *Quartus sententiarum* (Paris, 1509, ed. Ponset, Le Preux), dist. 15, q. 19, fol. 4, 99.
26 C. Lacroix, S.J., *Theologia moralis* (reprint Köln, 1929), Bk. 3, Part 1, dubium 2, n. 1101.
27 This question is more profoundly treated in chapter V on Fundamental Option.
28 See *Dutch Catechism* (1910), q. 284 and 287, *Dutch Catechism* (1948), q. 381; *Baltimore Catechism* (1884), q. 56.
29 A.M. Meier, l.c., 227-243; 336-345.
30 Thomas Aquinas, *De malo*, q. 15, a. 11.
31 l.c., q 2, a 10.
32 Cf. overview of the various comments: R. McCormick, "Notes on Moral Theology", in *Theol. Studies* 38 (1977), 100-114; Ch.E. Curran, "Sexual Ethics: Reaction and Critique", in *Linacre Quarterly* 43 (1976), 147-164.
33 K. Rahner, l.c. 367.
34 Salmaticenses, *Cursus theologicus*, tr. 13, "De vitiis et peccatis", disp. 10, dubium 5 (Paris, 1877, vol. VII, tit. 374, n. 185).
35 Paul VI, *Poenitemini* (February 17, 1966), AAS 58 (1966), 177-198.
36 l.c., 183.

37 Cf. G. Troxler, *Das Kirchengebot der Sonntagspflicht als theologisches Problem in Geschichte und Gegenwart*, Freiburg/Schw., 1971.

38 Cf. I. Tubaldo, in *Nuova Alleanza*, Oct. 10, 1972, 387ff.

39 Cf. A. Feuillet, "Metanoia", in *Sacramentum Mundi* IV, 17.

40 Cf. chapter V on Fundamental Option. Cf. also K. Rahner, "Conversion", in *Sacramentum Mundi* II, 4; K. Rahner treats there very clearly the "implicit" conversion to Christ of all those who without coming to explicit faith make however an authentic fundamental option for the good; l.c., 5f.

41 Cf. A. Feuillet, l.c., 19.

42 Essential aspects and dimensions of conversion are treated in chapter IV under the heading "From what and for what did Christ set us free".

43 A. Feuillet, l.c., 20.

44 Cf. R. Schnackenburg, *The Truth will make you free*, New York, 1966.

45 This important dimension of sin and conversion is more extensively treated in my book *Sin in the Secular Age*, New York and Slough, 1974: "Sin as alienation and sins of alienation", 37-105.

46 About the abiding content of this central message and the special historical context in which we have to proclaim it and to put it into praxis, cf. my book *Evangelization Today*, Notre Dame and Slough, 1974, last chapter.

47 See chapter IV, where liberty and involvement in liberation-redemption are treated as harvest of the Spirit.

48 This perspective is emphatically treated by Justin in his book *Dialogue with Tryphon*; cf. J. Daniélou, *The Theology of Jewish Christianity*, Chicago, 1964, 163-166.

49 Among the many outstanding recent books on original sin see: A.-M. Dubarle, *The Biblical Doctrine on Original Sin*, New York, 1964; K. Schmitz-Moormann, *Die Erbsünde. Uberhoite Vorstellung und bleibender Glaube*, Olten-Freiburg, 1969; K.-K. Weger, *Theologie der Erbsünde*. Mit einem Exkurs "Erbsünde und Monogenismus" von Karl Rahner, Freiburg, 1970; A. Vanniste, *Le dogme du péché originel*, Paris, 1971 (English tr. *Dogma of Original Sin*, 1977); M. Flick and Z. Alszeghy, *Il peccato originale*, Brescia, 1972; G. van der Velde, *Original Sin: Two Major Trends in Roman Catholic Reinterpretation*, Amsterdam, 1975; P. Guilluy (ed.), *La culpabilité fondamentale: péché originel et anthropologie moderne*, Gembloux, 1975; all these authors show awareness that one of the main reasons for reinterpretation or at least reformulation of this doctrine is the new knowledge regarding evolution. This aspect is the main focus of the book of S. Trooster, *Evolution and the Doctrine of Original Sin*, Glen Rock/N.J., 1968. I have treated this problem extensively in my book *Sin in the Secular Age*, 106-134.

50 A.-M. Dubarle, l.c., 28ff.

51 l.c., 72.

52 l.c., 224.

53 *Lumen gentium*, 1.

54 Ch. Journet, *Théologie de l'Eglise*, Paris, 1958, 236.

55 Y. Congar, *Sainte Eglise: Etudes et approches sociologiques*, Paris, 1963, 471; Id., "Die heilige Kirche", in *Mysterium Salutis* IV, Part I (Einsiedeln, 1972), 469ff.

56 Vatican I, Denz. Sch. 3013.

57 Decree on Ecumenism, 6.

58 K. Rahner, "The Church as Sinner", in *Theological Investigations* vol. VI, Baltimore, 1969, 261.

59 For a more detailed treatment see B. Häring, *The Sacraments and your everyday Life*, Liguori, 1976, 73-135; *The Sacraments in a secular age*, Slough, 1976.

60 Justin, *Dialogue with Tryphon*, 14, 1.

61 S.Th.,II II, q 84 a 6.

62 Cf. Poschmann, *Penance and Anointment of the Sick*, New York, 1964; A.B. Come, *Agents of Reconciliation*, Philadelphia, 1964; O. Betz (ed.), *Making Sense of Confession. A New Approach for Parents, Teachers and Clergy*,

Chicago, 1969; B. Häring, *Shalom - Peace. Sacrament of Reconciliation*, New York, 1969; E.C. Bianchi, *Peace. Sacrament of Reconciliation; the Function of the Church*, New York, 1969; E. Schillebeeckx (ed.), "Sacramental Reconciliation", in *Concilium*, New York, 1971; F. Buckley, *The Sacrament of Penance Today*, Notre Dame/Ind., 1972; W. Freburger (ed.), *Repent and Believe. The Celebration of the Sacrament of Penance*, Notre Dame/Ind., 1972; B. Basset, S.J., *O Lord, Yes I Still Go to Confession*, Garden City/N.Y., 1974; D.W. Barry, *Ministry of Reconciliation: Modern Lessons From Scripture and Sacrament*, New York, 1975; Theologische Fakulttät Trier, im *Dienst der Versöhnung: Umkehr und Beichte. Beiträge zu ihrer Theologie und Praxis*, Trier, 1974; S. Maggiolini, *La riconciliazione sacramentale nella Chiesa*, Brescia, 1974.

⁶³ J.M. Tillard, "The Bread and Cup of Reconciliation", in *Concilium* 61 (1971), 38-54; F. Nikolasch, "The Sacrament of Penance: Learning From the East" in *Concilium* 61 (1971), 65-75; D.A. Tanghe, "L'Eucharistie pour la rémission des péchés", in *Irenikon* 34 (1961), 65-81.

⁶⁴ Cf. L. Vencser, "Bewertung der Generalabsolution im Lichte der Bussgeschichte", in *Studia Moralia* 15 (1977), 469-482.

⁶⁵ Denz. Sch., 1673-1675; 1704.

⁶⁶ Augustine, *Epistola* 118, 22 PL 33, 442.

⁶⁷ Augustine, *De catechizandis rudibus*, Cap. XV PL 40, 343.

⁶⁸ M. Scheler, *Vom Ewigen im Menschen*, 41.

⁶⁹ Council of Trent, Denz. Sch. 1676.

⁷⁰ Quoted by I. Hausherr, *Penthos. La doctrine de la componction dans l'Orient chrétien*, Rome, 1944, 28.

⁷¹ M. Scheler, l.c., 43.

⁷² Denz. Sch. 1671-1672.

⁷³ Denz. Sch. 1679-1680; 1707.

⁷⁴ R. Pettazoni, *La confessione dei peccati*, 3 vols., Bologna, 1935/6; R. Mohr, *Die christliche Ethik im Lichte der Ethnologie*, München, 1954, 26-37.

⁷⁵ Gertrud von Le Fort, *The Veil of Veronica*, New York, 1935, 298.

⁷⁶ J.B. Hirscher, *Christliche Moral*, Tübingen, 3rd ed., II, 467.

⁷⁷ Fourth Council of the Lateran, Denz. Sch. 812; Council of Trent, Denz. Sch. 1679-1680; CJC, can. 901 and 906.

⁷⁸ Cf. A. Lehmkuhl, *Theologia moralis*, II, n. 437: "If the patient fears that by pondering on his sins, especially those against purity, he will fall into sin by taking pleasure in them, he must refrain from a more detailed recollection of them even taking the risk of failing to make an integral confession".

⁷⁹ Pius XII, Allocution of September 13, 1952, *AAS* 44 (1952), 779-789; and of April 13, 1953, *AAS* 45 (1953), 278-286 (English tr. in *The Catholic Mind* 51 (1953), 305-313; 428-435).

⁸⁰ Denz. Sch. 1692 and 1713.

⁸¹ Denz. Sch. 1714.

⁸² E. Brunner, *Justice and the Social Order*, London and Redhill, 1945, 253.

⁸³ Denz. Sch. 1693.

⁸⁴ S.Th., III q 90 a 2.

⁸⁵ Cf. P. Galtier, "Satisfaction", in *DTC* XIV, 1142f.

⁸⁶ Cf. Leo the Great, *Epistola* 108, 2 PL 54, 1012A.

⁸⁷ Denz Sch. 1692.

⁸⁸ Denz. Sch. 1691-1692.

⁸⁹ Card. Cajetan, *Opusculum* 15, *De indulgentiis*, cap. 8.

Synthesis

Freedom, fidelity and adoration

The dimension of adoration and praise of God is present in all the previous chapters. Here it is offered as a matter of synthesis.

Adoration is not something that is added to the rest of moral life; it is the heart and strength of that life. It is the highest expression of faithful commitment to God, the source of creative freedom.

I do not intend to treat here the virtue of religion side by side with faith, hope and charity. Rather, my concern is to make clear to the reader that the theological virtues are the adoring response to God's self-revelation and self-bestowal. Adoration of God, our Father, in spirit and truth is faith, hope and love of God, insofar as they mark and transform our life. It is integration of faith and life. And if I say "faith", I mean faith that is alive in its structure of hope and in its dynamic of love for God and fellowmen. I speak of worship, and especially of the Eucharist and the sacraments, in this dimension of adoration that frees all our energies for the service of God, for love of our neighbour and for faithful commitment to justice and peace.

I. FREEDOM AND ADORATION

We understand adoration as "honouring God as God" (Rom 1:21). In adoration we praise God for what he is and for what he has done for us; we rejoice in him and render thanks or, as Dietrich Bonhoeffer expressed it, we "let God be God in all our life".[1] For Christians, adoration means honouring God as he has taught us to do through Jesus Christ.

Adoration is thoroughly dialogical and expresses the highest freedom. In his own transcendence — that is, in his utter freedom — God reveals himself, his glory, his name and his holiness. Adoration is the creature's free response and the condition for sharing in God's freedom.

God revealed progressively the mystery of his awesome transcendence (mysterium tremendum) and his blissful and fascinating nearness (mysterium fascinosum). Holy Scripture describes these events mainly in terms of three key concepts: the name (shem), his being the Holy One (qadosh), and his glory (kabod). And Israel was to experience uniquely how exalted the Lord is and how absolute is the people's obligation to dedicate themselves to divine worship.

God's name is ineffable. Man cannot claim a right to learn and to experience it. When Jacob asks God, "What is your name?" the Lord answers, "Why do you ask my name?" (Gen 32:30; cf. Jgs 13:17f). In a tremendous historical moment, when God chose to communicate the marvel of his mystery to his people and his promise to liberate them, he disclosed his name to Moses: "I am who am (Yahweh)" (Ex 3:14). Thus he reveals his transcendence and his freedom to be with and for his people.

He who is absolute sovereignty and fullness of being decides in a supreme act of freedom to intervene and to show mercy to his people. "I show favours to whom I will, I grant mercy to whom I will" (Ex 33:19). Awesome and terrifying is the divine name in its sovereign grandeur for those who refuse to honour it: "You shall not take the name of the Lord, your God, in vain. For the Lord will not leave unpunished him who takes his name in vain" (Ex 20:7; Deut 5:11).

God is holy (kadosh). He is totally Other. Therefore he is absolute freedom to be present to us in his holy love. His presence is dynamic, striking people with awe and holy fear (mysterium tremendum). This means terror for the unconverted sinner but purifying fire for those who turn to God with a sincere heart.

Sinful man cannot dare to face God, the All-Holy. "Who can stand in the presence of this Holy One?" (1 Sam 6:20). For sinful man to face God is to die, unless God protects him by the power of his mercy. Jacob says, "I have seen God face to face, yet my life has been spared" (Gen 32:31). When God spoke to Moses as to a friend, Moses dared to beseech him, "Do let me see your glory". God answered, "I will make my spendour pass before you, and in your presence I will pronounce my name, 'Lord'; I who show favours to whom I will, I who grant mercy to whom I will. But my face you cannot see, for no man sees me and still lives" (Ex 33:18-20).

God manifests his awesome majesty to the prophet to purge his lips, his thoughts, his heart and his very life with the glowing coal from the altar of his sanctity (Is 6:3-6).

God reveals his glory in the dark cloud which is at the same time a glowing pillar of fire (Ex 13:21). Sign of mercy to the chosen people, this cloud is a portent of destruction for God's enemies (Ex 14:19f). "And the sight of the Lord was like a burning fire upon the top of the mount, in the eyes of the children of Israel" (Ex 24:17). After Moses had seen the glory of God from the "back" and "passing" before him, the reflection of the divine glory remained impressed on his countenance (Ex 33:23; 34:5f). So awesome was it that when Aaron and the other Israelites saw Moses and "noted how radiant the skin of his face had become, they were afraid to come near to him" (Ex 34:30).

When Solomon dedicated the temple to the Lord, "the glory of the Lord had filled the house of the Lord, then Solomon said: 'The Lord said that he would dwell in a cloud'" (3 Kgs 8:11). God reveals his glory for the exiled captives, so that they turn to him with all their hearts and give him due honour. And the Lord promises to manifest his glory anew in the temple at Jerusalem for those who have returned to the Lord (cf. Ez 10:18; 11:23; 43:1f).

God's disclosure of himself is more than a bare intellectual instruction on the divine magnificence; it is the dynamic manifestation of the hidden mystery which fills the people with holy awe and reverence, and is an impelling invitation to adore him in all their life. Thus God writes his commandment into their inmost being. "The Lord your God shall you fear; him shall you serve . . . you shall not follow other gods . . . for the Lord, your God, who is in your midst, is a jealous God" (Deut 6:13-15).

With his glory, God reveals also his name and the attractive power of his love (mysterium fascinosum). He dynamically invites his people to call upon him and to put their trust in him, for the Holy One of Isreal is the Saviour: " 'I will help you', says the Lord; 'your Redeemer is the Holy One of Israel' " (Is 41:14; cf. 54:5). The revelation of his glory and his name is an act of sovereign freedom by God who is Love and who, thus, calls us to holiness. "For I, the Lord, am your God; and you shall make and keep yourselves holy, because I am holy" (Lev 11:44; cf. Deut 7:6f).

God glorifies himself precisely in bringing salvation to humankind; and this constitutes the most compelling commandment written into the human heart to seek salvation wholly and only in the adoration of God. So we come to salvation and freedom only in the measure that we adore the all-holy God and dedicate our existence to him in response to the revelation of his glory.

The fitting response to God's self-revelation, which is at the same time the disclosure of his saving justice and mercy, is holy fear and jubilant love. For God glorifies himself by drawing us into his tender embrace with the ineffable and purifying power of his love. "Hear, O Israel. The Lord is our God, the Lord alone! Therefore you shall love the Lord, your God, with all your heart and with all your soul and with all your strength. Take to heart these words which I enjoin on you today. Drill them into your children. Speak of them at home and abroad, whether you are busy or at rest" (Deut 6:4-7).

The noted Dominican exegete, C. Spicq, sums up the Old Testament revelation this way: "Thus it is evident that the love of God is the one thing important. One is to think of nothing else. Nor is there anything else of which to speak. This is man's unique, life-long occupation, his agape that embraces faith, worship of God and the whole moral life . . . The bond of love with the virtue of religion is obvious. Love for God, ardently longing to manifest itself in prayer of praise and in good works, adores and serves him, submits to him, and makes his will the loftiest motive of daily conduct and of all virtues . . . The love of the Israelites is a love of adoration, of worship. It is truly a cultal love, the worship of praise for the sovereign, transcendent God and dedication of life to his service".[2]

It is from this loving, grateful adoration that Israel draws her strength, peace, joy and the whole vision of life. If she falls back into slavery and alienation, it is because of lack of gratitude. Since God reveals his glory through his saving action, man's response in loving adoration cannot be satisfied with anything less than total consecration to the God of love. The whole life of the people, individual and communal, should reflect, in the freest love, God's sovereign self-revelation.

The religious experience of the best of Israel is "dominated by the conception of a God who is free, transcendent, ordering will, and whose explicit aim is the creation of a freely responsive and ordered community of men".[3] All who gratefully adore God and joyously celebrate in praise of his liberating action will enjoy freedom and peace.

God's revelation and the experience of his glory and of salvation teaches us that "freedom becomes significant only through love".[4] We acquire our true stature and freedom by acknowledging humbly, joyously and gratefully that both our freedom and our capacity to love are gifts coming from God's sovereign freedom.

II. "WE SAW HIS GLORY, FULL OF GRACE AND TRUTH"

"When in former times God spoke to our forefathers, he spoke in fragmentary and varied fashion through the prophets. But in this, the final stage, he has spoken to us in the Son . . . who is the effulgence of God's splendour and the stamp of God's very being" (Heb 1:1-13). The Father who, in absolute freedom, gives himself wholly to his Word, reveals to us his boundless transcendence and freedom to love by giving us his only-begotten Son as our brother and redeemer. Christ is the sacrament of the Father's freedom to be for us and with us. This freedom is our salvation if it becomes the life-giving law of our conduct: total freedom for God and our fellowmen.

"The Word became flesh; he came to dwell among us, and we saw his glory, such glory as befits the Father's only Son, full of grace and truth" (Jn 1:14). The Word Incarnate is the new temple in which God's majesty is now enthroned. He is the presence of the Most High among us, the *shekinah*, the holiest of the holy. Christ is totally consecrated to glorify the Father on earth through the task given him by the Father, to manifest the height and the depth, the length and the breadth of his love.

In his freedom to be the servant of all and to give himself up for his brothers and sisters, entrusting his life wholly to his Father's hands, Christ both reveals the glory of the Father and responds in the name of all humankind. And the Father glorifies his Son, raising him from the dead and giving him a name above all names. Christ expresses this mystery of God's glory and his own freedom for the glory of the Father. "Father, glorify me in thy own presence with the glory which I had with thee before the world began. I have made thy name known to the men whom thou didst give me out of the world" (Jn 17:4-6). The resurrected Christ is "the Lord of glory" (1 Cor 2:8).

By sending us the Holy Spirit, the Spirit of glory, Christ takes us into his mission of glorification which is fulfilled if we live in the freedom to love as Christ did. "The glory that thou hast given me, I have given to them" (Jn 17:22). And if, guided by the Spirit who bears fruit in love and in all the dispositions that come from love, we are ready to share in Christ's sufferings, "that is cause for joy; and when his glory is revealed, our joy will be triumphant . . . then that glorious Spirit which is the Spirit of God is resting upon you" (1 Pt 4:13-14).

It is the Spirit "that makes us sons, enabling us to cry 'Abba! Father!' ". In that cry the Spirit of God joins with our own spirit in testifying that we are God's children (Rom 8:14-16). The Holy Spirit is the Spirit of truth. If, with Jesus Christ, our main purpose is to glorify the Father, then we are truly free to love one another as Christ has loved us.

III. ADORATION IN SPIRIT AND TRUTH

By revealing himself as the perfect adorer in spirit and truth, Christ does away with alienating disputes and rivalries between priestly castes and conflicting sacred mountains. He calls us all to be wholly consecrated to the honour of the Father and the service of his brothers and sisters, as he is. "The time approaches, indeed it is already here, when those who are real worshippers will worship the Father in spirit and truth. Such are the worshippers whom the Father wants. God is spirit, and those who worship him must worship him in spirit and in truth" (Jn 4:23-24).

In his self-giving love, to the glory of the Father, Christ is the source, the real symbol and the compelling norm of adoration in freedom, of the free gift of ourselves. The Church is called to be a community of adoring faith, adoring hope, adoring fraternal love. "Christ indeed always associates the Church with himself in the truly great work of giving perfect praise to God and making men holy".[5]

The "religionless Christianity" envisaged by Dietrich Bonhoeffer is freedom from alienated religious ritualism and formalism: true faith as the gift of God to those who accept the crucified Christ as the norm of their life. "God will do and be everything for men; therefore he alone must be adored. God alone will be God, because he alone is God".[6] It is the privilege of the community of the disciples of Christ to respond to the absolute freedom manifested in the crucified God, by freely praising God with their whole life and proclaiming Jesus as their Lord, through worship and through all their acts and attitudes. The Spirit of adoration enables them to give full witness of faith, a witness of freedom to be *for*.

Christ's utter freedom for us, to the glory of the Father, is the revelation of his divinity. To adore in spirit and truth means, then, to integrate worship and witness of living faith, hope and love. The Church thereby joins Christ in glorifying the Father. That such witness can lead men to the knowledge and adoration of God is the miracle of grace in the encounter of divine and human freedom.[7]

God has so abundantly revealed his glory and the freedom of his love because he wants the free response of his creatures. The truly free and the true adorers are those who learn, in loving adoration, to be free to love all their brothers and sisters. This is the synthesis of Pauline theology. "What should be man's answer to God's love so freely given to him?" The Apostle speaks in the perspective of cultal gratitude: one must sacrifice one's self, one's body, as a living, holy oblation well pleasing to God. "I implore you by God's mercy to offer your very selves to him, a living sacrifice, dedicated and fit for his acceptance, the worship offered by mind and heart" (Rom 12:1). All the moral dispositions that are subsequently mentioned spring from gratitude and praise as sacrificial oblations.[8] For Paul, moral life as well as prayer is marked by joy, peace, gratitude and that sacrificial spirit that arises from our configuration with the Paschal Mystery. The faith-experience, and especially the spirit of adoration, pervades the whole moral life.

The spirit of adoration is not only an essential note of faith, hope and love; it also gives shape, direction and strength to all moral life. As Thomas Aquinas expresses it, "The virtue of religion commands all other virtues".[9] For Thomas, moral life can be virtuous in the full sense only if it receives its final form and strength from the spirit of adoration. "Every virtuous work belongs to religion or, in other words, to the adoration of God. The proper end of divine worship is to order everything to the divine majesty . . . The ordering of the acts of any virtue whatsoever to the service of God makes them properly acts of adoration".[10] To be truly virtuous, one must be an adorer in all one's life.

IV. THE PRIORITY OF THE SACRED

One of the main concerns of all great theologians of our time, and especially of Karl Rahner and Dietrich Bonhoeffer, is to assert adoration in its own right. While one may, like Immanuel Kant, come to faith in God through a deep understanding of the ethical dimension, one should never subordinate adoration to morals. James Gustafson puts this clearly: "One is not a religious person in order to have reasons of mind and heart to be moral; rather, one is religious as a consequence of experience of the reality of God, and this experience requires that one be moral".[11]

The undeniable fact that the saints are models of morality for religious reasons,' and that their faith has enabled them to enrich the world with moral values, does not say that they were religious for moral reasons. They were saints because they came to understand adoration in its own right. "The notion that men are to do all things to the glory of God, for example, is not simply a moral command. God is glorified in religious communities by praising him, offering prayers of thanksgiving, celebrating his presence in the world with joy and thanksgiving".[12]

Adoration is the free human response to God revealing the glory of his freedom and love. It is our creaturely response to God. When God turns his countenance to us, we can truly respond, entrusting ourselves wholly to him, praising him with our whole being. The authenticity of this religious event is manifested by the experience of wholeness. Faith-experience, even more than a profound conscience-experience, is characterized by this dimension of wholeness. It seizes all of one's faculties, mind and will in that profound emotion that joyfully realizes the unity between intelligence (intuition) and will.

The Christian faith-experience which finds its climax in total adoration is encounter with God who, in Jesus Christ, has revealed all his love. To this love of the crucified and risen Lord, the adoring response can only be to answer his call to love one another as he has loved us. The faith-response in adoration can never be deprived of the horizontal dimension of co-humanity without being thoroughly dissolved and falsified.[13]

The more thoroughly we are open to the religious dimension as such — to adoration in its own right — the more will the fruitfulness of worship for the moral life be ensured. If our whole being proclaims the greatness of God and rejoices in the wonderful privilege we share with Jesus, to call the almighty God "dearest Father", then we shall be led into the covenant morality with all those dispositions that befit the sons and daughters of God. Religious conversion engenders moral renewal.[14]

Those who are filled with hope and are willing to work for a better tomorrow receive the gift of the present, a time of repose, of contemplation, of pure joy, not just for the sake of the tomorrow or the sake of any other time. There is a need to rest in the present "in order not to lose the future".[15] But out of the present gratitude grows the strength to walk and to work together in hope for the future. Only those who first seek God's glory will enter into the dimensions of the kingdom and be able to grasp their active role in it.

These truths shed abundant light on the self-understanding of the Church. A model that gives first importance to the institutional dimension — the Church as "perfect society" — leads to many dangers of "organized religion". The Church is meant to be, above all, the community of true adorers of God, and her sacraments are privileged signs of adoration in faith, hope and love. Priority given to cult in, with and through Christ, the prophetic High Priest, will then mould all the other functions of the Church and prevent the institutional aspect from being misunderstood.

V. THE SACRAMENTS AS PRIVILEGED SIGNS OF ADORATION

God has created us to be adorers of his name and, thus, to share in his beatitude and his boundless love. He calls us to adoration not so much through a commandment as through the many signs in which he reveals his glory, his faithful love, his design to make us all one grace-filled family, and thus to glorify him, the one Father.

God has given us the one great sign that enables and urges us to praise him as Father, in the name of all his creation. This supreme sign and sacrament is Jesus Christ, the Prophet and High Priest who offers himself up to the Father in the name of all creation. The more we know Christ the more we shall desire to join him in all the ways in which he glorifies the Father. And it is also true that the more we celebrate our gratitude to Christ and join him in praise of the Father the more we come to know him and to learn from him how to honour the Father with our whole life.

Gathered by the sacrificial love of Christ, the Church is, in him and through him, the primordial sacrament of adoration. Through the Church the Christian enters into intimate friendship and union with Christ and participates in the consecratory power of his passion, death and resurrection. All human history thereby becomes, by the grace of the Holy Spirit, an economy of salvation to the glory of God the Father. Inserted into Christ, the believer becomes a sharer in the cultic gift of self which the beloved Son, the Anointed, offers to the Father in the Holy Spirit. Hence the Christian understands himself as "a member of a community and of a creation which sing the praise of the triune God".[16]

It is the Church's mission to lead us to Christ in whom the Father has revealed the fullness of his glory and has received the full response given in the name of all. By leading us to Christ, the Church helps us to discover all the wonderful signs, works and events through which God glorifies his name and invites us to honour him.

The sacraments of the Church are privileged signs of adoration. They are not to be regarded as something besides our life, for they teach and enable us to adore God in and through our life. As Thomas Aquinas wrote, "The sacraments belong to the adoration of God according to the religion of Christian life".[17] They have a double purpose: to consecrate us to the cult of God that includes our whole life, and to liberate us from our sins which are the great obstacle to true adoration.

The sacraments ordain us to a corporate worship in which, united in Christ, we are enabled to be and to become ever more "a kingdom of priests, a holy nation" (1 Pt 2:9). The distinctively Christian character flows from adoring faith, hope and love experienced in the community of faith. There we celebrate the marvels done by the Lord and accept with joy our wonderful vocation to adore God in spirit and truth. It is not just the content of faith expressed in abstract concepts but faith celebrated and expressed in compelling symbols. The content of faith then gives us not only reasons but effective motives to discover in daily life all the opportunities to give praise to the Lord.[18]

The sacraments do not monopolize the signs of God's gracious presence and his call to adoration. Rather, as privileged signs, they lead us to discover the countless ways in which God comes into our life and calls us to honour him by a right ordering of our relationships and by participation in the ongoing work of creation and redemption.[19] Also through the sacraments, Christ enables us to participate in the joys and sorrows, the hopes and anguish of all people, in a way that gives meaning to all this in the light of the Paschal Mystery.

When we rightly celebrate the sacraments as privileged signs of hope, then we realize that we can truly respond to God's promises with hope that unites us all in a saving solidarity to the praise of God, the Liberator and Redeemer. Celebrating these signs of unity and love, the Spirit of adoration makes us realize ever more that we can adore God in spirit and truth only if we are sincerely and actively committed to the good of all our brothers and sisters: that is, to peace, justice and the promotion of human rights in our own small world and in the world at large. Only through the dynamics of adoration is our morality truly grounded in our faith and in the divine gifts of hope and love.

The liturgy is "the primary and indispensable source from which the faithful are to derive the true Christian spirit".[20] "The liturgy is the summit towards which the activity of the Church is directed; at the same time, it is the fountain from which all her power flows".[21]

(1) The celebration of the *Eucharist* is the basis and centre of the Christian community, and the most privileged school of adoration in spirit and truth. "If this celebration is to be sincere and thorough, it must lead to various works of charity and mutual help, as well as to missionary activity and to different forms of Christian witness".[22] Participation in the Eucharist should give us such a vital and inspiring experience of worship, praise and thanksgiving that it provides us at all times with the most illuminating motives and criteria for our personal decisions: Can I bring this thought, desire or action home into

the Eucharistic celebration and offer it to God as praise and thanksgiving with Christ?

From a vital celebration of the Eucharist, we learn to discern almost spontaneously by what kind of life we can be the "light to the world" so that people, seeing our faith, our hope, our love and commitment to all that is good, will praise the Father in heaven. In the light of the Eucharist, we understand all the sacraments as privileged signs celebrating the joy of Christian faith, hope and love. In it, we accept our mission to let the sacraments be, for us, effective signs of the covenant morality.

(2) Celebrating the sacrament of *baptism*, we enter into vital contact with the baptism of Christ who, by his baptism in the Jordan, publicly manifested and accepted his mission to be the covenant of the people and to bear the burden of all. The Spirit has anointed him for the baptism in his blood, the blood of the new and everlasting covenant.

The baptism we receive in the Church is a privileged sign of faith that defeats the godless world and enables us to profess Jesus Christ as the Son of God, as the Lord, and to do so in all our life. "This is he who came with water and blood: Jesus Christ. He came not by water alone but by water and blood; and there is the Spirit to bear witness, because the Spirit is truth" (1 Jn 5:6-7). By virtue of our life in Christ Jesus, we are entitled to call the almighty God "our Father" and to glorify his name if we join Christ in his faithful and saving solidarity.

(3) Through the sacrament of *confirmation* we are taught and enabled to live on the level of the Spirit and to live as active members of the faith-community. If we honour and praise God as mature Christians who, by creative liberty and fidelity, solidarity, discernment and generosity, manifest to the world what it means to adore God in spirit and truth, then we truly belong to the Church who is baptized by the Holy Spirit.

(4) According to traditional doctrine, the sacraments of baptism, confirmation and *Holy Orders* imprint on the life of the recipients a character of adoration. They enable and oblige

us to bring all our life, personal and corporate, into the dimension of adoration in Christ Jesus. Therefore the priest is meant to be, above all, a man of prayer who lives in an exemplary way the integration of faith and life. He is both a learner and a teacher of the Eucharistic style of life marked by the spirit of joy, thankfulness and solidarity. He honours Christ the prophetic Priest by being a man for others.

(5) In the sacrament of *reconciliation,* God reminds us that, in Jesus Christ, he has reconciled us to the praise of his fatherly mercy and justice. Receiving and celebrating this sacrament, we accept life's tensions and troubles as active signs of reconciliation and as harbingers of peace. Knowing that these are not possible without self denial and sacrifice, we accept this price to the glory of the name of Jesus who is the Reconciler, the Prince of Peace, the Victim and the Sacrifice for our peace.

(6) For believers, *matrimony* is marked by this same dimension of adoration that is life and shapes all of life. The spouses accept each other gratefully as gifts of the Father and, trusting in the Holy Spirit, they promise to offer each other and their children that love, kindness, gentleness, patience, forbearance and respect that truly honour God, the giver of all good things.

Every Christian home should be truly a "house of prayer", a source of joy and encouragement to praise God in all events. The Christian family will pray and reflect on God's word in such a way that they all discover in the daily events the coming of the Lord, inviting them to give to all their efforts and their joys the meaning of praise of God. "Be filled with the Spirit, addressing one another in psalms, hymns and inspired songs. Sing praise to the Lord with all your hearts. Give thanks to the Father always and for everything. Defer to one another out of reverence for Christ" (Eph 5:18-21).

(7) The *anointing of the sick* should be, for the sick person and his friends a comforting sign of adoring faith, hope and love. It should be celebrated in such a way that, in view of the suffering, death and resurrection of Jesus Christ, we are enabled to grasp the meaning of suffering and even of death, and thus enter effectively into the dimensions of the Paschal Mystery,

to the praise of the Father and the salvation of all humankind. Through the sacraments we should learn that, united with Jesus Christ, we reach the full stature of co-humanity and truly become Christians by sharing that suffering of Christ which reveals the compassion of God.[23] Thus we become free for one another, humble mirrors of God's wonderful freedom to enter into the suffering of our world, and manifest there the fullness of his love. For, in grateful praise of the Creator and Redeemer, we learn that freedom for God means also freedom of love for our fellowmen.

NOTES

1 D. Bonhoeffer, G.S. (Gesammelte Schriften, ed. by E. Bethge, München, 1958 ff.) III, 257, 344; V, 218.
2 C. Spicq, *Agapé, Prolégomènes à une étude néo-testamentaire*, Paris, 1955, 94; cf. 205.
3 R.B. Laurin, *Contemporary Old Testament Theologians*, Valley Forge, 1970, 31.
4 M. Nédoncelle, *God's Encounter with Man. A Contemporary Approach to Prayer*, New York-London, 1964, 179.
5 Vatican II, *Constitution on Liturgy*, 7.
6 Bonhoeffer, G.S., IV, 603 (June 1944).
7 Cf. J.W. Mödlhammer, *Anbetung und Freiheit, Theologisch-anthropologische Reflexionen zur Theologie Dietrich Bonhoeffers*, Salzburg, 1976, 49.
8 C. Spicq, "La morale de l'agapè selon le Nouveau Testament", in *Lumière et vie* 21 (May 1955), 103-122; cf. D.M. Stanley, *Boasting in the Lord*, New York, 1973, 100-107.
9 S.Th., II II, q 81, a 4 ad 1.
10 l.c., q 88 a 5.
11 J. Gustafson, *Can Ethics Be Christian?* Chicago, 1975, 173f.
12 l.c., 140.
13 This is one of the central themes of D. Bonhoeffer; cf. Mödlhammer, l.c., 46ff.
14 Cf. J. Jeremias, *The Lord's Prayer*, Philadelphia, 1969, 20.
15 R. Alves, *A Theology of Human Hope*, Washington/D.C., 1969, 31.
16 D. Bonhoeffer, *Ethik* (ed. E. Bethge), 7th ed., München, 1966, 129.
17 S.Th., III, q 95, a 1.
18 J. Gustafson, l.c., 147f.
19 Cf. L. Gilkey, *Catholicism Confronts Modernity*, New York, 1975, 22.
20 Vatican II, *Constitution on the Liturgy*, 14.
21 l.c., 10.
22 Vatican II, *Decree on Priests*, 6.
23 Cf. D. Bonhoeffer, *Widerstand und Ergebung* (ed. E. Bethge), new ed., München, 1970, 402.

Index